THE MAKING AND BREAKING OF THE AMERICAN CONSTITUTION

The Making and Breaking of the American Constitution

A THOUSAND-YEAR HISTORY

MARK PETERSON

PRINCETON UNIVERSITY PRESS
PRINCETON & OXFORD

Published by Princeton University Press
41 William Street, Princeton, New Jersey 08540
99 Banbury Road, Oxford OX2 6JX

press.princeton.edu

GPSR Authorized Representative: Easy Access System Europe - Mustamäe tee 50, 10621 Tallinn, Estonia, gpsr.requests@easproject.com

ISBN 9780691180014
ISBN (epub) 9780691287515
ISBN (Web PDF) 9780691208466

British Library Cataloging-in-Publication Data is available

Editorial: Priya Nelson and Emma Wagh
Production Editorial: Terri O'Prey
Jacket/Cover Design: Karl Spurzem
Production: Erin Suydam
Publicity: James Schneider
Copyeditor: Christina Nichols

This book has been composed in Arno

Printed in the United States of America

10 9 8 7 6 5 4 3 2 1

In memory of Edward Gray and Trevor Burnard,
and in gratitude to Eric Hinderaker, Lige Gould,
and Peter Mancall for their friendship.

CONTENTS

THE MAKING AND BREAKING OF THE AMERICAN CONSTITUTION

Introduction

"LIKE A GARMENT TO THE BODIE": ON CONSTITUTIONAL RELATIONSHIPS

> Remember my Countrymen, the present aera—perhaps the present struggle will fix the constitution of America forever.—think of your ancestors, and of your posterity.
>
> —BENJAMIN RUSH ON THE TEA ACT CRISIS, *PENNSYLVANIA JOURNAL*, OCTOBER 20, 1773

CONSTITUTIONS CARRY great emotional weight. Words like faith and love are not too strong to describe the feelings they inspire. Constitutions connect traditional objects of devotion—a beloved community and its history and customs—with cherished principles. The rights and liberties constitutions protect allow people to imagine and live better lives. Constitutions are living traditions, linking the present to the past and offering a vision of a society's future.

Over two centuries, through sectional crisis and civil war, depression, world wars, and cold war, Americans of all stripes have voiced their pride in their constitution, often hailed as the world's oldest written constitution still in effect. A national Constitution Day (September 17) is observed every year in its honor. It even has its own museum in Philadelphia. The version of the text inscribed on parchment in 1787 is a prime relic of the nation's civic religion.[1] When the Library of Congress transferred the document to a specially built exhibition hall at the National Archives in 1952, it was delivered in an armored personnel carrier, escorted in a procession of tanks, and placed in a fifty-ton, custom-built safe, from which it could be lowered nightly into a bomb-proof vault and raised again each day into a display case filled with argon gas.[2] Much of this veneration stems from the fact that Americans have looked to their constitution's provisions, especially those spelled out in the Bill of Rights, as tools to defend and expand the scope of freedom and to empower a wide range of people within the republic.

America's tradition of constitutional veneration has deep roots in the nation's colonial past. Like modern Americans, eighteenth-century Britons—in the home country and in the colonies—took enormous pride in the British constitution. With Britain's perfectly balanced sovereign triad of king, Lords, and Commons keeping tyranny, oligarchy, and anarchy in check, with traditions such as the common law preserving English rights, and with historic victories for liberty enshrined in documents from Magna Carta (1215) to the Bill of Rights (1689), Britons boasted of greater freedom than any other nation: "The constitution of our English government (the best in the world) is no arbitrary tyranny like the Turkish Grand Seignior's, or the French King's."[3] In the words of the future King George III, "The pride, the glory of Britain, and the direct end of its constitution, is political liberty."[4] The king's subjects in the colonies were quick to agree. In 1759, *The New American Magazine* declared Britain's constitution to be "the best model of Government that can be framed by Mortals."[5] For John Adams writing in 1766, "Here lies the difference between the British constitution, and other forms of government, viz. that Liberty is its end, its use, its designation, drift, and scope, as much as grinding corn is the use of a mill, the transportation of burdens the end of a ship, the mensuration of time the scope of a watch, or life and health the designation of the human body."[6]

During the "Glorious Revolution" of 1688–89, after a century of violent conflict, the monarchy's status was redefined by Parliament and the relationship between the Church of England and dissenting religions was settled in a major revision to the British constitution. Over the subsequent eight decades, Britain's empire grew ever larger, richer, and more powerful. Britannia ruled the waves, rose "more majestic" from each "foreign stroke," and refused all attempts of "haughty tyrants" to "bend thee down." "Britons never will be slaves"; this, in the words of the poet James Thomson, was "the charter of land." "Rule, Britannia," Thomson's 1740 anthem, presaged the empire's tremendous victories in the Seven Years' War (1756–63), when British arms drove the Gallic foe from North America and opened vast reaches of territory to further expansion. In the immediate wake of these victories, colonists reveled in the empire's glories and sang the virtues of their unparalleled constitution. In 1764, while writing an impassioned defense of the rights of the British colonies, Bostonian James Otis took care to observe that "the finest writers of the most polite nations on the continent of *Europe*, are enraptured with the beauties of the civil constitution of *Great Britain*." Otis concurred: "The *British* constitution in theory and in the present administration of it, in general comes nearest the idea of perfection, of any that has been reduced to practice."[7]

Yet within little more than a decade, Britain's authority over thirteen of its colonies and a huge swath of American territory would collapse. The breakdown occurred not because colonists rejected the British constitution but because they claimed to defend it against an imperial government that had failed to uphold its principles. The American Revolution was a constitutional crisis within the first British Empire, an imperial civil war in which the combatants came to blows over differing interpretations of a constitution both sides cherished.

How could this happen? How could Britain's venerable constitution—the best model of government, perfectly designed to promote liberty—suffer such a grave crisis? In the generations after 1688, the British Empire had changed in dramatic ways, but its framework of government had failed to adapt. The colonists of British North America, roughly 200,000 people at the time of the Glorious Revolution, ballooned to 2.5 million by the American Revolution, growing from statistical insignificance to a quarter of the population of the British realm in less than a century. With a booming economy, the colonies became both vital producers of goods for the British homeland and major consumers of British manufactures. Growing at a ferocious pace, the American territory Britain claimed to govern more than doubled in area with the conquest of New France. Yet the place of the colonies within British governance had not been adjusted. England and Scotland had been formally united under a single parliament in 1707; England and the colonies had not, though the colonies were now larger in population and size than Scotland and growing much faster. King and Parliament together transformed taxation and state finance on the home island, empowering Britain's imperial rise. The colonies had never been formally included in this taxation system. Each individual colony spawned legislatures that mimicked (imperfectly) Britain's Houses of Lords and Commons. The status of these legislatures in relation to king and Parliament remained undefined. When, in the wake of the Seven Years' War, George III and his parliamentary ministries attempted to reform the empire, each of these constitutional gaps, each yawning chasm between old institutions and practices and new realities, provoked conflict.

The flash points, the infamous events that triggered a revolution, will be familiar to many, if not most, readers: The Royal Proclamation of 1763 that foreclosed colonists' access to newly conquered territories. The Stamp Act (1765) and Townshend Duties (1767) that asserted Parliament's right to tax the colonists over the objections of colonial legislatures. The formation of new colonies without representative assemblies in Quebec and Florida. Royal interference in colonial courts. The use of royal troops to enforce Parliament's laws, resulting in the Boston Massacre of 1770. With respect to all these controversial measures, the colonists' opposition was rooted in their claims to possess the "rights of Englishmen" guaranteed by the ancient customs and written documents of the British constitution. But the sovereign right of king and Parliament to impose these measures had been resolved in the Glorious Revolution of 1688 and the subsequent century's development of settled practices of government. Neither side was wrong under the British constitution, but neither could their conflicting positions be reconciled. The British Empire had expanded beyond its constitution's capacity to encompass it and, as a result, tore itself apart from within.

The emergence of an independent American nation may seem inevitable today, 250 years after the event. But we should not underestimate just how wrenching, in emotional terms, the break from Britain and its vaunted constitution was to Americans, even among those determined to achieve independence. Love for Britain was strong. The principles of the British constitution were of necessity intertwined in the popular imagination with the institutions and persons who represented and defended them, including the royal dynasty. Across the developing landscape of America, colonists had strewn the names of members of the House of Hanover across their new settlements and rising cities, from Hanover, New Hampshire, to Hanover Street in Boston to Hanover Square in New York. Lunenburg, Massachusetts, and New Brunswick, New Jersey; Frederick, Maryland, and Fredericksburg, Virginia; Charlotte, North Carolina, and Charlottesville, Virginia, all derive their names from the royal family.[8] The Hanoverian dynasty had defended Britain against invasions by the Catholic Stuart pretenders and fought wars against France and Spain that expanded and enriched the colonies.

The depth of this affection for Britain, its constitution, and its history made the experience of separation excruciating. The colonists struggled to disentangle the virtues, ideals, and principles of the British constitutional tradition from what they saw as its corruption by the recent practices of the king's ministers. Even after the outbreak of war at Lexington and Concord on April 19, 1775, the Continental Congress sent the "Olive Branch Petition" to King George III on July 8, pouring out its continuing affection in the hope of reconciliation:

> Attached to your Majesty's person, family, and Government, with all devotion that principle and affection can inspire; connected with *Great Britain* by the strongest ties that can unite societies, and deploring every event that tends in any degree to weaken them, we solemnly assure your Majesty, that we not only most ardently desire the former harmony between her and these Colonies may be restored, but that a concord may be established between them upon so firm a basis as to perpetuate its blessings, uninterrupted by any future dissensions, to succeeding generations in both countries.[9]

George III responded by declaring the colonists to be rebels and traitors and promised "to bring to condign Punishment the Authors, Perpetrators, and Abettors of such traitorous Designs."[10]

Only then, when cast out of the constitution's protection and threatened with gruesome forms of execution, did the delegates to the Continental Congress move slowly toward a Declaration of Independence which at last named the king as a tyrant. Even then, in the very act of separation, the colonists' wounded feelings seep through their list of grievances, the "long train of abuses" identified in the Declaration. Its concluding paragraphs remind "our Brittish brethren" of how the colonies "have appealed to their native justice and magnanimity, and conjured them by the ties of our common kindred"—all in vain. Now the rebels must "mutually pledge to each other our Lives, our Fortunes, and our Sacred honor" to carry out the task of throwing off a government that had descended into despotism, and "provide new Guards for their future security."

The constitution of the United States is in a precarious condition today, for reasons much like those that threatened the British constitution 250 years ago. Americans' long-standing reverence for the U.S. Constitution as a bulwark against tyranny is not misplaced. In countless ways, domestic tranquility, the common defence, general welfare, and the blessings of liberty have been the better for it. And yet, like the British constitutional order in the late eighteenth century, the American constitutional order teeters on the verge of collapse. With hindsight, we can readily diagnose the constitutional flaws and identify the political crises that undermined Britain's constitutional order in America. In our present predicament, clarity of this sort is beyond our reach. Nevertheless, over the first quarter of the twenty-first century, Americans' faith in their government has plummeted amid escalating conflicts over fundamental constitutional issues. In recent years, attacks on the constitution's foundational structures by sitting governments have commenced as well, exceeding even some of the abuses that George III was accused of in the Declaration. Many Americans feel the same anguish and fear experienced by our forebears in the 1770s, worrying that the constitution can no longer protect them and that our ancient and venerable constitutional tradition, for all its virtues, may not be capable of containing the forces that threaten to pull it apart.

The purpose of this book is not to diagnose the political crisis of the moment or catalogue the present symptoms of an ailing constitution. Rather, the book before you is a historical investigation of how the constitutional order of the United States came together and changed over time, ultimately to reach its twenty-first century crossroads. It follows the story of the American constitution from its origins to the present. But it differs from many constitutional histories in steering away from court cases, Supreme Court decisions, and interpretations made by legislators, lawyers, and judges. They are not the sole proprietors of constitutional history. This book is grounded in the premise that our present crisis, like Britain's in the 1770s, emerged from long years of dynamic and comprehensive change, change located as much in expanding and mobile populations, shifting economies, and new environmental conditions as in the internal workings of legislatures and courts. It takes a long view, exploring social and political traditions that originated in Britain and evolved over many centuries. Rather than beginning in 1787, as if somehow Americans were inspired at that moment to create the world anew, we can better understand the origins of the United States Constitution—and even the question of what, exactly, constitutions are—by situating ourselves in the world from which an independent American nation emerged.

Two centuries before the American Revolution, indeed prior to the beginnings of English colonization in America, the scholar and diplomat Sir Thomas Smith unwittingly anticipated the eventual breakdown of the British constitution in a treatise on the Commonwealth of England, *De Republica Anglorum* (1583). Smith outlined the various forms of government that were combined and balanced within the English system—monarchy, oligarchy, democracy—and explained that changes to the form of government within a society are normal occurrences, not necessarily signs of foul play: "The mutations and changes of fashions of governement in common wealthes be natural, and do not alwayes come of ambition or malice." Because societies differ, "according to the nature of the people, so the commonwealth is to it fit and proper."[11] In early modern Europe, for instance, cities often had distinctive forms of government, spelled out in corporate charters or maintained by autonomous city-states. Urban life was different from rural life; merchants and artisans needed different rules and practices to govern their complex commercial society than peasants growing crops in the service of an aristocratic lord. A government suitable for a trading republic like Venice or Genoa would never do for the kingdom of France.

Smith offered a vivid analogy to convey this idea. A frame of government should suit the society to which it is applied "like a garment to the bodie or shoe to the foote, then the bodie politique is in quiet, and findeth ease, pleasure, and profit. But if a contrary forme be given to a contrary maner of people, as when the shoe is too litle or too great for the foote, it doth hurt and encomber the convenient use thereof." In Smith's view, the proper fit between a form of government and the nature of a society was critical. If a "free people" were "tyrannized or ruled by one against their willes, were he never so good," then they might "never rest untill they either destroie their king and them that would subdue them, or be destroyed themselves."[12] It's difficult to imagine a more succinct characterization of the constitutional crisis that would emerge within King George III's realm in the decade after 1763. Issue after issue tested the strength and flexibility of a constitution stretched to fit the distended body of the empire, until at last the fabric was torn asunder.

Amid one of these conflicts, the crisis over Parliament's Tea Act in 1773, Benjamin Rush of Philadelphia rallied his supporters, saying, "Remember my Countrymen, the present aera—perhaps the present struggle *will fix the constitution of America forever.*—think of your ancestors, and of your posterity."[13] Rush was a prominent physician, reformer, and civic leader but he was no soothsayer; we should not imagine that he could foresee how American colonists would successfully rebel and "fix the constitution of America" via drafting conventions, written documents, and popular ratification. Rather, Benjamin Rush, like all Britons, understood the British constitution to be fixed by virtue of the settled relationship among its several elements: first, the *body of society*—the land and people to be governed, their social conditions, how they earned their livings and organized their world (this was what Sir Thomas Smith meant by the "bodie" in his analogy); second, the *frame of government*—the institutions, practices, traditions, and customs that structured Britons' civic lives, including the king, the lords temporal and spiritual, the House of Commons, the common law, and all the customary rights and liberties that Englishmen loved to claim; and third, *written instruments* across the ages—from royal charters such as Magna Carta and the charters of cities, universities, and colonies to acts of Parliament such as the Act of Union with Scotland, the Bill of Rights, and the Act of Toleration of 1689 that declared and defended particular powers, rights, and liberties. These last two elements together—the frame of government and the written instruments that supported it—were the garment in Smith's analogy.[14]

When Benjamin Rush warned his fellow colonists that the struggle over the Tea Act would fix America's constitution forever, he meant that a fundamental constitutional issue was at stake—whether Parliament or the colonial assemblies had the ultimate power to levy taxes on the king's subjects in the colonies. What would fix America's part in the British constitution would not be a Supreme Court making a judicial decision on the constitutionality of Parliament's acts—no such body, no such concept, existed in the British constitution. Nor would it be a new written instrument rearranging the structure of the British government. This was theoretically possible, as when the parliaments of England and Scotland each voted in 1707 to pass Acts of Union, uniting to form a single Parliament for Great Britain, but unlikely in this situation. No, in this case, what Rush meant was that the outcome of the political standoff, either colonial acquiescence to the Tea Act or colonial resistance that forced Parliament to back down and repeal the law, would settle the question of Parliament's right to tax the colonies. The result would be an adjustment made to the British constitution through the establishment of a new precedent with lasting consequences. If the colonies acquiesced, they would see the diminishing power of their colonial assemblies and the growing authority of parliamentary legislation. Perhaps the colonial assemblies would wither away, and the older colonies would come to resemble the new ones in Quebec and East and West Florida, where royal governors ruled without assemblies.

We know the outcome. Colonists did "think of their ancestors, and of their posterity." Inspired by their own history of opposition to royal tyrants, Bostonians violently resisted the Tea Act to preserve for their posterity the rights their ancestors had won: the right to consent, through their own representatives, to any request for taxation. They destroyed the East India Company's tea rather than let it be unloaded, sold, and taxed. Parliament responded not with compromise but with punitive legislation, changing the constitutional relationship by attacking the rights granted to Massachusetts in its 1691 charter. One act cut off the lifeblood of Boston's economy by closing the port to all trade. Another struck down the institutions and practices of self-government in Massachusetts, from the town meeting to the elected council. A third revoked the power of Massachusetts courts to try the king's officers for crimes (up to and including murder) against colonists. In response, the people of Massachusetts rose in rebellion and convinced twelve other colonies to join them. In the ensuing war, the united colonies "never rested until they destroyed their king and them that would subdue them."

Amid this violent rupture, the former colonists began the process of "fixing" their American constitution in ways that Benjamin Rush could not have envisioned just a few years earlier. They created their own charters of government first as independent states and then as a confederated nation. During this process, each new state paid conscious, even obsessive, attention to the relationship of the elements that made up their constitutions. The thirteen states varied enormously in size: Pennsylvania's land area was thirty times the size of Rhode Island's. They varied greatly in population: Virginia had twelve times as many people as Delaware. Some states were exclusively agricultural, others were more urban and heavily commercial. In some states enslaved people were the majority of the population, their forced labor the heart of the economy. In others slavery barely existed. Some states had a strong established church, while others had none and fostered a chaotic array of competing religions. Some had long-cherished egalitarian self-government and widespread popular representation; others had more oligarchic traditions with elite gentry dominating small legislatures. Even amid the chaos of war, when the states set about framing new constitutions for themselves, each one strove to align the institutions of government they were creating and the written instruments that described them with the traditions, customs, and practices their framers deemed suitable to the conditions of their own state—not to some abstract ideal. As a result, the written instruments that declared rights and framed governments—the state constitutions—varied widely one from another.

When the states attempted to join together in a formal union, first with the Articles of Confederation and later with the Philadelphia Constitution, the wide differences among them made it difficult to agree on the principles, institutions, and powers suitable for a federal or "general" government. At the Philadelphia Convention in the summer of 1787, these differences generated fierce arguments. Regardless of the intensity of these disputes, there were two things that every delegate at Philadelphia, even those who refused to sign the final draft, agreed on. First, that a constitution should, indeed must, align the character of the land and people it governs with an appropriate frame of government; the garment should fit the body. It had been a grievous mistake for Britain's Parliament to attempt to rule directly a sprawling array of distant colonies whose conditions and interests were unknown to Parliament's members. The former colonies deserved governments suited to their own needs, not England's. Second, that it lay within the power of a people to alter a broken constitutional relationship, even in radical ways. It was in fact their duty to do so now that the people in America were independent and sovereign; they would tailor the constitutional garment in which they would clothe themselves.

This book offers a history of the United States Constitution that, in formal terms, was set in motion by the convention in Philadelphia in the summer of 1787.[15] But it does not define "constitution" simply or solely as the written document drafted by the convention, ratified the following year, and formally amended on rare occasions over the subsequent two dozen decades. Rather, it insists that in the Anglo-American tradition in which the United States emerged, a constitution is a *relationship* among the fundamental elements of a governing compact: the *body of society*, the nature and condition of the land and people; the *frame of government* as defined by its institutions, principles, practices, and customs; and the *written instruments* employed to define, describe, and delimit the government's powers.[16]

This view draws on the oldest English definitions of the word constitution, which refer to "the physical nature or character of the body."[17] Over time, the word came to describe bodies politic, "the mode in which a state is constituted or organized; especially as to the location of the sovereign power, as a *monarchical, oligarchical,* or *democratic constitution*"—these were the terms in which Thomas Smith described England's commonwealth in the 1560s.[18] It also encompasses the term's evolution across the long eighteenth century, when constitution increasingly came to refer to "the system or body of fundamental principles according to which a nation, state, or body politic is constituted and governed." After the American and French Revolutions, both of which generated written instruments delineating fundamental principles of governance, the word constitution came to be associated with these instruments: "In the case of a *written Constitution,* the name is sometimes applied to the document embodying it."[19] In other words, constitution has historically been taken to mean both the "body" and the "garment," further supporting the relational aspect of the concept.

The evolution of the word constitution might be taken to imply a historical narrative in which the term, in premodern times, meant the general composition of a state or society and its form of government, but in modern times came to mean a written document, a deliberately designed rulebook for government. This would be a mistake for two reasons. First, the older tradition lived on into modernity; Britain continued on its path to becoming the world's largest and most powerful empire in the nineteenth century without attempting to frame its system of government under a single written instrument. But second and more importantly, no written document can ever completely define, let alone create, a governmental system and the fundamental principles that shape its nature, functions, and limits. The structure of a society and the way it is governed always exceed the bounds of any written document, in the same way that maps are always inadequate to the terrain they depict.[20] Constitutions are more than just written instruments; they take the form of relationships between the body of a society, its frame of government, and its written instruments, the last of which always and necessarily fail to encompass the whole.

In exploring the evolution of American constitutional history, this book pays special attention to the significance of *land* to the body of society—the first element in the tripartite relationship—that is, those characteristics and qualities of a particular nation which a frame of government should be made to fit. The heightened significance of land is deeply rooted in English history and in the long process whereby constitutional practices that developed in England were transplanted to North America.

Governments marshal the resources of societies in order to govern them. At the most fundamental level, these resources consist of the land and the people—the natural endowments of a particular place and the productive labor of its population in generating wealth and power. Arrangements can vary widely; in countries where land is plentiful and human population slight, governments often focus on the control of people, the scarcer resource in the equation. Medieval England faced the opposite condition: an island kingdom with limited arable land, its population already exceeded two million at the time of its conquest by the Normans nearly a millennium ago. Power was determined by who possessed and controlled that limited and valuable land. As a result, England's constitutional evolution in the centuries before American colonization was shaped profoundly by struggles among the possessors of the land—the monarchs, the great aristocrats, and the church—as well as by the efforts of commoners to win or retain "liberties" against the overweening power of the landholders.

English efforts to colonize North America began five hundred years after the Norman Conquest of 1066. The colonists, guided by charters granted by the crown, attempted to recreate systems of government drawn from their English experience but ill suited to conditions in the colonies. Unlike England, the territory of North America was immense, essentially limitless as far as the first colonists could judge. Compared to England's, North America's Indigenous population was sparse—perhaps no larger than that of insular England at the time colonization began—but spread across a vast continent. Indigenous societies were not organized around the permanent and continuous occupation of fixed tracts of cultivated land. But such was the system, the constitutional order, that English colonists sought to impose on the land of North America. For the subsequent two centuries, this system, rooted in medieval doctrines of land and governance that were replicated in the colonial charters, evolved under the new conditions of life in America—conditions that were extraordinarily different from those in Britain.

The most significant difference for understanding the distinctive qualities of American constitutionalism lay in the astonishing dynamism of the American colonial population and its insatiable hunger for land. The explosive growth of settler society across the eighteenth century, doubling every twenty-five years, and its ceaseless quest for new and better land put tremendous pressure on the Indigenous peoples of North America, generating conflict that the imperial government struggled (and failed) to contain. In 1086, the new sovereign, King William, sought to impose his authority over England as it was, a stable agrarian kingdom. But in 1783, the now-sovereign former colonies sought to transform a continent. Their aspirations were based on territorial boundaries promised in their colonial charters that extended far beyond what they currently controlled. Although colonization had barely reached the Appalachians, the Treaty of Paris that ended the Revolutionary War in 1783 confirmed the United States' claims all the way west to the Mississippi River. The new nation aimed to displace Indigenous authority over the trans-Appalachian West to make way for white American settlers to develop the land and for new states to join the expanding union. Americans developed their new constitution with the *purpose* of creating a frame of government aligned with this envisioned transformation of the land and people of a continent.

The remarkable dynamism of the body of colonial American society, its extraordinary population growth and territorial expansion, was itself a challenge for English constitutionalism. When Benjamin Rush worried that the Tea Act crisis would "fix the constitution of America *forever*" and urged his fellow colonists to think of their "ancestors" and their "posterity," he was participating in a long tradition of constitutional discourse that staked claims to permanence and eternal validity. The Domesday Book, which was the result of William's efforts to consolidate his rule over England, acquired its name because its judgments were imagined to be as final and permanent as God's judgment of sinners at the Second Coming; English rights were believed to be unchanged from time out of mind. The liberties granted in Magna Carta in 1215 were to extend "in perpetuity." When Parliament declared the people's "ancient rights" in the Bill of Rights of 1689, they claimed to be acting "as their ancestors in like case have usually done." The constitutions drafted by the newly independent American states followed this tradition: Pennsylvania's new constitution would "remain in force therein forever, unaltered"; the Virginia constitution's Bill of Rights would "pertain to the good people of Virginia and their posterity." The Northwest Ordinance of 1787 claimed that its terms would "forever remain unalterable." And of course the Articles of Confederation created a "Perpetual Union." It lasted seven years.[21]

Two factors encouraged this rhetoric of permanence while also revealing tensions within it. First, the authors of constitutional documents across the generations were always aware that these were mere words on paper—"parchment barriers," as James Madison called them in *Federalist* no. 48. Words alone could never restrain "the encroaching spirit of power," let alone prevent the world itself from changing. Bold claims for permanence, assertions in writing that rights were both ancient and eternal, were nonetheless aspirational ways to lend force and durability to the agreements of a moment, to cast the resolution of a current crisis as a form of enduring truth. Second, during the long centuries of the premodern British world, it was more than plausible to think that the body of society went along relatively unchanged. There was no reason that rights or liberties already believed to be ancient at the time of Magna Carta should not be equally valid and applicable centuries into the future. Why not call them perpetual or eternal? In the premodern historical imagination, time's cycle of recurrence and return loomed larger than time's arrow flying forward into an unknown future.

By contrast, one of the most significant factors driving the American Revolution and the constitutional order created in its wake was the dynamic growth of the colonial population and its capacity to transform the land of North America. This is what changed the political meaning of the term "revolution" from a restoration—a turn of the wheel back to an earlier condition—to the creation of an utterly new and altered condition, a sharp break from the past after which people could, in the words of Tom Paine's *Common Sense,* "begin the world over again." As a result, the constitutional frameworks and documents produced during the American Revolution have a speculative, forward-looking quality. The express language of the Philadelphia Constitution's preamble looks to "ourselves and our posterity" as its audience, but not, as Benjamin Rush recommended, to our ancestors. Despite this tension with the tradition, the ancestors are present in the U.S. Constitution, lurking in the most fundamental aspects of how this new frame of government defines the sources of the nation's wealth and power in the relationships between land and people even as it tries to imagine their future.

Britain's constitutional order broke apart rather suddenly in the decade after 1763, unable to contain its expanding North American empire. But in remaking their own constitution, the newly independent former colonies built upon their historical legacy while attempting to apply it to a society experiencing rapid expansion. Neither the state constitutions begun in 1776 nor the Philadelphia Convention of 1787 was a stroke of originary genius, the creation of an utterly new constitutional order. Rather, independent American constitutionalism began as an effort to realign the bodies of their particular societies—the land and people of America, shaped by the outcome of the War of Independence and the Treaty of Paris that defined the new boundaries of the United States—with frames of government suitable to their new conditions. These would be drawn from the former colonies' historical past but modified to fit the challenges of the present and expressed in written instruments suited to their changed situation.

To understand the great realignment of 1776–87, we need to begin with the emergence of England's (and later Britain's) constitutional traditions and how they framed the colonists' inheritance, the institutional and ideological toolkit they brought to bear on the challenge of constitution making. This side of the story, the making of the "garment," has long been a focus of the work of early American historians and has produced an extremely rich body of scholarship. But we also need to consider more deeply a less studied element: the land and people of eastern North America and the unique challenges the states and incipient nation faced in aligning the ever-growing body with the garments they were fabricating from the torn remnants of their constitutional past.

Part I begins with the Domesday Book, the massive document generated by William the Conqueror's survey of England in 1086. By cataloguing the land and enumerating its people, the Domesday Book defined the relationship between the productive power of the land and people of England and the pyramid of dependencies by which the king's government was organized. The colonies transferred these British assumptions about constitutional relationships to a North America remarkably ill suited to their replication. Nonetheless, Britain's colonies embarked on a project to remake America into a landscape resembling the one recorded in the Domesday Book. The long-term success of these efforts so transformed the colonies that the fabric of Britain's constitution could no longer contain them.

The U.S. Constitution of 1787 was the product of that long transformation, a realignment of British constitutional principles to suit the land and people that the colonies had become across two centuries. Part II describes this realignment, following the process of state constitution making between 1776 and 1789 and the creation and reform of a federal union designed to meet the new nation's challenges. The resulting constitution fostered the continuous expansion of this new frame of government and form of land ownership across the continent and into the indefinite future. Part III follows the unfolding of this project across the nineteenth century, as the "Domesday Machine" of American expansion altered the constitution, drove the union into civil war, and transformed the land and people. Expansion radically altered the body of American society, but its frame of government and written constitution changed very little. The twentieth century, as part IV describes, witnessed yet another massive transformation of the body of society: the rise of modern, urban, industrial America and the wholesale redistribution of the country's population. An enormous and enduring expansion of the national government and its functions mirrored the changing society. Yet the nation barely adjusted the written instrument, the third element of the constitutional relationship, to redefine the structure, powers, and limits of national government in line with this century of dramatic change in the government itself.

By 1990, at the end of the second century under the Philadelphia constitutional order, a widening gulf separated the body of the land and people from the frame of government and from the written instrument. The representational structure of the elective branches of national government failed to adapt to the nation's changing populations. Within the written constitution's simple structure of three branches of government—legislative, executive, and judicial—there was little explicit provision for the administrative capacity necessary to carry out the government's immense new range of tasks. The capacious garment of the Philadelphia Constitution, designed by American citizens in 1787 to empower an agrarian nation to transform a continent, has more recently become a straitjacket in the hands of courts, lawyers, and politicians who see the constitution as nothing but words in a written text and use the written text to prevent a modern nation from pursuing the ends its people desire.

We are now only a third of the way through a third century under the Philadelphia constitutional order. The epilogue of this book, looking forward toward 2090, is, needless to say, speculative. The past thirty-five years have shown at first steady and now rapidly accelerating signs that the American constitutional relationship has, like its British predecessor in the 1770s, come apart. Can the American people in our current configuration defend the best constitutional traditions of our ancestors and preserve them for our posterity? Can we realign the body of the nation under new frameworks of government and new written instruments? To address these questions, let alone find answers to them, promises to be a difficult political and intellectual challenge. It will also be an emotionally wrenching one, given the faith and trust Americans have placed in their constitution. It will require courage to embrace the beliefs held by the framers of America's constitutions of the 1770s and '80s: that a society deserves a constitution suited to its own needs and challenges, not those of its distant ancestors, and that it lies within the power of a free people to alter a broken constitutional relationship, even in radical ways, to form a more perfect union.

PART I

From Domesday to Independence, 1066–1776

There seemed to be nothing to see; no fences, no creeks or trees, no hills or fields. If there was a road, I could not make it out in the faint starlight. There was nothing but land: not a country at all, but the material out of which countries are made. No, there was nothing but land. . . . I had the feeling that the world was left behind, that we had got over the edge of it, and were outside man's jurisdiction.

—WILLA CATHER, *MY ANTONIA*, 1918

1

Land, Conquest, and the Substance of Constitutions

FROM ENGLAND TO AMERICA

> Our whole constitutional law seems at times to be but an appendix to the law of real property.
>
> —F. W. MAITLAND, *THE CONSTITUTIONAL HISTORY OF ENGLAND*

ON OCTOBER 14, 1066, William, Duke of Normandy, defeated Harold Godwinson at the Battle of Hastings. Harold had reigned as England's king for a brief nine months after the death of Edward the Confessor. William and his conquering army of Norman knights (or "a French bastard" and his "armed Banditti," as Thomas Paine would later describe them) seized the throne of England.[1] He spent much of his subsequent reign consolidating authority over his new kingdom.[2]

To reinforce his control, William ordered a survey of what he had conquered. Twenty years after the Battle of Hastings, the register—later named the Domesday Book—was completed. It enumerated each of the realm's fifteen thousand named places, the human and livestock occupants of each place, and other resources such as ploughlands, woodlands, and meadows (fig. 1.1). It reckoned the expected annual yield of each landholding in pounds, shillings, and pence. And it identified each

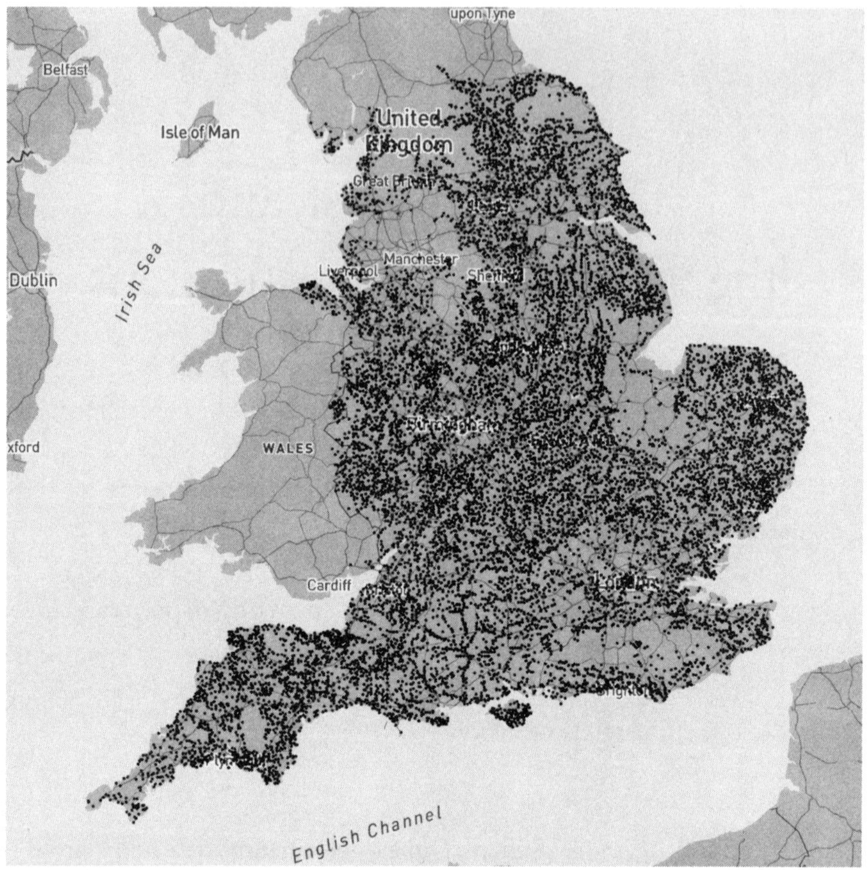

FIGURE 1.1. Modern map showing all named places in the Domesday Book. The map depicts how thoroughly developed England's eleventh-century landscape was, with its thousands of bounded estates yielding predictable annual agricultural revenues.

owner, including the new Norman owners of confiscated lands, the tenants-in-chief or lords to whom rent was due. Domesday was, in short, an immense rate book. It calculated the sources of revenue and delineated the chains of obligation and allegiance bound to each acre within a land-scarce realm. This critical compendium catalogued King William's newly won power.

The Domesday Book was also a constitutional document. It spelled out in excruciating detail how the body of the English realm was constituted, what its parts consisted of, and how each related to the whole. It described the sources and arrangement of wealth and power on which the king's sovereignty rested. Yet even though the Norman Conquest was a recent event when Domesday was assembled, its "constitutional" quality lay not in the projection of radical change. It did not announce an attempt to create a novus ordo seclorum, a new order of the ages, as the Great Seal of the United States would proclaim seven centuries later. William wanted to preserve in writing the conditions of property relations as they had evolved over the centuries in Anglo-Saxon England, up to the time when he seized the throne for himself and rewarded his Norman supporters by granting them lands of defeated Anglo-Saxon nobles. Even though the conquest brought about enormous changes in England's land ownership, the Domesday Book was designed to emphasize continuity with the kingdom's ancient past. The book's acquired name, Middle English for "Doomsday" or "Judgment Day," conveyed that the reckonings drawn from it were final: "For as the sentence of that strict and dreadful last examination, cannot be eluded by any art of equivocation: so in like manner, when any dispute should arise in the kingdom concerning the things there set down, upon recourse had to the book, the sentence of it could not be rejected or avoided, without punishment. . . . You cannot disagree with it, any more than you can to the aforesaid judgment."[3]

Of course, nothing in history is ever final. But many landholding practices of medieval England were still in place five centuries after the Norman Conquest, when English colonists began their slow conquest of North America, and they exerted a powerful influence on England's evolving constitution. In the words of Frederic Maitland, the great nineteenth-century historian of English law, "Our whole constitutional law seems at times to be but an appendix to the law of real property."[4] To understand America's constitutional development, we need to know how it emerged from England's. Domesday is the place to start.

We can take, for example, the village of Groton in the hundred of Babergh and the county of Suffolk, about seventy miles northeast of

London.[5] Groton was but one of the more than fifteen thousand places identified in the Domesday compilation. (John Winthrop, the first governor of Massachusetts Bay and an important figure in shaping land ownership and governance in colonial America, would be born there five centuries later.) According to Domesday, in 1086, the village of Groton had a total of forty-three households, perhaps around two hundred people, placing it among the top fifth of all settlements in England by population—not an insubstantial place.

The lands in Groton were owned—or, more properly, held—by three different entities. In medieval England, anyone who possessed land held it "of" the king, who was considered the rightful owner of all the lands in the realm.[6] In the case of Groton, however, one of the three local landholders was the king himself. William held the most valuable part of the village directly. It was not the most populous part, as only seven households lived on the king's Groton land, with a single plough team. But 363 sheep grazed on William's 100 acres. Wool was medieval England's most valuable export commodity,[7] and these 100 acres annually yielded twenty pounds, six shillings, and seven pence to the king, roughly seven times as much as the next most valuable parcel in Groton. Before 1066, this parcel of land had been held not by William's predecessor, Edward the Confessor, but by one of his Anglo-Saxon nobles, the Countess Aelfeva, who owned fourteen other estates in the region northeast of London. William seized her Groton property and several other valuable estates for himself and gave others to his supporters. After the Conquest, the Countess Aelfeva was left with only two of her less valuable estates.[8]

The second most valuable portion of Groton, yielding three pounds annual revenue in 1086, was held by the Abbey of St. Edmund, a Benedictine monastery in the nearby town of Bury St. Edmunds. The abbey's holdings comprised the largest and most populous part of the village, with thirty-three households on 180 acres of land, four plough teams for its ploughland, a meadow, a "winter mill," woodland for ten pigs, as well as one horse, six cows, and thirty sheep—one-twelfth the number of sheep on the king's neighboring Groton land. This portion was held by the abbey directly of the king—the abbot was "tenant-in-chief," as the terminology went. This arrangement was slightly different from before the conquest, when these holdings had been shared between the abbey and a small number of individual freeholders. The Norman Conquest consolidated the abbey's holdings in Groton, turning fourteen freemen who had formerly held their lands directly of the late king into tenants of the abbey. This change increased the abbey's revenues—before the conquest, the annual yield of the abbey's lands had been only half the amount.[9]

There were two more distinct parcels of land in Groton. Before the Conquest, each had been held of the king by a single freeman, but the Domesday Book records that in 1086 both parcels were held by one person, Richard FitzGilbert. Richard was one of those Paine later called "armed Banditti"—a Norman baron who served under William during the conquest. He was handsomely rewarded for his military service by the grant of some 185 separate estates, which he held directly of the king as tenant-in-chief. These two parcels in Groton were small, totaling sixty acres, supporting only three households with no recorded livestock, and yielding slightly less than one pound annually. These were two of Richard FitzGilbert's smallest holdings in England, but collectively his 185 landholdings made him very rich. The two freemen who had formerly held this land directly of King Edward were now Richard's tenants.[10]

As a written document, the Domesday Book was a great novelty—nothing quite like it existed in Europe's other kingdoms. But the landholding *practices* in England that it recorded in Groton and across fifteen thousand other places like it were not new.[11] Domesday offered a painstaking written description of the existing constitution of England. It spelled out everything that was known about its land and its people, its resources, and its hierarchical structure of authority—a pyramid of obligations and relationships with the new monarch at its summit. Virtually all the arable land in England was already owned and had an established monetary value, an expected annual yield. Although the Norman Conquest changed the identity of the personnel, from William on downward (to nobles, tenants-in-chief, lords, and freemen), the basic structure of the relationships among these individuals and the roles they played in governing the realm remained largely the same.

Notice another stable feature of the constitution Domesday describes that might too readily be taken for granted: the monetary system that measured the productive value of England's land. The relationship of pounds, shillings, and pence—twelve pence to the shilling and twenty shillings to the pound—was already well established. The system was based on the English silver penny, the most common form of money in the preconquest Anglo-Saxon kingdom. These would remain Britain's standard monetary units for another nine hundred years. But the apparent continuity in England's money across the centuries should not disguise the fact that money too was part of the constitution. Money served as a technology of rule generated and maintained by the power of the kingdom's rulers. England's silver pennies were made and issued by the crown and its agents. Mintmasters turned bullion into royally endorsed coins for customers (merchants mostly), who then circulated them through the markets of England. By requiring that the coins be used to pay the dues that the king collected from all those who held land directly from him, and that his lords collected from their tenants, the crown's money stitched together the relationships recorded in Domesday's words.[12]

Despite the massive scale of William's undertaking, the Domesday Book is not a complete description of the English constitution at the time of the Norman Conquest—no written document ever could be, for England or for any other country.[13] Domesday focused on the fundamentals necessary to support William's reign: England's well-developed land and the landholding relationships that yielded the revenues the king could use to keep the peace and defend the realm—in the medieval world, that is what government was. But Domesday did not attempt to record the laws, made under the Anglo-Saxon kings, which continued to be in force; the division of authority over the lives of England's subjects between crown and church; or institutional structures, such as courts, through which authority was exercised. Nor did it describe the many customary practices, obligations and duties, rights and privileges by which myriad forms of governance had taken shape, including the common law—the cumulative decisions of courts on the cases that came before them.[14] We know that such things existed, in part because any form of government needs norms, customs, and institutions in order to function.[15] But we also know about them because, in an equally significant constitutional moment more than a century after Domesday was completed, these concerns came to the fore in a series of fierce disputes among King John, the English barons, and the Roman Catholic Church. Out of these disputes emerged the great charter, Magna Carta.

Magna Carta was originally drafted in 1215 by Stephen Langton, Archbishop of Canterbury, to resolve the dispute between King John and the barons who had rebelled against him. It was subsequently annulled by Pope Innocent III, relaunching the war between the barons and the king. It was reissued in revised form in 1217 as part of the peace treaty ending that war, and then again in 1225 by John's successor, Henry III, and once more by Edward I in 1297, when it became part of English statutory law. Underlying the conflicts in each instance were objections by the powerful men of England, the barons and the bishops, to the king's consolidation of power and demands for revenue. King John's disastrous wars on the European continent, where he lost the Duchy of Normandy and other holdings in France, generated ever-increasing demands for revenue. These levies included scutage, money a knight paid as a substitute for direct military service. King John's demand for scutage even in peacetime, along with other efforts to squeeze money from the barons, were major causes of the rebellion. In addition, the king angered the pope by insisting on his right to control the election of a new Archbishop of Canterbury; the pope, in turn, excommunicated King John. By capturing London and other important cities, the rebellious barons forced John to negotiate in 1215 at Runnymede, a meadow along the Thames west of London. The great charter issued there was the result.[16]

Magna Carta frames its concessions to the barons as grants from the king to be in force in perpetuity: "TO ALL FREE MEN OF OUR KINGDOM we have also granted, for us and our heirs for ever, all the liberties written out below, to have and to keep for them and their heirs, of us and our heirs."[17] The specific liberties to which Magna Carta refers were considered ancient rights and privileges, customary ways in which England had always been governed, and they included norms surrounding the taxation of those holding land of the king. King John's recent conduct had eroded these older norms, and now the great men of the realm wanted them back.

The charter begins with an expansive grant from the king "to God" (generous, that!): "The English Church shall be free, and shall have its rights undiminished, and its liberties unimpaired" by any actions of the king.[18] Given that the Roman Catholic Church in England long predated the Norman Conquest, Magna Carta's recognition of the church's ancient rights set the model for the subsequent listing, over sixty-some clauses, of the equally ancient rights, privileges, and liberties of the "free men" of the kingdom.[19] For example, one of Magna Carta's clauses, still in force in British law today, asserts that "The city of London shall enjoy all its ancient liberties and free customs, both by land and by water. We also will and grant that all other cities, boroughs, towns, and ports shall enjoy all their liberties and free customs."[20] Another clause provides assurance that "no man shall be forced to perform more service for a knight's 'fee', or other free holding of land, than is due from it," thereby restoring the rates assessed by the Domesday Book to their rightful authority. In similar fashion, two other clauses guarantee that "no town or person shall be forced to build bridges over rivers except those with an ancient obligation to do so," and that "every county, hundred, wapentake, and tithing shall remain at its ancient rent, without increase."

Even clauses that do not refer expressly to "ancient" liberties or obligations nonetheless rely on basic principles of English society that recent royal incursions had violated, including two still in legal force today:

> No free man shall be seized or imprisoned, or stripped of his rights or possessions, or outlawed or exiled, or deprived of his standing in any way, nor will we proceed with force against him, or send others to do so, except by the lawful judgment of his equals or by the law of the land.
>
> To no one will we sell, to no one deny or delay right or justice.

And in clauses that are perhaps Magna Carta's most famous, at least in their legacy for American constitutionalism, King John promised that henceforth "no 'scutage' or 'aid' may be levied in our kingdom without its general consent." Both scutage and aid were taxes levied on landholders above and beyond the annual revenues laid out in the Domesday Book. The traditional rationale for kings to request such "aid" lay in the heavy costs of war making. King John promised:

> To obtain the general consent of the realm for the assessment of an 'aid' . . . or a 'scutage,' we will cause the archbishops, bishops, abbots, earls, and greater barons to be summoned individually by letter. To those who hold lands directly of us we will cause a general summons to be issued . . . to come together on a fixed day (of which at least forty days notice shall be given) and at a fixed place. In all letters of summons, the cause of the summons will be stated.

In other words, Magna Carta expressed in writing the principle that any taxation beyond those perpetual obligations of landholding due annually to the king and documented in the Domesday Book required the consent of those freemen who would be burdened by the additional tax. That consent would be expressed by representatives gathered in a single place to assess the "cause" for which aid was requested. The expenses of any royal ambitions beyond the crown's basic duty of keeping the peace in England, for which the customary revenues in Domesday should suffice, required the freemen's approval.[21]

From these practices would later evolve the institution of Parliament and the principle that taxation required the consent of the governed, which formed one of the chief constitutional arguments in the colonial American rebellion against the crown. But we're getting ahead of ourselves. For now, it's enough to see how Magna Carta, as a constitutional document, was a reaction to the king's violation of English rights, liberties, and obligations long since established by customary practice, including those concerning landholding recorded in the Domesday Book. To the extent that Magna Carta generated new liberties and obligations, these were rooted in fundamental premises of government from England's past, dragged into the light, and inscribed on parchment in response to a crisis. This was the English constitution: a combination of ancient customs and practices, formal institutions of government, and occasional written instruments that clarified or adjusted them.

In subsequent centuries, even moments of truly revolutionary change were justified by reference to England's ancient customs and liberties, a time-honored rhetorical practice.[22] In the 1530s, King Henry VIII seized control of England's church and expelled all papal authority, reversing Magna Carta's grant "to God" of the church's liberties. But the statutes drafted by Thomas Cromwell to achieve Henry's goals cited evidence from historical archives—"divers sundry old authentic histories and chronicles"—to declare "that this realm of England has always been an empire." According to these ancient authorities, England's king was under no superior earthly authority, and the king already "is and oweth [i.e., ought] to be the Supreme Head of the Church of England." The acts of Parliament merely corroborated established facts.[23] At stake in this rejection of Rome was the remaking of landholding relationships in England on a scale not seen since 1066. Henry confiscated immense amounts of property from the Roman Catholic Church for redistribution among the English nobility to cement their allegiance to the crown, much as William had done by giving the land of Anglo-Saxon nobles to his Norman knights.[24]

Similarly, during the Civil Wars and revolutions of the seventeenth century, Parliament justified its challenges to crown authority as attempts to uphold ancient rights and liberties. In 1628, Parliament's Petition of Right denounced Charles I's demand for forced loans by referring to Magna Carta and to statutes going back to Edward I. Parliament was objecting to Charles's attempt to impose taxation beyond what the traditional land-based revenue system yielded in order to pursue wars on the continent, as King John had done before Magna Carta. Charles continued to press for funds, extending the use of feudal instruments such as ship money over new territories, even in peacetime, thus starting down the road to Personal Rule that would end in civil war.[25] The Petition of Right joined the list of written constitutional documents that declared the rights of Englishmen, clarifying elements that were present but inchoate in Magna Carta. These included the right to consent, via Parliament, to any royal request for loans or taxes. It also reaffirmed the right to due process of the law and trial by peers in cases where a subject might be deprived of life, liberty, or property, and the right of private households to be free from the quartering of soldiers.[26]

The cycle of conflict and violence between the Stuart monarchs and Parliament finally ended six decades later, in 1688, when William of Orange, much like his namesake six centuries earlier, crossed the channel with an army, invaded England, and seized the throne. James II was deposed and fled to France. To justify this dynastic change and to recast Parliament's future relationship with England's kings, Parliament passed the "Act Declaring the Rights and Liberties of the Subject and Settling the Succession of the Crown." In this act, known as the Bill of Rights (1689), Parliament insisted that it was acting "(as their ancestors in like case have usually done)" to vindicate "their ancient rights and liberties." In other words, not only were the rights themselves ancient, but so too was the tradition of Parliament acting to assert them against usurping monarchs. Like Magna Carta, the English Bill of Rights enumerated a long list of ancient norms that James II "did endeavor to subvert and extirpate, . . . utterly and directly contrary to the known laws and statutes and freedom of this realm."[27]

Again and again in the course of England's history, authors of significant constitutional documents sought to declare that they were merely restating the rights and liberties of Englishmen that had existed since time immemorial, portraying them as somehow outside of time. Yet in every case, these constitutional interventions were entirely of the moment, brought about by a conflict or crisis within the polity that required resolution, often in the form of a transactional compromise that allowed the disputing parties to move forward. At heart, these conflicts were usually disputes over land, the wealth it produced, and the terms under which the state could extract that wealth for its own purposes. The written instruments these conflicts generated intertwined with the ancient customs and institutions of royal government, defending the rights and liberties of the people by placing fetters upon the king.

England's North American colonies were founded in the years after Henry VIII's radical restructuring of England's church and state but before the English Bill of Rights defined the modern sovereign as the

"King-in-Parliament." By formally requiring Parliament's consent to legislation, the Bill of Rights effectively shifted British sovereignty from the king to the combined will of the king and Parliament's two houses acting in concert—the King-in-Parliament. But where the colonies stood in this newly defined constitutional relationship was unclear. All the colonies were structured as large grants of land from the king, expressed in charters or patents outlining the terms by which this land would be held and governed. Some charters were granted to wealthy individuals such as Cecil Calvert, Lord Baltimore, founder of Maryland, or William Penn, son of Sir William Penn, Admiral in the Royal Navy. Others were granted to groups of investors organized as joint-stock companies, such as the Virginia Company of London and the Massachusetts Bay Company.[28] To convey the right of landholding to the colonists, the charters employed the language of feudal land tenure reaching back to Domesday. As in England, land in America would be held of the king by these individuals or organizations, received as a gift from the royal sovereign.[29]

In a typical example, the Massachusetts Bay Company Charter (1629) specified that the land granted to the colony would "be houlden of our saide most Deare and Royall Father, his Heires and Successors, as of his Mannor of East Greenewich in the County of Kent, in free and comon Soccage, and not in Capite nor by Knight's Service."[30] Let's unpack this mouthful of feudal legalese. Over the centuries since Magna Carta, the trend in English landholding practices had slowly moved away from the more burdensome forms of tenure, such as "knight's service," which required military service from the tenant, and tenure "in capite," which awarded the crown substantial fees if the tenant wanted to sell or transfer the land to anyone else. Instead, tenure in free and common socage was becoming more common. This was essentially a fee simple estate without feudal impediments, the least burdensome form of land tenure. Any residual obligations the landholder might have to the king could be paid in money, and there were few, if any, restrictions on the holder's ability to sell, or alienate, the land. The phrase "as of his Mannor of East Greenewich" was a legal form of conveyance designed to avoid any fees should the holder wish to grant, sell, or divide the land.

This generous and flexible form of land tenure turned out to be crucial for attracting settlers to a new colony. It provided incentives to investors by offering a secure and autonomous form of landowning that was still relatively scarce in England. It also allowed for necessary experimentation and change as colonists slowly came to understand America's landscape.[31] In 1086, Englishmen already knew where to find and how to use the country's best land. English colonists moving to Massachusetts in 1629 did not; they were reliant on Indigenous inhabitants' profound knowledge of the unfamiliar landscape, and often built their settlements on lands previously farmed by Indians.[32]

The king's granting of royal charters that conferred specific privileges and rights on particular subjects was an ancient institution as well. When Magna Carta protected the "ancient liberties and free customs" of the city of London, it was referring to this practice. London had enjoyed such privileges since a "time whereof the memory of many runneth not to the contrary"—far longer than anyone could remember. In 1067, King William had granted a formal written charter to the city, confirming this tradition. Henry III, King John's son and successor, granted royal charters to the universities at Cambridge (1231) and Oxford (1248), awarding them special governing privileges over their own members and exemptions from some forms of taxation. In the Tudor era, the crown extended the use of royal charters to the creation of overseas trading companies such as the Company of Merchant Adventurers to New Lands (1553), the Muscovy Company (1555), and the East India Company (1600). As with the cities and universities, these charters offered companies of merchant investors the power to govern their own members (the East India Company's charter referred to itself as a self-governing "fellowship") and exempted them from certain taxes, while specifying their obligations to the crown in return.

This form of conveyance was next extended to the American colonizing projects of the early seventeenth century, beginning with Virginia. The recipients of these charters, the prospective colonists and their financial backers, adopted the ancient practice of looking upon their charters as constitutional bulwarks, guarantees that the rights and liberties granted by them were inviolate—just as Magna

Carta had enshrined the ancient rights and liberties of the city of London.[33]

For someone like John Winthrop, born and baptized in 1588 in the village of Groton, the complex legal world of landholding and chartered corporations would have been familiar. His grandfather, Adam Winthrop, knew the value of corporate privileges. He was a citizen of London, a successful clothier, and a member of the Worshipful Company of Clothworkers, which had been incorporated by a royal charter in 1528. With the wealth he made in the city, Adam purchased Groton Manor in 1544, specifically the part recorded in Domesday as the landholdings of the Abbey of Bury St. Edmunds. (The abbey's property had been taken over by Henry VIII in 1533 and put up for sale.) As lords of the manor, the Winthrop family (Adam's heirs) gained the right to appoint the rector of the parish church and to preside in the manorial court over legal cases among their tenants.[34]

Both John Winthrop's father, also called Adam, and John himself studied law at London's Inns of Court. In 1627, John Winthrop became an attorney of the Court of Wards and Liveries in London, which oversaw the assignment of guardians over minors who had inherited estates where the land was subject to forms of feudal tenure. Thus, the Massachusetts Bay Company Charter, with its grant of lands in feudal language to the twenty-nine original investors in the Company and its delineation of the rights and privileges of corporate governance, spoke directly to the training and experience of the colony's first governor. Under Winthrop's direction, Massachusetts used its power to convey land to its colonists in the form of incorporated townships. The company also revised its corporate governing structure to include an assembly to represent the increasingly dispersed colonial settlements. In 1632, Winthrop commented that he and his fellow magistrates had transformed Massachusetts from its corporate origins, resembling an English city with a mayor and a corporate council, into something "in the nature of a parliament."[35]

Colonists understood perfectly well the ancient forms under which their grants to land in America were conveyed. But where did English monarchs get the authority to convey these distant lands? What right had the king to grant them? At the time of the Domesday Book, the answers had been obvious: William's authority derived from his military conquest of England. He and his army had defeated the prior king and seized power over the realm. England's land was already fully owned, or held, in a complex system that defined land as the fixed property of individuated households and valued it by reference to money. This was not true of North America before English colonization began. Native American peoples owned, occupied, and used the land of this immense continent, divided among thousands of polities ranging in size from single villages to extensive confederacies of tribes or nations.

The forms of Indian land ownership differed considerably from the permanent agricultural fields, meadows, and woodlots catalogued in Domesday. Land ownership also varied among the many different Indigenous polities across the continent. In much of eastern North America, Indian societies tended to be seminomadic. They farmed plots of ground during growing seasons, then moved to hunting and fishing territories to take advantage of seasonally shifting food and resource supplies. In other regions, such as the pueblos of the arid Southwest, permanent settlements were more common. Land ownership and use rights among Indigenous people often pertained to units larger than the individual household or family lineage, such as the village, clan, or tribe. Although America was very rich and the land yielded abundant resources for its human population, Indian polities were not in the business of making or using money, and land was not valued in monetary terms.[36]

Native American landholding and usage practices looked so strange to English eyes that they had difficulty recognizing them as forms of ownership. Instead, they would sometimes insist that Indians roamed across the earth like wild animals, gleaning its resources but no more possessing or holding it than did the abundant deer of the forests. This claim was patently false, but it offered European colonists a convenient, self-serving way to project their own landowning practices onto an unfamiliar world.[37]

When the colonization of North America began, it was obvious that England's monarchs had in no way conquered the land (in fact, no reigning British monarch would even visit the continent until 1939).[38] Instead, the crown derived its territorial authority from claims similar to those that Spain's monarchs, Ferdinand and Isabella, had made after the voyages of Christopher Columbus. Spanish and papal documents enunciated a doctrine of discovery, later taken up by England, that lands "inhabited by a Savage people, and not in the possession or government of any Christian Prince or State," when discovered on behalf of such a prince, fell under his sovereign power.[39] Although Columbus had claimed almost all of the Americas for Spain (save Brazil, which went to Portugal by virtue of the Treaty of Tordesillas of 1494), the English used a flimsy set of historical pretexts to assert prior discovery of the northern parts of America. Here John Dee, the alchemist, astronomer, and courtier, did for Queen Elizabeth's territorial ambitions what Thomas Cromwell had done for her father's ambition for supremacy over the church. Dee unearthed "historical" accounts—ranging from John Cabot's voyages of 1497 to North America's coast all the way back to legendary voyages of King Arthur and Prince Madoc—as a basis for English sovereignty, publishing them in his *General and Rare Memorials Pertayning to the Perfect Arte of Navigation* in 1576. Likewise, Sir Francis Drake, on his 1579 voyage up the Pacific coast north of Mexico to San Francisco Bay, claimed for Queen Elizabeth the immense and unknown territory he named "New Albion."[40]

In 1606, on the basis of these claims, Elizabeth's successor, James I, granted charters to two branches of the Virginia Company for the land north of Spanish Florida, stretching from present-day South Carolina to Maine (from the 34th to the 45th parallel). A revision of Virginia's charter in 1609 specified that this land grant would stretch "from Sea to Sea"—that is, from the Atlantic to the Pacific.[41] Of course, at that time, long before the invention of a method for determining longitude on sailing ships, no one knew how immense the distance was "from Sea to Sea." More than half a century into the English colonization of Virginia, a popular map suggested that it might not be more than about "ten days' march," or two hundred miles (fig. 1.2). In subsequent decades, the royal charters of Massachusetts and Connecticut likewise awarded these colonies territory stretching "to the South Sea on the West Part."[42]

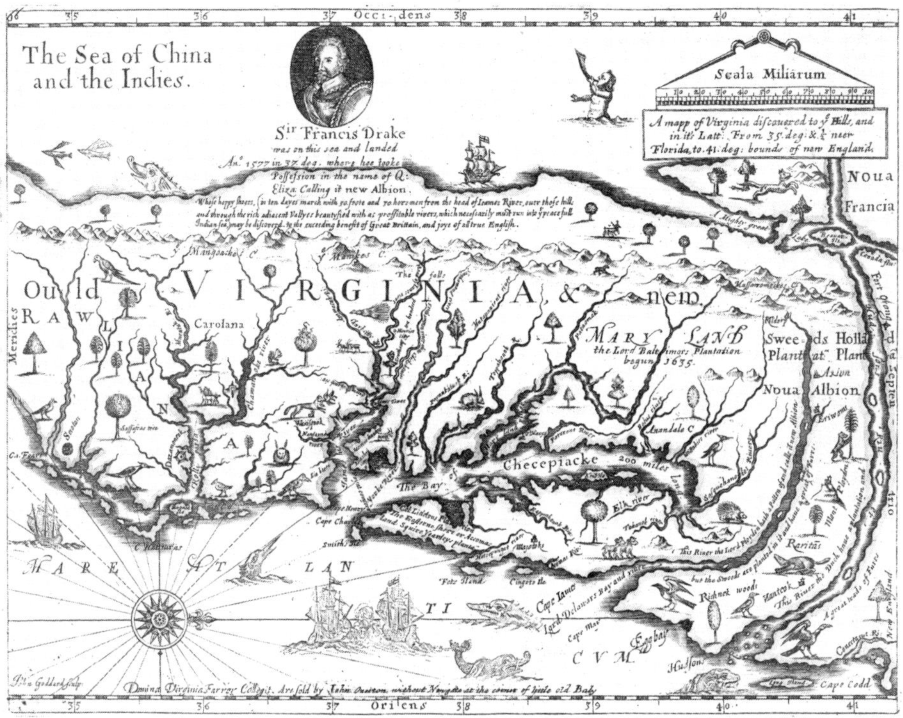

FIGURE 1.2. Thomas Farrar's map of Virginia, 1667. This map, like many early modern maps, is configured with north to the right and west at the top. The markers for latitude that run across the top and bottom edges of the map are reasonably accurate. But there are no longitude markers on the left and right edges, which accounts for the curious proximity of the "The Sea of China and the Indies" to the Blue Ridge Mountains, where Virginia's principal rivers begin.

England's North American colonies thus began as an extension of ideas about landholding that went back to the Domesday Book and before. The legal doctrines under which new territory was incorporated into England's realm followed the examples of earlier European empires in the Americas. The doctrines had been rehearsed by the English in earlier centuries through attempts at conquest and colonization in near-overseas places such as Ireland. This new land, though, whose features seemed to the colonists as strange and unknowable as its people, would confound their best efforts to stretch the English constitutional tradition to govern it.[43]

2

Colonies and Constitutions from Charter to Independence

[The colonists] were contented, therefore, to hold their lands of their king, as their sovereign lord; and to him they were willing to render homage, but to no mesne or subordinate lords; nor were they willing to submit to any of the baser services.

—JOHN ADAMS, *A DISSERTATION ON THE CANON AND FEUDAL LAW*, 1765

THE FICTION at the heart of England's claims to land in the colonial charters quickly became obvious. From the Chesapeake Bay to New England, colonists were dependent for their survival on the farming skills of America's Indigenous peoples; they were kept alive by the surplus grain produced by the true owners of the land.[1] To transform America from wilderness and waste, as the English imagined it, into something resembling the landscape recorded in the Domesday Book would require a massive project to acquire land from the Natives who possessed it, to move English colonists onto it, and to perform the work of surveying, dividing, distributing, bounding, recording, and valuing the land. Eventually, this process would transform the land into a country (to paraphrase Willa Cather) by creating the conditions for a European-style state. The granting of the colonial charters was the barest beginning.

What was clear from the outset was that the colonist-invaders of Indian lands would not treat the Indigenous inhabitants the way William and his conquering knights had treated England's Anglo-Saxon population. The Domesday Book recorded a new set of Norman overlords placed atop an existing system. This was roughly the approach of the Spanish conquerors of the populous, densely settled, and hierarchical societies of the Mexica and Inca Empires.[2] But the English colonists, organized into corporate trading companies rather than militarized bands of adventurers, would not have been up to such a task—and certainly not across the immense territories and diverse polities of North America in the seventeenth century, where there was no Tenochtitlan, no capital or administrative center to be seized.

Nevertheless, Indigenous people were everywhere the English went. Their presence was the first and most obvious sign that a particular stretch of land was a good place to "settle." As the settler populations gained a foothold and expanded their footprint, a similar process took place everywhere across the new colonies; colonists began to buy land from Indians. Through these purchases, the English acknowledged the obvious—that Natives did in fact have ownership and use rights in land, rights that could be valued, fairly or not, in money (the same English pounds, shilling, and pence used since Anglo-Saxon times). English purchasers did not always pay in sterling coinage, which was scarce in the colonies, and instead offered goods. Nevertheless, when deeds were recorded for the land acquired, they often specified a monetary amount, initiating the process of commodifying American land.[3]

These land purchases often accompanied land grants or allocations to colonists. For example, the Massachusetts Bay Company brought colonists in family groups to America in large numbers (nearly twenty thousand between 1629 and 1640). The colony quickly developed the practice of creating townships as sub-corporations of their chartered company. As designated holders of all the colony's land, Massachusetts's governing body (the General Court) would make a specific grant to a group of colonists—perhaps a few dozen families, not unlike the population of the English village of Groton in the Domesday Book. The court would set these colonists up as a corporate township with a defined amount of land (the town of Concord's grant in 1636, for instance, was six miles square) and then transfer to the township the power to distribute this land among themselves.[4]

At this stage, the new townsmen, usually the richer and more prominent among them, would seek out Indigenous owners of this land and try to extinguish their claims through purchase. Sometimes colonists attempted to do this fairly and with integrity, negotiating with leaders of local villages or bands, even paying several competing Native claimants to make sure all titles were extinguished. Other times they did it cynically or fraudulently, using liquor to make Indigenous owners pliant in negotiation or purchasing the land from Natives who had no authority to sell it.

Not all Indigenous land was purchased; some was taken by force, whether in small-scale conflicts or in large-scale wars. And as diseases that accompanied European colonists devastated Native communities, the English considered some land to be abandoned. Famously, the land on which the so-called Pilgrims of Plymouth settled had been a Patuxet village and farmland until the late 1610s, when a plague wiped out most of its people.[5]

Through purchase or seizure, land transfers took place throughout all the English North American colonies. In Virginia, after various experiments in creating corporate townships or private manors failed, counties became the organizational unit (sometimes subdivided into hundreds, as in Domesday). In 1618, a headright system emerged there to deal with a labor shortage—without labor to produce commodities, the land was worthless in English terms. The headright system granted the right to claim land to anyone who could afford to import servants (and later slaves) in large enough numbers to support commercial agriculture. For every servant or slave brought to America, the sponsoring planter would receive fifty acres, a practice later replicated in Maryland and the Carolinas. In colonies farther north, from Pennsylvania through New Hampshire, townships and family farms prevailed. In all cases, the colonial governments set to work to create a Domesday-like system of land ownership. They registered deeds and titles held by the new English owners (making possible a market in land), set up court systems to adjudicate disputes, and rated the value of landholdings for the sake of colonial taxation to raise the revenue necessary for these new colonial governments to function.[6]

Unlike King William after the Norman Conquest, the governments of the colonies could not rely on a steady stream of revenue already being produced by the tenants of a long-developed agrarian society. The high cost of colonization meant that the early colonial governments, whether corporate or proprietary, were often deeply in debt. Colonists felt pressure to generate valuable cash crops to reimburse their English creditors. It was hard enough simply to survive in this strange new world, let alone to generate profits to pay off creditors and fund a rudimentary government. Many early colonizing ventures simply failed.

In a new colonial settlement such as Springfield, Massachusetts, it was common for a wealthy colonist family, in this case the Pynchons, to take the lead in developing the land. The Pynchons had the resources to pay Indigenous claimants and build necessary infrastructure such as mills and roads. The Pynchons became magistrates in the local courts, employers of many wage laborers, merchants to the farmers of the region, and major players in the real estate market. They were American colonial variants of the tenants-in-chief or manorial lords of Domesday's England, power brokers who connected local colonists to the government in Boston. Over time, every colony developed some sort of speculative market in land, where individuals or even groups of investors took advantage of the lenient terms defined in the colonial charters, the "free and common socage" tenure that allowed for easy and unencumbered sales of land. Speculators began to buy and sell the rights to undeveloped land—land still occupied and possessed by Indigenous people who had not sold or ceded it to colonists.[7]

In every colony, as new colonists arrived and spread across the landscape, there emerged some form of assembly to represent the landholders in the government's meetings. A regional power broker like John Pynchon, whose Springfield home was then on Massachusetts's farthest frontier (several days' journey west of Boston, where the General Court met) would hold a virtually permanent seat in the upper house of the legislature. The ubiquity of these legislatures across the colonies was not the result of a widespread commitment among the colonizers to republican ideas of self-government. In some colonies, such as Massachusetts and Connecticut, republican ideas were present from the beginning, a by-product of the Puritan ideals of church government, where local congregations governed themselves and elected their own religious leaders.[8] But in all the colonies, including the proprietary colonies held by wealthy aristocrats and those directly under crown control with royally appointed governors, the assemblies emerged from the necessity of enlisting the new landholders in the tasks of government. It required an enormous effort to create an ordered, bounded, and revenue-yielding landscape, to transform North America's wilderness (as the colonists saw it) into something resembling the England of Domesday. As a consequence, these colonial legislatures, operating as something "in the nature of a parliament," to quote John Winthrop again, became far more *active* governing institutions than England's premodern Parliament.[9]

From the time of the Domesday Book through the American Revolution, the main function of the government in Britain "was virtually restricted to preserving the constitution (which meant doing nothing in home affairs) and conducting foreign policy"—in other words, keeping the king's peace and defending the realm.[10] The crown's annual budgets reflected these limited aims. In the century after the Glorious Revolution of 1688, as Great Britain grew into a global empire, the overwhelming majority of its expenses were for military purposes, even in peacetime. For example, in 1730, amid the longest stretch of peacetime in the eighteenth century, Britain's government spent a total of £5.4 million. Of this, £2.2 million went toward defense and £2.3 million toward interest on the debt (mostly incurred in the previous war). Only £900,000, 16 percent of the total, went toward general domestic government—operating the king's courts and the administrative functions of the state.[11]

Thirty years later, during the Seven Years' War, the largest war Britain had ever fought, the comparable annual amounts were £14.7 million for defense (a more than sixfold increase), £4.4 million for interest (nearly doubled from 1730), but still only £900,000 for general government, now less than 5 percent of the total. Indeed, Britain's domestic spending saw almost no change for the entire eighteenth century, fluctuating between £700,000 in 1701 and £900,000 in 1800 even as the annual budget grew from £3.4 million to £49.5 million and the public debt grew from £14 million to £441 million.[12] The legislation that the eighteenth-century Parliaments did pass tended to be private and local. It addressed the concerns of aristocrats and gentry who served in the Lords and Commons rather than instituting sweeping programs for the nation as a whole that required great expenditures; these were rare.[13]

In comparison, the legislatures of Britain's American colonies conducted far more vigorous and general forms of domestic development and spent relatively little on defense or foreign policy. The colonies relied on the crown and the Royal Navy for protection against external threats from European powers, although they did raise militias, some more vigorous than others, for the sake of defense (or aggressive assaults) against their Indigenous neighbors. But unlike England's Parliament, the colonial governments took an active role in shaping and extending their own societies, exercising a vigorous administrative function. In the words of the historian Bernard Bailyn:

> There devolved upon them, out of the necessity of the situation, the power of controlling the initial distribution of the primary resource of the society: land. . . . The colonial governments in one or another of their branches came to exercise this essential power; much of colonial politics was concerned with the efforts of individuals and groups to gain the benefits of these bestowals.

Beyond carrying out their primary function of land distribution, the colonial assemblies engaged directly or contracted to build material infrastructure such as "wharfs, roads, ferries, public vessels, civic buildings." The assemblies also legislated for and developed social institutions, such as schools and religious institutions, at a scale and speed unlike anything Britain's Parliament had ever attempted.[14]

Creating a local money supply was another central preoccupation of the "parliaments" of colonial America that Britain's Parliament very seldom engaged in.[15] The silver coins—the pounds, shillings, and pence—issued by the English crown from time immemorial, did not readily follow the colonists to America. The silver money that did drift into colonial British America (mostly the king of Spain's coins, acquired through trade with or plundering of the Spanish colonies) quickly passed to England in payment for imported goods. The primary way British silver came to the colonies was through military expenditure. But until the major imperial wars of the mid-eighteenth century, the Royal Navy's presence in the colonies was limited, and the army's virtually nonexistent.[16]

To ease their chronic shortage of money, colonial legislatures from Massachusetts to the Carolinas developed various schemes to generate currency that would serve as legal tender within the colony and be collected in taxes. These efforts ranged from the Bay Colony's careful coinage of its own sterling-grade shillings beginning in the 1650s (despite this being repugnant to English law) to endless schemes in the eighteenth century to issue colonial paper money backed either by silver reserves in the colony's treasury or by land owned by a bank's subscribers. The politics of paper money was immensely complex and a major source of the roiling factional conflicts that plagued colonial governance. The crown and Parliament tended to discourage these fiscal experiments and in 1764 ended them for good with the Currency Act, which prohibited the colonies from issuing paper money as legal tender.[17]

By the time of the Currency Act, much of the work presaged in colonial charters had been accomplished. Through the vigorous activities of the colonial legislatures; the continued migration of colonists, free and bound; natural population growth; and the spread of agriculture, the colonies extended westward from the Atlantic coast toward the Appalachian Mountains. The settler population grew from virtually none in 1600 to nearly two million in 1763, similar in size to England's population at the time of Domesday but spread over an area five times as large as England.[18] The king's colonial subjects in North America now amounted to almost a quarter of the population of England itself. They had turned the Atlantic seaboard of the continent, from the 34th to the 45th parallel, into something resembling the landscape that the Domesday Book described (fig. 2.1). The burgeoning lands of colonial America were held *of* the king, *through* "tenants-in-chief," *in* "free and common socage." And they now yielded revenues to the colonial governments

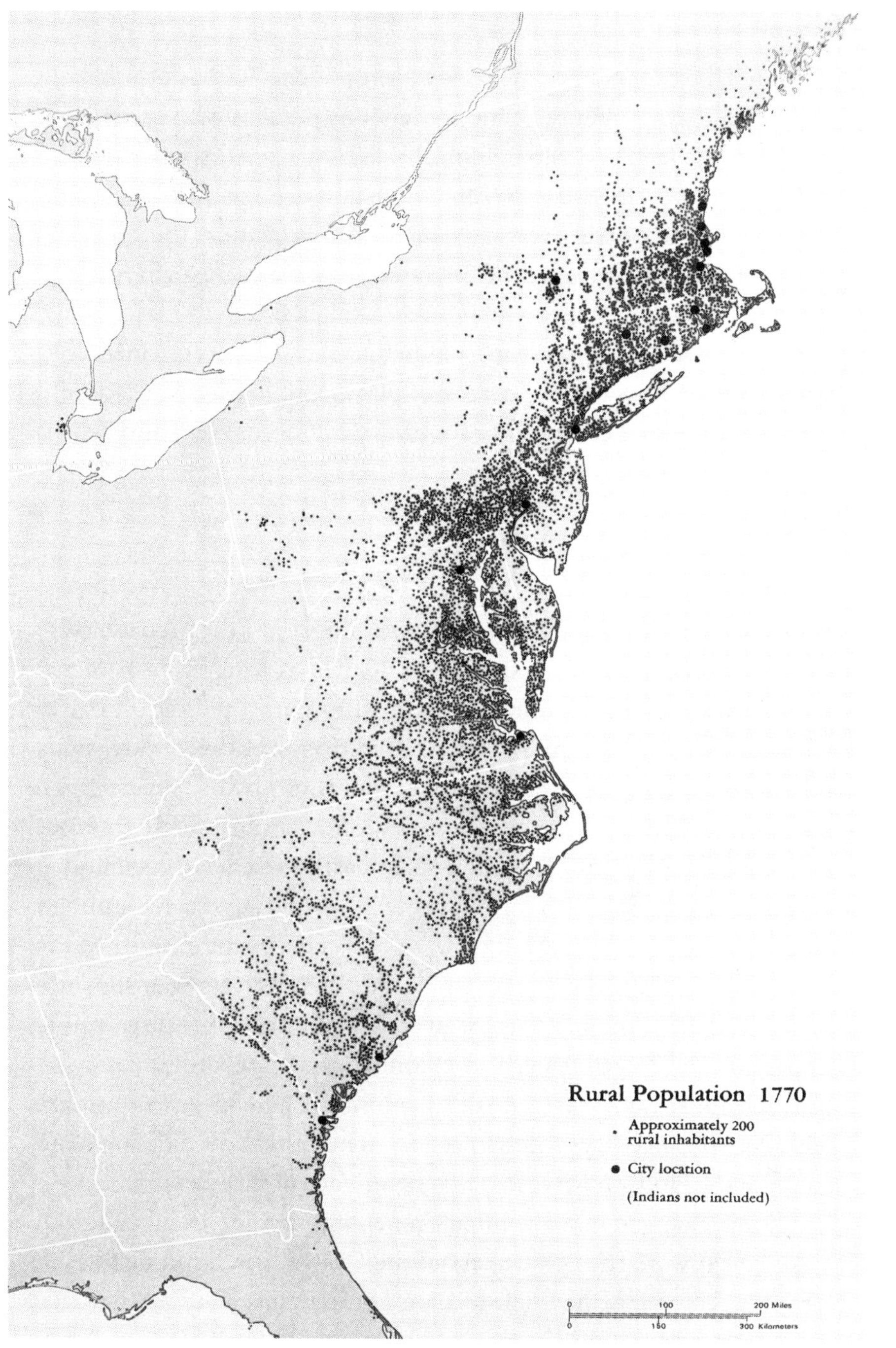

FIGURE 2.1. British North America, rural population, 1770. After a century and a half of colonization, the coastal region east of the Appalachians, especially from the Chesapeake to New England, had come to approximate the England of Domesday depicted in Figure 1.1.

that rated the properties and levied taxes on them.[19] This development came at the dire expense of the Indigenous peoples who owned and occupied the land prior to colonization. They were dispossessed in a way that most of the Anglo-Saxon population of England never experienced in the wake of the Norman Conquest. The far more thorough and transformative conquest of the eastern coastal plain of North America came not by way of armed and mounted knights led by a martial king, but through relentless pressure—punctuated by spasms of violence—from the steadily grinding forces of plows and livestock, roads and fences, money and commodities, surveys and deeds, laws and courts, churches and towns.

Starting in 1763, the British sovereign (no longer just the monarch as in the days of King John, but since 1689 defined as King-in-Parliament) began to make changes in its relationship with the colonies. The Currency Act of 1764 marked one alteration, but there were many others. They took the familiar form of incursions by the sovereign on the ancient rights and customs of the barons, the "barons" in this case being the trans-Atlantic colonies. As in past moments of rebellion in English history, conflict arose in response to the sovereign's military ambitions, the costs incurred by wars, and subsequent changes to the governance of the realm. Before about 1750, Britain's wars against France and Spain, its Catholic rivals for overseas empire, had relatively little impact on the North American colonies. New England, the crown's northernmost (and least valuable) colonies, had engaged in warfare with New France beginning in 1689.[20] The other colonies west and south of the Hudson River had less experience in these affairs.

All this changed in 1754, when French military forces moved from Lake Erie toward the headwaters of the Ohio River, building forts in territory claimed by the English colonies of Virginia and Pennsylvania. This was exactly the region where a westward bulge in the frontier of English settlement was expanding into land that speculators were eyeing for rapid development. There, a French military company encountered one of these speculators, a young Virginia surveyor named George Washington. Washington was leading a company of Virginia provincial soldiers on a mission to warn the French off King George's territory. The violent debacle that ensued in this remote forest touched off a global war, with Britain and France as principal combatants. The trans-Appalachian interior of North America was among the rich prizes at stake.[21]

During the war, the British crown requested a form of "knight's service" from its artificial barons, the colonies. The colonial legislatures complied. They raised taxes from their wealthy merchants and landholders and enlisted soldiers from among their subjects to fight alongside His Majesty's regular troops. By 1763, British forces had defeated the French and driven them from North America. Britain now had three more continental colonies: East and West Florida (gained from Spain, a later entrant in the war) and Quebec, the heartland of New France, along the St. Lawrence River Valley and the Great Lakes. By the Treaty of Paris that ended the war, Britain held undisputed claim to the continent from the Atlantic to the Mississippi River—undisputed by other European powers, that is. The Indigenous peoples who actually owned, occupied, and ruled the territory between the Appalachians and the Mississippi went unrepresented at the peace negotiations despite having formal diplomatic alliances with the European combatants. They saw things differently.[22]

Native nations responded forcefully to British military efforts to impose authority over the trans-Appalachian territory and to the simultaneous rush of colonists onto their lands. In Pontiac's War, named for an Ottawa chief who was among this rebellion's many leaders, Indigenous warriors in April 1763 began attacking British forts and colonial settlements in the trans-Appalachian West. Rather than fight further expensive wars now that the French war was settled, the crown chose to cordon off this territory. The Royal Proclamation of 1763, issued in October, drew a line along the ridge of the Appalachian Mountains, prohibiting colonists from settling or purchasing land beyond the line for the indefinite future. In a less well known but equally significant clause, the Proclamation overturned a common practice of the previous 150 years, prohibiting private subjects from purchasing land directly from Natives, even within the already "settled" colonial territory east of the Appalachians. Henceforth, only the crown or its agents, the colonial governments, could purchase land, and only "at some public Meeting or Assembly of the said Indians." Negotiations with Native peoples for land would no longer be understood as private transactions within a land market, but as treaty negotiations between sovereign powers.[23]

The Royal Proclamation was meant to keep the peace and prevent the "great frauds and abuses" in private land purchases that historically had provoked violence. But its effect was to deny to the colonies the right to develop enormous amounts of land that had been granted to them in their charters by earlier kings. This was an abrupt and sweeping change to a long-established set of fundamental customs and practices—a change, that is, in the imperial constitution. It was reminiscent of Henry VIII's seizure of the Roman Catholic Church's property (which his royal forebears had promised in Magna Carta to leave free) and distribution of it to his supporters.

The king could plausibly claim to have conquered these trans-Appalachian, Canadian, and Florida territories—unlike the older colonies—by military force. The crown now chose to govern its conquests directly, as William the Conqueror had done seven hundred years earlier. Rather than create new artificial barons (in the form of colonies—corporate, proprietary, or otherwise) and confer on them the right to distribute land, King George III chose to rule these territories himself. He would use some of this conquered land to reward his soldiers, the same tactic William of Normandy used.[24] The new colonies would be ruled by a governor and council appointed directly by the crown. They would have no representative assembly until such time as the royal governor determined that the colonists were ready to create one. The largest and most populous of these colonies, Quebec, consisted mainly of French habitants who, as Roman Catholics, were prohibited by law from civic participation in the British realm. The two Florida colonies also held mostly Catholic subjects and Native Americans, who had always been excluded from colonial governance. It was therefore unclear when and how assembly government of the kind seen in the first colonies would ever become possible in these new colonies.[25]

These were enormous spaces. The Quebec Act of 1774 revised the Royal Proclamation of 1763, making a single royal colony out of all the territory north of the Ohio River—what would become the states of Ohio, Indiana, Illinois, Wisconsin, and Michigan, as well as major parts of the present-day Canadian provinces of Ontario and Quebec. All told, the new Quebec was larger than all the pre-1763 colonies combined. Most of Quebec's land between the Ohio River and the Great Lakes had originally been granted to Virginia, New York, Connecticut, and Massachusetts in their charters. Now this land would be beyond the power of these colonies to develop and govern, as they had been doing piecemeal for a century and a half (figs. 2.2 and 2.3).

The sovereign King-in-Parliament also began to demand revenue directly from colonial subjects, and not just in the new colonies that the king had conquered and now ruled directly. These new measures violated the ancient English right of consent to taxation. The colonists understood their colonial charters as constitutional bulwarks, their own versions of Magna Carta and the Bill of Rights. The assemblies provided by those charters were their own parliaments, the only bodies through which they could express their consent. The new taxes began with the Stamp Act of 1765, an excise tax passed by Parliament and designed to raise revenue through the selling of stamps required for use on all public transactions on paper, from newspapers to legal contracts to college diplomas. The king and Parliament insisted that colonial subjects pay part of the cost of keeping royal soldiers in the colonies, and the Stamp Act would be a means to raise this money. From the colonists' perspective, the Stamp Act seemed reminiscent of the forced loans or ship money demanded by Charles I or the scutage demanded by King John. These were new demands to pay the expenses of the Seven Years' War, even though the colonies had already provided "knight's service" and yielded up substantial contributions of money, men, and material during wartime.[26]

From New England to the Chesapeake, an immediate outcry arose in response to the Stamp Act. In the Virginia House of Burgesses in May 1765, the twenty-nine-year-old Patrick Henry introduced resolutions declaring that Virginia's colonists "brought with them and

FIGURE 2.2. New and accurate map of North America, 1768, by Peter Bell. Note that this map, drawn prior to the Quebec Act of 1774, shows Virginia's land claims stretching northward around the western Great Lakes, and New York's claims encompassing Lake Ontario and the eastern side of Lake Huron. The Province of Quebec is limited here to the lower St. Lawrence Valley and does not reach as far as Lake Ontario.

transmitted to their posterity . . . all the liberties, privileges, franchises, and immunities that have at any time been held, enjoyed, and possessed by the people of Great Britain." Two royal charters from James I had expressly confirmed this. Henry asserted that "taxation of the people by themselves," or by representatives "chosen by themselves . . . is the only security against a burdensome taxation, and the distinguishing

FIGURE 2.3. The British colonies in North America, 1777, by William Faden. This map, produced after the Quebec Act of 1774, shows the Province of Quebec now stretching to encompass all of Virginia's claims north and west of the Ohio River and almost all of the Great Lakes, limiting New York to the south and east of Lake Ontario.

characteristic of British freedom, without which the ancient constitution cannot exist." The House of Burgesses was the one and only body so chosen by Virginia's people (white English colonists, that is, not Indians or enslaved Africans), and had been exercising this right for well over a century. Henry boldly asserted that "any person who shall, by speaking or writing"—such as Parliament in the Stamp Act—"maintain that any person or persons other than the General Assembly of this Colony, have any right or power to impose or lay any taxation on the people here, shall be deemed an enemy to His Majesty's Colony." This was a strong rebuke. Henry's fellow burgesses feared it was treasonous to call Parliament an enemy of Virginia. But it was no stronger than the barons' rebellion that led to Magna Carta, no stronger than the Petition of Right in 1628. It fell squarely within the range of protest that had shaped England's constitutional tradition.[27]

Three months later, John Adams (also twenty-nine at the time) voiced similar complaints, though somewhat less boldly, in his *Dissertation on the Canon and Feudal Law*, published anonymously and serially in a Boston newspaper. Adams feared the Stamp Act was a sign that the gains for liberty won by the English Reformation and by the civil conflicts of the seventeenth century, culminating in the Bill of Rights of 1689, were in danger. The "two greatest systems of tyranny," the twin forces of despotism named in his title, were threatening English liberty again. Adams was a trained lawyer and deeply schooled in British constitutional history. He understood that colonial subjects held their lands "of the king":

> To have holden their lands allodially,[28] or for every man to have been the sovereign lord and proprietor of the ground he occupied, would have constituted a government too nearly like a commonwealth. They were contented, therefore, to hold their lands of their king, as their sovereign lord; and to him they were willing to render homage, but to no mesne or subordinate lords; nor were they willing to submit to any of the baser services.[29]

But now, with the Stamp Act, Parliament was acting as a "mesne or subordinate lord" ("mesne" is an ancient legal term meaning "intermediate"), another body interposing itself between the king and his colonial subjects, demanding payment to the king without the colonies' consent, and enforcing "baser services."

The constitutional problem was that in England itself, the Glorious Revolution and Bill of Rights had firmly settled the King-in-Parliament as sovereign over the realm. The 1707 Acts of Union had brought Scotland under this umbrella as well, merging Scotland's parliament with England's. But the colonial charters and the assemblies they created long predated the Glorious Revolution. As Adams rightly pointed out, no act of union had ever joined the colonies to Britain or merged their legislatures with the parliament in Westminster. In addition, British military officers had treated American colonists "like servants, nay more like slaves than like Britons." Crown customs officers had place them under "the most abject submission, the most supercilious insults." Two months later, Adams would quote Magna Carta in complaining that the king's Vice-Admiralty Courts had suspended the colonies' rights to trial by jury: "No freeman shall be taken, or imprisoned, or disseized of his freehold . . . but by lawful judgment of his peers."[30]

The monetary demands of the Stamp Act represented another constitutional threat. The Currency Act of 1764 had voided the colonies' power to issue legal tender of their own, despite their chronic monetary shortage. During the Seven Years' War, from 1754 to 1761, the crown had spent large amounts of silver in the colonies to pay the enormous costs of supplying the troops in America. But with the war's end the specie rapidly began to drain away again; British merchants wanted to be paid in silver for goods shipped to the colonies. The Stamp Act doubled down on the demands, requiring that the mandatory stamps be purchased with sterling silver, precisely the thing the colonies lacked. When Benjamin Franklin testified against the Stamp Act before Parliament, he asserted that "in my opinion, there is not gold and silver enough in the Colonies to pay the stamp duty for one year." Even if the money raised by the Act were spent in America, he said, "it will be spent in the conquered Colonies [Quebec, East and West Florida], where the soldiers are, not in the Colonies that pay it." The result would be no better for the older colonies than sending the silver back to England—it would still drain away their scarce currency.[31] In addition to denying the colonists the right to consent to taxation, the Stamp Act in conjunction with the Currency Act threatened to rob them of any legitimate form of money, an essential instrument of their own self-governance.

The protests from American colonists along with persuasive arguments from British merchants and manufacturers that the tax was damaging their businesses led Parliament to repeal the Stamp Act in 1766. But Parliament expressly rejected the constitutional argument that only the colonial legislatures had the right to tax the colonists. In the

Declaratory Act of 1766, passed alongside the Stamp Act's repeal, Parliament claimed the absolute right to make laws that would "bind the colonies and people of America . . . in all cases whatsoever."[32]

After 1763, in Britain's older North American colonies, new measures threatened the fundamental constitutional elements that had knit the king's realm together since the time of the Domesday Book: land and the terms under which it was held and distributed, the people's obligations to the government that protected them, the rights and liberties owed them by their protectors, and the monetary system through which the obligations of government were transacted. Despite efforts on both sides to resolve their differences over the next decade, rebellion broke out in 1775. Thirteen of Britain's colonies, the artificial barons of North America, rose up against their sovereign.[33] But unlike in 1215 or 1689, there was to be no negotiated settlement. By using their internal taxing power, by borrowing from their own citizens, by issuing their own currency (however unstable), by raising their own troops, and with large doses of foreign aid borrowed from England's traditional enemies (France and Spain), the colonies made war on the king's forces and launched a fight for their independence.

These colonies now called themselves "states." They were no longer dependent subjects, the equivalent of barons owing fealty to the king. They were now parliaments, as John Winthrop had put it in 1632, in their own right. Effectively, they had become the commonwealths that John Adams had described in 1765. Their relationship with the king was dissolved, and therefore they no longer held their land of the king. This change raised a fundamental question: of whom or of what did the individual landholders within the former colonies now hold their land?

Perhaps the former colonists imagined that, without a king, they now had allodial rights to their land, that they owned it, as Adams put it, as "sovereign lord and proprietor of the ground [they] occupied." But that theory would not, could not, account for the vast tracts of land claimed under their original charters, land still held and occupied by Native nations. For many colonies, especially the largest ones, most of the land granted by their charters had not yet been ceded, purchased, developed, and transformed into revenue-producing real estate. For this reason, all the land claimed under the colonial charters, whether already developed or not, would no longer be held of the king, but rather of the new states. Therefore, the first revolutionary task taken up collectively by the former colonies, even before they declared their independence from the crown, was to begin writing constitutions as new states, to define exactly what they were so that these fundamental relationships between land, people, and government could be newly aligned.

In the ancient traditions from which colonial America developed, sovereignty had always been located at the top of the societal pyramid, in the hands of whoever could wield sufficient force to gain the submission and allegiance of all others.[34] The king was the allodial holder of all of England's land, "sovereign lord and proprietor of the ground he occupied." All others held land of him. But the North American rebellion was staged by the force of the many: many different colonies as coequal partners in the war and many different subjects of the crown willing to risk all for independence. Among the former colonists there were few categorical or legal differences of status and rights, chattel slavery and Indigeneity being the obvious and oppressive exceptions. The legal equality of white colonists limited the prospects for the creation of a new American royal lineage or privileged aristocracy in which to vest sovereignty. Consequently, the new states would need a new definition of sovereignty suitable for these kingless and lordless republics, if for no other reason than to define who or what it was that held the land that they claimed.

Beginning immediately in 1776, the former colonies made various attempts to solve this problem. Two of them, Connecticut and Rhode Island, essentially retained their colonial charters as new state constitutions, since in neither case had the crown played a role in their internal government as colonies—they had elected their own governors and assemblies all along. There was no urgent need to alter frames of government that had suited the people for generations, and they were content with the constitutions they already had. But the other eleven crafted new frames of government for themselves because they could no longer function under colonial charters that mandated royally appointed governors, lieutenant governors, councils, and other offices. The new states often drew on their colonial charters for inspiration in the process of remaking legislatures, executives, and court systems, which meant that the new constitutions, like the colonial charters, varied widely across the states. The most radical of them, Pennsylvania, dispensed with a single (king-like) executive altogether, and opted for a unicameral legislature, a single assembly to make all the laws. Most of the other states mimicked aspects of their colonial charters as well as the general outlines of Britain's government by (re)creating bicameral legislatures, single executives (governors), and independent court systems. But the initial delineation of governmental institutions and new procedures to fill their offices by no means completed the task of forming new constitutions.[35]

One of the principal remaining questions was the fundamental one of where sovereignty lay. In the ancient tradition, sovereignty belonged to the king—the wielder of sufficient force to dominate the ground he occupied and the final authority in all governing decisions. England's evolving constitutional tradition had largely been a process of placing fetters on the king, restraining the monarch's power through a combination of ancient and customary relationships, rights and principles, liberties and obligations, some written and formally enacted, others traditional.[36] But if the states' newly created organs of government were no longer understood to be servants of a sovereign king, but representatives of the sovereign people, how could fetters be placed on the people? What would be the American equivalent of Magna Carta or the English Bill of Rights that could prevent the people from exercising despotic power (i.e., mob rule)? And what could restrain their legislatures from becoming overweening oligarchs?[37]

The states were addressing all these questions in the midst of war, rebuilding the airplane that they were already flying. In some of the states, governing themselves through ad hoc provisional legislatures in the wake of royal government's collapse, the legislatures themselves took up the task of drafting new constitutions to legitimate their own actions. These new drafts borrowed directly from English constitutional tradition by first declaring the people's rights—in many cases drawn directly from England's 1689 Bill of Rights—and then carefully delimiting the powers of governors, legislatures, and courts. But a major question loomed over this process: what would prevent a subsequent legislature, a different group of lawmakers elected in future years, from loosening the fetters the previous one created by revising, or completely rewriting, the constitution drafted by its predecessor? If the legislature of 1776 could write a new constitution, then why not the legislatures of 1777, 1778, and 1779 as well, ad infinitum?[38]

After trial and error, Massachusetts eventually arrived at an answer. Its citizens rejected a first attempt at constitution making in 1778 precisely because it failed to answer this fundamental question. On its second try, Massachusetts developed an innovative process for representing the people in a way that was separate from any legislative representation. The state legislature called for a convention of the people. Numerous representatives from every part of the state came together for the sole purpose of drafting an instrument of government. The document they drafted would be simultaneously the people's grant of political power to a governing body, much as a colonial charter had been a grant of power from the king, and a set of fetters upon that governing body, like Magna Carta or the Bill of Rights. Once drafted, the written constitution was then returned to the people, effectively a congregation of all the heads of household in the state, assembled in their towns. Their town-by-town ratification would be a popular validation that the work of the special convention did in fact express the people's will. The resulting Massachusetts Constitution, ratified in 1780, broadly empowered all further elected governments to perform their defined functions. But it gave them no power to alter the constitution itself. Only another convention of the people, and then ratification by the people, could have that power.[39]

The result was a profound redefinition or, rather, *relocation* of sovereignty, as well as a dramatic revision of the Anglo-American understanding of what a constitution is. Far more than ever before, the written constitutions of these new states were understood to be the documents that both empowered and limited governments. This amounted to a narrowing of the more capacious understanding of a constitution as an amalgam of traditions, customs, institutions, and practices in conjunction with formal documents. Before, what empowered the government had been power itself—the king's demonstrated martial authority. When sovereignty had rested in the king, or the King-in-Parliament, the instruments of power—the tools of government—were held and wielded by the sovereign. In a monarchy, the acts of government were *necessarily* expressions of the sovereign's will, as the sovereign himself was performing them. With American sovereignty lodged in "the people," an abstract body capable of actual embodiment only in extraordinary conventions, the instruments of power were now separated from the source of sovereignty. Governing power was held by agents—elected representatives and governors, appointed or elected judges—who were (in theory) the mere servants of the people's sovereign will. But the people could not easily express their sovereign will in the same immediate way that a king could. This difference heightened the importance of written constitutions (both state and federal) and the forms and institutions of government they described because these documents were now the only definitive statements of the sovereign people's will available to be consulted at any given moment. The particular actions taken by any government in power might not in fact be consistent with the will of the sovereign people as expressed in a written instrument of government. A gap had opened between the concept of sovereignty and the ruling force of government.[40]

With this innovative procedure, Massachusetts became the last of the thirteen states to create its initial constitution. During this time, the states gathered in the Continental Congress had drafted Articles of Confederation among themselves. These articles were not a framework of government of the sort that Massachusetts and the other states had developed. They created what was effectively a treaty organization for mutual defense in which each state had an equal voice. The states united under these articles were not a single, representative republic; they had no taxing power, no executive branch, and no court system or judicial power over individuals. But they could make treaties with foreign governments, and their success in this effort gave the United States the power to prevail in the War of Independence. By the spring of 1781, all thirteen states had ratified the articles, authorizing the first constitutional framework for the United States.[41] That fall, the decisive French victory over the British fleet in the Battle of the Chesapeake and Lord Cornwallis's subsequent surrender of his army at Yorktown initiated the negotiations that would end in the Treaty of Paris of 1783. Great Britain recognized the independent existence among the powers of the earth of the United States of America. But the initial constitution-making process within the United States was completed before the Treaty was signed and independence was assured.[42]

In Paris in 1782, the French diplomats, Rayneval and Vergennes, eager to bring an expensive war to an end, offered a proposal for a general settlement among all the parties—Britain, the United States, France, and Spain.[43] In their proposal, the United States would be granted the territory east of the Appalachian Mountains to the Atlantic coast. This was essentially the territory the colonies had already settled and developed, the area that the new country could legitimately claim to have conquered from Britain by military force. Britain would return East and West Florida to Spain, but keep all the territory north of the Ohio River and west of the Appalachians, essentially the region defined as British Quebec in the Quebec Act of 1774. South of the Ohio, an independent Native American territory would be created, under the guarantee of Spanish protection—it would be adjacent to West Florida, where Spain had exercised significant influence for centuries (fig. 2.4).[44]

Had the United States accepted this offer, with its territorial limits defined by the region that the colonists had already developed into something resembling the England of Domesday, it is plausible that their first constitutional system, the state constitutions plus the Articles of Confederation, might have endured for many decades. Under the terms the French proposed, the collective governments of the United States might have been sufficiently empowered and restrained to keep the republic's peace within the territory that its citizens already owned and occupied. After all, under this initial constitution, the United States

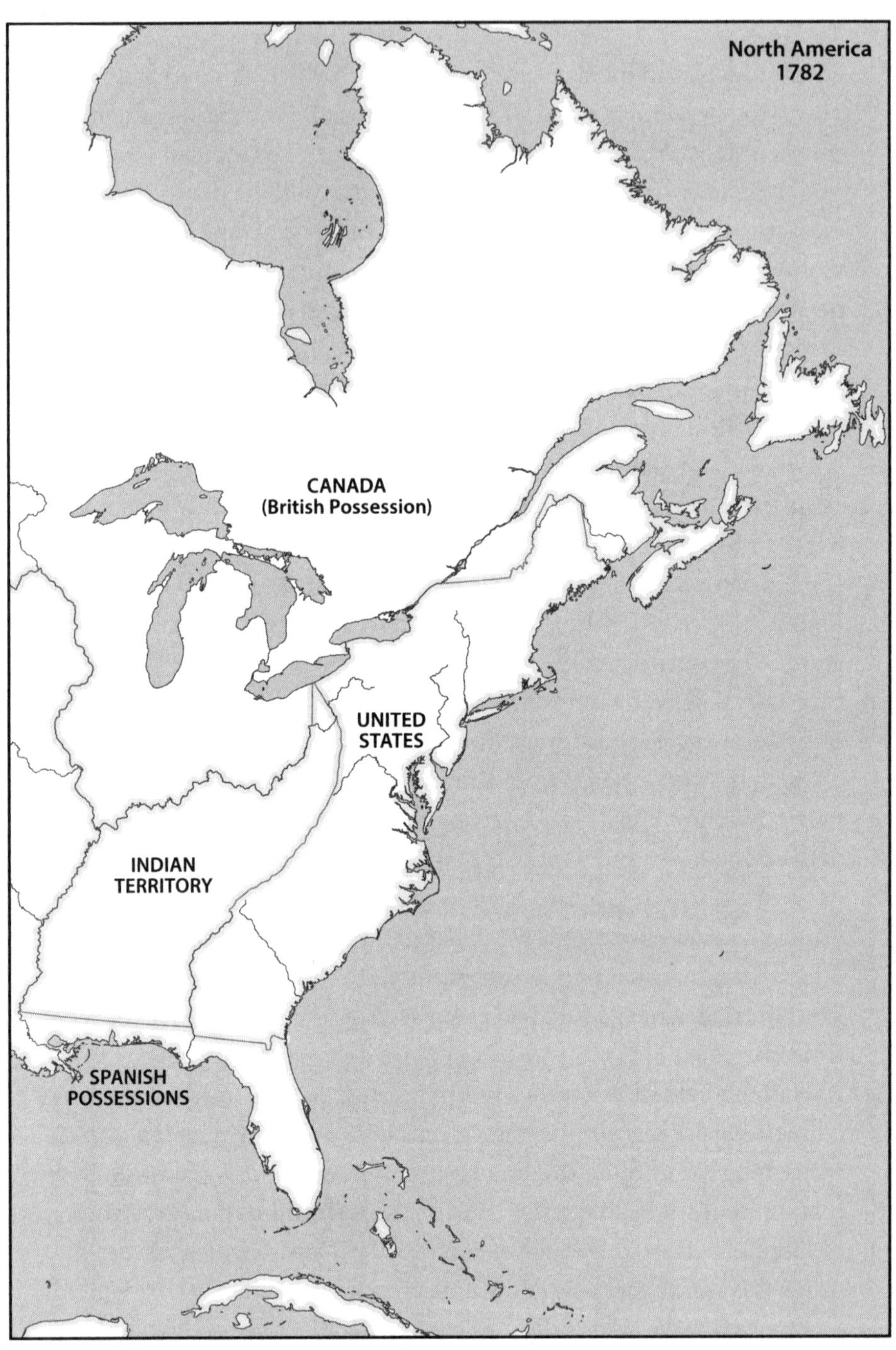

FIGURE 2.4. Map of territorial cessions proposed by Rayneval and Vergennes at Paris negotiations, 1782. The trans-Appalachian "Indian Territory" proposed by the French diplomats extends all the way from the southern shores of Lake Erie to the boundary of Spanish Florida, an area that would have been similar in size to that of the proposed United States.

had managed to win a military victory over the world's most formidable power and to conduct complex diplomacy among Europe's leading empires. These were no small achievements. If they had accepted this offer made by their French ally, the United States would have become a nation similar to (though larger than) others in Europe, as defined under the terms that emerged with the Peace of Westphalia in 1648 that ended the Thirty Years' War. It would have established a government over territory that its subjects actually occupied and controlled, an area where the states had effectively won a monopoly on the legitimate use of force. Even as a confederation of states (as opposed to a consolidated kingdom), the new United States would not have been so different from other confederacies in Europe, such as the Dutch Republic, the Swiss Confederacy, or the Holy Roman Empire.

John Jay and the other American negotiators, Benjamin Franklin, John Adams, and Henry Laurens, knew that most of the American states—especially those with extensive Western land claims—would not accept Vergennes's proposed boundaries. Given that the Royal Proclamation of 1763's barrier to the colonization of trans-Appalachian lands had been among the causes of the rebellion, it was difficult to imagine now-independent Americans accepting this line as their western boundary. Jay and his colleagues believed they could get better terms by negotiating with Britain directly. Jay proposed to Lord Shelburne, Britain's prime minister and chief negotiator, that the United States would make a separate peace with Britain (despite the fact that this violated the 1778 treaty the United States had made with France). Shelburne agreed. In the resulting treaty, signed in September 1783, Britain ceded to the United States all the disputed land west of the Appalachians, south of the Great Lakes, and north of Florida (Britain returned Florida to Spain in a separate treaty) (fig. 2.5).[45]

Compared with Vergennes's proposal, the final treaty more than doubled the land area claimed by the new United States. It restored to the states the Western land claims from their colonial charters—if not to the Pacific Ocean, then at least to the Mississippi River. This was undoubtedly a better "deal." For countless new American citizens, from the wealthiest land speculators to the poorest farmers, it redeemed at

FIGURE 2.5. New and correct map of the United States of North America, 1784, by Abel Buell. Buell's map is as effective as any contemporary map in depicting the contrast between the enormous claims of some states, such as Virginia, the Carolinas, and Georgia, and the limited territory of "small states" like New Jersey, Delaware, and Maryland. But given the confusing and shifting nature of these territorial claims, no two U.S. maps from this period are alike.

long last the promise of the West that the king and Parliament had denied, or indefinitely postponed, in 1763.

Looked at another way, this new Treaty of Paris was as disastrous for the Indigenous peoples of the trans-Appalachian West as the Treaty of Paris in 1763 had been; it ceded claims to their land to a power that had by no means conquered them.[46] Vergennes's proposal called for an extensive, permanent Indian reserve in the West guaranteed by Spain, one of Europe's strongest empires, with a continuing British presence north of the Ohio as well. The presence of multiple and competing empires in North America had for two centuries afforded Indigenous nations considerable strength, through the ability to play one empire's interests off the other. They had long used these strategies to slow the onslaught of colonization and generate favorable trading relationships between Native nations and their Euro-American partners. The separate peace devised between the United States and Britain dramatically reduced these prospects. By granting exclusive claims to this vast territory to a single new power and limiting Spanish and British authority to the remote northern and southern extremes of the continent, the treaty formally recognized the fictive claims to Western lands embedded in the ancient charters of the former colonies.[47]

The decision of the U.S. diplomats to reject the terms proposed by France for a peace settlement had momentous consequences for the new country's future, and for our understanding of the meaning of the American Revolution. France was the first ally of the United States, the first foreign power willing to put its own prestige and honor on the line to recognize, in formal diplomatic terms, the existence of this new political entity. By rejecting Vergennes's vision of a permanent Indian reserve west of the Appalachians and south of the Ohio River with Britain in possession of claims north of the Ohio, the United States definitively signaled its commitment to completing the work that Britain had failed to manage in the two decades after 1763. The rebellion against British rule in 1775 had begun as something like an anti-colonial rebellion by a coalition of dissatisfied colonies. But the terms that ended the war made it clear that the new United States would continue Britain's imperial project. So strong was this commitment that the nation's diplomats had to break their first (and at the time *only*) treaty with an overseas ally to make this separate peace with Britain.[48] By recognizing the territory of eastern North America as an independent nation, even though it was only half-colonized, with its western half under Indigenous control (fig. 2.6), the Treaty of Paris gave legitimacy to a very strange entity, utterly unlike any of the existing members of what is often called the "Westphalian System."

FIGURE 2.6. Map of population density recorded by the United States Census, 1790. This map, drawn from the first census under a new political regime, not unlike the Domesday Book compiled seven centuries earlier, reveals how little of the territory claimed by the United States had yet to be developed and controlled by U.S. citizens.

From the point of view of the new governments of the United States, the Treaty of Paris saddled them with the very same colonial problem that Great Britain had faced after the Seven Years' War—a problem that had appeared so challenging to king and Parliament that they had willingly upended centuries of constitutional practices and principles in their efforts to solve it. From the time the peace treaty was signed in 1783, the first constitutional system of the new United States faced urgent questions: would the combination of powers and fetters it had created for its new sovereign state governments, with their conflicting and overlapping Western land claims, be sufficient not just to keep the peace in the settled parts of the states, but to develop the lands across the mountains without Britain's protective umbrella? Would the states, under their league of mutual defense, have the power to overcome Native American opposition inflamed by the Revolutionary War and the treaty's betrayal of their rights—resistance that was more intense than ever before? Could they keep at bay the grasping designs of Spain (to the south) and Britain (to the north) on land the states had been ceded by treaty but had yet to conquer? It was clearly the intention of these new American citizens, no less than of William and his armed banditti in 1066, to conquer this land and make it their own. Under this new constitutional order in which the people were sovereign, how would they do it?

PART II

Making the United States, 1776–89

We are representatives, sir, not merely of the present age, but of future times; not merely of the territory along the seacoast, but of regions immensely extended westward. We should fill, as fast as possible, this extensive country, with men who shall live happy, free, and secure. To accomplish this great end ought to be the leading view of all our patriots and statesmen.

—JAMES WILSON, SPEECH AT THE PENNSYLVANIA RATIFYING CONVENTION, 1787

3

Independent States and the Challenge of the West

If we could lay aside our local prejudices, and heave up all our lines that were fix'd by Charters when the Geography of the country was not known, and fix them upon generous principles throughout the whole of your territory, it might be a mutual advantage, and would have a tendency to enlarge our ideas, to destroy animosities, and strengthen the interest of the Union.

—*FALMOUTH GAZETTE*, MAINE DISTRICT, 1785

THE UNITED STATES and France emerged from the Revolutionary War as the ostensible victors. But by the time the Treaty of Paris was signed, both nations found themselves in debt. For the United States, this meant that the new government it launched in 1789 under a new constitution was an experiment intended (among other things) to solve its debt problem. For France, the postwar debt crisis triggered a chain of events, also beginning in 1789, that caused its ancien régime to implode. It has been common among historians ever since that fateful year to search for affinities between the American and French Revolutions. But to understand the purpose of the new framework of government drafted in Philadelphia in 1787 and the distinctive nature and goals of the nation it helped to create, it may be more useful to ponder the significant *differences* between the United States and their first ally. Exploring these differences will reveal the distinctive constitutional challenges faced by the United States as they moved toward independence and nationhood.

Eighteenth-century France was Western Europe's largest and richest country, more than twice the size in land and population of its rival, Great Britain. Stretching from the Mediterranean to the North Sea, this extensive kingdom was well watered by rivers, blessed with some of Europe's best agricultural land, and home to twenty-eight million people. (Britain had fewer than ten million people in 1789; the new United States, about four million.) The material assets of the French state were enormous. The king and the Roman Catholic Church were the largest landholders, and the estates of France's nobility were extensive as well. France had no Domesday Book, but French tenants and lords remained more deeply intertwined in feudal arrangements than their counterparts in England, where the religious and political upheaval of the sixteenth and seventeenth centuries accelerated the movement away from restrictive forms of land tenure.

France's debt from the American Revolutionary war was 1.3 billion livres, roughly equal to £100 million sterling. When this sum was added to the country's prior debt left over from the Seven Years' War, France's total national debt came to about 3.3 billion livres, or £250 million.[1] France faced a political crisis in the 1780s not because it lacked the resources to honor these debts, but because the country's stupendous wealth was encumbered by forms of privilege that prevented its mobilization in service of the state.[2] The French Revolution was (among other things) an attempt to dislodge and redistribute this vast wealth. The new revolutionary government confiscated the holdings of crown and church to create a national domain, which it intended to sell to private citizens to finance the nation's debt. The revolution ended all feudal forms of landholding in order to create unencumbered private property and make it available to a far wider proportion of the population. It also eliminated the private ownership of public functions such as the administration of justice, the collection of taxes, and the occupation of state offices. These efforts to remake the state and redefine and redistribute its wealth caused the tremendous turmoil we associate with the French Revolution.[3]

By comparison, the debt the United States incurred from its War of Independence was tiny. France's entry in 1778 as America's ally expanded the war to global dimensions. Britain and France pursued combat on many fronts, including India, the Mediterranean, the North Sea, and the Caribbean. This escalation required Britain and France to spend huge sums of money on their far-flung navies and armies. Naval warships were the eighteenth century's costliest military technology. The United States spared itself great expense by relying on France's naval power rather than building its own navy from scratch.[4] And it was far less costly for Americans to defend their homeland than for Britain and France to mount expeditionary forces for trans-Atlantic warfare. As a result, the United States ended the war with a combined debt—money borrowed by the Continental Congress plus money borrowed by the individual states—of only about $75 million, equal to £15 million. This was only 6 percent of the £250 million debts carried by France and Britain. To put it differently, the total *principal* of the U.S. debt was slightly less than the amount of *interest* Britain and France had to pay every year to service their debts.[5]

Still, this small debt posed a large challenge for the United States. Unlike France or Britain, the newly confederated American government owned no assets—no wealth whatsoever. Under the Articles of Confederation the United States had no power to tax and no assets against which to borrow money or issue its own currency. When private citizens lend money to a government by buying its bonds, they do so because they want their surplus cash to generate a reliable form of income—the interest payments that the bonds promise. If a government cannot be relied on to make those payments, investors will put their money elsewhere. Before the age of stock markets and public corporations, those options included land, business investments, or interest-bearing loans to other private citizens. But in 1783, there was no American equivalent of the vast productive estates of the French kings that yielded large annual incomes and gave investors confidence in the government's credit. Nor was there any American equivalent of Britain's well-established system of customs and excise taxes that generated reliable revenue for the government to service its debt and keep investors willing to lend it money.[6]

This is not to say that those parts of the new United States already colonized by European immigrants and enslaved Africans were not themselves prosperous—they most certainly were. Starting in the 1750s, European empires fought expensive wars for control of North American territory precisely because the rapidly growing colonial populations made them realize what a rich country America was becoming. But at the end of the American War, the developed, income-producing land in America was mainly held by private owners who owed no fealty to the new national government.

Granted, the legislatures of each of the thirteen *states* did have the power to tax. Some, especially the New England states, had efficient mechanisms for assessing and taxing their citizens.[7] But the Continental Congress had no powers of taxation whatsoever. It could only *request* monetary contributions from its member states and make *recommendations,* based on the estimated wealth of the various states, for how much each state ought to contribute. During the war, when the need for military funding was urgent, this requisition system barely sufficed. With the war's end, the states were reluctant and often unable to tax their own citizens to contribute to national needs. Many states still had their own war debts to pay off.[8]

France, then, faced a crisis over a large national debt because it lacked a political structure to mobilize its immense but poorly distributed wealth. The United States faced a crisis over a small national debt because it lacked both state-owned wealth and the political power to tax its citizens. This left America's creditors unsure if they would ever be paid and reluctant to trust any future financial promises the United States might make. It left Americans with a national government helpless to remedy the situation as a deep postwar recession settled in.[9]

But perhaps we are overlooking something. Like France after its revolution, the new United States constructed a national domain—government-owned land it could sell to finance its debt. The Treaty of Paris in 1783 granted the United States preemptive claims to the immense territory west of the Appalachian Mountains, south of the Great Lakes, and north of Spanish Florida, all the way to the Mississippi River. This was a region twice the size of France, with land reported to be every bit as fertile, plentiful, and temperate as France. Before the war this region had been claimed by Britain. But unlike revolutionary France's national domain—the revenue-yielding land seized from the rich holdings of crown and church—America's national domain in 1783 was as much a liability as an asset. The land was *potentially* rich, in the terms by which European states measured riches. But neither the governments nor the citizens of the United States truly owned it. It belonged to dozens of autonomous Native nations, who maintained their own military, political, and economic authority over the land. Although it was already rich land for its Indigenous owners, it yielded no revenue accessible to the indebted American government. It produced little in the way of commercial products, the staple commodities that characterized the economy American colonizers wanted to construct. Despite the terms of the Treaty of Paris, both Spain and Britain still coveted this region and had hopes of gaining control of its trade, or even of the land itself.

In 1786, Philadelphian Benjamin Rush suggested that "there is but one path that can lead the United States to destruction; and that is their extent of territory. It was probably to effect this, that Great Britain ceded to us so much waste land."[10] By "waste," Rush did not mean that the land was spoiled or no good, but that it was still undeveloped, not yet enclosed or cultivated, not property. Moreover, as Britain's government and the leaders of the new United States could readily testify, the persistent desire among colonists to gain access to this land, to transform it into commercially productive property, raised the prospect of future military conflict—more wars and more debt. This was precisely what had happened when Britain asserted its claim to this territory after the Seven Years' War; Pontiac's rebellion was the result.[11] But now the problem was much more pressing. In the quarter century after the Seven Years' War, the colonial population of what was now the United States doubled, from two million in 1763 to almost four million by the first census in 1790. The pressure for access to trans-Appalachian land became far greater than when Britain first gained the rights to it.[12]

The situation was further complicated by the fact that every inch of this trans-Appalachian territory was claimed by at least one of the thirteen American states as part of its public domain. Any claim the national government made to the West was contested by the states, and sometimes the states asserted competing claims; New York, Massachusetts, Connecticut, and Virginia all claimed overlapping parts of the western region north of the Ohio River, for example (fig. 2.5). The complications did not stop there. Within the territory claimed by individual states, there was often conflict between speculators and settlers, which led to secessionist movements among Western settlers, who felt neglected and unprotected by their state governments located in the East.[13]

It is also important to remember how difficult this trans-Appalachian region was to access, let alone govern, in an era before canals, steamboats, and railroads. From the seat of the Continental Congress in Philadelphia to the Mississippi River was an overland journey of nearly 900 miles. It was more than 1,000 miles up the Mississippi from New Orleans to the Falls of St. Anthony in Minnesota. (By comparison, France measures roughly 500 miles from east to west and 600 miles from north to south.) Any overland journey had to cross the Appalachian Mountains, which run for more than 1,500 miles from Newfoundland in the Northeast to Alabama in the Southwest. Although they are not as high as the Pyrenees or the Alps, the Appalachians' continuous length and their breadth—from 100 to 300 miles—made them a formidable barrier to travel, commerce, and communication. Rivers to the east of the Appalachians flow to the Atlantic Ocean, while rivers west of the mountains flow either north and east toward the Great Lakes, the St. Lawrence River, and the North Atlantic, or west and south toward the Mississippi River and the Gulf of Mexico. Before the invention of steam-powered travel, it was very difficult to reach the trans-Appalachian interior from east of the mountains. Trade in bulky or heavy goods across the mountains was impossible. Even written communication was slow and unreliable. In the 1780s, it took fifty-seven days for information from the new settlements in Kentucky to reach Congress in Philadelphia, while news from London could reach Philadelphia in forty-eight days or less.[14]

The difficulty of governing at a distance had been among the reasons the rebellious colonies had denounced crown rule: legislators and administrators thousands of miles away in Britain could not possibly know and represent the interests of American colonists. In Europe, natural barriers such as mountain ranges and divergent river systems had contributed to the evolution of separate and durable languages, cultures, and countries, dividing Germanic-speaking peoples from Romance language speakers, separating France from Spain and Italy. The geography of eastern North America had influenced comparable divisions among its Indigenous peoples for thousands of years. And remember, the individual states of the United States were very large by European standards. In 1783, before it ceded its trans-Ohio claims to Congress, Virginia was larger than France, Spain, the United Kingdom, Sweden, or Habsburg Austria, Europe's largest nations. Georgia, likewise, was larger than all these except France and Austria. New York and North Carolina, even without its trans-Appalachian claims, were each larger than England. The prospect that each of these states, or coalitions of a few of them, could plausibly be an autonomous country, where the majority of their commerce was internal to the state or to a group of a few states, made a great deal of sense in terms of contemporary precedents.[15] But the absence of any form of easy or rapid transportation across their vast distances, especially in light of the Appalachian barrier, made the challenge of their governance pressing. In 1786, Massachusetts congressional delegate Rufus King imagined that "an entire separation" between the regions east and west of the Appalachians was inevitable: "I should consider every emigrant to that country from the Atlantic States, as forever lost to the Confederacy."[16]

In 1763, after being awarded control of both sides of the Appalachian divide in the first Treaty of Paris, Britain had barely been able to establish a few outposts in the Great Lakes region, essentially renaming French forts as their own; these had been attacked by Indian resistance movements. The government of the Province of Quebec that the crown had declared into existence in 1763 was largely a legal fiction in the trans-Appalachian region. In Virginia, Pennsylvania, and New York, as a growing number of Anglo-American colonists worked their way up river valleys—the Potomac, the Susquehanna, and the Mohawk—that provided the deepest access into the mountains, their presence exacerbated long-standing conflicts with the land's Indigenous owners. The notion that the two regions on either side of the mountains, rich as they might be some day, could easily be made into a single republic seemed preposterous.[17]

In constitutional terms the body of American society—the land and people that made up the nation—was extraordinarily different in nature from European societies such as France or Britain. The relationship of that body to the existing frame of government—the states joined in confederation—was extraordinarily different from European frameworks as well. The challenge of aligning these fundamental constitutional elements seemed formidable. If the viability of the new United States depended on its claim to the immense trans-Appalachian region, then its value was still speculative in the 1780s.[18] That value could only be realized, turned into the kind of extractable wealth that sustained European-style state making, through labor, resources, and violent force—all at the expense of the people who already lived there and possessed it. If the United States expected to use its Western land claims to solve its debt crisis, it would have to develop plans and powers to make this happen.

In one sense, this problem was not new. Britain's entire colonization venture in North America had had a speculative quality. When Englishmen first launched American colonies in the late sixteenth century, colonial projectors had no reliable idea of how they would earn enough money to recoup the immense cost of overseas settlements. The contrast with the overseas empires of Spain and Portugal was striking. Starting in the fifteenth century, ventures sponsored by the Portuguese crown hopscotched down the west coast of Africa and quickly found African merchants willing to trade gold, ivory, and other lucrative goods. The Portuguese rapidly rounded the Cape of Good Hope and established a seafaring trade empire in the Indian Ocean, where the well-known riches of the East awaited them. Portugal's subsequent colony in Brazil was a trans-Atlantic extension of already profitable economic practices, especially sugar cultivation, brought from the

Mediterranean and the Atlantic islands to South America.[19] In Spain, Ferdinand and Isabella commissioned Columbus to find a westerly route across the Atlantic and around the globe to the same Eastern riches Portugal had reached. Columbus stumbled by accident upon the impediment of the American continent. But in Mexico and Peru, subsequent conquistadors also found large, rich Indigenous populations and gold and silver reserves, resources that guaranteed the value of these colonial pursuits.[20]

By contrast, European exploration of the northern parts of America revealed neither large populations rich in valuable trade goods nor plentiful supplies of silver and gold. In the age of sail, the expense of long-distance ocean voyages was so high that only goods having a significant gap between the cost of their production in one place and the price they fetched in another could make these journeys economically rewarding. Consequently, the dreams of England's early colonizers for North America were filled with fanciful notions of rich and exotic goods (exotic in England, that is) that colonies might produce—wines, spices, olives, silks, perfumes—along with persistent hopes that gold or silver lay just over the next ridge.[21]

The failure rate of these early colonies was high. The resources, both human and capital, squandered in the earliest ventures were chastening. It is therefore not surprising that the joint-stock company emerged for England's colonial enterprises. Joint-stock companies were risk-sharing devices, an early modern innovation for pursuing potentially lucrative but precarious ventures without ruining the fortunes of a single investor in the likely event of failure.[22]

The colonies in British America that did succeed generally required long, difficult, and costly periods of trial and error to discover how to produce valuable commodities that would make them viable economic ventures.[23] Given the enormous variation in climate conditions, growing seasons, and soil qualities across the Atlantic region, from the West Indies to Newfoundland, that Britons attempted to colonize, what worked in one locale often did not in another.[24] Tobacco could be Virginia's staple, but not New England's. Sugar made fortunes for Barbadian planters, but not for their sons who colonized Carolina. Every colony was a speculative venture, many failed outright, and even in the successful ones much was lost before they became sustainable, let alone profitable. The one feature that successful colonies shared was a lengthy gestation period.

Time was also a critical factor in the process of colonists' encounters with, and eventual displacement of, the Native populations of coastal North America. In the earliest years, the balance of power lay with Indigenous communities: Indians outnumbered colonists. They knew how to live sustainably on the land, and they produced food surpluses to share with the desperate newcomers.[25] Although relations between Europeans and Native Americans were marred by chronic violence and occasional outbreaks of gruesome warfare, most of the colonists' acquisition of Indigenous land happened incrementally, through the slow process of individual land sales, small-scale treaties, and agreements for bits and pieces of land here and there. Native land was taken and transformed into cadastral, developed land—real estate—not by massive wars of conquest but through the slow structural violence of piecemeal encroachment.[26] It took more than 150 years for British North America's settler population to grow from zero in 1600 to two million by 1763. In that time, colonizers managed to occupy and develop land that reached two hundred miles in from the Atlantic coast—in most regions considerably less than that. During this long development period, each individual colony engaged energetically in the work necessary to create governmental and commercial infrastructures.[27] But so long as they remained under the umbrella of the crown, the colonies were unburdened by the need to make themselves independent sovereign states and to shoulder the full cost of autonomy.[28] They could afford to develop slowly.

In the 25 years between the end of the Seven Years' War and the ratification of the U.S. Constitution, rapid population growth, escalating violence, and competition among empires ramped up the speed of the colonization project. The settler population of British America doubled in that time; it took 150 years to generate the first two million colonists but only 25 years to reach four million. Many colonists, including large waves of immigrants, were eager for land and looked to the West as the place to get it.[29] The Treaty of Paris more than doubled the land area claimed by the United States. Two decades of warfare on an unprecedented scale had armed and militarized the continent as never before.[30] The Revolutionary War also heightened Native nations' awareness of the threat to their territory and way of life, enhancing their interest in organizing at larger scales and moving toward pan-Indian confederacies to defend themselves.[31] Britain and Spain remained poised on the northern and southern borders of the United States, eager to win back territory lost in the peacemaking process and to that end ready to ally with Native nations. And now the United States had fought and won the right to bear the burden of sustaining a sovereign, independent government, a burden exacerbated by a load of debt and no means to pay it. The United States thus had to do rapidly what Britain and its colonies had done slowly—conduct a speculative project for transforming extensive claims to land, a fictive right to other peoples' territory, from a liability into an asset. With independence, a complicated problem had become an urgent one as well.

How would the newly independent United States tackle this urgent challenge? As with everything else in America's constitutional tradition, the answer begins at the state rather than the national level. The new constitutions created at independence by the thirteen states said remarkably little about their claims to land in the trans-Appalachian West. This is not surprising for New Hampshire, Rhode Island, New Jersey, Delaware, and Maryland, small states that never had any Western claims.[32] But the states south of Maryland had major Western claims derived from their colonial charters. And although it may seem preposterous today, so did Connecticut and Massachusetts, whose colonial charters located their western boundaries at the South Sea (i.e., the Pacific Ocean).[33] The situation was more ambiguous with New York, which had vague Western claims based on its supposed "suzerainty" over the Haudenosaunee Confederacy, and Pennsylvania, which had a fixed western boundary by its charter. Both of these large states still had extensive uncolonized territorial claims within their original boundaries but beyond the Appalachians, areas difficult to reach and distant from the governing control of their coastal capital cities. In the Constitution of Pennsylvania (1776), brief provisions were made for adding additional representative members of the state's executive council, "in case new additional counties shall hereafter be erected in this state." New York's constitution (1777) provided that "all grants of lands within this State, made by the King of Great Britain" before the revolution were still valid. Because of the high risk of fraud and conflict generated by private land purchases from Natives, New York quickly adopted Britain's 1763 policy of allowing only the government, not private citizens, to purchase Indigenous land, but otherwise made no specific provisions for its legally vague Western land claims.[34]

Only Virginia and North Carolina addressed Western land claims directly in their new state constitutions. Not incidentally, these states had the largest number of colonists already moving into the trans-Appalachian backcountry (the regions that would become Kentucky and Tennessee). Virginia completed its new frame of government in June 1776, just before the states collectively declared independence. In this moment of plasticity, with the old order collapsing and monarchy repudiated, Virginia magnanimously allowed that it would recognize the right of Pennsylvania, Maryland, North Carolina, and South Carolina to exist—these colonies had been carved out of Virginia's original charter territory by subsequent English kings. However, with respect to the "western and northern extent of Virginia," the new Virginia constitution reaffirmed the 1609 charter's claim to all the land north of a line extending west from the Virginia–North Carolina border and south of the Great Lakes, all the way to the Mississippi River.[35] And it insisted on the right of Virginia's legislature (*not* the Continental Congress) to create additional new states (of unspecified number) in this territory. Virginia, like New York, adopted the policy that all future land purchases from Native Americans could be made only by the state, not by private individuals.[36]

North Carolina, which tended to follow Virginia's lead, claimed all the land between its northern and southern boundaries and west to the

Mississippi (the future State of Tennessee). Like Virginia, North Carolina reserved the right for its state legislature to form new states (not just one) in this Western territory. Georgia, by contrast, although it too had large Western land claims from its colonial charter, made no mention of them in its 1777 constitution, except to suggest how representation in its state legislature would be calculated should new counties be created in the future, much as Pennsylvania had done. South Carolina claimed a very narrow strip of land (about twelve miles from north to south) from its western boundary out to the Mississippi River but did not even mention this claim in its constitution.[37]

Taken together, these initial state constitutions of 1776–77 convey the sense that their framers were not yet preoccupied with trans-Appalachian expansion.[38] Given that they were drafted in the grim early days of a war centered on the northeastern seaboard, and before the French alliance brought hope for potential victory, the lack of attention to the West is understandable. That the coastal colonies might survive Britain's military onslaught, let alone seize the king's Western lands, could not have seemed likely at this point. The Articles of Confederation drawn up by the new states in 1776–77 confirmed this; they made no attempt to define what member states' boundaries might be or what land they claimed. But the Articles anticipated conflict over this issue and devised an elaborate mechanism for adjudicating boundary disputes between states.[39]

The Articles included only a single provision regarding the potential expansion of the confederation beyond the territory already claimed by the thirteen states. This provision did not focus on points west: "Canada acceding to this confederation, and adjoining in the measures of the United States, shall be admitted into, and entitled to all the advantages of this Union; but no other colony shall be admitted into the same, unless such admission be agreed to by nine States."[40] This clause was the product of the Continental Army's campaign in the winter of 1775–76 to drive the British out of Quebec, in the hope that its French inhabitants might want to rid themselves of British rule and join the American cause. No such response from the Quebecois was forthcoming. At the same time, this clause expressed the belief that the addition of any other colony to the confederation would significantly alter the basic nature of the Articles' "firm league of friendship,"[41] and thus require the approval of a supermajority of the existing states—an issue that would loom very large after independence was assured.

In sum, the early days of the Revolutionary War and the contemporaneous crafting of the initial state constitutions and Articles of Confederation generated no definitive answers to the problem of how an independent American nation would manage Western lands. This problem had vexed British imperial government after 1763 and for many Americans had been a major source of grievance against British rule. It was not until the years between 1777 and 1781, as the war itself moved to the south and west, military conflict with Native Americans became more frequent, and the states began to quarrel over boundary issues, that the Western lands question grew more prominent.[42] With the Treaty of Paris in 1783, which recognized U.S. authority over territory that only Virginia and North Carolina expressly claimed in their state constitutions, this issue moved to the forefront of politics in the new nation, exacerbating the constitutional challenges faced by these not very United States.

No one setting out to create an independent federal republic while declaring a commitment to equality among its citizens would ever have designed a set of member states as grossly unequal as the original thirteen. Virginia, easily the largest of the states, even setting aside its immense trans-Appalachian claims, entered the union with a land area of roughly 67,000 square miles and a settler population of about 750,000. Delaware and Rhode Island, the smallest states in population and land area, respectively, boasted land areas of 2,500 and 1,200 square miles, and populations of 59,000 and 69,000. Virginia already had more than fifty times as much land, and more than a dozen times as many people, as the confederation's smallest states. And Virginia's constitution claimed the right to expand its land area an additional five times over, an option unavailable to these small and bounded states. Furthermore, a state like Virginia (or even Connecticut) possessing Western land claims could sell land to its own citizens as a means to raise the revenue it needed to pay national requisitions (a win-win for citizen and state), whereas the small, landless states would have to tax their own people for the same purpose (a lose-lose proposition).[43] The inequity of this situation was obvious to all and would only get worse over time without reforms at the national level.

Of course, no one had set out to plan a self-governing republic when these colonies were created in the seventeenth century. The relative size of a colony had no particular significance when the colonies bore no governing relationship to one another and each was ultimately under the authority of the crown. But when resistance to crown rule caused royal government to collapse, it was the existing colonies, large and small, that assumed the risk of rebellion and then transformed themselves into states. The states framed a league of mutual defense, the states declared independence, and the states raised men and money to fight the war. The former colonies created their new constitutions under the doctrine of "state succession," based on the premise that these new states were essentially the same entities they had been as colonies, merely revised to eliminate vestiges of British rule and to reform their governments on republican principles.[44] There was never a "Lockean moment" when the people of colonial America reverted to a state of nature, when all was fluid and entirely new polities could be made. But critics of the new states and the confederacy wished there had been such a moment in order to rectify these troublesome inequalities. In April 1783, Congressman Jonathan Jackson of Massachusetts wrote to Continental Army General Benjamin Lincoln, wondering whether now, with the war ending, it might be possible "to throw the States into one large Family & the separate Sovereignties into one united (Forgetting Distinctions & swallowing up Names in one only that of Columbians if you please) laying out the whole into convenient districts, & as equal as possible for Territory & Inhabitants, . . . making the Representation always according to Numbers & equal in all deliberative Bodies throout the Nation?" In the same vein, a writer from Maine in 1785 recommended that Americans should "heave up all our lines that were fix'd by Charters when the

Geography of the country was not known, and fix them upon generous principles throughout the whole of [the] territory."[45]

Instead, the small states interested in creating a more equal confederacy turned to their strongest political tools: the equality among states as voting members in Congress and the requirement that every state ratify the Articles for the confederation to be formally established. Even if Virginia towered over the small states in land, wealth, and population, each had an equal vote. On this basis, the small states began a campaign to encourage the "landed states"—Virginia above all—to cede their trans-Appalachian land to the national government.

There were advantages for the landed states in making such cessions. Yes, if Virginia could have developed all of its trans-Appalachian claims by and for itself, it might have become enormously rich and powerful, a country in its own right larger than any in Europe. But Virginia already faced challenges in governing a massive territory divided by a huge mountain range. White settlers, both as individuals and under the auspices of organized land companies, were swarming into the Kentucky and Ohio regions that Virginia claimed. They complained about the inability of the government in Richmond to protect them. Speculators from competing states, such as Maryland and Pennsylvania, were investing in land companies and looking to the Continental Congress to support their claims in Virginia's western regions. And there were leading figures in the landed states, including most prominently Virginia's own governor, Thomas Jefferson, who believed that the survival of the republic depended on the states being proportional and moderate in size, and thought it best to generate new states in the trans-Appalachian territories. In addition to these incentives in favor of cessions, neighboring Maryland refused to ratify the Articles until a plan for the landed states to cede their Western claims was in place.[46]

These factors steered the politics of the confederacy toward land cessions. Between 1782 and 1786, New York, Virginia, Massachusetts, and Connecticut, the states with competing claims to the Northwest, all ceded their claims to Congress. In return, Congress promised that the states' current boundaries, over which there had been various running disputes, would be guaranteed by the confederation government.[47] As part of their cession agreements states also received rewards, such as the 1.5 million acres of Ohio lands granted to Virginia as a military reserve to compensate the state's Revolutionary War veterans. Through the internal politics of the confederation, the United States extinguished the states' preemption claims derived from the colonial charters—north of the Ohio River, that is—and created a national domain. Now there was a huge territory claimed by the United States collectively but not belonging to any state, and a process in place for the national government to acquire the remaining unceded trans-Appalachian regions south of the Ohio River.

Between 1775 and 1786, by way of a successful rebellion against British rule, the creation of new state constitutions as successors to the colonies, the framing and ratification of a confederation to unite the states, a peace treaty that granted the confederation the trans-Appalachian West, and the effective internal politics of the confederation, the new United States had substituted its own claims to authority over the eastern half of North America for those of Great Britain. This was a remarkable accomplishment. Through more than a century of colonial rule, the British crown had been the authority that had granted territorial rights to colonies, had guaranteed those rights by resolving disputes, and had gradually taken control over land cessions and treaties with Indian nations. Now, the new United States had assumed all these functions within the span of a decade. As George Washington said in his 1783 address to Congress on retiring as commander-in-chief, the "citizens of America" were now the "sole Lords and Proprietors of a vast tract of continent," and "acknowledged to be possessed of absolute freedom and independency." Wittingly or not, Washington echoed the ancient language of the king as sole lord and proprietor, the allodial owner of the lands of his kingdom, while substituting the people for the king.[48]

But *claims* to land—preemptive rights—are not the same as actual ownership, possession, and development. The value of these lands to the state-making and nation-building enterprise remained in the realm of speculation, even if the legal claims of states and Congress were now more clearly defined. The United States still lacked a plan to transform outsize claims into authority, ownership, and wealth. It also lacked the power to enforce such a plan in the face of resistance from Indigenous nations and imperial competitors. The urgency of this challenge pushed national leaders to make constitutional reforms. The future viability of their confederation was at stake.

4

Constitutional Solutions Before the Constitution

> The legislatures of those districts or new States, shall never interfere with the primary disposal of the soil by the United States in Congress assembled, nor with any regulations Congress may find necessary for securing the title in such soil to the bona fide purchasers.
>
> —THE NORTHWEST ORDINANCE, 1787

IN THE POPULAR mythology of the American founding, the U.S. Constitution is the "miracle at Philadelphia," a moment of originary political genius and a repudiation of the constitutional efforts that went before, especially of the "weak" or "failing" government under the Articles of Confederation.[1] But in reality, the effort to expand the original national government's power and codify that power through written instruments was an extended process, not a single charmed moment. The process began after the Treaty of Paris (signed in September 1783) clarified the new nation's challenges, with Virginia's cession to Congress in March 1784 of its land claims north and west of the Ohio River. Other states then followed suit. The process continued with Congress's enactment of land ordinances in 1784, 1785, and 1787 and with efforts in Congress to devise taxation plans and other revisions that might be added to Congress's powers.[2] The Philadelphia Convention of 1787 was a dramatic reworking and expansion of the national government, but it was one intense moment within a longer series of reforms to the constitution, all designed to expand the national government's power. The Philadelphia draft was no miracle—it incorporated many elements developed in the state constitutions and the Articles of Confederation and drawn from British constitutional history. Made public on September 17, 1787, the draft was a dead letter until it was ratified by the states in a contentious process that generated an overwhelming demand for amendments (a Bill of Rights) which were framed in the new government's first session and quickly ratified as well. To understand the nature and purpose of the far more powerful national government launched in 1789, it is essential to grasp this longer process of constitutional reform, especially in relation to the peculiar challenges posed by the nation's territorial claims.

The challenge of the West was one of three national issues about which Confederation Congress members felt hampered by their limited powers under the Articles. The other two were finance and diplomacy. All three issues were tightly intertwined.[3] Congress faced conflict with Britain, Spain, and Indigenous nations over control of the West, as well as the need to negotiate new international trade agreements in the postwar era. Britain's Orders in Council of 1783 prohibited American trade with British ports, including the West Indies—a major blow to America's Northern mercantile communities. In 1784, Spain closed the port of New Orleans to American shipping, which meant any Americans settling west of the Appalachians would be unable to use the Mississippi River to ship their products to international markets. Spain aimed to lure Western settlers away from U.S. allegiance, and had some success. Most famously, General James Wilkinson, a Revolutionary War veteran, swore allegiance to Spain and worked to promote its interests in the West.[4] In 1785, American diplomat John Jay attempted to negotiate a resolution. Jay proposed an agreement that would open Spanish ports to American merchants but preserve exclusive Spanish rights to the lower Mississippi for twenty-five years. The Southern states with extensive land claims and high expectations that their citizens would occupy the West rejected this plan as, in effect, a self-inflicted version of the Royal Proclamation of 1763—a further postponement of the promise of the West. Their opposition prevented the negotiations from going forward, embarrassing John Jay and making the United States appear feeble and indecisive in the world of international diplomacy.[5]

Enforcing treaties that Congress made with Indian nations was an equally frustrating diplomatic challenge. The Articles granted Congress the exclusive power to make treaties, denying this power to the states. In 1785, Congress negotiated the Treaty of Hopewell with the Cherokee, Choctaw, and Chickasaw nations, creating a western boundary in the South beyond which white settlers were prohibited. But since North Carolina had asserted its right to this territory in its state constitution, it considered Congress's treaty to be "repugnant to our [North Carolina's] Bill of Rights and Constitution."[6] On this point the Articles of Confederation were ambiguous. While Article IX did grant Congress the power to "manag[e] all affairs with the Indians," it limited this power to Indians who were "not members of any of the states; provided that the legislative right of any state, within its own limits, be not infringed or violated." Georgia's legislature used this language to declare the Treaty of Hopewell to be "null and void." Meanwhile Georgia's citizens continued to occupy Indian lands, escalating the threat of war and making the state and confederation governments appear ridiculous and incompetent in the eyes of Indian negotiators.[7]

In April 1787, James Madison drafted "Vices of the Political System of the United States," a handwritten document, in preparation for the convention scheduled that summer to revise the Articles and report their proposals to Congress and the states. Madison listed "Encroachments by the States on the Federal Authority" as the second of eleven major problems facing the nation.[8] He singled out "the wars and treaties of Georgia with the Indians" as a prime example of this encroachment. Months later, at the Philadelphia Convention, Alexander Hamilton put the problem more bluntly: "Let us take a review of the variety of important objects, which must necessarily engage the attention of a national government. You have to protect your rights against Canada on the north, Spain on the south, and your western frontier against the savages. You have to adopt necessary plans for the settlement of your frontiers, and to institute the mode in which settlements and good government are to be made."[9]

If America's diplomatic challenges were inextricably linked to its tenuous claims over the trans-Appalachian West, so were its financial challenges. The postwar debt crisis would have been solved if the United States had secured the power to transform its national domain into revenue by selling or leasing rights to develop its immense territory. As William Ellery, a congressional delegate from Rhode Island, wrote about Virginia's proposed northwest land cession, "Some men who are acquainted with that country assert that the value of it is sufficient to discharge our whole public debt."[10]

Since control of the West remained elusive, Congress looked for other solutions. America's leading financiers, Robert Morris of Philadelphia foremost among them, devised proposals to amend the Articles of Confederation to grant the national government the right to levy an impost—uniform national customs duties on imported goods. These proposals raised ideological concerns; colonists had resisted this form of taxation when Parliament imposed it in the 1760s. But the chief stumbling block, given that the states would now be agreeing to impose such duties on themselves, was the small and heavily commercial State of Rhode Island. Rhode Island would bear a much heavier burden from a customs-based taxation system than would large landed states with little mercantile activity. To nationalize the customs duties Rhode Island collected at its ports would rob the state of its primary source of tax revenues. Amending the Articles of Confederation required a unanimous vote, and Rhode Island consistently blocked every effort to add the impost to Congress's powers.[11]

Lacking a guaranteed source of revenue, Congress risked defaulting on its international debt—yet another diplomatic crisis in the making. It also lacked the resources to take charge of the national domain. After postwar demobilization, the remaining U.S. Army consisted of about four to six hundred men, while, to cite just one example, the Creek Nation could field upwards of four thousand warriors to defend its territory in the Southwest.[12] For political reasons, Congress wanted to insist on its control of the national domain; this would prevent conflict among the states, avoid antagonizing Native nations, and someday become a source of wealth. But without an immediate revenue source, Congress had no power to exercise this control.

The revenue problem and the challenge of diplomacy both prompted calls to revise the Articles of Confederation. But neither issue necessitated the full national representative republic that emerged from the Philadelphia Convention. A simpler and less ambitious modification of the Articles would have sufficed to solve these problems. We know that the power to levy national customs duties would have managed the national revenue problem because that is exactly the form of national taxation that the U.S. government under the 1787 Constitution relied on for its first century. But none of the proponents of the impost imagined that it was necessary to change the Articles' structure as a confederation among sovereign states just to add a uniform impost to Congress's powers.[13] Similarly, it would have been possible to create a larger and more professional diplomatic corps under the existing authority of Congress. And a two-thirds supermajority of representatives of the states (embodied in the U.S. Senate) remained the standard necessary to ratify treaties under the Constitution, just as it had been under the Articles.[14]

Of the three major challenges to effective national authority, only the problem of Western lands could not be solved under the Articles. During the 1780s, Congress managed to agree on a series of constitutional reforms on this issue—a series of land ordinances that took major steps toward creating a governing framework over the national domain it gained from the states' Western land cessions. But the increasingly obvious limitations on the power of Congress to *implement* these plans in the actual world of the trans-Appalachian West would demonstrate the need to enhance the capacities and structure of the national government.

The Confederation Congress's land ordinances specified how the national government would acquire title to land from Indigenous owners, transfer ownership to American citizens, and eventually create new states from these territories. If this process seems inevitable today, it was not in the 1780s. The United States under the Articles was a creation of the preexisting states—Britain's former colonies. It was plausible to imagine that a similar process might continue, that a new colony created by a private venture (much as the original thirteen had been created) would organize itself into a prospective state and then apply to join the union. Colonists in the region that would become Vermont were already concocting such a scheme, issuing their own constitution for a territory long claimed by both New Hampshire and New York.[15] In the trans-Appalachian regions of North Carolina and Virginia, there were two such prospective colonies, Franklin and Vandalia, being developed by settlers and investors. The State of Franklin went so far as to apply for admission to the union in 1785 but failed to receive the necessary approval of a two-thirds majority of states. In response to this chaotic situation, the Confederation Congress crafted a series of land ordinances to ensure that the national government would control land distribution and take the lead in crafting new states out of the national domain, rather than accepting petitions for admission from privately constructed colonies.[16]

The first of these ordinances was drafted by a committee headed by Thomas Jefferson and passed by Congress in April 1784, only a month after Virginia ceded the territory north and west of the Ohio River. The Land Ordinance of 1784 projected a grid of lines of latitude and longitude onto the trans-Appalachian West, defining future boundaries of new states (fig. 4.1). With the approval of two-thirds of the existing states, each new state could be admitted to the union once its population equaled that of the least populous of the original thirteen states. The new states would be equal members of the confederation and would be responsible for their share of the national debt. But the process for surveying land, selling it to settler colonists or investors, and creating townships, counties, and the like for governing these new states was left vague.

What was clear about the 1784 ordinance was its intention to claim the state-making process as part of the fundamental constitution of the United States. It concluded by asserting that its terms "shall be formed into a charter of compact; . . . and shall stand as fundamental constitutions between the thirteen original states, and each of the several states now newly described."[17] Note the fluid language of "constitutions" in

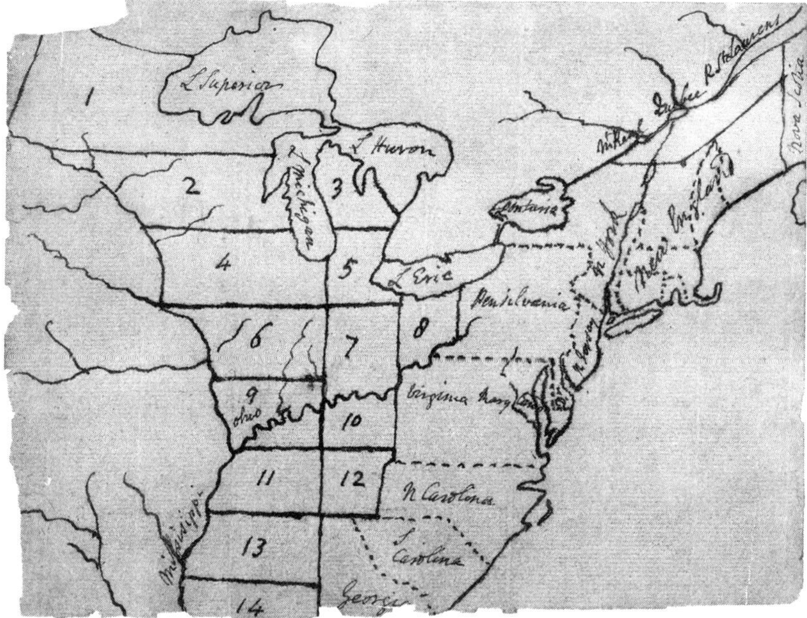

FIGURE 4.1. "A map of the United States east of the Mississippi River in which the land ceded by the Treaty of Paris is divided by parallels of latitude and longitude into fourteen new states / by David Hartley." The new states projected on this map were smaller and more numerous than the ones that would eventually come into being. This map also projects new states in territory south of the Ohio River not yet ceded by Georgia and North Carolina to the national government.

Jefferson's draft of the ordinance, used to describe these instruments elaborating the relationships among the states in the confederation. There is no mistaking that Congress saw these reforms to the Articles as part of an ongoing constitution-making process.

The following year, Congress extended this process with a second land ordinance, which clarified how land in these new territories would be surveyed and sold to colonists and investors. The Land Ordinance of 1785 specified that federal land sales would honor the financial promises made to the nation's soldiers and help to retire the national debt. This new ordinance projected a fine-grained geometrical land survey grid onto the larger state-making grid of the 1784 ordinance (fig. 4.2).

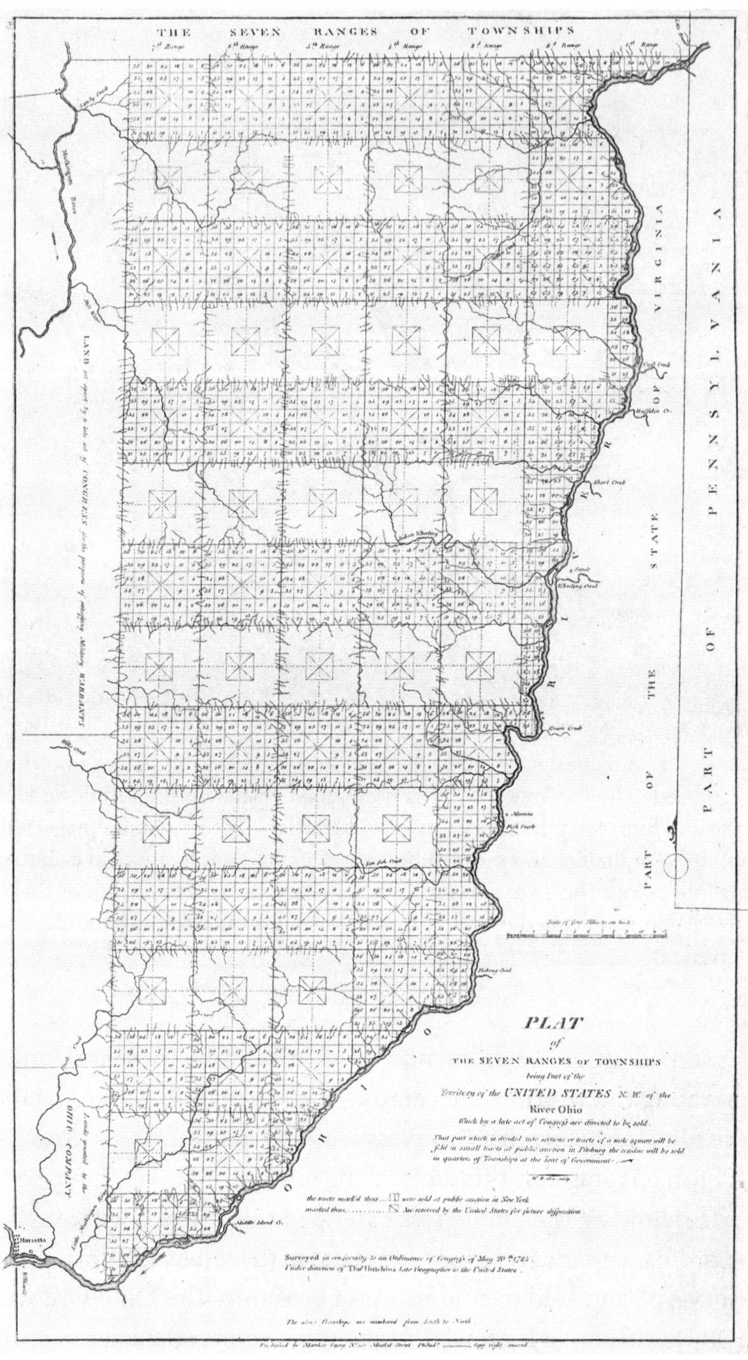

FIGURE 4.2. "Plat of the seven ranges of townships being part of the territory of the United States n.w. of the Ohio River which by a late act of Congress are directed to be sold."

Surveyors under the authority of a Geographer of the United States would measure square townships of six miles by six miles, divided into thirty-six numbered sections of one square mile each.[18] The sixteenth section of each township would be reserved for the support of public education. Four additional sections would be reserved for later sale (presumably at higher prices) once the township became more developed. The secretary of war would be given the opportunity to set aside surveyed land to satisfy promises made to Revolutionary War veterans. Then Congress's Treasury Board would be given the surveys to conduct orderly sales of the remaining townships and sections. Widely advertised sales were to be held within each of the thirteen states, making it possible for citizens across the nation to purchase land from the national domain. The smallest unit of land for sale, a 640-acre or one-square-mile section, would have a minimum price of one dollar per acre, meaning that purchase of land in the national domain would be restricted to people of means. (As events would show, this plan would ultimately favor large land speculators.)[19] Payment for the land could be made in specie, or in loan office certificates or "certificates of the liquidated debts of the United States," creating a direct mechanism linking Western land sales to the retirement of the national debt.[20]

The 1785 ordinance mandated standard forms for land deeds to be recorded by the Treasury Board and issued to purchasers: "which deeds shall be recorded in proper books, by the commissioners of the loan-office, and shall be certified to have been recorded, previous to their being delivered to the purchaser, and shall be good and valid to convey the lands in the same described." This cadastralization of land would be the method whereby legal title for settler colonists would be overseen by the United States. It was a system designed to favor speculators, large investors, and those with the means to purchase land directly, while discouraging squatters. In effect, the Land Ordinance of 1785 inaugurated the making of a speculative, rationalized, forward-looking Domesday Book for America, seven hundred years after William the Conqueror had issued the orders for his own "Great Survey" of England. Until the land was purchased, settled, and developed, it was not yet the real estate the Domesday Book had catalogued for the sake of taxation and state building, but the new land ordinance projected this future onto the national domain. The surveying process, which would become the U.S. Public Land Survey System and continues to the present day under the auspices of the U.S. Bureau of Land Management, was scheduled to begin on the northwest bank of the Ohio River, in territory ceded by Virginia to Congress, on what was then the border between Virginia and Pennsylvania's western edge.

Though originally intended to implement the prior year's ordinance, the 1785 ordinance actually demonstrated how inadequate the earlier measure was. On one hand, the 1784 ordinance had overreached by projecting a large number of new trans-Appalachian states, including ones in the territory *south* of the Ohio River that had not yet been ceded to Congress. Virginia's trans-Appalachian territory south of the Ohio (the future State of Kentucky) was rapidly filling up with American settlers. By the time of the first national census in 1790 there were already seventy-three thousand non-Indian residents there, more than the population of Rhode Island or Delaware, and a tenfold increase over the preceding decade.[21] White settlers were also colonizing the western parts of North Carolina, the future State of Tennessee. These settlements were just as much part of Virginia or North Carolina as the district of Maine was part of Massachusetts, or the Mohawk Valley was part of New York. The notion that the Confederation Congress could dismember existing states by fiat and generate new states out of yet-to-be-ceded state territory was an obvious flaw in the 1784 ordinance. So too was its vague description of how settlers moving into this new grid of states-to-be would organize themselves into governmental units. To remedy these flaws, even as delegates from twelve of the thirteen states were meeting at the convention in Philadelphia to revise the Articles of Confederation, a committee in the Confederation Congress (then meeting in New York) chaired by James Monroe drafted another new land ordinance exclusively for the territory north and west of the Ohio River, land that was no longer claimed by any state and was clearly in the national domain.

The resulting Northwest Ordinance enacted in July 1787 superseded the 1784 ordinance, formally declaring it to be "repealed . . . null and void."[22] In its stead, the new ordinance offered a plan for Congress to supervise the eventual creation of three to five states in this region, with a specified method of generating territorial governments for the transitional period between settlement and statehood. At first, Congress would appoint a single territorial governor over this enormous region, together with a secretary and a court consisting of three judges. The governor would be commander-in-chief of the territorial militia and have the power to appoint all local magistrates in the territory's emerging counties and townships, "necessary for the preservation of the peace and good order." The territory would be ruled in this autocratic way until such time as its free adult male population reached five thousand (probably about twenty to twenty-five thousand settlers all told). At that point these men could elect representatives from their townships to a general assembly. The assembly, together with the appointed governor and a five-man council nominated by the assembly and approved by Congress, would legislate for the territory, with the governor retaining veto power over the assembly's bills. Whenever the population of one of the three to five proposed future states in the territory reached sixty thousand free inhabitants (not just free adult males), then, in the words of the ordinance, "such State shall be admitted, by its delegates, into the Congress of the United States, on an equal footing with the original States in all respects whatever, and shall be at liberty to form a permanent constitution and State government."

Note that admission of new states to the confederation no longer required a supermajority vote of two-thirds of the existing states, as the 1784 ordinance had required, presumably because the confederation itself had taken full control of the process, and it was confederation land being formed into new states. With the Northwest Ordinance, the process of state making within the national domain became fairly routine, a matter of numbers and procedures, so long as the prospective states' governments were republican. The ordinance supplied guidelines for what republican government required in the form of a proto–Bill of Rights, including religious freedom, habeas corpus, trial by jury, property rights, and a series of other protections similar to the Bills of Rights in the constitutions of the original thirteen states. The ordinance prohibited slavery in the Northwest Territory, although it also included a fugitive slave clause to prevent the region from becoming a haven for enslaved people escaping from neighboring states[23]—a topic we will return to later. Even though the ordinance affirmed that newly admitted states would be "on an equal footing with the original States," it nonetheless created one stark distinction between the future states and the original thirteen:

> The legislatures of those districts or new States, shall never interfere with the primary disposal of the soil by the United States in Congress assembled, nor with any regulations Congress may find necessary for securing the title in such soil to the bona fide purchasers.

By contrast, the original thirteen states retained complete authority over the distribution of lands within their boundaries but not yet occupied by white settlers. These were very substantial amounts of land, from Massachusetts's Maine district in the Northeast (larger than the rest of New England combined) to Georgia's immense reserves in the Southwest, along with large parts of the Carolinas, Pennsylvania, and New York. But within all the newly created states as outlined under the Northwest Ordinance, the national government under Congress's authority would insist on the right to control this land distribution process, using the procedures outlined in the Land Ordinance of 1785. The national domain would remain national, even while states proliferated within it. In that sense, new states formed by the national government would lack a significant power that the original thirteen states retained. This was a clear sign of the growing power of national government (as opposed to state power), a significant structural reform to the nation's constitution that preceded the drafting and ratification of the Philadelphia Constitution.[24] Congress had asserted the same kind of sovereign authority over the trans-Appalachian West as King George III had in his Royal Proclamation of 1763, but with a much more careful and detailed plan for its future development.

Over the three years in which the Confederation Congress was creating these deliberate and rational land ordinances for the trans-Appalachian

West, the situation on the ground was deteriorating. Violence between white settlers and Native Americans was exacerbated by the frustrating inability of the states or the nation to contain the flood of colonists moving westward. The United States was in the midst of a population explosion produced by a combination of postwar immigration and natural growth. The fastest-growing regions were in the western reaches of Pennsylvania, Virginia, North Carolina, and Georgia, a population boom that skewed white, male, and young. At the small army garrison of Fort Harmar, built in 1785 at the confluence of the Muskingum and Ohio Rivers to prevent squatters from settling north of the Ohio, soldiers recorded that from October 1786 to December 1787, more than 5,500 settlers passed the fort in flatboats, bringing their horses and cattle with them. Another 4,000 passed the fort in the single month of April 1788.[25] They were ostensibly heading for the Kentucky district south of the Ohio River, still part of Virginia, but the national government had no power to stop them from settling north of the river. George Washington described the teeming thousands of colonists as "a parcel of Banditti, who will bid defiance to all authority."[26] Dozens of separatist and secessionist movements arose in the West. Settlers violated Indian treaties that the national government had negotiated, generating a growing sense, reminiscent of 1763, that authority had collapsed over the newly acquired national domain.[27]

Powerful Americans felt this collapse personally, none more so than Washington, the now-retired commander-in-chief of the victorious Continental Army. From his youthful days as a surveyor, he had been obsessed with Western lands. His family's homestead at Mount Vernon, on the banks of the Potomac River, placed him along one of the primary avenues for expansion westward. By the time the war ended, Washington had amassed ownership of nearly sixty thousand acres in the trans-Appalachian region, mostly in southwestern Pennsylvania and the Ohio River Valley.[28] At the same time, his personal finances were in disarray from wartime neglect, and he hoped his Western land investments would generate income from sales or rent from tenants to help right the ship. In September 1784, Washington made a tour of the region, heading up the Potomac from his Mount Vernon home and crossing into

Pennsylvania to inspect his landholdings. From there he planned to reach the Ohio River and float down to his westernmost and largest holdings, forty thousand acres at the junction of the Kanawha River with the Ohio.

Throughout the trip Washington planned to scout out likely routes for building canals that would connect the Potomac to the Ohio. For visionary speculators like Washington, who agreed to head a joint Maryland-Virginia company to expand the Potomac's navigation, canal building offered a strategy for joining the West and East together in the new nation. The *Virginia Journal* exhorted in 1784, "[The canal] will be one of the grandest Chains for preserving the federal Union[;] the Western World will have free access to us, and we shall be one and the same people, whatever System of European Politics may be adopted."[29] Note the subtext in this passage: specific forms of government for the new nation mattered less, to this writer, than any government's capacity to develop the nation's economy and maintain communication and trade across the Appalachian divide. The continuing integrity of the social body was more important than the details of the frame of government—the garment in the constitutional relationship. This region between the headwaters of the Potomac and those of the Ohio was precisely where the great flood of colonists was moving, "like a plague of locusts in the territories of the Ohio River," as Indigenous people from the region complained to the Spanish governor of St. Louis.[30]

Washington's scouting journey was cut short. Rumors of Indigenous violence spurred by settler intrusions in the Ohio country prevented his small party from attempting the trip down the river from Fort Pitt (the violence was a major reason why Fort Harmar would be built the following year). They turned back from western Pennsylvania, where Washington discovered squatters occupying his land (some had even fraudulently sold some of Washington's acres) and returned to Mount Vernon by a safer route through the Allegheny and Blue Ridge Mountains. Washington's enthusiasm for canal building through this region was undimmed, and he recruited to the cause other powerful Virginians, including James Madison, Thomas Jefferson, and Benjamin Harrison. A viable transportation system to the East from the West seemed like the only way to keep the flood of America's westward migrants loyal to the United States, given the likelihood that once beyond the mountains, "the Spaniards on their right, & Gt Britain on their left" would "hold out lures for their trade and alliance" unless they had some convenient and profitable means to trade with the Eastern states.[31]

Other prominent figures had similar experiences. In 1785, James Monroe accompanied a congressional commission down the Ohio River to negotiate a land cession treaty with Ohio Indians, and then toured his own speculative land investments in Kentucky. The treaty negotiators failed to make headway with the Shawnee, who opposed ceding any land north of the Ohio. Monroe feared the growing hostility of Western settlers to the Eastern governments; this convinced him of the need to revise the Land Ordinance of 1784 to strengthen Congress's hand in the development of this region. Monroe went on to chair the committee that drafted the Northwest Ordinance in 1787.

Another leading figure in drafting the Northwest Ordinance was Manasseh Cutler of Massachusetts. Cutler organized the Ohio Company of Associates in 1786 with a group of Continental Army veterans, many of them Society of the Cincinnati members.[32] They pooled their resources, acquired through speculation in Continental certificates—Congress's IOUs to soldiers for their military service—to purchase 1.5 million acres of Ohio land at a discount negotiated with Congress. They aimed to profit by selling these lands to colonists from New England, who might prove to be more orderly and law-abiding than the "willful and obstinate sinners" Washington found squatting on his western Pennsylvania claims.[33] Cutler strategically sold shares in the Ohio Company to leading members of the Confederation Congress, including Arthur St. Clair, Congress's president. St. Clair was then appointed by Congress as the first territorial governor of the Northwest Territory after the passage of the Northwest Ordinance.

Surveys of Ohio land commenced after the Land Ordinance of 1785 but were disrupted and brought to a halt by Indigenous hostility to the process. Altogether the federal government only had about four to five hundred troops to defend the surveyors, and even these soldiers grew increasingly mutinous because Congress lacked the money to pay them.[34] From New England to Georgia—where settler violations of the Treaty of Hopewell threatened to touch off war with the Creeks and neighboring Spanish Florida lured American colonists with secessionist plots—there were powerful incentives across the original thirteen states to augment the powers of the national government. On the critical question of Western lands, Congress had succeeded in reforming the national constitution, but only partially. They had added a new set of formal powers to the collective or "general" government of the union and asserted its exclusive authority over the national domain, but the confederation still lacked the financial resources, the administrative capacities, and the military power to turn plans into action. Without such changes, Congress's careful design for controlling the West could never be implemented, and the confederated national body of the United States might well be pulled apart.[35]

5

From Convention to Ratification

DRAFTING A BLUEPRINT FOR A SPECULATIVE EMPIRE

> I cannot consent to take two dollars a acre for the Land in Washington County. If the Government of this Country gets well toned, and property perfectly secured, I have no doubt of obtaining the price I have fixed on the land, and that in a short time.
>
> —GEORGE WASHINGTON TO JOHN CANON, LAND AGENT, SEPTEMBER 16, 1787, THE DAY BEFORE WASHINGTON SIGNED THE PHILADELPHIA CONVENTION'S DRAFT CONSTITUTION

OF THE THOUSANDS of books and articles that have been written on the origins of the U.S. Constitution, few tend to focus on the challenge of Western land claims or acknowledge that half the territory of the original United States belonged to Indigenous peoples who were formally excluded from citizenship in the new nation.[1] In a way, this is not surprising: the Constitution's text says relatively little about these subjects, at least not directly. But the document's reticence does not mean that these issues were unimportant at the time.

This wide blind spot in constitutional scholarship is the result of an all-too-common assumption that the Philadelphia text is somehow complete unto itself—that the document drafted by the convention *is* "the Constitution." But, as we saw in the previous chapter, the Philadelphia text was another step in an ongoing process of constitutional reform, building on the Land Ordinance of 1785 and the Northwest Ordinance of 1787—the latter completed by July 13, 1787, midway through the Philadelphia Convention's deliberations.[2] The Philadelphia Convention did not address these land issues because the Confederation Congress had already addressed them, at least formally. The Philadelphia Convention paid more explicit attention to the challenges that the confederation had been too conflicted to address under the Articles and to the powers necessary to implement the nation's authority over matters where it already had formal claims.

Nor is the frequency with which the Philadelphia Constitution mentions a subject necessarily a sign of its importance. Consider slavery. The word is nowhere mentioned in the document. The practice of slavery is obliquely alluded to in only a few clauses, even though one in every five Americans was enslaved—more than one in three in the states south of Pennsylvania. This unnamed but pervasive institution had a profound influence on the Constitution, including the most fundamental question in a self-governing republic: how to represent the people in the legislature. In recent decades, scholarship on the origins of the Constitution has increasingly attended to the significance of slavery. This focus has emerged in recognition of the growing conflict in the early U.S. over slavery, a rift between states that abolished slavery and those that embraced it, which made it all the more difficult to create a framework for a single, consolidated national government.[3] During the Philadelphia Convention, the ratification process, and afterwards, slavery was a controversial subject, testing whether the coalition that declared independence in 1776 could remain intact despite fundamental societal differences and generating conflict that would ultimately lead to civil war.

In contrast to their relationship with the fraught subject of slavery, the delegates at Philadelphia were neither squeamish nor divided about their intentions regarding Western lands and the dispossession of Indians. Article I, Section 2, avoided using the word "slaves" when describing the "other Persons" whose numbers were to be represented in Congress at three-fifths the rate of free persons. But the very same clause readily named "Indians not taxed" (i.e., Indians living as separate nations) when excluding them from any representation in Congress. The Constitution also enumerated the powers of Congress to "regulate Commerce . . . with the Indian tribes" (Article I, Section 8—in this clause equating Indian tribes with "foreign nations"), to admit new states to the union from Western territories, and "to dispose of and make all needful Rules and Regulations respecting the Territory or other Property belonging to the United States (Article 4, Section 3)." As with slavery, the few instances in which Western lands and Indian affairs are directly mentioned in the text belie the major importance of this subject for understanding the purpose of the 1787 Constitution.

Most obscure of all is the question of what empowering the national government was meant to accomplish: what was the Constitution for? All the major constitutional interventions in the Anglo-American tradition were meant to *do* something, to resolve a problem or address a crisis that seemed insurmountable. A polity does not produce a written constitution, or subvert an older one, simply to make an abstract statement of timeless truths about the science of governance.[4] In this regard, there was a critical difference between the problem of slavery and the issue of territorial expansion and Indigenous dispossession in the constitution-making process. Free white citizens were profoundly divided, mostly along regional lines, over the value of slavery to the union, and therefore divided on how or even if a new national constitution should address this subject. But U.S. citizens from all regions generally agreed on the value of dispossessing Natives and developing Western lands for white settlers.

As a result, there was little controversy at the Philadelphia Convention or in the ratification debates in the states over whether the extension of America's colonization and state-making project in the trans-Appalachian West should be the task of the national government. Even as the delegates were gathering in Philadelphia, the Confederation Congress was drafting a definitive plan for the political framework of expansion, the Northwest Ordinance. Each of the original thirteen states had been formed through some version of this expansionist process in the colonial period. Now they intended to empower their collective government—often called the "general" government in this era—with the tools to continue this westward colonization of the territory they claimed. There were varying opinions on the most expeditious policies for conducting this transformation, but all agreed on the fundamental importance of giving the national government the requisite tools.[5]

In May 1787, delegates from twelve states convened in Philadelphia to discuss reforms of the Articles of Confederation.[6] Only Rhode Island was missing. A convention to address the confederacy's commercial challenges had been held the year before in Annapolis, Maryland, but had attracted scant participation (five states, twelve delegates). Annapolis yielded no results beyond a call for another convention to revise the confederation government and render it "adequate to the exigencies of the Union." On February 21, 1787, the Confederation Congress authorized a second convention "for the sole and express purpose of revising the Articles of Confederation."[7]

As the delegates assembled in Philadelphia, they expected that these reforms would significantly enhance the powers of national government. But many delegates were unprepared for the plan presented on May 29 by Edmund Randolph, governor of Virginia and spokesman for its delegation.[8] The plan was drafted principally by James Madison and reflected the interests of other members of Virginia's powerful delegation, most notably George Washington, who was elected as the convention's presiding officer.[9] If the charge from Congress had called for the convention to *revise* the Articles, the Virginia Plan completely *overthrew* the confederation among equal states that the Articles mandated. In its place Virginia proposed a full and direct government over all the nation's citizens, with a bicameral representative legislature and separate coequal executive and judicial branches. Not only was Virginia's plan radically different from the Articles, but it also offered an alarmingly open-ended description of the government's enhanced powers: all the powers held by the existing Congress plus the power to

> . . . legislate in all cases to which the separate States are incompetent, or in which the harmony of the United States may be interrupted by the exercise of individual Legislation; to negative all laws passed

> by the several States, contravening in the opinion of the National Legislature the articles of Union; and to call forth the force of the Union agst any member of the Union failing to fulfill its duty under the articles thereof.[10]

This would include all national taxation, since the separate states were of course incapable of laying taxes on the nation as a whole. Legislation over control of the national domain would clearly fall under these powers as well. Essentially, this was carte blanche for Congress to legislate on any and all national matters and to force state compliance and overturn state laws. In other words, Virginia's plan was little different from the legislative authority "in all cases whatsoever" that Parliament had claimed over the colonies in the Declaratory Act of 1766.[11]

Some of the delegates, especially those from smaller states whose votes would be overwhelmed by the populous states in a general legislature, recoiled in opposition to the Virginia Plan. It was fear of a plan like this that had kept Rhode Island away from the convention. The small states, many of them lacking Western land claims or unlikely to benefit much from westward expansion, soon brought forward their own proposal. The New Jersey Plan presented by William Paterson on June 15 hewed to the convention's instructions and retained the Articles' *structure*—a confederacy of equal states assembled in Congress. But the enhanced *powers* the New Jersey Plan proposed to make the Articles "adequate to the exigencies of Government" were considerable. These included new taxation powers, an executive branch for the national government with military powers, a judicial branch with jurisdiction over national affairs, and the power to make treaties that would be the "Supreme Law" of the United States. The national government under the New Jersey Plan would have the capacity "to enforce and compell an obedience to such Acts or an observance of such Treaties"—tools necessary to project national power over the Western territories and to control the "admission of New States into the Union."[12]

This is the key point: the proponents of the Virginia Plan's vision of a national republican government as well as the opponents of such a "consolidated" union were *equally* in favor of granting the national government the necessary powers to take on the challenge of Western expansion. Even at the most fractious moment in the Philadelphia Convention, when the prospect of reconciling the division over the Virginia and New Jersey Plans looked doubtful, there was a strong underlying consensus on the need to expand the government's powers to meet this purpose.[13]

After several days of deliberations, the convention voted down the New Jersey Plan. But its supporters continued to insist that the Articles' principle of state equality must be retained. This impasse was breached with the "Great Compromise," which allowed for national representation in proportion to population for the House of Representatives but maintained equality among the states in the Senate. This modified version of the Virginia Plan would be the structural framework on which the new national government would rest. The delegates then turned to arguing over the fetters to be placed on the newly empowered government through the distribution of powers across the branches and their checks on one another, preventing any one branch of government from acting without cooperation from the others.

As recent historians of the Constitution have persuasively argued, this outcome was "a revolution in favor of government," an agreement that the exigencies of the union simply could not be met by the firm league of friendship the Articles had created. The delegates mostly agreed that the union needed to become a European-style state with a full panoply of powers, one that other countries would recognize as a "treaty-worthy" equal.[14] The Virginia Plan, modified by three months of intense bargaining and building upon the powers attained in the Land Ordinance of 1785 and the Northwest Ordinance of 1787, offered such a prospect. But as we saw with respect to America's post–Revolutionary War debt problem, American state-making needs differed significantly from European models, precisely because so much of the nation's land mass, its western half, took the form of "non-state" territory, occupied by people ("our Indian neighbors," in Jefferson's words) who ranked far below European states ("our sister nations") on the "treaty-worthy" scale.[15]

The completed constitutional draft, together with the simultaneous Northwest Ordinance, which was immediately affirmed by the new

Congress in its first session in 1789, thus divided the "United States" into two unequal parts, the states and the non-state territories. The terms of the Constitution applied fully to citizens who lived in places that were already states, excluding "Indians not taxed," such as the Haudenosaunee (or Iroquois) Confederacy whose homelands lay within the bounds of New York State but who governed themselves as a separate nation. But for the extensive national domain outside of any state's boundaries, the rules were different. In the national territories, people were excluded, either temporarily or permanently, from the normative system the Constitution created for American citizens.[16] For white settlers in the territories, the bargain was that they would live under territorial governments mandated by national authority. They could gain legal access to land only under the Land Ordinance system. When settler populations reached sufficient numbers they could participate in local territorial self-government, but any legislation their territorial assembly might pass could be vetoed by an appointed territorial governor. And they could not actively participate in national government—a territory was allowed to send only a non-voting representative to the House of Representatives.[17] When its population reached sixty thousand settlers, a territory could apply to Congress for admission to statehood.

The temporary disenfranchisement[18] of U.S. citizens who opted to move from states to territories was designed to avoid the problem that had undermined Britain's American empire—namely, the anomalous place of Britain's colonies within its imperial constitution and the ambiguous rights of colonial subjects and their governments. In the 1760s, Britain's colonists had protested against Parliament's legislation, claiming that in leaving the homeland and moving to America, they retained all their rights as Englishmen, including the right to consent to legislation that directly affected them. This would clearly *not* be the case under the new U.S. Constitution. American citizens who moved to the nation's territories could not claim all their rights until various stages of colonization had been reached. They would be governed by appointed magistrates, and the appointed governor could veto laws their assemblies passed and appoint judges who would decide their fate in court cases.

Above all, their right to consent to the laws passed by the new national government was forfeit until the territory achieved statehood.

For Indigenous people, who were to be permanently excluded from full participation in the constitutional bargain so long as they lived as separate nations, the Constitution and Northwest Ordinance promised only to protect them from squatters and insisted that the national government alone could acquire land from them through formal treaties. How that process fared in reality will be discussed in part III. But for the moment it is essential to understand that under the new Constitution, America was a bifurcated country, structured unlike any other nation of the time. The U.S. territories differed from the colonies of an imperial nation such as Britain in that there were fixed plans for their transformation into full membership within the realm; they were also unlike the colonies of the soon-to-be revolutionary French republic, where the "rights of man and the citizen" would be fully extended to residents of the overseas departments. The trans-Appalachian West on which the country staked so much of its future prosperity was part of the United States, but at the same time oddly outside of the new governing framework.

———

What new powers and tools did the draft Constitution provide for managing the challenge of Western lands?[19] Most directly, Article IV, Section 3, plainly gives Congress the power to admit new states to the union following the plan of the Northwest Ordinance (notably *without* the supermajority that had been required under the Articles). Congress is also empowered to "dispose of and make all needful Rules and Regulations respecting the Territory or other Property belonging to the United States." This clause includes the power to criminalize illegal settlement on Indigenous or federal land and to prosecute violators in the new federal court system—a power that appealed to land speculators, who feared that squatters would seize their land claims and provoke expensive and dangerous Indian wars.[20] At the same time, Section 3 protects the integrity of all the existing states, and any future states, by guaranteeing that Congress cannot make new states by carving up existing ones, or by combining two or more existing states, without the consent of state legislatures. Thus, Virginia's authorization was required for Kentucky to gain statehood in 1792, and Massachusetts's for Maine in 1820.[21]

The Indian commerce clause (Article I, Section 8) gives Congress the power to "regulate Commerce" with "the Indian Tribes," with foreign nations, and among the states. This clause granted the federal government its power to appoint Indian superintendents and oversee relationships that had traditionally been a source of friction between settlers and Indigenous people, gaining further control over Western development. Augmenting this capacity is the exclusive power that Article II, Section 2 gives to the executive branch to make treaties (pending Senate approval), and the corresponding prohibition in Article I, Section 10: "No State shall enter into any Treaty, Alliance, or Confederation." Thus, even if a state such as Georgia with extensive land claims wanted to acquire land from Native nations within its territory, only the national government could negotiate a valid treaty for legal land cessions.[22]

Under the new Constitution, states could not pass laws invalidating federal treaties, as Georgia had done with the Treaty of Hopewell in 1786. All state legislators and officials were required by Article VI to swear to uphold the Constitution's powers. Article VI also declared all ratified treaties to be "the supreme Law of the Land," binding judges in every state to uphold them. Under Article I, Section 8, Congress gained the power "to provide for calling forth the Militia to execute the Laws of the Union [which includes all treaties], suppress Insurrections and repel Invasions." This was a crucial change from the Articles of Confederation, where states could use military forces only to defend themselves against external invasions and the national government lacked the power to call on state militias to enforce laws or suppress insurrections. Now the federal government was committed to supporting states against Indian attacks, even if the state itself was responsible for instigating the violence.

Article II's creation of a separate executive branch provided crucial tools for implementing what had mostly been paper powers under the Articles of Confederation. It vested supreme military command in the president as head of the new executive branch, including ultimate authority over the state militias when called into national service. Combined with Article I, Section 8, Congress now had the power to raise and maintain armies in peacetime, and the president had the power to command them. Although the Land Ordinance of 1785 had provided a plan for surveying and selling lands in the national domain, the threat of Native reprisals in the Ohio country had prevented the first surveyors from completing their work; the confederation government lacked the money to raise troops to defend them. Under the new Constitution these challenges could now be addressed. The national judicial system created by Article III (also lacking under the confederation government) gave the federal judiciary authority to adjudicate disputes among states or individuals with conflicting Western claims, to complement the territorial judicial system mandated by the Northwest Ordinance. As the convention wound down and the drafting committee polished the final draft, its presiding officer, George Washington, wrote to his land agent. He instructed him not to sell his Western lands at a low price. Once the new Constitution was ratified, Washington had "no doubt of obtaining the price I have fixed on the land, and that in a short time."[23]

Washington made a shrewd decision. As the first president of the United States, he took charge of a system newly designed to seize control over the immense national domain generated by the terms of the Treaty of Paris and outlined by the Confederation Congress's land ordinances. With this new array of powers and tools, the national government became a technology for replicating the conditions described in the Domesday Book, by acquiring Indigenous land, transforming the land into marketable real estate, moving settlers onto the land, and organizing landowning settlers into new states. Under the national government's deliberate control, the United States could generate new territories and then make them into states while avoiding political turmoil among its own free citizens, the goal that Britain's empire had found no method for accomplishing over the territory it had won in the Seven Years' War. Over the course of the next century, this is exactly what the United States government would do, and with breathtaking efficiency. Before the nineteenth century ended, the United States had added thirty-two new states to the original thirteen and increased the territory under statehood from 365,000 square miles in 1789 to 3.4 million square miles in 1896. This astonishing, near tenfold increase in land under statehood accommodated the even more dramatic population growth between the 1790 and 1890 censuses from four million to sixty-three million people.

Of course, there was more to the new Constitution than its provisions for conquering and controlling the American West. My purpose here is not to provide a complete description and analysis of the Constitution's production and contents.[24] Yet it needs to be said that what is *in* the Constitution is not the same as what the Constitution was *for*. A great deal of the Constitution's content includes material directly carried over from the Articles of Confederation, as well as venerable concepts borrowed from the state constitutions and English constitutional history. The Bill of Rights, which Americans today consider an essential part of the Constitution—for many its most important part—was only produced in response to the backlash generated in the ratification debates over the Philadelphia draft. The defense of fundamental rights is not what the Constitution was *for*, not a reason why it was created to begin with. The appended Bill of Rights simply modified the content and format of earlier state bills of rights, which themselves were derived from English precursors.[25] By contrast, the creation of new structures and powers needed to meet the challenge of Western lands was clearly one of the chief purposes of the constitutional reforms of the 1780s. It was the national challenge for which the specific provisions of the Philadelphia framework were most essential.

The most fundamental element of the Philadelphia Constitution, as a departure from the Articles, was its creation of a representative republic with direct power over individual citizens, including the power of taxation, on a national scale. The initial United States constitution defined by the Articles of Confederation had left these powers of representation and taxation fully in the hands of the states, much as they had been in the colonial period. The Philadelphia Constitution's reasoning and method for extending this authority across the immense territory of the

United States were grounded in early modern assumptions about land, population, and power. Like England at the time of the Domesday Book, the United States in the 1780s was an overwhelmingly agricultural society. As of the 1790 census, there were only thirty-one places in the United States with an "urban" concentration of more than 2,500 people (few today would think of places that small as urban). The average population of these thirty-one places was about 7,200. Only six of them were to be found south of the Mason-Dixon Line. Eleven of the thirty-one were in Massachusetts, and nineteen were in New England. Of America's nearly 4 million people, 94.3 percent lived in rural communities of fewer than 2,500 people, a percentage that rose higher the farther south and west one went.[26] Most of the country's early leaders had every intention of keeping it that way, none more so than Thomas Jefferson, who believed that cities were "cankers" on the body politic. Jefferson envisioned America's future as an expanding agrarian republic stretching from sea to sea.[27]

It should come as no surprise that the framers of the Constitution made the same assumption as the Domesday recorders: that a given quantity of arable land plus a certain amount of human population yields a reasonable assessment of the wealth and power of a particular place. In the England of 1086, this assessment served a hierarchical purpose, defining the amount of revenue the king and his feudal lords could expect from their holdings based on the empirical evidence of the Domesday surveyors. The richest and most powerful lords had the most say in the kingdom's decision, but they also bore the heaviest burdens in defending the realm. Seven hundred years later, the Philadelphia delegates modified this formula to serve a republican version of the same purpose, to determine fairly both the amount of representation and the burden of taxation to be distributed across each part of the union, now that there was no privileged class of rulers with an outsize say in making the nation's decisions. The representation that a state received in the national government would be directly proportional to the amount of taxation it would have to pay under national legislation. Some of the convention's most consequential decisions emerged out of arguments over this question.

During the Revolutionary War, under the Articles of Confederation, this question had arisen in determining the amount of revenue each state was expected to contribute (voluntarily) to Congress's funding requests. This was a difficult problem, given the obvious inequalities among the states in land area, population, and wealth. Even though all the states had an equal vote in Congress, it would have been ludicrous to imagine that tiny Delaware could or should contribute to the war effort as much as massive Virginia. Consequently, the Articles declared that the contributions of the states should be made "in proportion to the value of all land within each State, granted or surveyed for any person, as such land and the buildings and improvements thereon shall be estimated according to such mode as the United States in Congress assembled, shall from time to time direct and appoint." In theory, this very Domesday-like process for assessing the value of each state's improved land would determine its share of the national expense burden.[28]

The system proved to be entirely unworkable. There was no Domesday Book for the colonies. Many colonies lacked the capacity (or the will) to assess their citizens' property holdings. The national government as yet had no resources, institutions, or bureaucracy to implement such a plan.[29] And there was a war going on. Under these circumstances, it was impossible to develop a national system for property assessment. In 1783, after the war had ended, Congress debated an alternative plan, substituting population for real estate as the basis for estimating each state's wealth. It was far easier to count people than to assess the value of land and its improvements.

But delegates in the Confederation Congress immediately disagreed over whether to count slaves as people or as property. Southern slaveholders claimed that enslaved people were property and therefore ought not be counted as persons for tax assessment any more than Northerners' horses and cows.[30] Northern delegates countered that the very reason to count people as a proxy for wealth was the value of the labor they performed. In that sense, not only were enslaved workers people, they were extremely productive people by virtue of masters' power over them—both to extract their labor by force and to restrict their consumption. Northerners further argued that excluding slaves from assessments for taxation would necessarily encourage slavery's expansion. Slave owners disagreed that slave labor was more profitable. They cited the many enslaved children and old or enfeebled slaves who produced little and were a burden to their owners. Haggling over this issue generated the infamous three-fifths ratio as a compromise on the revenue question. James Madison suggested that for the purpose of apportioning revenue requests across the states, every five enslaved people be counted as equal to three free people, a victory for slave owners' claim that slaves were less productive than free workers. But like so much else under the confederation government, this attempt to change the Articles failed to get unanimous approval from the states. It never went into effect.[31]

Four years later, Madison's proposal in the Virginia Plan for a national legislature forced the convention to determine how to apportion *representation* as well as taxation across the unequal states. No longer would revenue be requested from sovereign states; now elected representatives would vote to extract taxation directly from the nation's people. Revolutionary ideology had insisted on the ancient Anglo-American constitutional maxim that taxation required the consent of the governed; taxation and representation were inextricably linked. But Virginia's proposal that the lower house of the national government should be based on population reversed the terms of the earlier debate about the value of slaves. Slave owners now argued that for the purposes of *representation* slaves should be fully counted as persons, even though they had earlier insisted that for *taxation* purposes, slaves were not persons at all. To Charles Pinckney of South Carolina, slaves were "the labourers, the peasants of the Southern States: they are as productive of pecuniary resources as those of the Northern States. They add equally to the wealth, and considering money as the sinew of war, to the strength of the nation."[32] Pinckney expressed the prevailing conception that wealth, just as much as population, deserved representation in a legitimate legislature.[33] Counting slaves for the purpose of representation would also give white Southerners sufficient voting power to protect against the danger that Congress might threaten their property in slaves.

But Northern delegates reminded Pinckney that in 1783, when the issue was the allocation of tax burdens, Southerners had insisted that slaves were inferior to freemen in producing wealth. Nathaniel Gorham of Massachusetts noted that now, "when the ratio of representation is to be established, we are assured that they are equal to free men."[34] When the convention introduced the three-fifths taxation measure as a compromise to offset representation for slaves, Northern delegate James Wilson of Pennsylvania, who had taken part in the 1783 arguments over taxation, pointed out the absurdity of this notion; either the enslaved were citizens, and should be represented "on an equality with White Citizens," or else they were property, and then "Why is not other property admitted into the computation" for representation?[35]

Ultimately, when Gouverneur Morris of New York proposed to solve this dilemma by linking representation to direct taxation and counting five slaves as the equivalent of three free people for *both* purposes, a compromise was reached.[36] Direct taxation means any form of taxation extracted directly from the people, such as a property tax or an income tax, not unlike the annual yields the Domesday Book listed for each of England's thousands of estates. Such taxes, based on the fundamental resources and labors that sustain the people, are essentially unavoidable. Direct taxes are distinct from indirect taxes, such as customs duties or excise taxes levied on commercial goods, where a person can avoid the tax simply by choosing not to purchase the product. Governments often levy indirect taxes on luxury goods or non-necessities such as tobacco or alcohol; the closer an indirect tax gets to essentials like food and clothing, the more consumers resent it and (rightly) consider it to be a direct, unavoidable tax.

Reformers under the Articles had assumed that uniform national customs duties could be legitimately administered by the confederation government, as long as all the states agreed, because these would not be direct taxes on the people and therefore did not require direct representation of the people. But by granting the potential power of direct taxation to the national legislature, the Virginia Plan required a link between taxation and representation. Under Gouverneur Morris's compromise proposal, which became Article I, Section 2, of the Constitution, each state would be awarded representation in the lower house "according to their respective numbers, which shall be determined by adding to the whole Number of free Persons, including those bound to Service for a term of Years, . . . three fifths of all other Persons." To compensate for the additional voting power that large slaveholding states gained from their slaves, direct taxes would be apportioned among the states by the same ratio—if Congress ever voted to levy them, that is.

This was a big "if." The additional voting power gained by the free white men of the slave states became a tool they could use to prevent Congress from ever approving direct taxes. And indeed, the future United States Congresses almost never voted to levy direct taxes, relying instead on versions of the impost or customs duties on imported goods that members of the Confederation Congress had been proposing since the early 1780s. Until the Sixteenth Amendment of 1913, which gave the federal government the power to levy a national income tax without having the amounts be proportional to each state's population, virtually all the tax revenue raised by the federal government came from customs and excise—that is, indirect—taxes.

Despite the surface conflict at the convention over how to assess the value of enslaved people as productive laborers or property, there was deep consensus among all the delegates, Northern and Southern, on the question of how to define and allocate power in a republican government. Given the rudimentary administrative capacities of the nation; its immense size; the variation in its climates, crops, labor systems, and the varied forms of economic activity that characterized the different states, there could be no single method to assess the nation's wealth and population to make taxation and representation perfectly equitable. In *Federalist* no. 21 (December 12, 1787), Alexander Hamilton said as much: "The wealth of nations depends upon an infinite variety of causes. . . . There can be no common measure of national wealth; and of course, no general or stationary rule, by which the ability of a State to pay taxes can be determined." For that reason, Hamilton argued, the U.S. government ought to prefer indirect taxes such as the impost. Direct taxation was difficult to calculate fairly. But as of 1787 it was still an open question whether customs duties alone would be sufficient to raise enough money to address the national debt and perform the new functions that the Constitution awarded to the national government. When additional taxation was necessary, Hamilton recognized that "either the value of land, or the number of the people may serve as a standard" for apportionment because "the state of agriculture, and the populousness of a country, have been considered as nearly connected with each other." And since "in view of simplicity and certainty" it was easier to count people than to assess agriculture's value, then population provided the best available standard.[37]

The new Constitution claimed to express the sovereign will of the nation's citizens and greatly expanded the powers of the nation's government, including the power to tax the nation's wealth. At its heart lay the belief that it was imperative to represent, fairly and equitably, the nation's people and wealth—that is, the varied *interests* within the nation—despite the fact that they were distributed unevenly across the highly unequal states. This inequality among the states, and the understanding that different states had different interests, was the very thing that made it so difficult to distribute the power of representation and the burden of taxation fairly, to prevent some states from having too great a say in the government's policies, or from bearing too great a portion of the government's demands. In the 1760s and '70s, colonists had claimed that Parliament was incapable of representing their interests for similar reasons.[38] Even though the delegates at the convention argued over the specific terms of what would be fair and equitable, every delegate who engaged these questions shared the assumption that land plus population was the best equation for assessing the wealth and power of a given region and that this agrarian equation should form the fundamental basis for apportioning representation and taxation in a federal republic.

The convention never seriously considered enacting Jonathan Jackson's 1783 notion to redivide the nation into states of equal size and population.[39] But there was nonetheless agreement around the idea that a republic of states would endure longer and in greater harmony if its constituent elements were relatively equal in land and population. This view was advanced by leading international political theorists such as Emer de Vattel, author of *The Law of Nations* (1758). It was shared widely among the convention delegates, including George Washington, who borrowed a copy of Vattel's work from the New York Society Library when he assumed the office of the presidency.[40] This vision was plainly (if impractically) evoked in the grid system for future states that Jefferson projected in the abortive Land Ordinance of 1784. Even if Congress could not forcibly expand Rhode Island or shrink Virginia, at least the future of the nation might be bent toward greater equality through the admission of carefully designed new states. The more equal in area and population the states became, the less anomalous it would be for each of them to be equally represented in the Senate.

The Northwest Ordinance mandated the creation of three to five new states that would be roughly equal in area to the larger states in the original union, such as Pennsylvania, the largest state whose borders were already fixed and known.[41] The ordinance guaranteed that for admission, these new states would already have a population (sixty thousand) equal to the smallest of the original states (Delaware's was fifty-nine thousand) along with sufficient land and resources to encourage continued growth under a system administered by the national government. James Madison, delegate from the largest state, spoke out at the convention on June 28 in favor of the idea that a national government of "sufficient energy & permanency" would ensure that "gradual partitions of the large, & junctions of the small (States) will be facilitated, and time (may) effect that equalization, which is wished for by the small states."[42] Other delegates, including ones from large states, like James Wilson of Pennsylvania, Nathaniel Gorham of Massachusetts, and Pierce Butler of South Carolina, agreed.[43]

On this score, Madison proved to be at least partially prophetic. Throughout U.S. history, no small states have ever joined together into one new state—that would mean forfeiting two Senate seats between them in the process. Delaware and Maryland have not combined forces, nor have Rhode Island and Connecticut, nor, for that matter, North and South Dakota, huge in territory but tiny in population. But under processes overseen by Congress and agreed to by the states in question, Vermont was carved out from New Hampshire's and New York's land claims (1791); Kentucky split off from Virginia (1792), and Tennessee from North Carolina (1796); Mississippi (1817) and Alabama (1819) divided out from Georgia's formerly immense claims; and finally Massachusetts agreed to statehood for Maine (1820). Before Madison died in

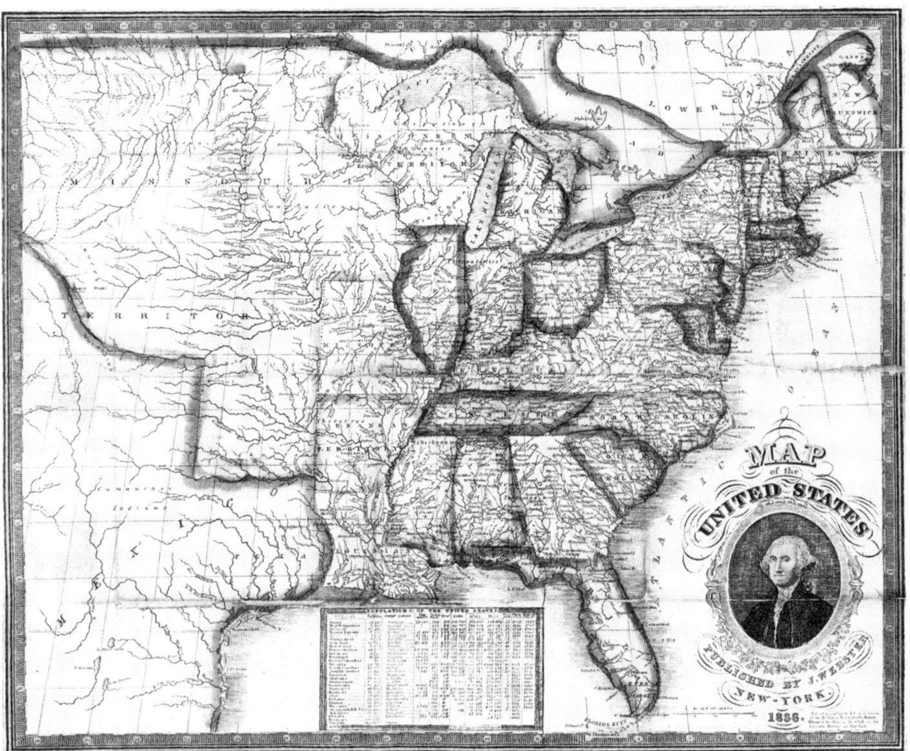

FIGURE 5.1. Map of the United States, 1836, by J. Webster. Note the roughly comparable sizes of all the new states west of the Appalachians, including the three from the Louisiana Purchase, in stark contrast to the 1784 geopolitical boundaries in depicted in Figure 2.5.

June 1836, all of the original territory of the United States from the 1783 Treaty of Paris had achieved statehood, with the exception of Michigan and Wisconsin, its northernmost reaches. And altogether the states were far more equal than the land claims of the states in 1783 had projected. Compare Figures 2.5 and 5.1.

But we're getting ahead of ourselves. There remained a major hurdle: ratification of the draft constitution by at least nine of the thirteen states.

Without ratification, the draft was a dead letter. The approval of only nine states for ratification, rather than the unanimity required by the Articles, was one of the convention's many extra-constitutional departures from their charge from the confederation, and a sign of the delegates' awareness that their radical break with the Articles would be controversial. But even though nine states' approval would officially put the Constitution into effect, a technical victory might not have been sufficient. There were five large and powerful states—Massachusetts, New York, Pennsylvania, Virginia, and North Carolina—that together held 63 percent of the U.S. population.[44] Four of these five, all but Massachusetts, were among the fastest-growing states in the union, with large numbers of immigrants and settlers moving rapidly into their western districts. Even Massachusetts had room to grow in its extensive undeveloped lands in the Maine district. If four of these large states had failed to ratify, the new government, with less than half the people of the United States represented in it, would likely have collapsed anyway.

In fact North Carolina did refuse to ratify the Constitution at its first state convention in July 1788, and would not do so until November 1789, well after the new government had begun. Of the other four large states, the outcome of the ratification debates was extremely narrow in three: Massachusetts, New York, and Virginia. In these three state conventions, a combined 580 votes were cast, and the Constitution was approved by a collective margin of only 32 votes. In Virginia and New York combined, only thirteen votes made the difference, even though in both states the votes were taken *after* nine states had already ratified.

The Constitution's ratification is a complex story, with intricate conflicts within each of the thirteen states. It generated an astonishingly rich literature of political debate, both in the popular press where the famous pamphlets of Federalists and Anti-Federalists were printed, and in the convention debates and correspondence among delegates.[45] For our purposes, it is vital to see how the nation's challenges regarding Western lands, and the powers created by the Constitution to address them, played a critical part in making ratification possible and reorienting the country's expectations for what the new government would accomplish.

The startled reaction of many of the Philadelphia delegates to the Virginia Plan presaged the response across the nation at large when the draft of the new Constitution was made public in September 1787. As state ratification conventions began to gather in the fall and winter of 1787–88, the Constitution's supporters, quickly self-labeled as Federalists, had good reason to fear that the anti-Federalist opposition would prevail. They mounted an intense publicity campaign undertaken by proponents such as Alexander Hamilton, John Jay, and James Madison, who composed their "Publius" essays (later collected as *The Federalist Papers*) for the New York press. Four states (Delaware, New Jersey, Pennsylvania, and Georgia) ratified quickly, before the year was out. Georgia's unanimous vote (26–0) on December 31 was the most surprising, and in many ways the most critical.[46] Surprising because Georgia had all along been the least supportive state with regard to national government under the Articles. Georgia never paid any of the money Congress requisitioned from the states for financial support. It also refused to cede to the national domain its immense Western territories, stretching across the mountains all the way to the Mississippi River. Georgia repeatedly violated and nullified treaties that Congress made with Indigenous nations, and still hoped to grow rich by selling its Western land claims to speculators and settlers in defiance of the confederation's authority.[47]

In the end, it was precisely these earlier habits of defying a weak Congress under the Articles that turned Georgians toward support of the Constitution. In the years before the convention (to which Georgia sent a rudimentary delegation that contributed little), Georgia's aggressive behavior toward the Indian nations of its Western territories, especially the Creeks, had provoked escalating violence. Alexander McGillivray, a Creek leader, formed an alliance with Spanish Florida against Georgia. The Creeks were supplied with arms by the British merchant firm of Panton, Leslie & Company, whom the Spanish allowed to operate out of Pensacola.[48] By the time the Constitutional Convention was underway, Creek attacks had "spread terror through every part of the state." By

October 1787 Georgia was engulfed in a "general Indian war." Georgia's rapid and unanimous ratification of the Constitution at year's end, a startling turnabout from its earlier position, was spurred by its desperate need for protection. As George Washington analyzed the situation, "If a weak state with powerful tribes of Indians in its rear and the Spaniards on its flank did not incline to embrace a strong *general* government there must, I should think, be either wickedness or insanity in their conduct." For Georgians, ever suspicious of a national government with power over their land claims, the Constitution was the lesser evil compared to "this great evil, an Indian war."[49]

The other states were not in Georgia's desperate straits, although the violence along the entire settler-Native frontier in these years after the Treaty of Paris should not be underestimated. (Roughly three thousand Anglo-Americans were killed or captured by Native peoples between 1783 and 1790, as were an untold number of Native Americans by colonizers.)[50] Even in Massachusetts, where, the winter before the convention, the resistance movement against the enforcement of punitive taxation measures (called Shays' Rebellion by its opponents) had caused widespread alarm over the failure of republican government, the threat of violence had diminished. Elections in May 1787 brought a new governor (John Hancock) and a new legislature to power, and they voted to ease the state's internal tax burden and suspend legal foreclosure on farms for unpaid taxes.[51] In the most critical states that held their conventions from January to July of 1788, Massachusetts, Virginia, and New York, it was argumentation and debate, not desperation over impending violence, that determined the outcome.

Opposition to the proposed Constitution was strong in Massachusetts, Viriginia, and New York. But concerns over Western territories, population, representation, and taxation varied widely. A range of different interest groups defended competing positions: large-scale investors and land speculators versus potential Western settlers and squatters; proponents and detractors of the three-fifths compromise; advocates of the Constitution's expanded powers versus those who feared a reversion to the distant tyranny that the Revolution had been fought to overthrow. On this last point, anti-Federalists universally expressed dismay that the new

Constitution supported powers equal to Britain's fiscal-military state, but lacked a Bill of Rights of the sort Parliament had promulgated in 1689.[52]

But the Federalists offered a persistent and ultimately winning (if only barely) set of arguments and countermeasures to address these fears. Massachusetts Federalists appended a set of recommended amendments, a Bill of Rights in the making, to the state's ratification statement, encouraging the new Congress to create protections for citizens' rights to balance the government's new powers. Federalists repeatedly emphasized the benefits of the new constitution for controlling the West and defeating British, Spanish, and Native American resistance. They pointed out that the Constitution gave the national government clear power to regulate commerce with Indian nations, make treaties that would be the supreme law of the land, and adjudicate land claims in federal courts. Speculators, investors, and land purchasers could expect a greater government capacity to keep the peace with Native nations, survey land, and supervise land deals in an orderly fashion—what George Washington and others like him had dreamed of for decades.[53]

This prospect raised concerns among the many thousands of white settlers who had already moved west or who feared that the financial power of wealthy speculators would overwhelm the interests of small family farmers—an old story in American colonization. Many Western colonizers knew that Eastern elites considered them little better than "white Savages" or "banditti," and feared the new government would be a tool for the elite to deprive them of land.[54] The Constitution's much enhanced military powers brought back memories of Britain's use of redcoats to police the boundary line of the Royal Proclamation of 1763 and keep settlers away from the land they coveted, as well as the use of regulars to enforce the hated Townshend Acts that had touched off revolutionary violence in cities like Boston.

But the Federalists countered these fears by warning of the Indian threat across the Western frontiers. Robert Livingston in New York and Edmund Pendleton in Virginia argued that the enhanced military power of the national government would be used to *protect* Western settlers and help them gain title to land, not keep them away. James Madison added that only the powers of the new Constitution could energize the national government to end Spanish and British support for Indians that hindered American expansion.[55] In the years since the Treaty of Paris in 1783, Britain had refused to give up possession of forts in the Northwest Territory because American states had failed to honor the treaty's provision for restoring lost property to Loyalists. The new Constitution would solve this problem, and in *Federalist* no. 24 and no. 25, Alexander Hamilton hammered this point home. An American standing army, he argued, would not resemble those of European monarchs, used to oppress their own subjects and involve them in endless wars of vanity. What's more, Hamilton pointed to Spain's and Britain's ongoing efforts to control the trans-Appalachian West and argued that "the savage tribes on our western frontier ought to be regarded as our natural enemies, their [Britain's and Spain's] natural allies." Only a national army, not state militias, could manage the "common" dangers (common to all the states) posed by the fact that "the territories of Britain, Spain and of the Indian nations in our neighborhood . . . incircle the Union from MAINE to GEORGIA."[56]

While they defended the need for a national army to secure the West, Federalists also acceded to anti-Federalist demands for a protective Bill of Rights. Virginia, one of the last states to hold its convention, generated the longest list of recommended amendments by building on the suggestions of earlier states.[57] Among them were two extensive provisions for ameliorating the threat of standing armies that deserve quotation in full:

> Seventeenth, That the people have a right to keep and bear arms; that a well regulated Militia composed of the body of the people trained to arms is the proper, natural and safe defence of a free State. That standing armies in time of peace are dangerous to liberty, and therefore ought to be avoided, as far as the circumstances and protection of the Community will admit; and that in all cases the military should be under strict subordination to and governed by the Civil power.
>
> Eighteenth, That no Soldier in time of peace ought to be quartered in any house without the consent of the owner, and in time of war in such manner only as the laws direct.[58]

As readers will notice, these recommendations became the basis for the Second and Third Amendments in the U.S. Bill of Rights.

James Madison had originally argued against the need for such a bill, but he immediately drafted one and ushered it through the House of Representatives once the new government came into effect. Though pared down in their ultimate form, Virginia's lengthier versions of these two amendments related to military power spell out the intention of these guarantees that were promised during the ratification debates: to reassure skeptical anti-Federalists that the defense of the existing states would ordinarily be the responsibility of state militias, just as under the Articles of Confederation. In no case would national standing armies directed by distant tyrants be tools of oppression within the states, as they had been in the colonies before the Revolution. The emphasis Federalists placed on the need for military force to take control of the West, together with the recommendations for fetters on the government to protect American citizens in the states from the abuses of standing armies, offered the implicit promise "that the United States Army would not be used to maintain public order within the states. It would instead be consistently employed in territories administered directly by the federal government."[59]

With Virginia's ratification in June 1788 and New York's in July, eleven states had approved the new Constitution. The new government began the following year. When soon thereafter President Washington reorganized the national "peacetime" army to fight against a confederacy of Native nations in the Ohio country, he renamed it the Legion of the United States. The word legion evoked the troops of ancient Rome that were especially adapted to conquering barbarians on the empire's frontier.[60] The military power that king and Parliament had used *against* the colonists as British subjects was now to be used *by* them and *for* them as American citizens, and in regions of the nation already marked out as having diminished rights prior to attaining statehood.

For many delegates in the state ratifying conventions, and especially in those Southern states that still retained major Western land claims, ratification was understood in transactional terms. They would offer the national government "loyalty and obedience so long as the government fulfilled what they considered its most basic function of protection"—exactly what beleaguered Georgians hoped for late in 1787 when they voted unanimously in favor of the new Constitution.[61] Through the ratification process, the creation of a Bill of Rights, and the launching of the first government, the new Constitution began to take shape as a framework under which the states would govern themselves for most domestic purposes, while the national government would attend to all matters beyond the capacities of the states. The latter would include managing the nation's debt. In fact, the debt crisis that had played a part in launching these constitutional reforms was easily resolved with the national government's taxing and fiscal powers and its regulation of overseas commerce and diplomacy.[62] But the largest, most pressing, longest-lasting, and costliest matter would involve taking control of the national domain and developing new states in the West.

By turning the nation's growing wealth and power to the conquest of trans-Appalachia, the United States was indeed creating something new under the sun, a novus ordo seclorum. By promising to use its power to transform the West—"Indian Country"—into private property for purchase, the United States created a welfare state for its free white citizens under the only terms in which welfare made sense in the 1780s. The government would make rich land easily available to white settlers and gradually incorporate them within the nation with the full privileges of citizenship. The new national government would work together with colonists moving into new territories and assist them in transforming the territories into self-governing states, full members of an expanding union. This was a promise no nation had made before.

Patrick Henry, a fierce opponent of the consolidation promised by the Constitution, thought he saw what lay in store: "The American spirit, assisted by the ropes and chains of consolidation, is about to convert this country into a powerful and mighty empire: If you make the citizens of this country agree to become the subjects of one great consolidated empire of America, your Government will not have sufficient energy to keep them together: such a Government is incompatible with the genius of republicanism."[63] If Patrick Henry pronounced this in anger and sorrow, fearing the loss of what he fought the revolution to gain, Federalist James Wilson at Pennsylvania's ratification convention sketched the same future in ecstatic terms: "We are representatives, sir, not merely of the present age, but of future times; not merely of the territory along the seacoast, but of regions immensely extended westward. We should fill, as fast as possible, this extensive country, with men who shall live happy, free, and secure. To accomplish this great end ought to be the leading view of all our patriots and statesmen."[64]

Whether they praised it or damned it, Americans understood what their new Constitution had been designed to accomplish.

PART III

The Domesday Machine in Action, 1790–1890

After our Constitution got fairly into working order it really seemed as if we had invented a machine that would go of itself, and this begot a faith in our luck which even the civil war itself but momentarily disturbed. Circumstances continued favorable, and our prosperity went on increasing. And this confidence in our luck with the absorption in material interests, generated by unparalleled opportunity, has in some respects made us neglectful of our political duties.

—JAMES RUSSELL LOWELL, ADDRESS TO THE REFORM CLUB OF NEW YORK CITY, 1888

6

Two Paths to Westward Expansion, North and South

> Fields a few years ago waste and uncultivated [are now] filled with inhabitants and covered with harvests, new habitations reared, contentment in every face, plenty on every board. To produce this effect was the intention of the Constitution, and it has succeeded.
>
> —RICHARD BLAND LEE, SPEECH IN U.S. CONGRESS, JANUARY 1794

THE FIRST DECADE under the new Constitution proved how difficult the challenge of transforming the trans-Appalachian West would be. Granted, three new states were readily admitted to the union during George Washington's two terms as president: Vermont, Kentucky, and Tennessee. The first two were regions already heavily populated with white settler colonists at the time of ratification; each had significantly more people at the 1790 census than Delaware or Rhode Island, the smallest states. Both were already part of existing states in the union. New York had long claimed (though New Hampshire contested) the region that became Vermont. Kentucky was the remaining western part of Virginia after Virginia's cession of its huge claims north of the Ohio River. Tennessee was the first state made from territory already ceded by a state to the national government, but it too had a burgeoning white settler population by the time of its admission in 1796 and had been under North Carolina's jurisdiction until 1790.

It was the Northwest Territory that presented the most formidable initial challenge. Various states—New York, Connecticut, and Massachusetts, in addition to Virginia—had already ceded all their claims to the region, so it was the national government's alone to deal with. The Ohio country was densely populated by an array of powerful Native American peoples determined to hold onto their land. For many of these Native nations, the land north of the Ohio River had been a refuge from earlier conflicts with European colonists and other Indigenous nations. During the three decades from the outbreak of the Seven Years' War to the end of the War of Independence, the Ohio country also became the center of growing pan-Indian movements, in some cases inspired by religious revivals committed to restoring older Indigenous ways of life and resisting further encroachment by Euro-American colonists.[1] The confederation of Native tribes in the Ohio country included Miami, Shawnee, Lenape, Potawatomi, Wyandot, Ojibwa, and numerous others, collectively determined to resist white settler encroachment north of the Ohio River.[2] The Ohio confederation received additional support from British military posts that remained in the southern Great Lakes region even after the Treaty of Paris in 1783 had mandated their removal.

In the first years of government under the Constitution, Washington's administration attempted to use the nation's newfound military and diplomatic powers to take control of the Ohio country and make the region's rich lands available to white colonists according to the terms of the Land Ordinances of the 1780s. Some of this land had already been promised to veterans of the war. Speculative groups like the Ohio Company had also purchased large tracts claiming millions of acres. But the ability of the federal government to eliminate Native resistance to white settlement was achieved only through a series of halting and violent steps requiring the repeated expansion of U.S. military power.[3]

In 1790, General Josiah Harmar, a Revolutionary War veteran, led an army of 320 U.S. soldiers (its small numbers reflective of the nation's limited funds at this early date) augmented by 1,100 short-term militia recruited from Pennsylvania and Kentucky. Harmar intended to mount a punitive expedition against the Miami and Shawnee, who had resisted white settlement in Ohio. The plan resembled the Continental Army's 1779 expedition against the Haudenosaunee in upstate New York, which had earned George Washington the nickname of "Town Destroyer." Harmar's expedition marched north in October 1790 from Fort Washington, the site of the future city of Cincinnati. They were badly defeated by confederated Native nations under Little Turtle, a Miami leader, whose forces killed or wounded over 300 soldiers and militia.[4]

The following year, a larger expedition was organized by General Arthur St. Clair, the newly appointed governor of the Northwest Territory. St. Clair received funding from Congress to add a second regiment of regular army soldiers. Like Harmar, St. Clair recruited 1,400 militia and short-term conscripts from Kentucky to augment his 600 regulars. He aimed to attack the principal Miami town of Kekionga, about 160 miles north of Fort Washington. But the forces of the Miami under Little Turtle and the Shawnee led by Blue Jacket destroyed St. Clair's army, killing or wounding nearly 1,000 soldiers and many civilian camp supporters as well. This was among the worst defeats in U.S. military history, with higher casualties than any suffered by the Continental Army at British hands during the Revolutionary War.[5]

In the wake of this humiliation, Washington's government tried to gain by diplomacy what it had failed to accomplish by military force. Negotiators from the federal government offered to make treaties with Native nations in the Northwest Territory but could not secure the concession they sought. One treaty was rejected by the U.S. Senate because it gave the Wabash and Illinois nations too much authority over their reserved lands, allowing them to sell (or not to sell) land to whomever they liked, including foreign nations, which would undermine exclusive U.S. preemption claims in the territory. Another proposal by Secretary of War Timothy Pickering to negotiate an Indian boundary line that would recognize existing U.S. settlements in southern Ohio was jointly rejected by sixteen Native nations. Emboldened by their victories against Harmar and St. Clair, and with the continuing support of the British at Detroit, the Ohio confederation in 1793 demanded that all white settlement remain south of the Ohio River, rejected the legality of existing trans-Ohio settlements, and insisted on their inherent right to their own territory, granted to them by the "Author of Life."[6]

Meanwhile, Congress authorized and funded the building of the Legion of the United States, a far larger "peacetime" army of over five thousand regular soldiers, a nearly tenfold increase of St. Clair's inadequate force. The War Department's expenditures multiplied from $632,804 for the three years of 1789–91 to $2,639,098 for the year 1794 alone, effectively a twelvefold increase. This investment indicated the growing commitment of the national government to Indigenous expulsion, as well as its growing fiscal strength thanks to import duties enacted under the new Constitution. The War Department budget in 1794 was fully 26 percent of all national expenses—only the payment of interest on the national debt, at 57 percent, was larger, a result of the federal government's recent assumption of all the individual states' remaining debt from the Revolutionary War. In 1794, the sum of all other national expenses aside from debt interest was less than the amount spent on salaries, food, clothing, and supplies for the Legion of the United States alone.[7] As this budget reflects, funding the military to remove Native people and gain ownership of the national domain was the principal function of the early U.S. government.

The new Legion of the United States was organized into four sub-legions—each with its own infantry, cavalry, riflemen, and artillery—designed to conduct complex warfare against Indigenous opponents. President Washington appointed revolutionary veteran Anthony Wayne as its commanding general. Other veterans of the revolutionary officer corps and future leaders in American expansion, such as William Henry Harrison, William Clark, and Zebulon Pike, joined the Legion as well. Unable to achieve its aims through diplomacy, the Washington administration sent the Legion in the summer of 1794 to secure the territory sought by Harmar's and St. Clair's disastrous expeditions. Wayne's well-trained and equipped professional army marched to the stronghold of the Ohio confederation at the Glaize, a site along the Maumee River in northwestern Ohio, and won a major victory at the Battle of Fallen Timbers on August 20. British officers at Fort Miami refused to aid or give refuge to the confederated Indians, signaling their unwillingness to support further Native resistance. The Legion of the United States destroyed Indigenous settlements at the Glaize and at the now-abandoned Miami town of Kekionga, much as the Continental Army had done across Iroquoia fifteen years earlier (fig. 6.1).[8]

At Kekionga, General Wayne built a permanent U.S. military fort and named it for himself—the future Fort Wayne, Indiana. The following year, Wayne negotiated with the defeated confederation to produce the Treaty of Greenville, formally opening most of Ohio to white settlement, while reserving part of northwestern Ohio for its Native owners. After Wayne's triumph, Virginia congressman, plantation owner, and land speculator Richard Bland Lee commented that "fields a few years ago waste and uncultivated [are now] filled with inhabitants and covered with harvests, new habitations reared, contentment in every face, plenty on every board. To produce this effect was the intention of the Constitution, and it has succeeded."[9] Of course, the fields of Ohio had been cultivated by Indians long before these wars. But the belief that Indigenous lands were "waste and uncultivated" was an emerging tenet of the early republic's ideology of dispossession.

The American Domesday Machine had been set in motion. Slow, expensive, and brutal warfare fueled Native expulsion, land commodification, and settler expansion in the Northwest Territory. Meanwhile, in the Southwest during the same period, a parallel but messier and more complicated process generated an alternative, though no less devastating, mode of expansion. In the trans-Appalachian South, land speculators continued to dream of interposing their private interests between the national government and Indian land acquisition.

Even after the ratification of the Constitution, the States of North Carolina and especially Georgia were reluctant to relinquish their claims to extensive Western lands beyond the mountains.[10] They ignored the Constitution's prohibition (in Article I, Section 10) on states' making treaties, as well as its allocation to Congress (in Article IV, Section 3) of the power "to dispose of and make all needful Rules and Regulations

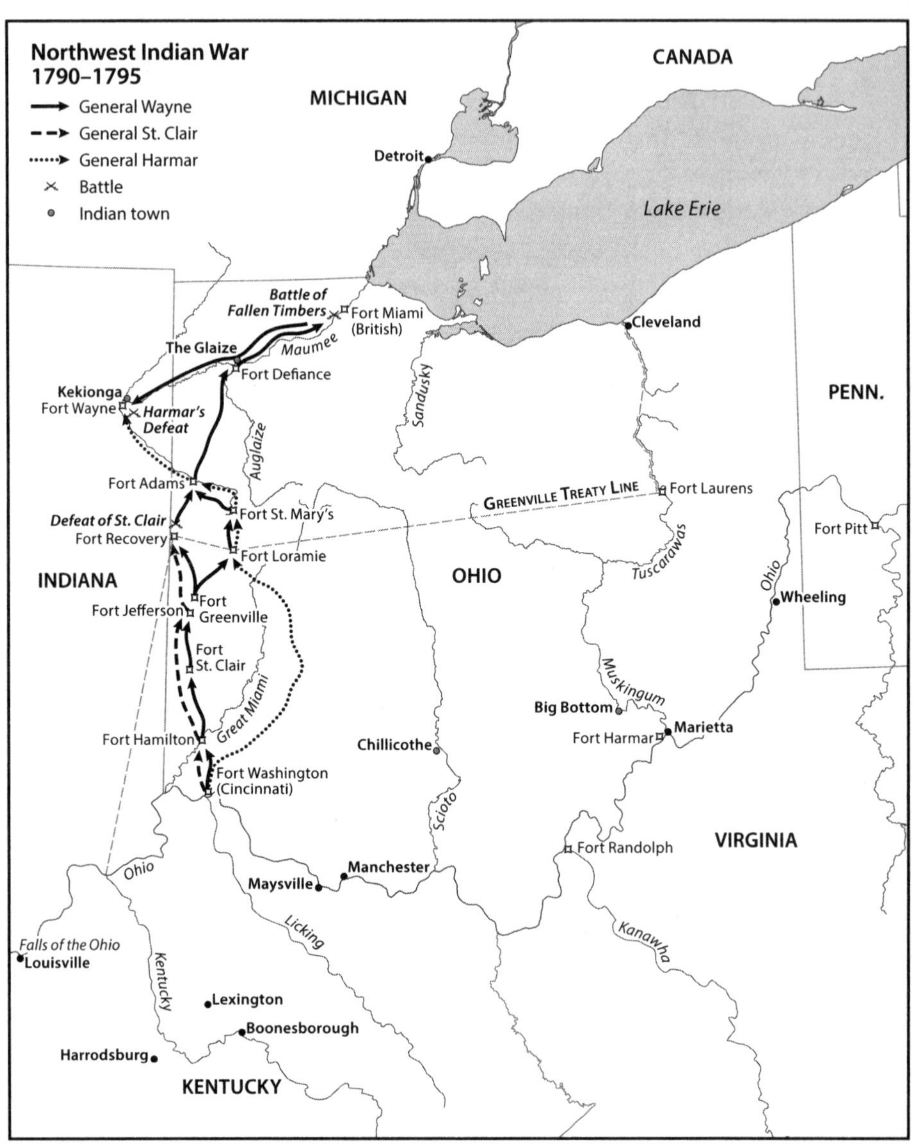

FIGURE 6.1. Map of the Northwest Indian War, 1790–95. The three U.S. military expeditions deep into the Ohio country were meant to gain extensive land cessions from the Ohio Indian confederation and discourage British intervention in the region.

respecting the Territory" of the United States. Part of the problem lay in the ambiguity introduced by the latter half of the very same clause: that "nothing in this Constitution shall be so construed as to Prejudice any Claims of the United States, or any particular State." The claims of the particular State of Georgia lay at the heart of an emerging conflict. Additional confusion arose over the exact northern boundary of Spain's claims in this region, as East and West Florida had reverted to Spanish control with the Treaty of Paris.

The State of Georgia marched directly into this ambiguous space, trying to take control over its enormous land claims stretching westward to the Mississippi River. The Creek Nation was Georgia's chief obstacle. Creek military prowess had forced Georgia into a rapid if reluctant ratification of the Constitution in 1787. Given Georgia's transactional view of the constitutional pact, its citizens now expected that U.S. military power would aid them in putting down the Creeks. But in the first years after ratification, the national government lacked the funding and military capacity to take on anything more than the Northwest Territory. While the campaigns were difficult in the Ohio region, where no state claims or private companies competed with federal authority, in the Southwest they were much more complex. Georgians and North Carolinians attempted to purchase land from or make treaties with Native nations, or to encroach directly on Indigenous lands, in disregard of the national government's authority. In the long run, the outcome would be similar—Native dispossession, land commodification, and the rapid expansion of white settlement—but the Southwestern process generated a more conflicted relationship between the states and federal authority.[11]

Before the Constitution was ratified, the State of Georgia had negotiated several treaties of dubious value with various Creek groups to secure title to their land. Speculative land companies had also claimed some of Georgia's western territory. In 1789, Georgia attempted to formalize these arrangements by selling preemption rights to twenty million acres of the so-called Yazoo Lands, named for the Yazoo River in what is now the State of Mississippi, at the westernmost extent of Georgia's claims. Three land speculation companies, the South Carolina

Yazoo Company, the Tennessee Company, and the Virginia Yazoo Company, bought the preemption rights to this immense region (equal in size to the State of South Carolina) from the State of Georgia for about a penny an acre, and began planning settlements in territory still owned by the Creeks, Cherokees, and Choctaws.

To counter this threat, a delegation of Creeks led by Alexander McGillivray journeyed in 1790 to New York City, where the national government was then meeting. The Creeks negotiated the Treaty of New York with Secretary of War Henry Knox; the treaty preserved their right to keep white settlers off their lands and thwarted Georgia's and the land companies' claims. The Creeks were awarded payments of $1,500 in goods per year, plus livestock and agricultural tools, and McGillivray himself was appointed as the U.S. agent to the Creeks, with an annual salary of $1,200 and a brigadier general's rank. At this moment when the U.S. war in the Northwest against the Ohio confederation was going badly and depleting the nation's limited treasury, the United States decided to farm out security over the Southwest to the Creeks—the only group strong enough to keep the peace in the region. The Treaty of New York simultaneously confirmed the national government's authority over Indian negotiations and voided Georgia's earlier treaties with the Creeks. It also solidified the Creeks' loyalty to the United States against possible Spanish influence in the region. At the same time, Congress passed the 1790 Indian Trade and Intercourse Act, which expressly banned states from purchasing land from Native people. Together, the Treaty of New York and the Trade and Intercourse Act clarified the ambiguity in the Constitution that Georgia had tried to exploit and strengthened the federal government's control over Indigenous affairs. Georgians protested and declared that the national government was reneging on the Constitution's "compact" to support settler rights. But the 1789 land company purchases of the Yazoo lands collapsed in 1792 when cash-starved Georgia refused to accept the land companies' depreciated paper currency as payment, insisting on specie, which these speculators lacked.[12]

The failure of the first Yazoo land sale did not resolve the larger issue; Georgians still wanted access to Indian lands sooner than the national government could afford to take action. Several years later, Georgia's legislature tried again. It passed a second Yazoo Act in 1795 that authorized the sale of preemption rights to forty million acres, twice as much as before, to four newly organized private land companies. Promoters smoothed the bill's passage through widespread bribery, granting large shares in the new land companies to state legislators. The blatant corruption caused a backlash. After elections the following year, the new legislature voted to rescind the Yazoo Act. However, the land companies had already sold shares to thousands of investors, including speculators and financiers in New York, Philadelphia, and Boston, and their European clients. The second Yazoo Act touched off further conflict with the land's Native owner-occupants, as the land companies sought to develop their claims by acquiring land title from Indians, despite constitutional and treaty prohibitions. And the act's recision in 1796 generated more than a decade of legal disputes over the legitimacy of these sales.[13]

By 1802, Georgia's legislature finally voted to cede its Western land claims to the national government. Georgia was happy to be rid of its legal entanglements. In return for the land cession, the national government promised to "extinguish the Indian title to all the other Lands within the state of Georgia," two-thirds of which were still occupied by their Creek and Cherokee owners.[14] The legal dispute over the Yazoo land company purchases would finally be decided in 1810 when the U.S. Supreme Court in *Fletcher v. Peck* declared the Georgia legislature's recision of the second Yazoo land sale to be unconstitutional because it violated valid property contracts made by the prior legislature's approval of the sale (regardless of how corrupt that process may have been). In 1814, the federal government agreed to pay off thousands of investors with outstanding claims from the sale by issuing $5 million in the form of "Mississippi Stock." These paper notes could be used to claim actual land in the Mississippi Territory but were frequently sold as securities.[15]

Chief Justice John Marshall's decision in *Fletcher* had momentous consequences. It was a key moment in defining the sanctity of contracts in U.S. commercial law, but it also called into question whether Native "occupants" had any true title to their land under American law. Marshall's opinion reversed centuries of Anglo-American legal practice supporting Indian land title, as the dissenting opinion by Justice William Johnson pointed out.[16] As the federal government took over the role of extinguishing what Marshall referred to as "Indian title" (a lesser form of occupancy right, not ownership in the Anglo-American legal tradition), the intensity of speculative trading in land titles granted by states or sold by land companies escalated, even before Indian title had been extinguished. The power of this securitized market in speculative land claims lay behind a later Supreme Court decision written by Marshall (himself a land speculator). In 1823, *Johnson v. M'Intosh* would confirm the power of the states "to grant the soil, while yet in possession of the natives."[17] Marshall's position was rooted in the obvious fiction that "the tribes of Indians inhabiting this country were fierce savages, whose occupation was war, and whose subsistence was drawn chiefly from the forest," and therefore Indians could not possess true title to lands they roamed as hunters and nomads.[18] At the time Marshall wrote these words, thousands of Indigenous Americans lived and worked as farmers on land their people had owned and farmed for generations. But for Marshall's court, the only legally recognizable title to land ownership belonged to Euro-American colonizing powers, even while Indians still lived on the land. Indians had a right to "occupancy" of the land as long as they chose to remain on it, a newly invented right that replaced the older doctrine that Indians were indeed the owners of their land. But this was the only right the U.S. government was required to extinguish before settlement could begin. A lively futures market in Indian-occupied land could flourish, with these speculative land titles now secure under federal law.[19]

Marshall and the court's majority claimed that "Indian title," a limited occupancy right, should prevent the violent ejection of Native Americans by white colonists. But the combined effect of the *Fletcher v. Peck* and *Johnson v. M'Intosh* decisions enormously expanded the number of speculators, investors, and potential settlers with an interest in removing Native occupants so that they might enjoy the fruits of their purchases, whether as productive farmland or as share values of land company stock.[20] In short, the very foundation of U.S. property law was laid by corrupt state legislation, private transactions, and court decisions that overturned centuries of prior legal practice regarding Native land ownership. The Marshall court flatly denied the reality of Indigenous land use and ownership practices which earlier generations of colonists had recognized. This change made Indian expulsion easier, cheaper, and more widely desired among white settlers, who did enjoy the full protections of the nation's constitutions.[21]

With the passage of the Organic Act of 1798, the U.S. Congress created the Mississippi Territory in the southernmost part of the trans-Appalachian West to assert its authority over these lands and deny Spanish claims to the region. The Mississippi Territory was to be governed in the same manner as the Northwest Territory, but without the Northwest Ordinance's prohibitions on slavery.[22] Following the Georgia legislature's decision to cede its Western claims in 1802, Congress enlarged the Mississippi Territory, adding Georgia's ceded lands to the national domain in 1804 (fig. 6.2). In other words, it had taken an additional seventeen years after the Northwest Ordinance for a similar process to be completed in the Southwest. The stage was now set for the use of military force by the national government to compel Native land cessions in this new national domain.

The process that the federal government would use to extinguish Indian title and open the Mississippi Territory to white settlement differed considerably from its takeover of the Ohio country in the 1790s. Expansionist interests in the Southwest became entangled with the mounting tensions between Britain and the United States that led to the War of 1812. That conflict stemmed in part from the Napoleonic Wars, in which Britain and France fought to control the terms of Atlantic commerce, leading Britain to discriminate against American shipping and forcibly impress American sailors into the Royal Navy. But the territorial interests of the United States, in both the Northwest and Southwest, played a part in the renewed war with Britain. The U.S. government's designs on securing more land for settlement in these regions would again require military force against Native confederations; at the same time, the

FIGURE 6.2. The lands ceded by Georgia in 1804 expanded the existing Mississippi Territory northward to the Tennessee border.

United States hoped to drive Britain's forces out of the southern Great Lakes and undermine Spanish power in the Florida territories.

The situation was further complicated by the rise of new pan-Indian movements to resist the expansion of U.S. settlement in the trans-Appalachian West. These new movements, while reminiscent of the Lenape prophet Neolin's message in the Ohio country in the 1760s, were far more expansive, attempting to unite northern and southern Indian confederacies across this enormous trans-Appalachian region. In the years before the War of 1812, the Shawnee brothers Tecumseh and Tenskwatawa (known as "The Prophet") worked to rebuild and extend the older Ohio pan-Indian confederation of the 1790s, with tacit support from the British in Canada. Tecumseh also made diplomatic journeys to the Creeks, Choctaws, and Chickasaws in the Mississippi Territory, aiming to extend the confederation across the entire trans-Appalachian region from north to south.

Even before the U.S. war against Britain formally began, the governor of the Indiana Territory, William Henry Harrison, led an American army on a mission to destroy the northern confederation's center, Prophetstown, on the Wabash River in present-day Indiana. Harrison's force of one thousand soldiers attacked Tenskwatawa's forces on November 7, 1811, while Tecumseh was away on his southern diplomatic mission, and destroyed Prophetstown, burning the village and its food stores. With Congress's formal declaration of war against Britain, Harrison became commander-in-chief of the Army of the Northwest and led U.S. forces into Canada, where Tecumseh was killed at the Battle of the Thames in 1813. Harrison's forces burned and destroyed Native villages, livestock, and crops much as Wayne's forces had done in 1794. With Indian resistance broken, the way was cleared for further rapid colonization of the Indiana and Illinois territories.[23]

The United States focused its national military resources, both army and navy, in the Northwest during the War of 1812, as that was where the British enemy had its strongest North American presence. But an equally significant set of conflicts occurred in the Mississippi Territory in the Southwest, beyond the federal government's immediate control. In 1812 and into 1813, a powerful group of militant Creek Indians, the Red Sticks, inspired by their own prophetic movement resisting European ways, struck out against settler intrusion into Creek territory. The Red Sticks attacked travelers on the "Federal Road" built across Creek-owned lands from Georgia into the Mississippi Territory, and destroyed Fort Mims, a U.S. military installation on the Alabama River near Mobile Bay.[24]

Fort Mims lay 250 miles south of Tennessee's border. But Andrew Jackson of Tennessee, major general of the state's militia, raised an army of 3,500 men to "repel the invasion of the state of Tennessee" by the Red Stick Creeks. This was a carefully worded statement. The Constitution forbids individual states from engaging in war "unless actually invaded, or in such imminent Danger as will not admit of delay" (Article I, Section 10). Tennessee had to claim a Creek invasion of its territory to justify Jackson's aggressive actions.

The Tennessee legislature approved raising sufficient troops "to carry a campaign into the heart of the Creek nation and exterminate them."[25] Jackson led his men into the Mississippi Territory, in present-day Alabama. At Creek sites such as Tallushatchee, Talladega, and Tohopeka (Horseshoe Bend), Jackson's armies, supported by Cherokee and Creek soldiers who opposed the Red Stick movement, killed some two thousand Creeks, more than ten percent of the entire Creek Nation, and destroyed their villages. To halt the devastation, Jackson demanded land cessions amounting to thirty-six thousand square miles in western Georgia and Alabama, regardless of whether the Creeks who owned this land had been Red Sticks or not. In a single bloody campaign, Jackson and his men, without the direct support of the federal government but ultimately acting on its behalf, completed in the Southwest the work that had taken two decades in the Northwest. They violently cleared enormous territories of "Indian title" and opened them to the white colonization on which statehood in the union depended. President Madison's administration later provided official endorsement of Jackson's troops by declaring them to be part of the war effort under formal U.S. military command. Within five years of Jackson's demand for Creek land cessions, the new states of Mississippi and Alabama were admitted to the union, matched in the North in the same period by Indiana and Illinois.[26]

These two modes of Native dispossession, Northern and Southern, demonstrate how the national government under the Constitution conducted its principal business at the time—land acquisition and state making. This was the Domesday Machine in action. Underlying this process was confidence among political leaders, speculators, and investors that "if you build it, they will come." The booming population of the early United States, which grew by roughly 35 percent in every decade between 1790 and 1860, and the potential commercial value of this incomparable farmland would together guarantee that thousands of eager white farmers would be enticed to settle anywhere the U.S. government extinguished Indian title.

Population figures from the newly admitted states bear this out; they grew far faster than the already staggering national averages. In the 1810s, the decade of Tecumseh's defeat and Indiana's statehood, its settler population grew fivefold, and then it more than doubled in each of the next two decades, increasing from 24,520 in 1810 to 685,866 in 1840. Illinois had a similarly rapid growth rate, tripling its settler population in the 1820s and again in the 1830s, from 12,282 in 1810 to 476,183 in 1840. In the Southwest, Mississippi more than doubled its settler population in the 1810s and replicated the feat in the 1820s and '30s, growing from 31,306 in 1810 to 375,651 in 1840. And Alabama saw a fourteenfold settler increase in the decade of Jackson's campaign against the Creeks, followed by doublings in the next two decades, from 9,046 in 1810 to 590,756 in 1840.[27] In just three decades, these four new states alone added two million settler colonists to the population of the trans-Appalachian West. The same feat had taken more than 150 years in the English colonization of North America's Atlantic seaboard. Empowered by the Constitution, the U.S. government had met the urgent challenge of the 1780s.

The result was almost exactly what American founders from Benjamin Franklin to Thomas Jefferson had envisioned, and what American colonists since 1763 had desired. But the dramatic expansion failed to live up to Jefferson and Franklin's expectations in one important way. Of Mississippi's 375,651 residents in 1840, 195,211 of them were enslaved, 52 percent of the settler population. In Alabama, 253,532 of its residents were enslaved, 43 percent of its total. During the decades of revolution and constitution making in the 1770s and '80s, many leading political figures, Jefferson among them, had expected that the wave of abolition measures begun in the Northern states, especially the gradualist plans of states like New York, New Jersey, and Pennsylvania, would spread southward into Maryland, Virginia, and perhaps beyond. In these states, with tobacco yields falling due to soil exhaustion and plantation owners shifting to less labor-intensive crops such as wheat and corn, and raising livestock, many slaveholders in the 1780s believed that enslaved workers exceeded the demand for labor.[28]

This vision of a future in which slave labor would decline had influenced the Northwest Ordinance's ban on slavery in the trans-Ohio region. In Kentucky, early white settlers from Virginia brought enslaved people to the territory, but a movement within Kentucky's 1792 constitutional convention led by Presbyterian minister David Rice attempted to prohibit slavery south of the Ohio as well.[29] Expectations for slavery's decline also prompted the Constitution's clause allowing Congress to tax the importation of enslaved persons and eventually to abolish this trade. But in South Carolina and Georgia, demand for new enslaved workers remained high in the rice, indigo, and long-staple cotton plantations of the coastal regions. At their insistence, Article I, Section 9, postponed Congress's power to end the slave trade for twenty years, allowing these states time for a slave-purchasing spree.[30]

Long-staple cotton, with only a single seed in each of its extensive "bolls," had long been the dominant American cotton crop, a luxury commodity used for producing fine cloth. But the long-staple variety only grew well in limited coastal regions with high humidity and rainfall, such as the Sea Islands of Georgia and South Carolina. At the time the Constitution was ratified, there was little prospect for greatly expanding profitable cotton production in the United States. However, Eli Whitney's patenting of an efficient cotton gin just a few years after the Constitution's ratification, combined with improvements in seed quality, soon made it much more profitable to grow short-staple cotton. This variety had formerly required labor-intensive (and therefore expensive) hand removal of the numerous small seeds or "staples" from its fibers. The new mechanized cotton gin vastly reduced processing costs for short-staple cotton, a hardier plant that could thrive in drier climates. It therefore opened millions of acres in upland regions of the trans-Appalachian West to commercial cotton production in unprecedented volumes. This technology allowed the colonizers of the Mississippi Territory to replicate the plantation model of South Carolina and Georgia. As soon as the federal government cleared title to these regions, planters from the Atlantic seaboard brought enslaved African Americans by the thousands into Mississippi and Alabama. Already in 1820, 32,814 of Mississippi's 75,448 residents, 43 percent of its population, were enslaved. In subsequent decades, this percentage would increase in conjunction with exponential growth in cotton production.[31]

Contrary to earlier expectations, the conflict of interest between slave and free states that had profoundly shaped the constitutional compact in 1787 now spread west across the Appalachians. The unexpected but explosive expansion of slavery in the Southwest meant that the states in this region would be *less* well represented than the Northwest in the House of Representatives because "only" three-fifths of each state's enslaved population would be counted for apportionment.[32] For example, Indiana's population in 1840 of 685,866 received full representation—seven seats in Congress. Alabama had 590,756 people according to that year's census, but 253,532 of them were enslaved. Their representation under the three-fifths ratio meant that Alabama only received representation for the equivalent of 489,343 people—five seats in Congress. As a result of this asymmetry, the South lost power in the House and became all the more reliant on each state's equal representation in the Senate to sustain a hold on national power. With the near simultaneous admission of the two pairs of twin states—Indiana and Illinois in the North, Mississippi and Alabama in the South—Congress acknowledged the importance of preserving the delicate balance of population and power within the United States that the framers of the Constitution had negotiated.

These admissions of new states from the original territory of the United States had been fully contemplated and expressly provided for in the Constitution of 1787—this was an explicit part of the constitutional compact. The land ordinances that preceded the Constitution had mapped out what this process should look like, including the relative size of states and thus the plausible limits to the potential number of new states north of the Ohio River. By the time Illinois and Alabama were admitted in 1818–19, the process was almost complete—of the original land within the United States, only Wisconsin and Michigan remained under territorial status. The Northwest Ordinance left no question about the future status of slavery in these areas.

Just as the framers of the Constitution and the land ordinances had planned, new states were admitted into the union with remarkable parity in both geographical size and population numbers. Of the nine states west of the Appalachians added to the union from the country's original territory after the Constitution's ratification, the average land area was 47,367 square miles, roughly the same size as some of the larger original thirteen such as New York, Pennsylvania, and Virginia. The largest of the nine new states, Michigan, measured 56,539 square miles, a bit smaller than Georgia, while Indiana, the smallest, encompassed 35,870 square miles, a bit bigger than South Carolina. By 1850, the average population of these nine states was 876,281, with states admitted to the union early, like Tennessee (1796) and Ohio (1803), having already attained more than a million residents. In 1850, the population of even the most recently admitted of the nine, Wisconsin (1848), already stood at 305,391, significantly larger than the smallest of the original thirteen, like Rhode Island and Delaware.[33] This work of state making was completed within three decades of the national government's inauguration in 1789, creating across this territory a federal republic of states that were far more equal and balanced in 1819 than they had been in 1787. The conquest of the trans-Appalachian West had gone almost entirely according to plan.

7

The President Who Failed to Bark

JEFFERSON, LOUISIANA, AND CONSTITUTIONAL CHANGE

> "Is there any point to which you would wish to draw my attention?"
> "To the curious incident of the dog in the night-time."
> "The dog did nothing in the night-time."
> "That was the curious incident," remarked Sherlock Holmes.
>
> —ARTHUR CONAN DOYLE, "SILVER BLAZE," 1893

THE CONSTITUTION'S provisions for expansion within the *original* United States territory had shown themselves to be remarkably effective. But could the United States expand into *foreign* territories that were not part of its original claims under the Treaty of Paris?

The question arose for the first time in the summer of 1803, when President Thomas Jefferson's government announced that it had purchased claims to Louisiana from Napoleon and the French Empire. This momentous event would help extend slavery and the cotton kingdom across the American South. But it would have an equally important, though much less well-known, influence in changing the constitution of the United States by defining a new process for territorial expansion and statehood beyond the boundaries established by the Treaty of Paris.

In April, 1803, American diplomats had negotiated a treaty with France to purchase the immense Louisiana Territory, equal in land area to the existing United States (which was already larger than any European nation). This purchase would give the United States preemption rights to some eight hundred thousand square miles of Native-owned and -occupied land, an inconceivably large addition to the enormous territorial claims the United States already asserted east of the Mississippi River. Initially, the entire Louisiana Purchase would become part of the national domain, vastly increasing the amount of non-state territory under Congress's direct control. The president and his Democratic-Republican allies were planning a strategy to move this controversial measure through Congress. To close the Louisiana deal, the Senate would have to ratify the treaty, and both House and Senate would need to approve a bill to fund the purchase.

The constitutionality of the purchase was much on Jefferson's mind. In the previous decade, he had taken a strong position as a strict constructionist. He fiercely opposed Treasury Secretary Alexander Hamilton's plan to charter a national bank, because the Constitution did not expressly grant the national government the power to do so. But neither did the Constitution bestow the power to purchase vast territories from foreign countries. The southernmost portion of the Louisiana Territory, in the vicinity of New Orleans, already had a population of around thirty thousand French, Spanish, and African American colonial settlers, and their numbers were rapidly increasing. Given the importance of New Orleans as a port for the commercial products of America's Western states, the population would continue to grow. The constitutionality of admitting a new state from this territory was sure to arise soon.[1] On this question as well, the written constitution is mute. By the time of the Louisiana Purchase, Congress had admitted the new states of Vermont, Kentucky, Tennessee, and Ohio. But these were all formed according to the explicit provisions in Article IV, Section 3, for managing the nation's original territory granted by the Treaty of Paris and, in the case of Ohio, under the terms of the Northwest Ordinance.

To understand the constitutional transformation at the heart of the Louisiana Purchase, we return to the summer of 1803 and Thomas

Jefferson's mountaintop estate in Virginia, where he composed several of the most revealing and consequential private letters in American history. That summer, Jefferson corresponded with Wilson Cary Nicholas, one of Virginia's two U.S. Senators and a fellow speculator in Western lands, about how to shepherd the Louisiana Purchase through Congress. Jefferson's letter to Nicholas of September 7, 1803, deserves quotation at length. First, he warned Nicholas that he and his party's colleagues should keep quiet about constitutional issues: "Whatever Congress shall think it necessary to do, should be done with as little debate as possible, and particularly so far as respects the constitutional difficulty." But at the same time, Jefferson disagreed with Nicholas's views on the constitutional question and explained why:

> I am aware of the force of the observations you make on the power given by the Constitution to Congress, to admit new States into the Union, without restraining the subject to the territory then constituting the United States. But when I consider that the limits of the United States are precisely fixed by the treaty of 1783, that the Constitution expressly declares itself to be made for the United States, I cannot help believing the intention was not to permit Congress to admit into the Union new States, which should be formed out of the territory for which, and under whose authority alone, they were acting. I do not believe it was meant that they might receive England, Ireland, Holland, etc. into it, which would be the case on your construction.

Jefferson's double negatives are confusing—"I cannot help believing the intention was not . . ." But he is reminding Nicholas that the Treaty of Paris granted the new United States a fixed territory, and that the Constitution's terms were agreed on by delegates from the states that claimed this territory—and nothing more. He believes that Congress's constitutional power to admit new states is therefore confined to the original "fixed" territory of the United States. If foreign territory is to be acquired by Congress and admitted to the union, then the existing states must be consulted directly.

Jefferson goes on to describe the only remedy he can see for the problem—a constitutional amendment:

> When an instrument admits two constructions, the one safe, the other dangerous, the one precise, the other indefinite, I prefer that which is safe and precise. I had rather ask an enlargement of power from the nation, where it is found necessary, than to assume it by a construction which would make our powers boundless. Our peculiar security is in the possession of a written Constitution. Let us not make it a blank paper by construction. . . . Let us go on then perfecting it, by adding, by way of amendment to the Constitution, those powers which time and trial show are still wanting.[2]

Senator Nicholas, like many other Virginians, including Jefferson's Secretary of State James Madison, had argued that no such amendment was necessary. He believed that the Louisiana Purchase and the admission of future states from its territory were already constitutional, part of the implied powers of Congress despite the absence of specific language to that effect—following the same logic Hamilton had deployed in favor of a national bank.

But Jefferson was deeply skeptical of implied powers, especially in this case, when he was sure they were opposed to the clear intention of the Constitution. If there were no limits to the amount of foreign territory that the United States government could acquire, whether by purchase, treaty, or conquest, and if there were no limits on Congress's ability to create new states out of such territory, then there was no reason why "England, Ireland, Holland" or any other country in the world might not someday become states in the United States, merely by Congress's say-so. This, Jefferson reasoned, could not possibly be what the Constitution's framers, acting on behalf of the sovereign American people, intended. The thirteen colonies had broken from England's rule because they were sure they could not be governed under the same constitution as England; their fundamental conditions were simply too different. Adding new states to the union from foreign territory would alter the body of the nation, remake the society, and shift the balance of power among the states, thereby changing the nation's constitution.

In his view, a formal amendment to the written instrument, granting such powers in explicit terms and thereby aligning the written instrument with the altered framework of government and the new social realities of this additional territory, was required by the novelty of the Louisiana situation and the Constitution's silence on such an important matter.

This was no idle or momentary speculation on Jefferson's part. A month earlier, on August 12, he had expressed identical sentiments in a letter to John Breckenridge, U.S. senator from Kentucky, arguing that after approving the Louisiana Purchase, Congress "must then appeal to *the nation* for an additional article to the constitution, approving & confirming an act which the nation had not previously authorised. [T]he constitution has made no provision for our holding foreign territory, still less for incorporating foreign nations into our Union."[3]

Then, on August 30, in a letter to his attorney general, Levi Lincoln of Massachusetts, the president sketched out a draft of such an article—that is, a constitutional amendment: "On further consideration as to the amendment to our Constitution respecting Louisiana, I have thought it better, instead of enumerating the powers which Congress may exercise, to give them the same powers they have as to other portions of the Union generally, and to enumerate the special exceptions." For his proposed amendment, Jefferson could find no general language to describe the powers Congress might safely exercise in all such situations in the future without also creating the "boundless" powers he feared. Instead his draft reads quite narrowly:

> Louisiana, as ceded by France to the US is made a part of the US. it's white inhabitants shall be citizens, and stand, as to their rights & obligations, on the same footing with other citizens of the United States in analogous situations. Save only that as to the portion thereof lying North of an East & West line drawn through the mouth of Arkansa river, no new state shall be established, nor any grants of land made, other than to Indians in exchange for equivalent portions of land occupied by them, until an amendment of the Constitution shall be made for these purposes.[4]

The Arkansas River joins the Mississippi about fifty miles north of the northern boundary of the present State of Louisiana. Jefferson was envisioning that this constitutional amendment would allow the admission of only a single state, a little larger than the eventual State of Louisiana turned out to be. Any future states, or even any future land grants to white settlers in the remainder of the vast territory north of this line (more than 750,000 of the purchase's 827,000 square miles), would require an additional constitutional amendment.[5]

It is obvious from the language here about limiting citizenship to "white inhabitants" in the region intended for statehood and about the potential for "exchange" of lands with Indians that Jefferson was already contemplating that the Louisiana Territory could be used for Indian removal—as a refuge for Native peoples expelled from territory east of the Mississippi. He had made the same suggestion in his earlier letter to Senator Breckenridge, arguing that the best use for Louisiana "will be to give establishments in it to the Indians on the East side of the M[is]s[issip]pi in exchange for their present country."[6] As we have seen, this is not how Andrew Jackson and his Tennessee militia would deal with this region's Indians during the War of 1812. During Jackson's presidency, this would become a subject of immense importance, which the next chapter will address. But first, let's dwell for a moment on what Jefferson meant, in his letter to Senator Nicholas, by his preference for "safe and precise" constructions rather than "dangerous" and "indefinite" ones, and by the "peculiar security" of a written constitution.

Jefferson firmly grasped the importance of a well-constructed relationship between a written "instrument" (the word he uses in his letter to Senator Nicholas), the framework of government, and the substance of the nation. As he would later put it: "Such indeed are the different circumstances, prejudices, and habits of different nations, that the constitution of no one would be reconcilable to any other in every point."[7] Of course, Jefferson was not alone in this opinion—this was the basic assumption underlying the great flurry of constitution making that began with the American Revolution and spread through the Atlantic world in subsequent decades. Americans including Jefferson had justified their colonial rebellion against Britain by arguing that Parliament wrongly asserted its authority over jurisdictions—the American colonies—where its power had never been "precisely fixed."[8] Jefferson used this same language in the letter to Senator Nicholas to describe the original boundaries of the United States established by the Treaty of Paris. That territory was precisely what the Constitution's framers understood to be the tangible object of the powers allocated by their document—the Constitution's proper jurisdiction. To extend that jurisdiction, by way of mere interpretation or implied powers, to territories and peoples that had played no part in the making of the nation and its Constitution, and who had not consented to being part of the United States, was "dangerous," Jefferson held, in just the same way that Parliament's usurpation of authority over the colonies had been. It would make the written constitution into a "blank paper" on which future presidents and Congresses could write what they wanted. They could add new territories, people, and states to it, conceivably even England itself, despite having just fought a war to rid themselves of English rule—a war prompted by the belief that nations with such different "circumstances, prejudices, and habits" as England and the American colonies could not be ruled under the same frame of government.

The delegates at Philadelphia in the summer of 1787, and those at the state ratifying conventions over the following year, had debated, framed, and modified the Constitution to promote the well-being of the "precisely fixed" territory of the thirteen states and the Western lands claimed by the nation. That written constitution was created voluntarily[9] by and for a specific people and place, defined by the outcome of the War of Independence and the Treaty of Paris. Among the framers, both at the Philadelphia Convention and more generally throughout American constitution making in the 1770s and '80s, there was a profound commitment to the idea that a written constitution should be closely aligned with the substantive constitution of the polity—its people, land, economy, and environment—for which it is framed. The garment should be carefully tailored to fit the body. But just as Parliament had never consulted with the American colonies on which it imposed taxation, no one in the United States government had consulted the inhabitants of French Louisiana to see if they wanted to join the United States, or inquired whether French Louisianans believed they could be well represented under the framework offered by the United States Constitution. As territorial subjects, their rights and liberties would be less than those of full U.S. citizens in the states. The interests of the people of Louisiana and the nature and qualities of its vast territory had played no part whatsoever in the complex agreements, the balances and compromises, that delegates from the original thirteen states had crafted in framing the Constitution. And the sovereign American people had not been consulted, in their constitution-making role, about whether they wanted Louisiana to be part of their political union.

In his desire for "safe and precise" amendments to the written constitution, Jefferson acknowledged that to add a new territory to the United States regardless of the wishes of the people who lived there or the wishes of the sovereign American people, and to make new states from that territory, would change the constitution of the union by remaking its component parts. It would add, as an equal partner in the federal union, a territory that for more than a century had been a French colony (and for a brief period a Spanish one), a territory whose people had "different circumstances, prejudices, and habits." Such changes should only be made if the written constitution were amended as well, to make the instrument conform to the altered nature of the nation that it governed and to express the consent of the sovereign people to this radical change in their condition. Without such an alteration, the old garment could not possibly fit the enormous new body that the accession of Louisiana augured. For, as Jefferson confessed in his private letters to his Democratic-Republican allies, a loose construction of the Constitution implied that there were no rules and no limits on the territory that might be acquired by the United States and admitted as additional states through simple acts of a sitting Congress.

This was not just technical quibbling. The "safe and precise" amendment process Jefferson favored required two-thirds majorities in both houses of Congress, as well as ratification by three-fourths of the existing states—a high bar for popular approval that acknowledged the momentous political and social consequences of any fundamental change to the Constitution. The formal amendment process laid out in Article V of the Constitution requires something approaching a national consensus, akin to what had been necessary for ratification of the document itself. By contrast, under the "dangerous" and "indefinite" construction that Jefferson feared, any sitting Congress could acquire new national territory and then generate new states from it with bare majority votes in Congress and the president's approval.[10] Given the voting qualifications in place across the states in the early nineteenth century, a narrow majority in Congress would represent a minority of the American people. If this loose construction were to prevail, then political factions would have incentives to pursue foreign conquest and state making as a means to entrench their own power and subdue their opponents. To give such power to transform the fabric of the nation to a sitting Congress and president was the opposite of the popular consensus the framers thought necessary for constitution making and amendments. It would turn the conquest and acquisition of foreign territory and its transformation into states into normal aspects of national politics in the United States.

But in 1803, despite the precision of his logic and the intensity of its expression in these letters to his allies, Jefferson chose *not* to defend his constitutional principles in public. Rather, he concluded his letter to Senator Nicholas this way: "If, however, our friends shall think differently, certainly I shall acquiesce with satisfaction; confiding, that the good sense of our country will correct the evil of construction when it shall produce ill effects."[11]

Jefferson's friends in the Democratic-Republican Party did think differently. They worried about opposition from regions of the country that expected to derive little benefit from the accession of Louisiana, New England included. They feared that a formal amendment process might not succeed and that the opportunity to expand would vanish. So they followed the initial instinct Jefferson expressed to Wilson Cary Nicholas: they said as little as possible about the "constitutional difficulty" and rushed the Louisiana Purchase through congressional approval by October, 1803, far too quickly for a serious national conversation on the question to occur.[12]

By the time of the Louisiana Purchase, the cotton gin was a decade old. With it, the expansion of plantation slavery beyond the original territory of the United States had become not only imaginable but technologically possible. And the rapid expansion of slave-based agriculture was spurred yet further by the flight from the Haitian Revolution of many slave-owning planters, who brought enslaved workers to Louisiana and began to establish sugar plantations along the fertile bottomlands of the Mississippi River.[13] Given the immense size of the Louisiana Territory, equal to the original United States and as yet unexplored by settler Americans, it was impossible to know how many more additional states, or how many new settlers, would spread across this land. By failing to insist on constitutional amendments, Jefferson left the answers to these questions up to Congress to decide.

Congressional politics increasingly centered on the contentious question of whether new states within the Louisiana Territory would permit slavery. Eight years after the Louisiana Purchase, Congress began to frame its answer when the Madison administration pushed forward a bill for the admission of the Territory of Orleans as the new State of Louisiana. Although he could not have known the contents of Jefferson's private correspondence from 1803, Massachusetts Congressman Josiah Quincy III, in arguing against Louisiana statehood, echoed Jefferson's logic precisely. On January 14, 1811, Quincy mounted a fierce attack against the bill in a subsequently famous speech on the floor of the House of Representatives.[14] Using quotations from relevant documents and specific historical events, Quincy demonstrated what Jefferson had privately asserted in his letters: that the clauses in the Constitution granting Congress the power to admit new states pertained only to the original territory of the United States, not to unspecified foreign acquisitions. He further endorsed Jefferson's concern that the addition of foreign territory to the union as equal states would fundamentally alter the constitution of the nation. Such an addition "materially affects the liberties and rights of the whole people of the United States," and should never be treated as "a common power, as an ordinary affair, a mere municipal regulation" for Congress alone to exercise.

Quincy cited words spoken by George Washington as president of the Constitutional Convention that related how careful and delicate the negotiations had been to balance the interests of every part of the union in drafting the Constitution. To Washington's words, Quincy added:

> The debates of that period will show that the effect of the slave votes upon the political influence of this part of the country [the South], and the anticipated variation of the weight of power to the West, were subjects of great and just jealousy to some of the best patriots in the Northern and Eastern States. Suppose, then, that it had been distinctly foreseen that, in addition to the effect of this weight, the whole population of a world beyond the Mississippi was to be brought into this and the other branch of the legislature to form our laws, control our rights, and decide our destiny. Sir, can it be pretended that the patriots of that day would for one moment have listened to it? They were not madmen.[15]

As it happened, while Congress was debating its future statehood, Louisiana was experiencing the largest slave revolt in American history. Hundreds of enslaved workers on the "German Coast" of the Mississippi River above New Orleans, mostly young men, armed themselves with farm tools and rose up in rebellion on January 8, 1811. They burned several plantations, killed two white planters, and marched toward New Orleans, only to be massacred by a mounted and armed militia raised to put down the rebellion. Dozens of slaves were executed, their heads put on pikes along the road from New Orleans to the German Coast to terrorize the rest.[16] Although Quincy and his fellow representatives in the nation's capital could not yet have heard this news, the enabling bill for Louisiana's admission had unwittingly addressed the issue by adding the word "white" to the qualifications for free male voters eligible to select delegates to write a state constitution. New Orleans was home to a large population of free people of color—nearly half of New Orleans's free population, and 10 percent of the total population of Louisiana by the 1810 census. Congress had no intention of allowing Louisiana to replicate the Haitian Revolution, which had been precipitated by the political demands of free men of color, nor did it imagine that Indians could have a say in framing its government.

Josiah Quincy believed that the Territory of Orleans, and any other part of the Louisiana Territory, could be admitted to statehood only by a constitutional amendment. He even believed that in the single case of Orleans, such an amendment would succeed: "I do suppose that, in relation to the objects of the present bill (the people of New Orleans), no great difficulty would arise. Considered as an important accommodation to the Western States, there would be no violent objection to the measure." Yet, knowing full well how much slavery had expanded since 1787, Quincy predicted that his fellow congressmen would not be satisfied by the admission of just one state by constitutional amendment:

> But this would not answer all the projects to which the principle of this bill, when once admitted, leads, and is intended to be applied. The whole extent of Louisiana is to be cut up into independent States, to counterbalance and to paralyze whatever there is of influence in other quarters of the Union,—such a power I am well aware that the people of the States would never grant you. And therefore, if you get it, the only way is by the mode adopted in this bill,—by usurpation.[17]

Quincy rounded out his oration with dire warnings about the union's future if the Louisiana bill, "upon a principle pretended to be deduced from the Constitution," should pass: "This government, after this bill passes, may and will multiply foreign partners in power at its own mere motion, at its irresponsible pleasure; in other words, as local interests, party passions, or ambitious views, may suggest." The result, in Quincy's view, would be disastrous: "This Constitution . . . was never constructed to form a covering for the inhabitants of the Missouri and the Red River country; and whenever it is attempted to be stretched over them it will rend asunder." As we shall see, this is exactly what would happen.[18]

Having already served three terms in Congress, Quincy was under no illusions that his speech would sway Southern congressmen. He later reflected that "the *Southern*, as then called, but now *the Slave-holding States*, were omnipotent in this Union."[19] And indeed, while his fellow New England representatives supported his position by a vote of twenty to seven, and while the other Northern states were evenly split on the matter, the farther south and west the districts they represented, the more unanimous were the congressmen in favor of admitting Louisiana as a "common power" of Congress. The bill passed the House easily on March 20, 1812.

In the Senate debates, Samuel Dana of Connecticut took up Quincy's (and Jefferson's) principle. Dana introduced an amendment to the bill to prohibit Louisiana's admission "unless each of the original States shall consent to the same, or there shall be a Constitutional amendment empowering the Congress to admit into the Union new States formed beyond the boundaries of the United States, as known and understood at the time of establishing the Constitution for the United States." The Senate split this proposal into its two alternatives for debate, then voted both of them down. But in each case there was substantial support for the idea—ten of twenty-eight senators present voted in favor of requiring unanimous approval of the original States, and eight of twenty-five senators present were in favor of requiring a constitutional amendment. Considering the Senate as representing the states, it would seem that roughly a third of the states, perhaps more, opposed this form of admission, which suggests it lacked the degree of consensus that a constitutional amendment ought to require. The regional biases in the Senate mirrored the votes in the House, and the Senate passed the bill on April 2, 1812.[20] Although they did not win the day, substantial minorities in both houses of the national government agreed with Jefferson and Quincy that acquiring foreign territory and making new states from it would seriously alter the nation's constitution and therefore required an amendment. Former president Jefferson, despite his strong convictions on this matter expressed in his private letters to colleagues in the summer of 1803, and notwithstanding his revered status in the party pressing for Louisiana statehood, remained silent during these debates—this was the curious incident of the dog in the night-time. Instead, Louisiana was admitted as "an ordinary affair, a mere municipal regulation." A precedent was set that in due time would tear the union apart.

The Anglo-American tradition going back to the Middle Ages made the relationship between land and people—the ultimate sources of power in an agrarian world—a central element in constitutional practice. Constitutional documents gained their legitimacy by their ability to both accurately represent these relationships and define limits to the power inherent in them. The position that Thomas Jefferson, Josiah Quincy, and Samuel Dana all favored (though with varying degrees of candor) was entirely consistent with this tradition. They and their supporters in Congress believed that the potential addition of immense new territories and unimagined new peoples to the union would amount to a radical constitutional alteration. Such a dramatic change in power relations, and in the "character, prejudices, and habits" of the union's constituent parts deserved recognition and approval in the written constitution through the amendment process.

By shielding the purchase from an amendment process, Congress in 1811 exposed a growing bifurcation between two different understandings of what a constitution is: on one hand, a broader and older definition of constitution meaning a description of the fundamental qualities of a society, people, land, or nation, and how its parts and interests are represented in a system of government and expressed in written instruments; on the other hand, a newer and narrower understanding of a constitution simply as a written document amounting to a rulebook for how a nation's game of politics and government is to be played.[21] By choosing not to require an amendment for the admission of previously foreign territory to statehood, the congressional majority in 1811 showed that it did not really care about the characteristics of the land, people, and society of the Louisiana Territory, or how its admission into the union might change the body of the nation, as long as this majority could extend this political rulebook to cover Louisiana's governance in a way they found advantageous. This was an extraordinary decision, given that the rulebook itself, a written document not yet twenty-five years old and produced by a set of men still alive and active in politics—not least of them President Madison—was the product of careful negotiations among a varied assortment of states, each looking out for their particular interests and negotiating a balance among them.

The British Empire had broken apart in 1776 because it had failed to resolve an issue much like that of Louisiana's statehood: how to incorporate a newly acquired large landmass and its growing population within the governance of the realm in a way that respected ancient constitutional traditions and the rights of all British subjects to the constitution's protections. The distinctive American innovation to this constitutional tradition lay in the creation of special conventions to draft and to ratify constitutions, devised as a method to express the general will among a sovereign people, and to remove from the hands of any sitting legislature the power to dramatically alter such fundamental aspects of the constitution. Constitutional amendments required the state and federal governments to meet high thresholds of popular consensus, ratified state by state, before they could take effect.

By confirming Louisiana's admission to statehood as a simple legislative act, a majority in Congress, with the approval of a willing President Madison, seized for itself a power to change the constitution that rightfully belonged to the sovereign people. Jefferson, in his optimism, hoped that "the good sense of our country" would correct any evils that this constitutional "construction" might generate. Quincy was sure that it would destroy the union, and he wanted no part in it. He withdrew from national government and returned home, where he had a distinguished career as Boston's mayor and later as president of Harvard.

By not speaking up in favor of amendments and allowing territorial acquisition and the making of new states to become what Quincy called a "common power" of Congress, Jefferson and his party changed the constitution—they usurped on behalf of Congress a fundamental power of the people. One more passage in Jefferson's private correspondence about Louisiana in 1803 reveals the constitutional thinking behind this change. In his letter of August 12 to Kentucky Senator John Breckinridge, while defending the need for a constitutional amendment, Jefferson described the logic behind his purchase of an immense territory without the authorization or consent of the people—"an act beyond the constitution," as he called it. Jefferson argued that the executive branch was only doing for the people "what we know they would have done for themselves had they been in a situation to do it." He turned to a metaphor: "It is the case of a guardian, investing the money of his ward in purchasing an important adjacent territory; and saying to him when of age, I did this for your good." But Jefferson believed that if the people would ratify an amendment in favor of the Louisiana Purchase and "incorporating foreign nations into our union," then such an "act of indemnity [would] confirm and not weaken the constitution."[22]

The usurpation is plain. Jefferson and his correspondents knew that they were treating the sovereign American people like children, minors incapable of handling their own affairs, doing for them "what we know they would have done." This is the constitutional logic of monarchy. Jefferson at least wanted to absolve himself and his party from guilt by means of a constitutional amendment that would demonstrate the people's consent after the fact. But because Jefferson's party did "think differently," no such amendment ever occurred. Through this broad construction of the Constitution, Congress would forever exercise a power that the people never granted: to pursue expansion and state making like squabbling guardians over their wards, continually changing the fundamental body of the nation in the pursuit of their own momentary political advantage, and not the people's considered interests.

This modification of the workings of the Constitution regarding territorial expansion generated fierce rivalries between Southern slave states and Northern free states. Contrary to Jefferson's expectation, no amount of "good sense of our country" would "correct the evil of construction" and the "ill effects" it produced. Even after the Civil War, the competing national political parties would resume the expansionist rivalry, pushing the United States to complete its continental dominion. In doing so, they fulfilled the Constitution's mandate under the interpretation—the construction—that Jefferson had allowed to advance despite his strongly held preference for the safety that a stricter construction promised. This is not to say that had Jefferson spoken up and insisted on the necessity of an amendment for the admission of Louisiana to statehood, expansion would not have continued, or that any such amendment would have been as restrictive as the ones he sketched in his private correspondence of 1803. But given his political power over the party he created and still led, and the fact that there was already considerable support for such an amendment among a substantial minority in Congress, it's more than plausible that the expansion process might have been slower and less easy to use as a tool for regional and partisan domination of national government.

The strategic broad construction of the constitution in this case was similar to the reasoning used by Hamilton in defense of his economic program of the 1790s. But there was a critical difference. The government institutions Hamilton created by broadly interpreting Congress's powers, such as a national bank, could be and in fact were undone by future legislatures and presidents. Statehood, by contrast, is forever. Once admitted, a new state becomes a permanent and equal member of the union. A state's right to equality in the United States Senate remains the one element of the written constitution that can never be altered, even by formal amendment, as the last clause of Article V plainly states. By usurping the people's power to make these decisions, Congress, without altering the written instrument, changed it in the most substantive and fundamental way possible. It allowed the political process controlled by sitting legislatures and presidents to remake the body of the nation over and over again. In the decades after Louisiana's admission to statehood in 1811, the politics of expansion would become ever more entangled with the nation's growing divisions over slavery. The escalating struggle to control Congress's unwritten but now confirmed power over expansion and state making would drive the union into civil war.

8

The Machine Runs Amok

EXPANSION, SLAVERY, AND CIVIL WAR

> Cuba is as necessary to the North American republic as any of its present members[;] . . . it belongs naturally to that great family of states of which the Union is the providential nursery.
>
> —OSTEND MANIFESTO, DRAFTED BY U.S. MINISTERS TO BRITAIN, FRANCE, AND SPAIN, OCTOBER 1854

AT THE TIME of the Louisiana Purchase, the area around New Orleans was densely populated by European and African American colonists—and eligible for statehood as a result. The same could not be said for the rest of the Louisiana Territory. President Jefferson sent the famous Corps of Discovery expedition led by Meriwether Lewis and William Clark to explore the new territory's farthest reaches and forge commercial ties with its myriad Native peoples. Less known is the way the United States government deployed its now fully developed Domesday Machine to transform its new trans-Mississippi possessions. After the voyage of discovery, William Clark became the governor of the new Missouri Territory (renamed in the wake of Louisiana's statehood) as well as the chief administrator of the St. Louis Superintendency of Indian Affairs.

This now obscure institution was created by the federal government to manage the transfer of Indian land title into government hands and to oversee the movement of white American colonists into this region. The government used the twin tools of diplomacy and military force to pressure Native nations, such as the Osage, Sauk, Meskwaki, and Iowa, into ceding their most desirable and accessible lands in the Missouri River Valley and to move them onto less attractive, more remote reservations farther west and south. With land cessions in hand, the territorial government opened the region to colonization. A population boom quickly followed.

In the few years after 1815, when William Clark declared large tracts in Missouri to be in the public domain and available for purchase, the little settlement of Boon's Lick, on the north bank of the Missouri about 160 miles west of St. Louis, grew from fewer than a thousand to more than twenty thousand settlers, making it the fastest-growing place in the United States at the time. Boon's Lick alone supplied a third of the population necessary for Missouri to apply for statehood in 1819. A second state from the Louisiana Purchase now threatened to leapfrog ahead of other regions from the original United States, such as the Michigan and Wisconsin Territories, in the race to gain full representation and political equality in the union. Unlike Michigan and Wisconsin, Missouri's white colonists, many from neighboring Kentucky and Tennessee, brought enslaved African Americans with them in large numbers. By 1820, one of every three adults in Boon's Lick was enslaved. If Missouri were to be admitted as a state, it would become the second slave state from the Louisiana Purchase, an ominous fulfillment of Josiah Quincy's worst fears only nine years after his denunciation of Congress's usurpation of this constitutional power.[1]

Missouri's prospective statehood touched off a crisis when an antislavery congressman from New York, James Tallmadge, introduced an amendment to the House bill for Missouri's admission. The Tallmadge Amendment echoed the Northwest Ordinance of 1787 in aiming to prohibit the further introduction of slaves into Missouri and granting freedom by age twenty-five to all children born there to enslaved parents. The House of Representatives approved Tallmadge's amendment on a starkly sectional vote, carried by the North's growing advantage in the House. But in the Senate, a unified South defeated it. Congress admitted

Missouri as a slave state, but only after these sectional tensions were eased by a compromise bill, negotiated by Henry Clay of Kentucky. The Missouri Compromise of 1820 provided for the simultaneous admission of Maine as a new free state—Maine's citizens had long expressed their desire to break away from Massachusetts and form their own state. In addition to maintaining a balance of free and slave states, the Missouri Compromise mimicked the Northwest Ordinance by creating another national dividing line, prohibiting slavery in the remainder of the Louisiana Purchase north of 36°30′—Missouri's southern boundary line.[2]

Missouri's statehood followed the precedent set by Louisiana's admission in 1811–12. Without a formal amendment, an ordinary act of Congress altered the constitution of the union yet again, making fundamental changes to the nature of its population, its political economy, and the balance of power among the states. The line drawn over slavery's future in the remaining Louisiana Purchase territories, an immense region, had been determined by a sitting legislature, which meant that a future legislature could just as easily undo it. Statehood was permanent—the Constitution guarantees it. But a boundary line between slave and free territories could be changed by future Congresses. The split between House and Senate over the desirability of slavery in the case of Missouri created additional incentive for each region to strive for domination in *both* houses of Congress. There were sure to be similar battles over future states, and over the organization of future territories. To Thomas Jefferson, who had hoped in 1803 that the "good sense of our country" would correct any evils that came from a loose construction of the Constitution, this sectional conflict over the admission of another slave state was deeply troubling. Jefferson heard the fight over Missouri as "a fire bell in the night" that "awakened and filled me with terror. I considered it at once as the knell of the Union."[3] The constitutional process Jefferson had unleashed by his (and his party's) earlier failure to insist on amendments would turn the Domesday Machine into a wrecking ball.

The story of how the union went from the fire bell of the Missouri Compromise to the death knell of civil war is among the most familiar in American history; it need not be retold in detail here. Yet it is essential to understand that though the Civil War was caused, most obviously, by the growing division between North and South over slavery, it was also caused by a less obvious factor. Slavery as an institution had inescapable economic, infrastructural, cultural, and gendered, to say nothing of religious and moral, aspects that collectively deepened the nation's political divide. A more subtle, though no less significant, force in the march to civil war was the structure of the Constitution as a land-developing, state-making engine that, with the Louisiana Purchase, had been informally but enduringly modified to put the acquisition of foreign territory and the admission of new states at the mercy of congressional politics. In the 1770s, the absence of a method for resolving the position of the American colonies within the British constitution had been an underlying cause of the thirteen colonies' rebellion. By the 1860s, the struggle within Congress over gaining territories and making new states would motivate the rebellion of eleven Southern states.

Contrary to Abraham Lincoln's assertion, a political house divided against itself can stand for quite a long time. Many profoundly bifurcated nations endure for long periods, so long as the state sufficiently guarantees the rights and security of the differing parties.[4] However, the U.S. Constitution's expansionist capacities under Jefferson's loose construction generated political contests that steadily undermined a divided but stable American house. As the controversies over the admission of Louisiana and then Missouri demonstrated, it was possible for one side in the increasingly intractable argument over slavery to gain a lasting political advantage—not by persuading existing voters of the virtue of its position, but by controlling the expansion process and thereby producing new states sympathetic to that position, adding representatives, senators, and Electoral College votes from new territory to their cause. This curious, high-stakes method for continuously reshaping the union's constitution provided the persistent subtext for the politics of expansion through the decades leading to civil war.

Congress admitted Arkansas to the union in 1836, which was in theory balanced by Michigan's statehood the following year. But Michigan, of course, was part of the original territory of the United States. Slavery had been prohibited there even before the Constitution went into effect. So Arkansas was now the *third* new slave state in twenty-five years carved out of the Louisiana Purchase, with no free states. The United States gained the Florida Territory from Spain through a combination of military conquest (Andrew Jackson's illegal invasion that began in 1816) and diplomatic negotiation (the Adams–Onís Treaty of 1819).[5] In 1835–36, slaveholding Anglo-American settlers in the Mexican state of Texas broke away from Mexico to defend their right to hold human beings in bondage. Texas became an independent republic for the next nine years, under a constitution that defended slavery and denied citizenship to Blacks and Indians. In 1845, following the victory of Democratic President James K. Polk, who had run on an expansionist platform, the United States annexed Texas, using a joint resolution of both houses of Congress to avoid the need for a formal treaty and a two-thirds vote in the Senate for ratification. The acquisition of Florida and Texas, two very large regions (each, like Louisiana, the former colony of a European empire) led to movements for statehood, immediately in the case of Texas. Congress balanced the admission of Florida and Texas as slave states in 1845 with the admission of the free states of Iowa in 1846 and Wisconsin in 1848. This made Iowa, part of the Louisiana Purchase, the first free state created out of foreign territorial acquisitions, against the combined weight of Louisiana, Missouri, Arkansas, Texas, and Florida. For the first sixty years following the Constitution's ratification, newly acquired foreign territory yielded a ratio of five new slave states to one free state, with new land area for colonization in these slave states exceeding Iowa's area by a ratio of nine to one.[6]

Behind the slave states' relentless drive for new territory and more representation in Congress lay Southern planters' and politicians' belief that the institution of slavery had to expand to survive. This belief stemmed in part from an accurate assessment of the ecological ravages of plantation agriculture. Cotton production on an industrial scale undermined soil quality and pushed capitalist planters to search for new fertile lands.[7] The promise of expansion also encouraged poorer whites to believe that they might join the plantation aristocracy if they could migrate to rich new lands. But politics was equally important, for the dominance of slavery as a labor force in the South meant that in many of these new states, roughly half the population was enslaved. Combined with the effect of the three-fifths clause on representation levels, this meant that each new slave state tended to gain fewer seats in the House of Representatives than each new free state; the Northern population was booming due to natural growth and high levels of immigration. Immigrant numbers to the United States mounted rapidly decade by decade: 128,502 in the 1820s, 538,381 in the 1830s, 1,437,337 in the 1840s, and 2,814,554 in the 1850s. Very few of these immigrants moved to the southern slave states given the limited demand for free labor there.[8] To sustain its power in Congress—to avoid having the next iteration of a Missouri crisis end with both houses voting to keep slavery out of new territories—the South needed to admit new slave states to keep its advantage in the Senate. Southern politicians came to believe that they could never afford to lose this contest. If they did, a free-state majority would make its advantage permanent by admitting more free states.[9]

Slaveholders in Congress continually pressed for federal government action to gain new foreign territories. Their cause was abetted by the military leaders, Southerners, and expansionists who served as U.S. presidents. From Andrew Jackson's election in 1828 until Lincoln's in 1860, every man elected to the presidency, with the exception of Martin Van Buren (Jackson's vice president), had experience either fighting wars for expansion or serving as diplomats to promote expansion. And Southerners reacted with increasing hostility to every Northern attempt to limit slavery's expansion.

After President Polk (1845–49) of Tennessee pressed for Texas statehood, he launched an invasion of Mexico in 1846. Victory in the Mexican War added 530,000 square miles of new territory to the United States, another immense accession, nearly two-thirds the size of the Louisiana Purchase.[10] In 1846, Congressman David Wilmot of Pennsylvania offered a reprise of the Tallmadge Amendment, adding a proviso to an appropriation bill for the war declaring that any territory gained from Mexico should be off-limits to slavery. As in the case of Missouri, the House of Representatives supported the Wilmot Proviso, but the Senate voted it down. This round of sectional hostility was resolved in 1850 by another tense and temporary congressional compromise: California was admitted to the union as a free state, balanced by the creation of the Utah and New Mexico Territories. "Popular sovereignty"—a vote by eventual settlers—would decide whether slavery would be permitted in these territories. With most (though not all) of the extensive New Mexico Territory falling south of 36°30′, the Missouri Compromise line, Southerners assumed it would be open to slavery.[11]

Similar attempts at foreign expansion continued apace, promoted by Southerners who, in the tradition of Andrew Jackson in the Creek country and Spanish Florida, did not wait for official support from the federal government. A group of Southern senators, congressmen, and American diplomats with Southern sympathies issued the Ostend Manifesto in 1854, calling for the United States to purchase the island of Cuba from Spain or, failing that, to "wrest" it from Spain by force. The manifesto asserted that "Cuba is as necessary to the North American republic as any of its present members, and . . . it belongs naturally to that great family of states of which the Union is the providential nursery."[12] In 1853–54, William Walker, a Tennessee freebooter or filibuster, attempted to colonize the Mexican state of Sonora, which was not part of Mexico's cession to the United States in 1848, and annex it to the United States as a slave state, much as colonizers of Texas had done. Walker was inspired by the efforts of Narciso López, a Venezuelan-born adventurer, who with support of Southern Mexican War veterans had made several unsuccessful attempts to invade Cuba in the early 1850s. When Walker's Sonoran venture was suppressed by the Mexican government, he led a small mercenary army to join an ongoing civil war in Nicaragua. By 1856, Walker had succeeded in taking control of Nicaragua's government and reinstating slavery there to garner support from the American South. U.S. President Franklin Pierce recognized Walker as Nicaragua's legitimate ruler. Walker was eventually defeated by a coalition of Central American governments and executed in Honduras in 1860. But his remarkable, if temporary, success inspired other American political figures, such as Kentucky Senator John J. Crittenden (whose nephew was among the filibusters executed in Cuba alongside Narciso López). Crittenden took a hemispheric view, arguing that all of the Americas south of the Missouri Compromise line, not just the parts currently claimed by the United States, might be fair game for the expansion of slavery from America's "providential nursery."[13] Crittenden's position spoke directly to the problem that Jefferson had foretold in his private correspondence of 1803: the loose construction of Congress's powers to acquire territory and admit new states favored by Jefferson's fellow party members provided no limits whatsoever to the union's potential for expansion beyond its original boundaries.

The expansionist impulse finally pushed the union into civil war when slavery's promoters encroached upon territories thought to be settled in favor of free labor. Congress passed a revised Fugitive Slave Act as part of the Compromise of 1850. The new act, unlike earlier versions of this law, required citizens of free states to assist Southern slave catchers in returning escaped slaves or else face severe punishment. This act brought the violence of slavery into the heart of the free North in an escalating series of incidents, including the use of U.S. Marines in May 1854 to return Anthony Burns, an escaped slave arrested in Boston, to his Virginia owner.[14]

At the same moment, the Kansas-Nebraska Act, passed by the House on May 22, 1854, upended the Missouri Compromise by organizing the Kansas and Nebraska Territories. Both territories lay north of the 36°30′ parallel (the Nebraska Territory at that time reached all the way to the Canadian border). But under the new doctrine of popular sovereignty, new settlers would be allowed to vote to determine the legality of slavery in these territories and, therefore, in any future states to be formed there. This position seemed, even more than the admission of Louisiana in 1811, not merely a loose construction of the Constitution but an abandonment of the Constitution's formal provisions. Article IV, Section 3, expressly gives Congress (not territorial colonists, whose rights to influence national government policy through representation in Congress were deliberately, if temporarily, suspended when they moved to the territories) the power "to make all needful Rules and Regulations" for U.S. territories and to control the admission of states. The land ordinances of the 1780s had been designed to put control over the public domain in the hands of the national government and to discourage individuals from forming their own colonies and then seeking admission as states. Texas slaveholders had evaded these restrictions by colonizing part of a foreign country—Mexico—and then violently breaking away from it to join the United States. Promoters of slavery in Kansas made a blatant attempt to do something similar, but within U.S. territory. The Republican Party Platform of 1856, which opposed the doctrine of popular sovereignty, resolved "that the Constitution confers upon Congress sovereign powers over the Territories of the United States for their government; and that in the exercise of this power, it is both the right and the imperative duty of Congress to prohibit in the Territories those twin relics of barbarism—Polygamy, and Slavery," with the first of the two barbs aimed at the Latter-day Saints in the Utah Territory and the second at the Slave Power forcing its way into the Kansas Territory.[15]

The Kansas-Nebraska Act generated intense competition between slave owners and anti-slavery activists to populate the fertile region of eastern Kansas as rapidly as possible. To combat slave owners from neighboring Missouri, who could quickly move into Kansas, Boston merchants and industrialists organized a corporation, the New England Emigrant Aid Company, to move anti-slavery colonists to Kansas, echoing the way New England itself had been colonized in the 1630s. The competition for settlement quickly devolved into guerrilla war between the factions—Bleeding Kansas. Supreme Court decisions such as Chief Justice Roger Taney's 1857 opinion in the *Dred Scott* case assured slaveholders that they could bring their human property anywhere in the union without fear of loss. Taney's opinion declared that African Americans could not be U.S. citizens and "had no rights which the white man was bound to respect."[16]

Collectively, the Slave Power was on the march, pressing to expand not only into newly acquired foreign territories but into parts of the union where slavery's prohibition had long been settled. Radical attempts to fight back by threatening slavery in its heartland, such as the abolitionist John Brown's 1859 raid on Harper's Ferry, Virginia, that aimed to raise a massive slave insurrection in the South, were put down by the military force of the United States government. These circumstances made the national election of 1860 the most starkly sectional contest in U.S. history. Abraham Lincoln of Illinois campaigned on a promise to leave slavery unmolested in the states where it currently existed, but to prevent its expansion into any new territories. Lincoln won the presidency without a single electoral vote, and virtually no popular votes, from anywhere south of the Ohio River. In ten of the eleven future Confederate states Lincoln was not even on the ballot as a candidate.[17]

For slave owners, Lincoln's victory was a catastrophe, a sign that the union was inexplicably deranged. The South had dominated the presidency for sixty years, from Jefferson's election onward. Even presidents elected from Northern states, like Ohio's William Henry Harrison, had been sympathetic to expansion and slavery—Harrison was descended from one of Virginia's oldest and wealthiest slave-owning families. How could a candidate who was not even on Southern ballots have won the presidency? The outcome drove eleven Southern states to secede from the union, even though the Southern-leaning Democrats would have retained a Senate majority and could have blocked any national legislation detrimental to their interests that Lincoln or a Republican House of Representatives proposed. South Carolina and Mississippi, the states with the highest percentage of enslaved people in their populations, led the way. Both states modeled their declarations of secession on the U.S. Declaration of Independence, first stating a set of principles on which they justified withdrawal from an existing polity and then describing a set of grievances that demonstrated their case—what the Declaration called "a long train of abuses." But compared with the U.S. Declaration, these secession statements were oddly lacking in solid constitutional grounds; they were hard-pressed to identify specific examples of how the national government had violated their rights in any way analogous to George III's depredations upon the American colonists.

South Carolina's declaration, adopted December 24, 1860, fixated on Article IV of the U.S. Constitution, specifically its fugitive slave clause in Section 2, which guaranteed that slaves who escaped their masters and crossed state lines would be returned, regardless of whether slavery was legal in the state to which the slave escaped. According to the South Carolina declaration, "This stipulation was so material to the compact [the Constitution], that without it that compact would not have been made." South Carolina complained that despite national legislation supporting the fugitive slave clause, individual free states had passed contrary laws and failed to comply with their national obligations (even though President Franklin Pierce of New Hampshire had used federal troops to enforce the law): "Thus the constituted compact has been deliberately broken and disregarded by the non-slaveholding States, and the consequence follows that South Carolina is released from her obligation."[18] To put it another way, the state that in the Nullification Crisis of 1832 had passed an ordinance asserting its right to nullify federal laws detrimental to its interests—only to back down in the face of federal intransigence—now proclaimed its right to secede from the union because other, anti-slavery states had attempted (likewise unsuccessfully) to do the same thing.[19] In both cases, the federal government had upheld the Constitution and prevented states from violating it.

Mississippi's declaration of secession, adopted January 9, 1861, was, if anything, less subtle than South Carolina's. Its principle of secession, if such it can be called, was that "the institution of slavery" was "the greatest material interest in the world," and that a "blow has long been aimed at the institution, and was at the point of reaching consummation."[20] Mississippi does not mention that this "blow" seemed to have done very little damage to its material interests. In 1860, the Cotton Kingdom was booming, the State of Mississippi had the highest per capita income of any state in the union, and the enslaved population of the United States was at an all-time high.[21] By focusing on its "material interest" and the institution that undergirded it, Mississippi supported the idea that a constitution was not just a rulebook, a set of words on paper, but also encompassed the land, its people, and relations of wealth and power among them. But who or what entity was responsible for aiming this blow at slavery, Mississippi's prized institution and the heart of its constitution as a state?

In the U.S. Declaration of Independence, the culprit was clear, both in historical and constitutional terms. The king was the source of the colonies' legitimate ties to Great Britain, the sovereign who had granted them their charters. Therefore, the king must finally be to blame if the governing compact had been violated. Consequently, each of the "long train of abuses" in the Declaration began with the word "He," describing the specific violations to colonists' rights and government's obligations that George III had perpetrated. Even when the Declaration's grievances were aimed at Parliament, it took care to state that "He," the king, had *allowed* Parliament to act. In the earlier words of John Adams, George III had allowed another "mesne lord," Parliament, to interpose itself between the king and his colonial subjects and pass legislation destructive of the constitutional relationship.

But in Mississippi's secession declaration, modeled after the Declaration of Independence, the perpetrator of the "blow" aimed at slavery was not "He" but "It." And "It" was neither the federal government nor the free states nor the Republican Party. Rather, the mortal foe in Mississippi's declaration was much more ethereal—"It" was literally a "hostility" that had arisen against its prized institution, a "feeling" of opposition to slavery that had grown within the union over the preceding decades. According to the Mississippi declaration, "It," this hostile feeling, had committed such grave offenses as "advocating negro equality" and "enlisting its press, its pulpit, and its schools against us." Worse come to worst, "*It* [this feeling] has recently obtained control of the Government, by the prosecution of its unhallowed schemes, and destroyed the last expectation of living together in friendship and brotherhood."[22] None of what Northern anti-slavery politicians had actually done violated the Constitution in any formal sense. The one thing they *could* do to harm slavery would not be a violation of the Constitution, precisely because Thomas Jefferson had failed to bark in the night, granting Congress and not the people power over expansion: the most powerful constitutional change that the North could make under Lincoln's leadership would be to use its congressional majority to admit additional free states from the nation's territories, and thereby permanently dilute the South's power in the national government. But if the Southern states remained in the union, they could use the Democrats' Senate majority to prevent that from happening.

Take away the hypercharged rhetoric, and Mississippi's complaint is that anti-slavery forces, by electing Lincoln, had finally won a major victory in the game of national politics. The slaveholding states had lived and prospered by this game since 1803. They had taken the lead in making unwritten revisions to the constitution by way of expansion, insisting that territorial conquest and the making of new slave states was simply the normal course of national politics, even though it radically changed the character of the nation and upended the careful balance created in 1787. Expansionists in favor of slavery had eschewed formal constitutional amendments in favor of simple congressional majorities, insisting that this process was legitimate under the constitutional rulebook. Now they had lost a round in the game and plausibly feared they might never win again.

The population growth of states north of the Mason-Dixon Line and the Ohio River had allowed Lincoln to win an Electoral College majority easily, despite receiving less than 40 percent of the national popular vote, the lowest winning percentage in American history.[23] The Constitution had designed the Domesday Machine to require forceful leadership from the executive branch, which used diplomatic and military power as well as institutions such as the Indian superintendencies to acquire new land and extinguish Indian title. Without control of the presidency, the South could not gain more new potential slave territory or make new slave states from the land the nation already claimed, and therefore no longer wished to remain in the union. Josiah Quincy's 1811 prediction had turned out to be stunningly accurate. When the South attempted to stretch the Constitution, under the slaveholding terms it desired, to cover the colonization of the Red River and Missouri River Valleys, the fabric was rent asunder.

It would stand to reason, then, that when the newly formed Confederate States of America (CSA) wrote a constitution of their own, they might address the problem that had caused such trouble for half a century—not slavery but control over expansion. And, in fact, they did. The CSA's constitution of 1861 closely mimicked that of the USA, but with key changes to specific articles and clauses, most obviously to protect slavery throughout the Confederacy. Into Article I, Section 9, the

CSA constitution directly imported the U.S. Bill of Rights as a list of prohibitions on the powers of the Confederate Congress. (To this it made several additions, including "No bill of attainder, ex post facto law, *or law denying or impairing the right of property in negro slaves shall be passed.*")[24] But whereas Article IV of the U.S. Constitution had been silent on whether Congress had the power to acquire foreign territory and make new states from it, the CSA made these powers *explicit* in its own constitution's Article IV, Section 3:

> The Confederate States may acquire new territory; and Congress shall have power to legislate and provide governments for the inhabitants of all territory belonging to the Confederate States, lying without the limits of the several States; and may permit them, at such times, and in such manner as it may by law provide, to form States to be admitted into the Confederacy. In all such territory the institution of negro slavery, as it now exists in the Confederate States, shall be recognized and protected by Congress and by the Territorial government; and the inhabitants of the several Confederate States and Territories shall have the right to take to such Territory any slaves lawfully held by them in any of the States or Territories of the Confederate States.

The issues that had plagued the politics of the United States by their omission in its Constitution were resolved in the Confederate Constitution in favor of slavery and expansion without the need for constitutional amendments. In addition, the CSA replicated the same machinery of expansion that the U.S. Constitution had created, including the power to raise peacetime armies and navies commanded by the president. And despite Southerners' vaunted support for states' rights, the CSA, like the USA, prohibited its states from making treaties, acquiring land from Indians, or controlling lands in the public domain, instead reserving these powers for the Confederate national government.[25]

But having just lost the political game of control over expansion and state making, the Confederacy made an additional alteration to its Constitution—it required that new states could be admitted only "by a vote of two-thirds of the whole House of Representatives and two-thirds of the Senate." In other words, the founders of the Confederacy recognized the truth of Jefferson's unspoken belief, of Josiah Quincy's passionate conviction, that adding new states from foreign territory does inevitably change the nature of the compact. It is not merely "municipal regulation" or a "common power" of legislation. It alters the fundamental constitution of the nation and should therefore only be done with a wide consensus among the sovereign people in favor of the change, not as a political power play to make partisan advantages permanent.

Needless to say, the Confederacy's violent bid for independent nationhood failed; its constitution had a short life. The Union effort to suppress the Southern insurrection has its own constitutional history. Much of it involves the question of whether the eleven states in rebellion had actually departed the union, and whether the United States government could live up to its constitutional principles in the midst of civil war. Warfare on this unprecedented scale also altered the operations of the national government in ways that had constitutional implications for banking, the monetary system, taxation, the conscription of soldiers, and the expansion of national government (to be discussed in part IV). But with respect to formal constitutional changes, the most important results of the Union victory were the three amendments passed by congressional supermajorities and ratified by the states in the war's aftermath, from 1865 to 1870. Indeed, these were the only formal amendments to the Constitution of any substance passed in the whole of the nineteenth century.[26]

These three amendments were designed to deal with the more obvious cause of the war, the conflict over slavery, and to manage the consequences of ripping this institution out of the heart of the Constitution.[27] President Lincoln's Emancipation Proclamation had freed enslaved people as a wartime measure, but only in places within the United States deemed to be in rebellion. Therefore, when the proclamation went into effect on January 1, 1863, it left slavery intact in the nonseceding slave states (Missouri, Kentucky, Maryland, and Delaware) and in places where the insurrection had already been suppressed by

Union troops (such as Tennessee and Louisiana). As a presidential proclamation, it could be reversed by Congress or by future presidents. Given the extent to which slavery had been embedded in state and federal law, only a constitutional amendment could reliably and permanently eradicate it. Any amendment required two-thirds majorities in both houses of Congress and ratification by three-fourths of the states—twenty-seven of the thirty-six, counting the Confederate states, that were in the union by 1865.

The Thirteenth Amendment banned slavery or involuntary servitude in the United States or any of its territories, "except as punishment for a crime whereof the party has been duly convicted," language borrowed directly from the Northwest Ordinance of 1787.[28] It moved through Congress in 1864–65, when many of the Confederate states were absent from the national government, and was ratified by three-fourths of the states by December 1865. The fact that several pacified Confederate states had already formed new Reconstruction governments that banned slavery helped to make ratification by twenty-seven of the nation's thirty-six states possible—Georgia became the twenty-seventh. The Thirteenth Amendment also included a second clause, which granted Congress "power to enforce this article by appropriate legislation." While it may seem innocuous, this clause marked a significant shift in constitutional history. The preceding amendments, especially the Bill of Rights, had generally *restricted* the powers of Congress. When the First Amendment declared that "Congress shall make no law respecting an establishment of religion," it did not bar the states from doing so, and several of them did. The Thirteenth Amendment was the first to *expand* federal power and restrict the rights of states to conduct their own internal affairs, the doctrine under which slavery had been staunchly defended. Whereas in 1787, the essential constitutional pact had involved the states' retaining full police powers and the federal government acting mainly as an outward-facing agent of expansion and mediation, the Thirteenth Amendment offered a dramatic change, turning the power of Congress toward the internal policing of the states.[29]

But merely ending the institution of slavery left unresolved many issues that had been shaped by it—questions of citizenship, civil rights, and representation, as well as the aftermath of the war itself. The Fourteenth Amendment addressed these issues. Its first clause provided the Constitution its first definition of national citizenship: "All persons born or naturalized in the United States and subject to the jurisdiction thereof" would henceforth be citizens of the United States "and of the State wherein they reside." Former slaves, now free men and women, could not be disowned or expelled by their states. States were prohibited from making laws that would "abridge the privileges and immunities" of citizens, and from denying citizens "due process of the law" or "equal protection of the laws." These provisions were designed to defeat the Black Codes that former slave states were already using to restrict the freedom of former slaves after emancipation. Like the Thirteenth Amendment, the Fourteenth continued the trend of enhancing national power and restricting what states could do, in the interest of equality before the law for all (still excepting "Indians not taxed").

The Fourteenth Amendment's second clause repaired the rift in the Constitution made by slavery's excision. Each state's representation in Congress and the Electoral College had depended on the calculation of "three fifths of all other persons" in addition to the "whole number of free persons." Ironically, the freeing of slaves meant that former Confederate states would now enjoy greatly enhanced representation in Congress. The biggest former slave states (and most vehement rebels) would get the largest bonus. Because Republican reformers feared that the former slave states would deny freedmen the vote—voting rights having yet to be defined among the "privileges and immunities" of citizenship—the amendment's second clause also provided that if any state denied the vote to any class of male citizens, then "the basis of representation therein shall be reduced in the proportion which the number of such male citizens shall bear to the whole number of male citizens." Though well-intentioned, this clause still left control over voting rights in the hands of the states. It also failed to prevent states from using other means, such as literacy tests, poll taxes, or property requirements, to do the work of disenfranchising African Americans. The clause was never enforced, even during the height of Jim Crow. Southern states gained new representative power in Congress but would never pay the price for subsequently disenfranchising Black men under the new, full-representation regime, just as they had never paid the price of higher direct taxes under the old three-fifths regime.[30]

The third clause of this lengthy amendment barred any person from holding office "who, having previously taken an oath, as a member of Congress, or as an officer of the United States, or as a member of any State legislature, or as an executive or judicial officer of any State, to support the Constitution of the United States, shall have engaged in insurrection or rebellion against the same, or given aid or comfort to the enemies thereof." Given recent events, it was obvious that former Confederate politicians and military officers were the immediate target of this clause—remember, major constitutional interventions tend to arise from the need to resolve a problem or crisis. But the language of the clause was made general enough for applicability to other events and circumstances.

The fourth clause of the Fourteenth Amendment dealt with the debts incurred in the war, affirming Congress's power to pay the debts of the United States, including pensions for Union veterans, but barring states or the federal government from paying any debts incurred by the insurrection or compensating slave owners for the loss of their human "property." Together, these last three clauses were designed to prevent any future Congresses, dominated by former Confederate states with enhanced representation, from defaulting on the debts of the United States, ending pension payments to Union soldiers, or showering national revenue on former slave owners or Confederate veterans. These clauses were an unsubtle reminder of how recently, and for how long, the South had dominated the federal government. But here too, the general language of the clause transformed the response to the crisis into an enduring principle: "The validity of the public debts shall not be questioned."

Most of the former Confederate states were initially unwilling to ratify the Fourteenth Amendment. In response, the Radical Republicans used their strength in Congress to pass legislation that required its ratification as a condition for the Confederate states' readmission to the union. This and the other Reconstruction Acts of 1867 imposed military government on the former Confederacy and mandated voting rights for free Black males over age twenty-one, to be enforced by Union soldiers. But once again, the Republicans feared that any congressional legislation could be overturned in the future, and the newly enfranchised freedmen's votes would be essential to the Republicans' ability to retain future congressional majorities. Congressional Republicans therefore proposed a Fifteenth Amendment, designed to prevent state or federal governments from denying voting rights to any citizens "on account of race, color, or previous condition of servitude." By omitting sex as one of these attributes, this amendment rebuffed the women's suffrage movement, which had been campaigning for decades in favor of women's enfranchisement. The Fifteenth Amendment was further weakened by its failure to ban poll taxes, literacy tests, property ownership requirements, religious tests, or other devices of voter discrimination. But without compromises on these issues, the likelihood of its ratification was slim, as even Northern states had generally been unwilling to grant voting rights to free Blacks. With these limitations, and with military government in the former Confederacy enforcing the right of freedmen to vote, African Americans were able to cast ballots in favor of the Fifteenth Amendment. Under these conditions, Louisiana ratified it before Massachusetts did, and the amendment went into effect in 1870.[31]

The Reconstruction Amendments, flawed and compromised as they were, did eliminate slavery—the most obvious cause of the Civil War—from the Constitution, though they failed to provide lasting remedies for slavery's legacy in American society. As we know all too well, their omissions and limitations left room for the post-Reconstruction return of systemic discrimination, exploitation, and oppression of African Americans in the form of Jim Crow. But in constitutional terms, what is seldom noticed is that the postwar settlement, including the three Amendments, left the Civil War's other, less obvious cause untouched. The standing interpretation of the Constitution's Article IV, fixed in perpetuity (in the sense used by Benjamin Rush) by Congress's response to the Louisiana Purchase, which allowed for the acquisition of foreign territory and state making as simple acts of Congress, remained uncontested despite the damage it had done in pushing the union into civil war—damage that the Confederate constitution had tellingly attempted to avoid.

In addition, while the Reconstruction Amendments attempted to prevent racial discrimination against African Americans, no comparable effort was made to address the brutal treatment of Native Americans and the abuse of their land rights over the preceding two and a half centuries of Anglo-American colonization, which had also been accelerated by the expansionist interpretation of Article IV. In fact, the only recognition of this issue in the Reconstruction Amendments came in the Fourteenth, which affirms the continuing exclusion of "Indians not taxed" from representation in Congress. This oversight—or, rather, persistent blindness—confirms how universal the belief was among the Constitution's framers, and among the nation's white citizens ever after, that the workings of the Domesday Machine to convert Indian land into U.S. property lay at the heart of the Constitution's purpose.

9

The Machine Stalls Out

THE CHALLENGE OF THE ARID WEST

> [T]he waters of the arid lands flowing in the great rivers must somehow be divided among the States. How can this be done? Lands can be staked out, corner-posts can be established, dividing lines can be run, and titles to tracts in terms of metes and bounds can be recorded. But who can establish the corner-posts of flowing waters? . . . The farmer may brand his horses, but who can brand the clouds or put a mark of ownership on the current of a river?
>
> —JOHN WESLEY POWELL, "INSTITUTIONS FOR THE ARID LANDS," MAY 1890

THE THIRTEENTH AMENDMENT eliminated slavery, the main issue over which the political contest of expansion and state making had been fought. But the expansionist contest itself continued through the Civil War and afterwards. Rather than slavery's promoters and opponents, the contestants were now the Republican and Democratic Parties. It remained the case that the admission of new states could be manipulated to bolster a party's vote totals in Congress and the Electoral College. This device always bore the potential to transform temporary political victories into durable ruling majorities.

During the Civil War the Republican majority in Congress (enhanced by the absence of representatives from the rebel states) rushed through the admission of Nevada. In October 1864, Nevadans spent over four thousand dollars to send a telegraph message conveying a complete last-minute draft of their state constitution to Washington, DC. This was done just in time for Nevada's three electoral votes to contribute to Lincoln's contested reelection bid, as most of Nevada's settler population was affiliated with the Republican Party. Congress approved the constitution even though Nevada had only ten to twenty thousand settlers at the time, most living near the recently discovered silver deposits in the boomtown of Virginia City, on the California border. Nevada's population fell far short even of the original sixty thousand standard for statehood derived from the Northwest Ordinance of 1787. Given that most of its territory is desert, there was little likelihood for any significant population growth.[1]

By contrast, the Wisconsin Territory had more than 150,000 settlers at the time of its admission to statehood in 1848. This larger number reflects the evolution of statehood admission standards over time. As the nation's population grew, the Northwest's Ordinance's standard of 60,000 settlers—based on the population of the smallest states in the 1780s—gradually gave way to a number known as the ratio of representation or "National Ratio," the average number of people represented by each member of Congress. The prevailing notion was that to qualify for statehood, a territory should have a sufficient population to "deserve" at least a single representative in the House. By 1860, this number had grown to 127,381. But since the number was not fixed in the Constitution, politics could, and did, subvert the process. The Republican Party created Nevada as a rotten borough, giving it two senators and one representative despite its having a population perhaps one-tenth the size of 1864's ratio of representation. A quarter century later, Lord Bryce, the Anglo-Irish member of Parliament, diplomat, and author of *The American Commonwealth* (1888), an insightful description and analysis of American government in the late nineteenth century, referred to Nevada in just these terms, as "a State whose inhabitants number only about 40,000, and which is really a group of burnt out mining camps. Its population is obviously unworthy of sending two men to the Senate, and has in fact allowed itself to sink, for all practical purposes, into a sort of rotten borough, which can be controlled or purchased by the leaders of a Silver Ring." Republicans in Congress designed Nevada to strengthen their hold on the presidency and Congress and thus set a pattern for the remainder of the vast Western territory.[2] On the eve of the removal of slavery as a source of derangement in the Constitution's design for representation, this new problem emerged.

The first great problem of minority rule in national government—the excessive power of large slave owners through the three-fifths clause—had been eliminated by the Civil War amendments. But with the admission of Nevada, a new version was rising to take its place. Partisan politics in Congress could create new states regardless of whether territorial populations warranted national representation. Before the Civil War, the careful admission of new states that were relatively equal in size had succeeded in resolving some of the inequality among the states that had been such a challenge at the time of the Constitutional Convention. Overall, the land area and populations of the states were far more equal in 1860 than they had been in 1790. But the politics of state making in the arid West would reverse this trend and make inequality in state populations, despite state equality in the Senate, a persistent problem in American representative government.

Two years after the Treaty of Guadalupe Hidalgo that ended the Mexican War in 1848, the enormous new State of California joined the union, driven by the Gold Rush that generated a huge population explosion of new colonists in this once sparsely populated region thousands of miles away from the other states in the union.[3] From this moment forward, the United States began to grapple with an issue unforeseen at the time of the Philadelphia Convention. By 1850, the original territory of the United States defined by the Treaty of Paris had been almost entirely transformed into states in the union—only a portion of what would become the State of Minnesota in 1858 remained in territorial status. Beyond the country's original territory, west of the Mississippi River, a tier of new states—Iowa, Missouri, Arkansas, and Louisiana—was arrayed along its banks. But to the west of these states, stretching out to California and the Pacific, the landscape of America changed dramatically because levels of annual rainfall were far lower west of the

100th meridian. In the nineteenth century, this region was often called the Great American Desert. Over the second half of the century, it would gradually become clear that the careful plans for systematic expansion laid out in the constitutional realignment of the 1780s, plans that had been remarkably effective over the eastern half of the continent, would be inadequate for the colonization of the Great American Desert.

America's wars of expansion, together with the politics of statehood admission, made the United States into a very strange looking country on the eve of the Civil War (fig. 9.1).

California and Oregon were admitted in 1850 and 1859, but between these Pacific coast states and the rest of the union lay an immense arid region of mountains and desert—at this point divided up in very unfamiliar shapes of long forgotten territories. Try, if you can, to look at this map with 1860 eyes, and not mentally fill in what you know of the subsequent Western state making. Its strangeness becomes apparent. Most of the arid West at the time just before the Civil War was already organized into federal territories. Some of these, like the Nebraska Territory, were almost as large as the original thirteen states. But this region had very little in the way of settler population. A population density map (fig. 9.2) of the United States at the time reflects a similar geography. The Latter-day Saints in the Great Basin of the Salt Lake and the longstanding Hispanic settlements of New Mexico dating back to the seventeenth century constituted the only substantial non-Indigenous populations between eastern Kansas and California's central valley.[4] A third map (fig. 9.3) made in 1880 illuminates the reason for this striking settlement distribution pattern by showing the average annual rainfall across the United States.

The wavering edge of the Eastern "green" section across the middle of the country, which lies roughly between the 99th and the 101st meridians, separates the well-watered East from the arid West. By 1860, the Domesday Machine had reached nature's western limit. Beyond it, agricultural practices common in the original United States could not

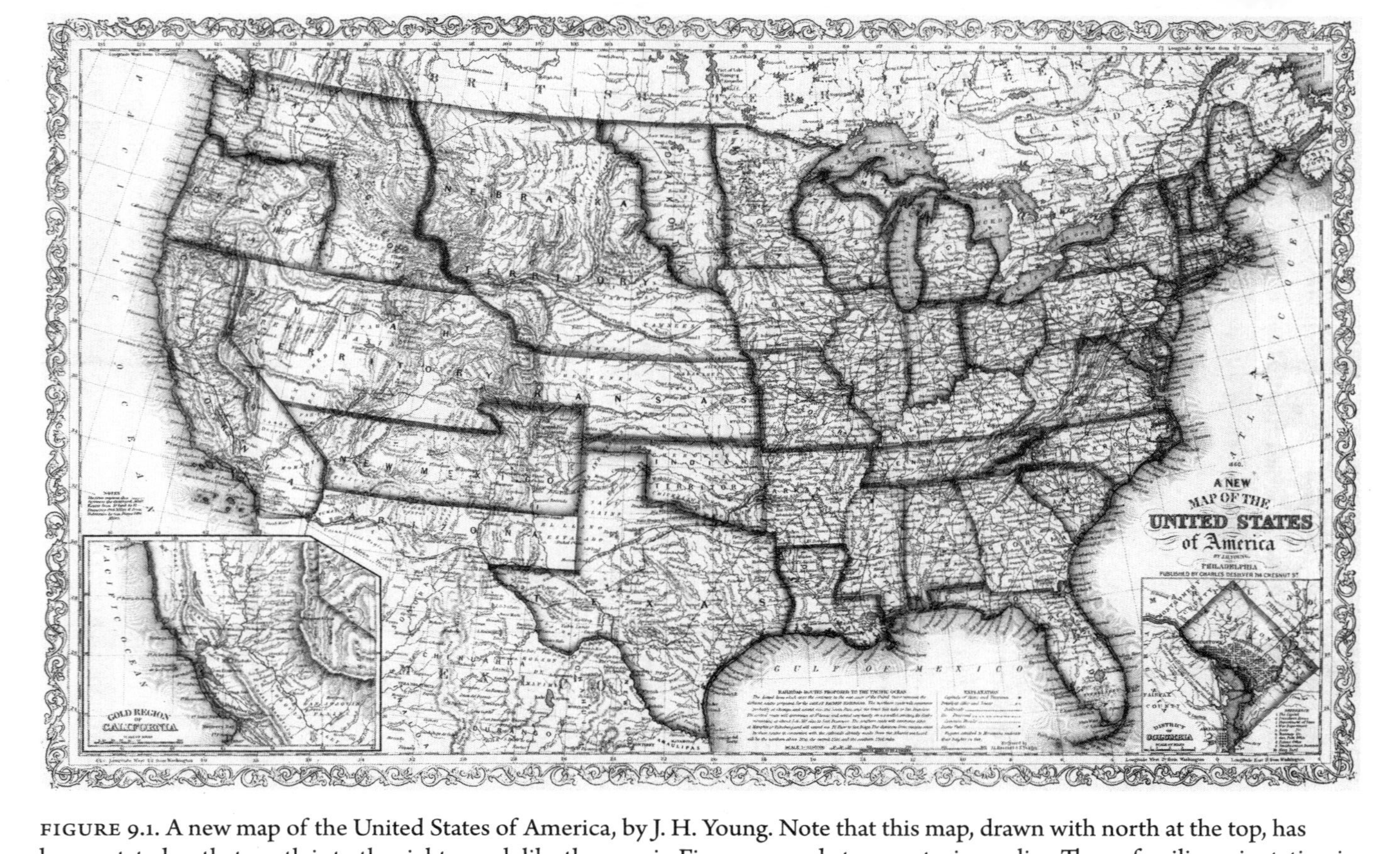

FIGURE 9.1. A new map of the United States of America, by J. H. Young. Note that this map, drawn with north at the top, has been rotated so that north is to the right, much like the map in Figure 1.2 made two centuries earlier. The unfamiliar orientation is meant to highlight for the reader the enormous distance between the new State of California and the existing states bordering the Mississippi River east of the 98th meridian. (Philadelphia, 1860).

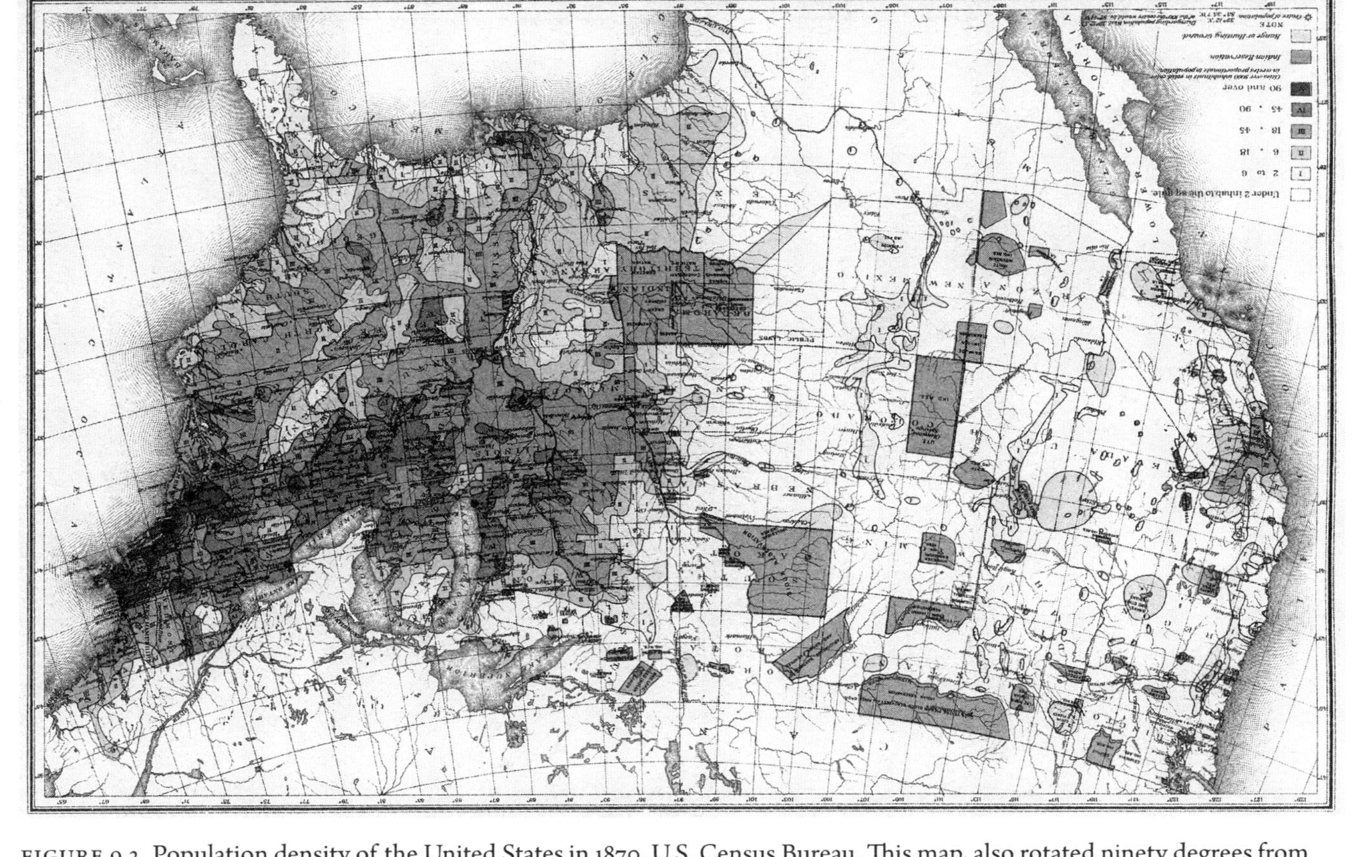

FIGURE 9.2. Population density of the United States in 1870, U.S. Census Bureau. This map, also rotated ninety degrees from the conventional orientation to highlight the dramatic regional population differences across the U.S., shows the relative density of the nation's "Constitutional Population," excluding "Indians not taxed." It depicts land areas reserved for Indigenous people, but not the size of Indigenous populations.

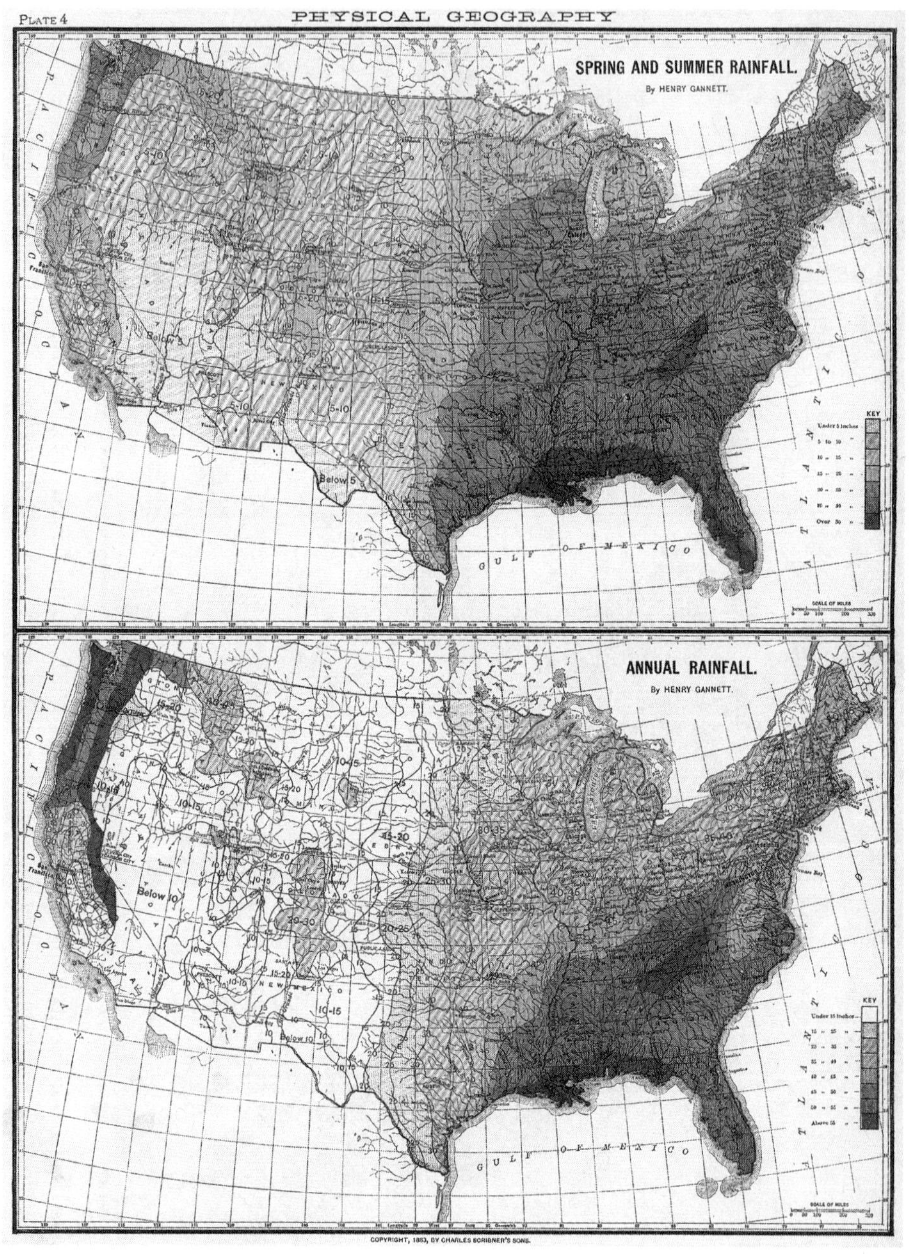

FIGURE 9.3. Average annual rainfall, 1880. Between the 99th and 101st meridians, marked across the top of the map, the average annual rainfall drops below twenty inches per year, making agriculture without irrigation untenable.

easily be sustained. At the northern end of this zone, Minnesota had been admitted to the union in 1858. Although Texas at the southern end had been admitted earlier, in 1845, by 1860 its settler population had not significantly expanded beyond its eastern portion, where rainfall is greater, despite the immensity of the state itself.

From the time of the land ordinances of the 1780s, United States territorial expansion had a simple working premise: once the federal government extinguished Indian title and organized land into territory for sale, white settlers in large numbers would purchase and move onto this land of their own volition; they needed no further incentives from the government. Settler populations sufficient to form self-governing states and sustain a vigorous political economy would naturally follow. For eighty years, the system had worked with remarkable efficiency throughout the original United States and the first tier of states formed west of the Mississippi. But by the 1860s, the Domesday Machine was stalling out. New Western land available for settlers was no longer sufficiently attractive to entice them to leave their homes and, like Huckleberry Finn, light out for the Territory. The phenomenon of Missouri, where rich farmlands opened for white settlement in 1810 achieved statehood population levels within a decade, would not be easily repeated farther west.

Nevertheless, with the Mexican War the political boundaries of the United States vaulted across the Great American Desert. California statehood was spurred, of course, not by its suitability for family-based agriculture but by the discovery of gold at Sutter's Mill in 1848. The Gold Rush brought thousands of new settlers to California from around the world, with the side effect of enhancing Oregon's prospects for statehood as well.[5] The result was the peculiarly bifurcated geopolitical nation of 1860. In world historical comparison, it would be as if the Ottoman Empire had annexed sub-Saharan West Africa, so that its territories in the Maghreb were separated from Nigeria and Ghana by the Sahara Desert. Indeed, the distance from Kansas City to Sacramento is roughly the same as the distance from Tripoli to Timbuktu, at the southern edge of the Sahara. Although traversing the Great American Desert was less uniformly formidable than an overland crossing of the Sahara, in 1848 the journey by sea—around the tip of South America—from the eastern United States to California was far longer and more difficult than an ocean voyage from Morocco to the Gulf of Guinea.[6]

The national government in the 1860s faced the challenges of linking the new Pacific states to the rest of the union and addressing the unsuitability of the arid West for Eastern-style agriculture. With the Confederate states absent from Congress, Republicans had the majority needed to pass a series of measures to promote settlement of public lands in the territories. These included the Homestead Act of 1862, which granted free land from the public domain, in 160-acre sections, to settlers who would agree to occupy, improve, and farm the land. Southern interests had opposed these grants for fear that they would encourage free labor at the expense of slavery. The idea stemmed from a Free Soil and Republican Party belief going back to the 1840s that making land freely available would prevent rich slave owners from monopolizing the newly available territory, developing it with slave labor, and marginalizing small farmers.[7] But by the time Southern secession made passage of the Homestead Act possible, the available public domain lands were mainly west of the Mississippi and stretching into the arid zone. The fact that the federal government was now willing to give this land away for free to any head of household who would farm it (except for those who had taken up arms against the Union) was a sign of diminishing market demand. Even with the offer of free land, the rush of migration and development in the old Northwestern and Southwestern regions between 1810 and 1840 (described in chapter 6) would not be repeated in the arid West. In 1890, almost thirty years after the Homestead Act was passed, the State of Ohio alone still had more than twice as many farms as all eleven far-Western states and territories combined.[8]

Congress passed the Pacific Railway Act of 1862 to support the creation of transportation and commercial linkages between California and the Eastern states, but it did so in a way to promote settlement in the West as well. Congress granted two corporations, the Union Pacific Railroad and the Central Pacific Railroad, enormous tracts of public land. This was the first time the U.S. government had given land from the public domain to corporations.[9] These enormous land grants provided not only the right-of-way on which to build railroad tracks, but also adjacent tracts of 6,400 acres for every mile of railroad line, land that the railroad companies could sell to settlers.[10] The presence of a railroad would make the adjacent land more profitable for farmers or ranchers wanting to ship crops or livestock to Eastern markets, promoting new settlement on formerly undesirable or inaccessible Western lands.[11]

In addition, Congress passed the Morrill Act of 1862, designed to create public universities across the nation by awarding states the title to large tracts of land from within the public domain, much of it in the West. States could sell or rent the land, with the proceeds to be used to fund higher education. This act likewise aimed to stimulate the market in Western lands, and the new universities would, it was hoped, produce useful knowledge to promote farming, ranching, mining, and manufacturing in the West. The Lincoln administration's simultaneous creation of the Department of Agriculture in 1862 also furthered these efforts to promote farming, an endeavor that few in the 1780s imagined would ever need much promotion. But the growth of an industrialized and urbanized America, together with the expansion of the nation's population to the edge of the arid zone, were leading indicators that the country's future was diverging from its first four score and seven years.[12]

From the far West in the years after the Civil War, two new voices emerged, two radical thinkers who recognized these changes in the fundamental pattern of American development and called for new approaches to national government that would recover and sustain the republican vision of the 1780s: the political economist Henry George and the geologist John Wesley Powell. Between them, George and Powell would offer bold new plans for an egalitarian and sustainable America, plans that would require substantial changes to the agrarian vision of the 1787 Constitution.

Henry George was born in 1839 to a middling family in Philadelphia, went to sea at age fifteen, and eventually washed up in San Francisco, where he found work as a printer, barely scraping by while trying to support a growing family. Working for newspapers gave George the opportunity to express himself in editorials, where he began to diagnose the social ills he saw all around him. He made his name in 1868 with an article on "What the Railroads Will Bring Us." Unlike much of the boosterism of the time, George argued that only the fortunate few showered by government land grants would profit from the railroads. Californians in general would be impoverished by the inflated land prices caused by giving away the public domain to land monopolizers. Several years later, George had an epiphany while out riding in the Oakland hills, when a passerby pointed out a tract of undeveloped land that was selling for $1,000 per acre—this at a moment when the federal government was giving away free land under the Homestead Act and the price for marketable land in the public domain was only $1.25 per acre. The Oakland land was undeveloped—unchanged from what it had been a decade or two earlier. Its grossly inflated price was the product of two factors: the boom in the Bay Area's population initiated by the Gold Rush, which generated greater demand for use of the land and expectations of further growth; and the opportunity for monopolization that speculators and railroad companies had seized.[13]

This moment of clarity led Henry George to write his first major publication, *Our Land and Land Policy: National and State,* published in 1871. In this pamphlet, George analyzed the situation in California. He showed how speculators had taken advantage of the vagaries of Mexican land grants from the pre-U.S. era and railroads had been given enormous grants by state and federal charters. Despite California's immense territory, the forces of monopolization had driven land prices so high that California's new settlers were becoming impoverished, as George himself had experienced. The golden promise of California had already devolved into a division between haves and have-nots. From California's dramatic recent transformation, George then generalized to the entire American experience since the Constitution went into effect.[14]

The roots of George's method of analysis lay in the eighteenth century. He followed the mode of reasoning from Benjamin Franklin's *Observations Concerning the Increase of Mankind* (1751). George used the most recent census data to project future American populations even larger than Franklin had imagined a century earlier, and described the pressure future generations would put on public domain land. He borrowed from Anne-Robert-Jacques Turgot and the eighteenth-century French physiocrats the idea that land, because of its fixed and finite supply, was the only form of productive wealth that could be taxed without the burden being shifted to others (labor or capital) via higher prices. George followed Adam Smith's emphasis on labor as a source of value, as well as David Ricardo's critique of rent as a tax on labor and capital, and thus an impediment to economic development. And he echoed Thomas Paine's position in his pamphlet on *Agrarian Justice* (1797) that the earth's finite supply of land should be considered the "*common property of the human race*" and that rent earned on land should be confiscated from landowners and returned to the public—in effect, a land tax—"*as compensation, in part, for the loss of his or her natural inheritance, by the introduction of the system of landed property*."[15] In sum, the ideas behind George's proposal for a "single-tax" on the value of land were present at America's founding. But it was only in the wake of the Civil War—with the federal government's immense new land grants to corporations and the nation's emerging encounter with the arid West—that George was able to assemble, in *Progress and Poverty* (1879), these older ideas into a distinctive new proposal to address growing concerns about inequality in America.

Time—a challenge for any constitutional order—played a critical part in Henry George's understanding of the emerging problem. As he explained in *Our Land and Land Policy*, the mistake that the United States had made at the nation's founding was in believing that the available land for its growing population, even augmented several times over by vast acquisitions through purchase and war, would always be sufficient to sustain the more equitable access to land ownership on which republican government depended, and on which it had been nurtured in the colonial period. Overconfidence in America's vastness, together with the urgent challenge of controlling the trans-Appalachian West in the republic's early years, encouraged the national government to drift toward policies allowing speculation in land rather than restricting purchases to what owners could actually use.[16]

The Yazoo scandals of the 1790s, when the State of Georgia sold claims to tens of millions of acres of Indigenous land to speculative companies at a penny an acre, had foreshadowed this outcome. Although the federal government eventually took over this territory after Georgia's cessions in 1802, the Supreme Court's decisions resolving the Yazoo debacle affirmed the legality of the sales contracts. These decisions permitted the formation of futures markets in unceded Indian lands, an extreme form of commodification guaranteed by the government's promise to extinguish Indian title. Abstract land claims now had a legally recognized monetary value and could be bought and sold in the expectation of future increase, once the land was "improved," "cultivated," or "civilized." From that point forward, state and national governments had been in a rush to sell or give away rights to land long before the land was actually needed, a process highlighted by the transcontinental railroads and land monopolization in post–Gold Rush California.

George described California in 1871 as the "greatest land state in the Union." As of 1871, California remained the state with the largest amount of land still in the public domain (there was no national domain land in Texas, which retained all of its own land claims at the time of annexation). While land monopolization proceeded "at an alarming rate" in all the "new States of the Union" (those other than the original thirteen), "none of them so fast as in California, and in none of them, perhaps, are its evil effects so manifest." So much of the land of California had been reserved in grants to the railroad, tied up in the "unsettled Mexican grants," or cornered by speculators "under the possessory laws of the State," that new arrivals could not find land suitable for cultivation without paying exorbitant amounts to one of these rent-seeking "middlemen." Already in 1871, "a large part of the farming is done by renters," or by industrial-scale operations, "men who cultivate their thousands of acres in a single field."[17] Yet on a per-acre basis, the human population of California remained tiny; the state had less than half the population of Massachusetts living in an area twenty-four times its size. Extrapolating from California's situation, George argued that "the prices of land in the United States today are not warranted by our present population, but are sustained by speculation founded upon the certainty of the greater population which is coming. . . . We are thus compelled to pay in the present, prices based on what people will be compelled to pay in the future."[18]

To heighten the irony of this American dilemma, George made a striking comparison of "our land policy" in the United States to that of England after the Norman Conquest. Not that George longed for feudalism's restrictions on workers—the freedom of labor and the worker's right to the value of his or her own production were central to his political convictions. But George argued that "the spirit of the Feudal System dealt far more wisely with the land than the system which succeeded it" because "the Feudal System annexed duties to privileges." Modern speculative ownership of commodified land, land represented by paper titles that could be bought and sold like any other form of stock, but nonetheless excluded potential users from the actual land, was pure privilege without duties.[19] By contrast, in the feudal system, "ownership of the land involved the necessity of bearing the public expenses." The crown lands yielded revenue that "defrayed the expenses of the State," the aristocracy's land supported armies when the state needed defense, and the church's lands supplied relief for the sick and the poor.[20]

George also noted that the famous Cincinnatus of Republican Rome "left his two-acre farm to become Dictator, and after the danger was over and the State was safe, returned to his plough."[21] George Washington, the modern Cincinnatus, likewise gave up military power to return to his farm. But Washington was no two-acre ploughman. His plantation at Mount Vernon consisted of some eight thousand acres worked by hundreds of slaves, and as a speculator he owned claims to another sixty-thousand acres on the trans-Appalachian frontier.[22] The Constitutional Convention over which Washington presided gave the United States government (that Washington would soon lead) the powers necessary to realize his land's potential value. Essentially, Henry George argued that in its transformation from monarchical to republican government, and from the colonial period's slow, demand-driven process of land development to the rapid, speculative form unleashed by the independent United States, the American constitutional order had shed the duties and obligations to support the public weal that had once been intrinsic to land ownership. Rich speculators could now own claims to vast tracts of the nation's finite (if undeveloped) land but pay nothing to support the common good.

Thomas Paine, writing during the tumultuous decade of the French Revolution, had realized how difficult it would be, especially in a long-settled and -cultivated country such as France, to separate the right to *property*—the improvement and cultivation brought about by human labor—from *land* itself, the "common property shared by the human race." As Paine put it in *Agrarian Justice,* the common right to land is "that kind of right, which, being neglected at first, could not be brought forward afterwards, till heaven had opened the way by a revolution in the system of government."[23] Paine devised a scheme for the French legislature to compensate the landless for the loss of their birthright with money drawn from a tax on land. This was an attempt to recognize "that kind of right" in the wake of a revolution that had initially focused on legal, procedural, and political rights. The seventeen articles of the *Declaration of the Rights of Man and of the Citizen,* issued in 1789 by the French National Constituent Assembly and echoed in the U.S. Bill of Rights in 1791, had guaranteed civil and political rights but not the less obvious, though equally important, right to land as the common property of mankind.

It would have been far easier in revolutionary America than in France to distinguish between humankind's common ownership of *land* and the rights to *property* generated by labor. At the time the United States formed its constitution, and for the century afterwards, most of the land claimed by the United States was *not* already cultivated or improved as "property" in the European sense. The large trans-Appalachian land cessions granted by Virginia, Connecticut, New York, and Massachusetts after 1784 that became the national domain, owned collectively by the United States, could have been the basis for such an experiment, separating individual ownership of property from common ownership of land. Instead, the tendency had been exactly the opposite—not only to rush as rapidly as possible toward Indigenous expulsion and cultivation by European settlers, but also to make land into property by way of speculation rather than by development, to commodify it in the abstract, even before the application of labor or cultivation associated with "civilization." Henry George's ferocious critique of American land policy was driven by his outrage over this difference. The opportunity afforded by the American Revolution had been squandered by the founding generation in their rush to claim and occupy the continent:

> Yet nobly and well as our fathers reared the edifice of civil and religious liberty, true ideas as to the treatment of land, the very foundation of all other institutions, seem never to have entered their minds. In a new country where nothing was so abundant as land, and where there was nothing to suggest its monopolization, the men who gave direction to our thought and shaped our polity shook off the idea of the divine right of kings without shaking off that of the divine right of landowners.

Now, looking back from the western edge of the United States' breathtaking leap across the continent, an unprecedented expansion driven by the powers vested in the national government by the Constitution, Henry George could see clearly that the land policy framed by the United States was undermining the principles of the founding:

> Of the political tendency of our land policy, it is hardly necessary to speak. To say that the land of a country shall be owned by a small class, is to say that that class shall rule it; to say—which is the very same thing—that the people of a country shall consist of the very rich and the very poor, is to say that republicanism is impossible. Its forms may be preserved; but the real government which clothes itself with these forms, as if in mockery, will be many degrees worse than an avowed and intelligent despotism.[24]

Henry George was an autodidact with a middle-school education driven by his experience of poverty amid great riches to extemporize a new sociology focused on the economic problem of land in America. By contrast, John Wesley Powell was a university-trained scientist who brought his background in geology and geography to bear on the challenges of America's arid Western lands.[25] But he shared with George an intense encounter with the landscape of the West as the basis for a new vision for the nation's future. Powell explored the region in the aftermath of the Civil War, in which he had served as a Union officer, losing his right arm at the Battle of Shiloh in Tennessee. In his famous *Report on the Lands of the Arid Regions of the United States* (1878), Powell distilled his many years of observations:

> The eastern portion of the United States is supplied with abundant rainfall for agricultural purposes, receiving the necessary amount from the evaporation of the Atlantic Ocean and the Gulf of Mexico; but westward the amount of aqueous precipitation diminishes in a general way until at last a region is reached where the climate is so arid that agriculture is not successful without irrigation. This Arid Region begins about midway in the Great Plains and extends across the Rocky Mountains to the Pacific Ocean.[26]

The 100th meridian was the line that marked the beginning of Powell's arid region, where the pattern of settlement generated by the Constitution's Domesday Machine came to a halt. Powell understood the political, economic, and constitutional implications of this change for the United States. In his government reports and in writings for popular audiences, Powell identified a series of distinctive watersheds across the arid West. Geological features separated the West into naturally defined regions, each drained by a different river system. Irrigation, dams, canals, and reservoirs would be necessary to make agriculture successful here, in a way the East had never required. Water was the most precious Western resource, far more valuable than the land itself. Powell saw that arbitrarily drawn territorial or state lines would inevitably create conflict among states, as well as conflict among individuals, because water does not naturally flow in straight lines or obey human boundaries:

> [T]he waters of the arid lands flowing in the great rivers must somehow be divided among the States. . . . Contests are arising between different districts of the same State. But the waters must be still further subdivided in order that they may be distributed to individual owners. How can this be done? Lands can be staked out, cornerposts can be established, dividing lines can be run, and titles to tracts in terms of metes and bounds can be recorded. But who can establish

> the corner-posts of flowing waters? . . . The farmer may brand his horses, but who can brand the clouds or put a mark of ownership on the current of a river?[27]

Powell's language of "metes and bounds" harked back to the England of the Domesday Book, the source of the land-based practices that had shaped Anglo-American constitutionalism in the well-watered East where it began.[28] But if the Domesday Machine were to continue its progress across the West's very different environment and organize land in ways that would attract American farmers, then Powell anticipated that its arid conditions would have to be accommodated by a new political geography:

> This, then, is the proposition I make: that the entire arid region be organized into natural hydrographic districts, each one to be a commonwealth within itself for the purpose of controlling and using the great values which have been pointed out. . . . Each such community should possess its own irrigation works; it would have to erect diverting dams, dig canals, and construct reservoirs; and such works would have to be maintained from year to year. The plan is to establish local self-government by hydrographic basins.[29]

Such a plan (fig. 9.4) would be necessary if the United States were to avoid "piling up a heritage of conflict and litigation over water rights, for there is not sufficient water to supply the land."[30]

Already, the pursuit of water was "entering upon an era of unparalleled speculation, which will result in the aggregation of the lands and waters in the hands of a comparatively few persons," undermining the democratic political economy that the Constitution had designed for its white citizens. In words that unwittingly echoed Thomas Jefferson's expectation at the time of the Louisiana Purchase that "the good sense of our country will correct the evil of construction," Powell concluded, "Let us hope that there is wisdom enough in the statesmen of America to avert this impending evil."[31]

If we now allow ourselves to recollect how the United States actually did fill the spaces on the map between Missouri and California, we can

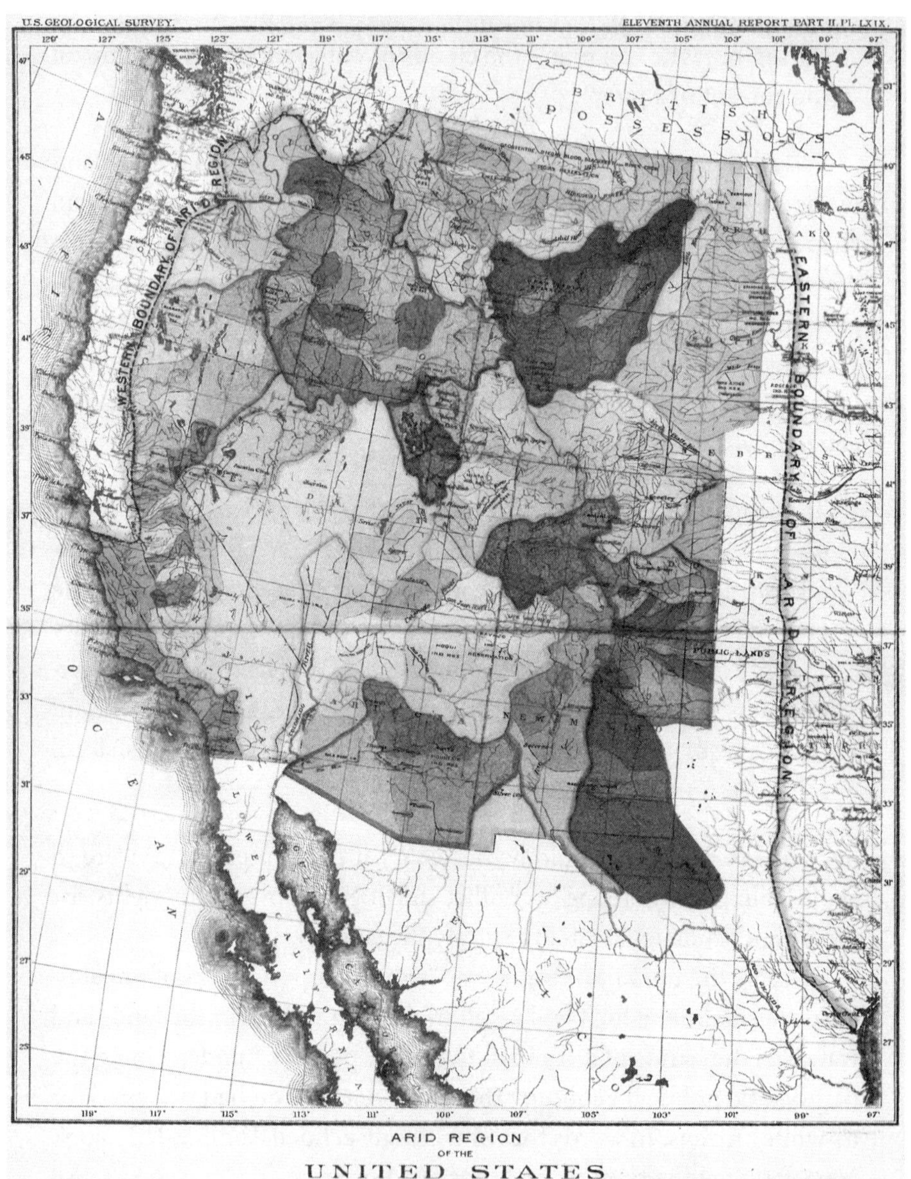

FIGURE 9.4. Arid regions of the United States, showing Powell's hydrographic districts.

instantly see how far America's statesmen fell short of wisdom. Congress produced nothing like Powell's watershed commonwealths. Instead, the nation continued to use arbitrary lines of latitude and longitude to define state boundaries in the arid West, without regard for the imperatives of water to define prospects for settlement or governance. Congress heeded Powell's recommendations no more than it adopted Henry George's single tax program. We can nonetheless see that the two reformers were pursuing a similar goal along parallel tracks. For John Wesley Powell, a wiser plan for managing and distributing the scarce water supply of the West was the only way to sustain anything like a Jeffersonian vision of a democratic society based on relative equality among numerous smallholders. Without such intervention by the national government, the environmental conditions of the arid West would favor rich speculators, heavily capitalized business enterprise, and the dominance of the few—just as Henry George had seen in California in the 1860s. Taken together, the work of George and Powell conveyed a growing awareness that the agrarian constitutional order created in the 1780s was breaking down in its encounter with unanticipated environmental conditions and unbridled inequality.

Compared to the populations of the new states created before the Civil War east of the Mississippi, the settler population of the arid West remained small through the nineteenth century. But the sparse population did not prevent parties in Congress from using their state-making powers to enhance their political majorities. After the Civil War, control of the two houses of Congress was frequently split between the Republicans and Democrats, making further state admissions difficult. Each party clearly wanted to use state admissions to strengthen itself. By the 1880s, the Dakota Territory was the most populous of the eight organized territories in the West. Its eastern region, like eastern Nebraska and Kansas, lay in the transitional rainfall zone friendlier to agriculture. The Republican Party hoped to make two states out of the region because its settler population trended Republican, while Democrats preferred to restrict it to one state.[32]

The stalemate was broken by the 1888 election. The Republican presidential candidate, Benjamin Harrison (grandson of President William Henry Harrison, the general who defeated Tecumseh's confederation in 1811) had been a major promoter within the Senate of creating two states from the Dakota Territory. Harrison's presidential victory was accompanied by a Republican takeover of the House, which would give the party a free hand in the next legislative session. Consequently, the lame duck Congress, with the House still run by Democrats, rushed forward an omnibus bill in the hope that Republicans' desire to admit the Dakotas as two states could be partially offset by the admission of New Mexico, where the heavily Catholic and Hispanic population favored the Democrats. In the congressional debates, the Republican Party, which had roots in the anti-immigrant Know-Nothing Party of the 1850s, voiced its opposition to New Mexico's statehood and managed to exclude it from the omnibus bill. In February, 1889, North and South Dakota were admitted along with Washington, all expected to be Republican states, offset only by Montana as a likely Democratic state.[33]

Eight months later in the next session of Congress after Harrison's inauguration, the GOP pushed through the admissions of Wyoming and Idaho, despite their having populations (measured in the 1890 U.S. Census) of only sixty-two thousand and eighty-eight thousand, respectively—far short of the ratio of representation at the time. Pointedly excluded were New Mexico and Utah, each far more populous than Wyoming or Idaho. As with New Mexico, Utah's Democratic-leaning population precluded its statehood under a Republican administration. As the South had done before the Civil War in the interest of slavery, the Republican Party (which had no presence in the South after Reconstruction ended) pursued statehood admissions instrumentally, as a way to make their congressional majorities permanent. One Democratic member of the House, Francis Spinola of New York, son of a Portuguese immigrant, complained that the admission of these six new states in 1888–89 "put the Senate of the United States where the Democratic Party cannot gain control of it in the next quarter century."[34] In the centennial year of the Constitution, party politics yielded the largest admission of territory to statehood since national government began, despite the absence of significant population in much of this region; Wyoming has never in its history reached the ratio of representation. After a century, the original model of 1789 had broken down. The territorial expansion for which the Constitution had been designed was reaching its end, and the inequality among states that had plagued the confederation in the 1780s was returning.

Further evidence of the Domesday Machine's decline lay in the specific patterns of Western settlement. As both Henry George and John Wesley Powell had foreseen, colonization of the West now relied far more heavily on investment by the federal government and by large corporations than expansion east of the 100th meridian had ever required. Massive land grants from the public domain to the transcontinental railroad companies, accompanied by similar grants to ranchers and mining interests, made these heavily capitalized forms of enterprise profitable.[35] Government intervention generated the infrastructure necessary to link these far-flung businesses to the new cities of the West, from Chicago to San Francisco.[36] Amid California's agricultural splendor there were very few family farms, as large corporations dominated the state's large-scale mechanized farm production.[37] With ranching, mining, and other extractive industries coming to dominate much of the arid West, the Eastern model of the family farm never took hold, fulfilling Henry George's and John Wesley Powell's dire predictions of the "aggregation of lands and waters in the hands of relatively few persons."[38]

Development of the West did closely resemble expansion east of the 100th meridian in one essential way: the dispossession of Native Americans from their land. This catastrophe was one subject for which Henry George and John Wesley Powell offered no solutions, no thoughts even, in their public writings, despite Powell's history of working closely with Indigenous people in his geological surveys of the West. Both men seemed to accept the idea of the "Vanishing Indian"—even these critics of the process of American expansion and its outcome for white colonists were unable to envision alternatives for Indigenous Americans.

In the post–Civil War arid West, the expulsion of Native nations from their homelands was driven even more directly by the federal government, with greater intensity and an accelerated pace. The infamous era of Indian removal in the 1830s, inaugurated under the presidency of Andrew Jackson, had been predicated on the belief that land reserves in the territory west of the Mississippi were virtually infinite. Promoters of removal from Thomas Jefferson onward reassured themselves that moving Eastern tribes to the limitless West would be an act of mercy, relieving Indians of pressure from white settlers on their lands.[39] Creeks and Cherokees; Choctaws, Chickasaws, and Seminoles; Delawares, Shawnees, Potawatomis, and Miamis—all these sovereign nations and many more would find permanent homes with plentiful land across the great river, while white settlers (and their enslaved African laborers) would fill up the original territory of the United States. But of course, in addition to the horrors of removal itself, the "Trail of Tears" on which thousands of forced migrants died, the trans-Mississippi lands allocated to these Eastern tribes by the federal government encroached upon territory that belonged to Western nations—Osage, Pawnee, Lakota, Cheyenne, Kiowa, Ute, Shoshone, and many others. Federal removal of Eastern Indians to the territories that would become Kansas and Oklahoma generated intertribal conflict and violence by putting immediate pressure on the scarce resources of these more arid lands. In response, the federal government developed the reservation system.[40]

In the Ohio country in the 1790s, when Native nations ceded land to the United States in the Treaty of Greenville, a line was drawn up to which white colonists could now settle, but beyond that line the land reserved for Natives was unrestricted. After the Civil War, with a dawning sense of both the limits to Western territory that Henry George identified in 1871, and the limited resources available on sometimes unpromising land, federal treaties increasingly restricted tribes to circumscribed areas that they would not be allowed to leave—the land reserve became a prison. Under such terms, the national government's acquisition of Indigenous land leapt forward at unprecedented rates. Between 1850 and the admission of the omnibus states in 1889–90, virtually all the land of the arid West—all the territory between Missouri and California—was either ceded to the government by Indians or designated as Indian reservations (fig. 9.5).[41]

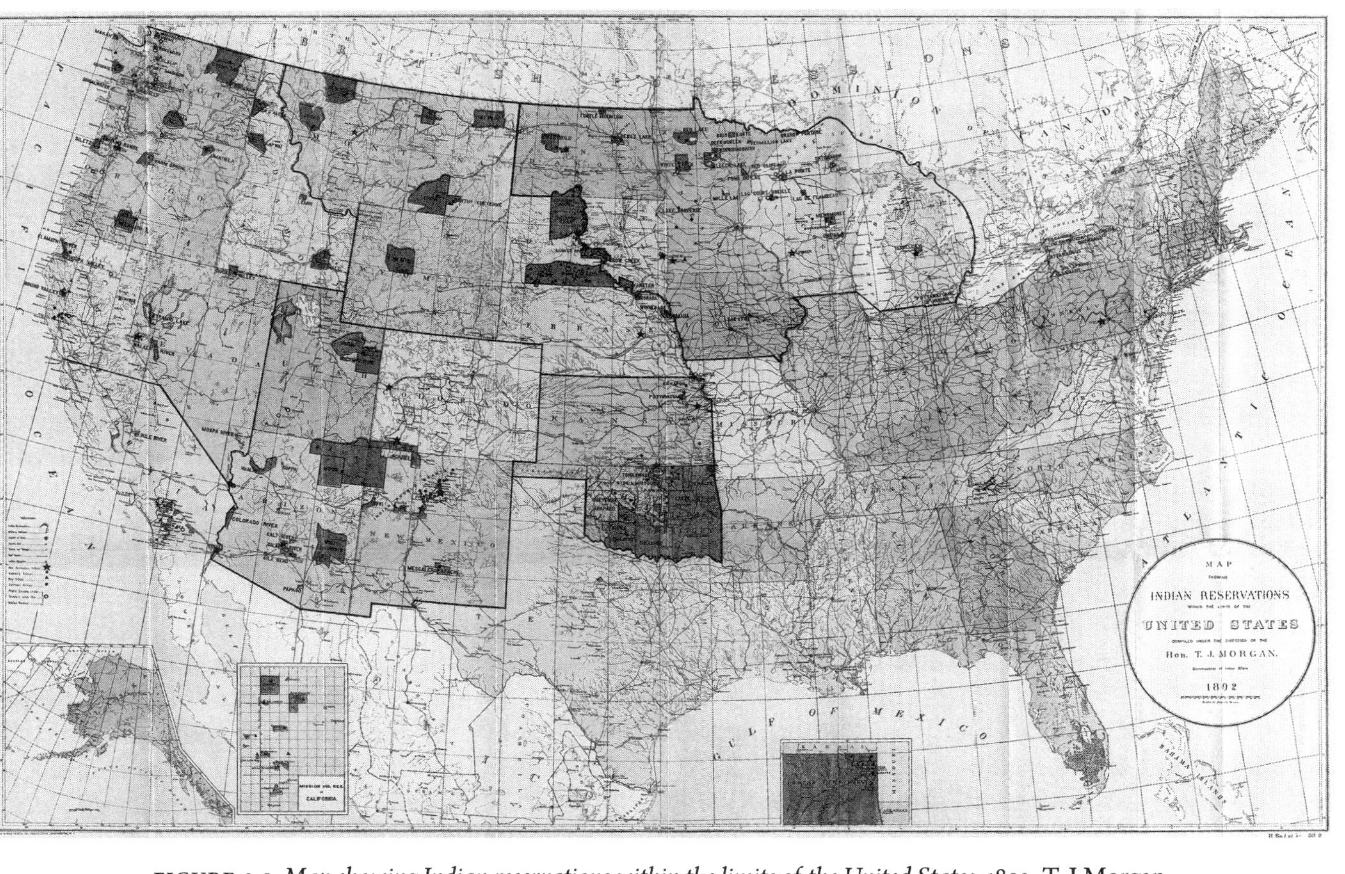

FIGURE 9.5. *Map showing Indian reservations within the limits of the United States*, 1892, T. J Morgan.

The United States Army played a critical part in this rapid transformation. Former Union generals such as Philip Sheridan and William Tecumseh Sherman adapted the scorched-earth practices they had learned in the campaigns of the Civil War and turned them against Native nations who resisted making land cessions or refused to remain on reservations. From the Red River Valley of the Southern plains to the Black Hills of the Dakotas, Sheridan's soldiers forced Comanches, Kiowas, Arapahos, Cheyennes, Lakotas, and others onto meager reservations, in part by destroying the buffalo on which Plains Indian lives depended. Unlike in the Eastern states, where white settler hunger for fertile farmland drove Indian dispossession, in the arid West it was often the discovery of precious metals that unleashed the violence. In California, the Gold Rush of 1849 inaugurated a genocidal wave of violence against the state's Indigenous population. In the Black Hills, the discovery of gold launched the wars of 1876–77 against the Cheyenne, the Lakota, the Dakota, and their allies, which ended with the Wounded Knee Massacre in 1890.[42] The exterminatory nature of this last phase of continental expansion punctuated a startling realization among white Americans: the seemingly infinite task of territorial expansion the Constitution had been designed to accomplish had abruptly reached its end. The census of 1890, a century after the nation's first, declared the frontier closed.

PART IV

A Domesday Book for the United States, 1890–1990

Naturally difficulties of division within state boundaries, unequal growth of population, migration from year to year, and slow adjustment to these and other changes, make equal population of these districts only approximate; but unless by and large, and in the long run, essential equality is maintained, the whole basis of democratic representation is marred and as in the celebrated "rotten borough" cases in England in the nineteenth century, representation must be eventually equalized or democracy relapses into oligarchy or even fascism.

—W. E. B. DU BOIS, *AN APPEAL TO THE WORLD!*, 1947

10

A Union of Three Distinct Sub-Nations and the Beginnings of Constitutional Reform

> I attended a funeral once in Pickens county in my State [Georgia]. The South didn't furnish a thing on earth for that funeral but the corpse and the hole in the ground. There they put him away and the clods rattled down on his coffin, and they buried him in a New York coat and a Boston pair of shoes and a pair of breeches from Chicago and a shirt from Cincinnati, leaving him nothing to carry into the next world with him to remind him of the country in which he lived, and for which he fought for four years, but the chill of blood in his veins and the marrow in his bones.
>
> —*ATLANTA CONSTITUTION* EDITOR HENRY GRADY, ADDRESS TO THE BAY STATE CLUB OF BOSTON, 1889

UNDER THE PHILADELPHIA Constitution, the United States government proved remarkably effective at acquiring land from Native and foreign nations and conveying it to American citizens, creating new territories and states as it went along. The United States transformed the continent at a speed difficult to imagine at the republic's origins. In these terms, during the nation's first century, the body of American society, its frame of government, and its written constitution had proven to be well aligned; the constitution worked as intended. It had become, in the words of James Russell Lowell on the centennial of its ratification, "a machine that would go of itself."

Yet not all had gone according to plan. The unwritten constitutional change that shifted control over foreign territorial acquisition and state making from the sovereign people to Congress had, through subsequent political contests, exposed the nation's profound conflict over slavery. The resulting civil war brought slavery to an end, but the failure of Reconstruction left the freed African American population impoverished and disenfranchised. Total war had devastated the American South, transforming the nation's richest region into its poorest and most stagnant.

As expansion continued into the arid West, a further drawback to the 1787 plan became apparent. No longer would clearing title to land automatically generate rapid settlement and small-scale farming by American colonists—in a region of such scarce rainfall, the machine would not go of itself. The agrarian nation envisioned in 1787 was unlikely to extend into the arid West without forceful government action and investment. The plan for relative equality among the states was breaking down. Furthermore, within the large new states of the arid West, growing inequality of wealth and power threatened prospects for democracy, as Henry George and John Wesley Powell had warned. What did continue, and at an even faster pace, was the dispossession of Native nations.

Across the Northeastern region of the country, from the Atlantic coast to the Mississippi River and north of the Ohio, other changes undermined the agrarian assumptions of the 1787 Constitution. This region witnessed rapid urbanization and industrialization, a shift away from rural life and from farming as the predominant occupation—changes that accelerated through the later decades of the nineteenth century. An ever-increasing flow of migrants from new areas of Europe filled the cities of the Northeast. As in the West, growing inequality within the states threatened the functioning of democracy, generating intense struggles between capital and labor.

Taken together, these dramatic changes in the second half of the nineteenth century created conditions across the body of American society unanticipated at the founding: by 1890, the United States had become a continent-spanning union of three very different sub-nations:

the old Northeast, the former Confederacy, and the arid West. A century later, in 1990, the nation and its government would be radically transformed yet again, in almost every way imaginable—every way, that is, except as described and defined by its written constitution. After a flurry of formal amendments in the early twentieth century, the written constitution remained remarkably static.

This final part of the book describes these fundamental social and governmental transformations as key to understanding America's changing constitutional order across the twentieth century. This may seem an impossible task—the majority of the American historians employed by colleges and universities work on the immense story of the making of twentieth-century America. Nevertheless, these chapters pursue this unlikely goal by returning to the approach with which the book began: looking to the Domesday Book as a model, a crude method for understanding the essential structure of a large and complex political entity.

In 1086, when William the Conqueror ordered the creation of a record of all his landholdings, he demanded that "no single hide nor a yard of land, nor indeed . . . one ox nor one cow nor one pig which was there [should be] left out, and not put down in his record."[1] Strict attention to detail would reveal the productivity of the entire human-built ecosystem, the object of royal governance. In addition, William wanted this information regarding three different moments: during the reign of King Edward (before the Norman Conquest in 1066), at the time William redistributed the land (1066 or after), and in 1086 when the survey was taken. The Domesday Book recorded what the conquest had changed, as well as declaring that its findings were henceforth to be permanent. It is difficult to get a clear picture of a complex subject (like the value of a kingdom) without comparing it to what it used to be. Following the Domesday example, part IV of this book uses data from the U.S. census between 1890 and 1990 to track changes in American society and government across the nation's second century under the Constitution.

When the United States took its first census in 1790, the country resembled the England of the Domesday Book more than it does the nation of today. The Philadelphia Constitution was suitable as the frame of government for a society at the end (though not *knowingly* at the end) of a long, stable agrarian era. It might be argued that it was the final flowering of a constitutional tradition shaped by the needs of agrarian societies. But the new nation differed from its English predecessor in that its agrarian future was speculative; the United States required the transformation of a continent to produce the conditions from which the England of Domesday began. The efforts made by the new nation to achieve this future would, ironically, change the nation into something radically new.

The Constitution mandated a decennial census for purposes similar to those of the Domesday Book: to assess the nation's population and wealth as the basis for a functioning government. Nor was the scale of this task in the new United States all that different from that in England seven centuries earlier. In 1086, England's population stood at about 2.5 million. London, the largest city, had about 18,000 residents. In 1790, America's population was just under 4 million, and New York City had 33,000 residents.[2] However, the U.S. population was spread across an area far larger than England; the new American republic was less concentrated, even less urban, than the world of Domesday. Like King William, the framers of American constitutions understood the connection between the size of a population, its agricultural endeavors, and its distribution on the land. This relationship was key to mobilizing the nation's wealth and power to "provide for the common defense and promote the general welfare." Given the explosive growth of America's population in the 1780s, the framers anticipated expansion in population and territory.

Americans' expectation of continuous population growth was another significant difference from the world of the Domesday Book. The Constitution's framers, among whom was Benjamin Franklin, a leader in predicting the growth of the American population, linked demographic growth to the fundamentals of republican self-government: representation and taxation.[3] A regular census was necessary for the United States to sustain equitable representation over time. The British Empire—which proved incapable under its ancient constitution of incorporating into its own framework of government an enormous colonial population that had not existed a century earlier—had foundered on this problem. The United States did not intend to repeat Britain's mistake. Unlike the Domesday Book, expected to be permanent, the constitution's census was designed to help the American government adapt to a growing and mobile population.

In the early years, U.S. census enumerators (650 agents were hired to conduct the first census) asked questions that differed little from those whose answers were recorded in the Domesday Book: how many people lived in each household? Was the land rented, owned, or mortgaged? As the capacity of the census administration grew, agents began to inquire into the value and qualities of the land: tilled land, meadow, pasture, woodland, and fisheries—the same categories as Domesday. In the U.S. census, race and slave status were the equivalent of the wider range of social categories recorded in Norman England (freeman, sokeman, villan, cottar, bordar, slave); the three-fifths compromise on representation and direct taxation made it necessary to account for race and slavery, so the census needed accurate information on this question.[4] Twice in these early years—once in 1798 during the "Quasi-War" with France, and again during the War of 1812—Congress used census figures to levy direct taxes on the American public. The amount each state owed was apportioned by state population adjusted by the three-fifths clause.[5]

Decade by decade, each census recorded the U.S. population's phenomenal growth. Congress would then use the new population figures to increase and reapportion the number of representatives in the House. In every decade from the 1790s to the 1910s, Congress admitted new states to the union, and population growth continued at high rates (35 percent per decade on average before the Civil War, 25 percent per decade afterwards). The number of members of the House of Representatives leaped from 106 to 435, and the Senate grew from 26 to 96. The adjustments to the House were not just to add new representatives for each new state but also to account for the increase in the nation's population. For instance, in the 1870s, only one new state was added to the union (Colorado, its small population entitled to a single representative), but the total number of representatives increased from 292 to 325 following the population growth registered by the 1880 census. Thirty-two of these additional 33 new representatives were apportioned among the existing states.[6]

By 1890, the census office required 46,804 agents to survey the U.S. population, a seventy-two-fold increase from 1790.[7] The population in 1890 was not seventy-two times as large as it had been a century earlier, although its sixteenfold growth, from 3.9 million to 62.6 million, had been extraordinary.[8] The even more rapid expansion of the census office reflected both the changing nature of American society and a revolution in statistical science, spurred by the vast mobilization of the Civil War, the growth of large business enterprises, and the rise of modern universities. The 1790 census results had been published as a single 55-page report, with tables listing the numerical results by county in five categories: free white males sixteen and older, free white males under sixteen, free white females, other free persons (i.e., people of color of both sexes), enslaved persons, and the sum of all these. A century later, census takers conducted far more extensive inquiries and recorded the results on dozens of different specialized "schedules." The published reports of the 1890 census amounted to 26,408 pages of information and analysis—five hundred times as much data as a century earlier.[9] From this vast trove of information, we can draw a portrait of the United States as its first century under the Philadelphia Constitution ended.

The 1890 census counted 62,622,250 Americans spread across forty-four states plus six federal territories. Although its population had grown sixteenfold since 1790, the nation's area quadrupled over this century.[10] Thus, the nation's population *density* had increased fourfold. But the spatial distribution of this population had changed in the nation's first century, led by the rapid growth of America's cities, mainly in the region north of the Ohio River and east of the Mississippi.

In 1890, the census defined urban areas as places with a population of 8,000 or more. In 1790, only 3.3 percent of Americans had lived in urban areas by this definition. By 1890, this percentage had grown to almost 30 percent: more than 18 million Americans lived in urban places by 1890, a 150-fold increase from 1790. To put it another way, the urban population grew more than nine times as fast as the very rapid growth of the overall population. The century's fastest increase in urbanization occurred between 1880 and 1890.[11] Urbanization was arguably the most dramatic transformation of any aspect of the nation's population over this century, and it was becoming ever more pronounced.

The geographical distribution of the cities, especially the largest of them, tells an important story about what the nation looked like in 1890. Of America's fifty largest cities, only five—New Orleans, Richmond, Nashville, Atlanta, and Memphis—were in the eleven states that attempted to secede in 1860–61. No Southern city was among America's ten largest.[12] Likewise, only five of the fifty largest cities lay in states west of the Mississippi River—St. Louis, San Francisco, Omaha, Kansas City, and Denver. Two others, Minneapolis and St. Paul, straddled the river near its source in Minnesota.

In other words, urban America in 1890 was mostly confined to the northern half of the original United States territory of 1783. State-level data from the 1890 census bears this out. With the exception of Louisiana (where New Orleans, with 242,039 inhabitants, was by far the largest Southern city), the remainder of the former Confederate states had urban populations below 10 percent of their total populations, not much changed from 1790. The arid West resembled the South in this regard. Apart from California, no Western state was even in the top half of U.S. state populations. Of the twelve least populous U.S. states and territories, all but tiny Delaware were in the arid West. These Western states had extremely small urban populations, comparable to overall U.S. levels a century earlier. By contrast, small Eastern states like Connecticut, Massachusetts, New Jersey, and Rhode Island had populations that were more than 50 percent urban (Rhode Island's was near 80 percent), though all had been at or below 10 percent in 1790.[13] This data on the changing distribution of urban versus rural population is but one among many indicators that the United States in 1890 was less a single integrated nation than three quite distinct sub-nations—the Northeast, the former Confederacy, and the arid West—loosely held together under a federal system. The data collected by the 1890 census demonstrates just how different and distinct these three sub-nations were.

Other demographic features such as sex ratio were also starkly differentiated along regional lines. In the states east of the Mississippi River, except for the most remote regions of northern Michigan and Wisconsin, the female population generally exceeded the male population. This pattern was a legacy of the Civil War's toll on the male population combined with the greater prevalence of males among westward migrants. Nearly everywhere west of the Mississippi, the male population exceeded the female population. In some of the West's more populous areas such as California, Oregon, and Washington, males exceeded females by more than 20 percent.[14]

The social category of race defined the nation's regional divisions even more starkly than sex. At the time the Constitution was drafted, nearly 20 percent of the U.S. population was African American, of whom most were enslaved. In 1860, on the eve of the Civil War, this figure had dropped to 14.5 percent. During the republic's first seventy years, internal growth rates of white and Black populations were nearly the same, but European immigration increased dramatically, while the abolition of the Atlantic slave trade in 1807 halted new involuntary migrants from Africa. This asymmetry explains the declining African American percentage of the overall population despite slavery's enormous expansion in the years before the Civil War. After the Emancipation Proclamation and the Thirteenth Amendment's prohibition of slavery, African American population growth further slowed in comparison to European-descended Americans, which continued to be augmented by immigrants. By 1890, the Black population was less than 12 percent of the nation's total.[15]

Emancipation for African Americans had not yet led to extensive geographical mobility. When the 1890 census mapped the racial distribution of the American population, it employed only two categories: the omnibus term "Colored," which included African Americans

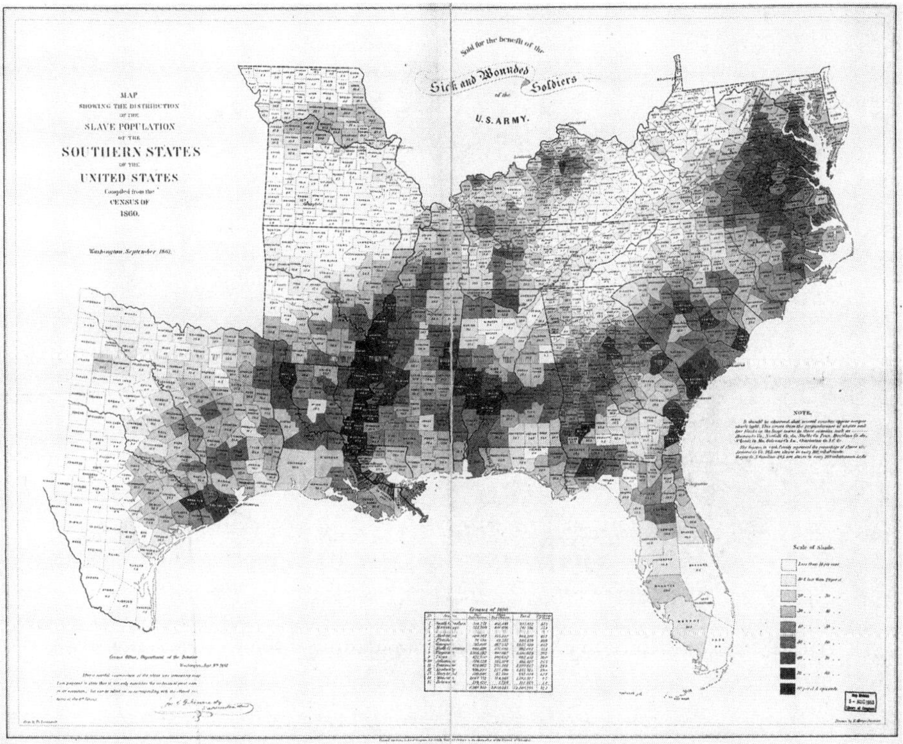

FIGURE 10.1. E. Hergesheimer, *Map showing the distribution of the slave population of the Southern states of the United States compiled from the Census of 1860.*

("Negroes"), Chinese, Japanese, and "Civilized Indians" (meaning Native Americans not living in tribal nations); and the undifferentiated "White" category, which included Americans of Hispanic descent. But the numbers of Chinese, Japanese, and "civilized Indians" were vanishingly small, about a quarter of a percent. "White" plus "Negro" together made up 99.73 percent of the nation's total population.[16] When these 1890 figures were projected onto the map, with the distribution of "colored" people across the nation measured in density per square mile (fig. 10.2), the result showed strikingly little geographical movement of African Americans since before the Civil War (fig. 10.1).

A closer look at the 1890 numbers of "colored" people per square mile as a percentage of the population, as shown in Figure 10.3, reveals low

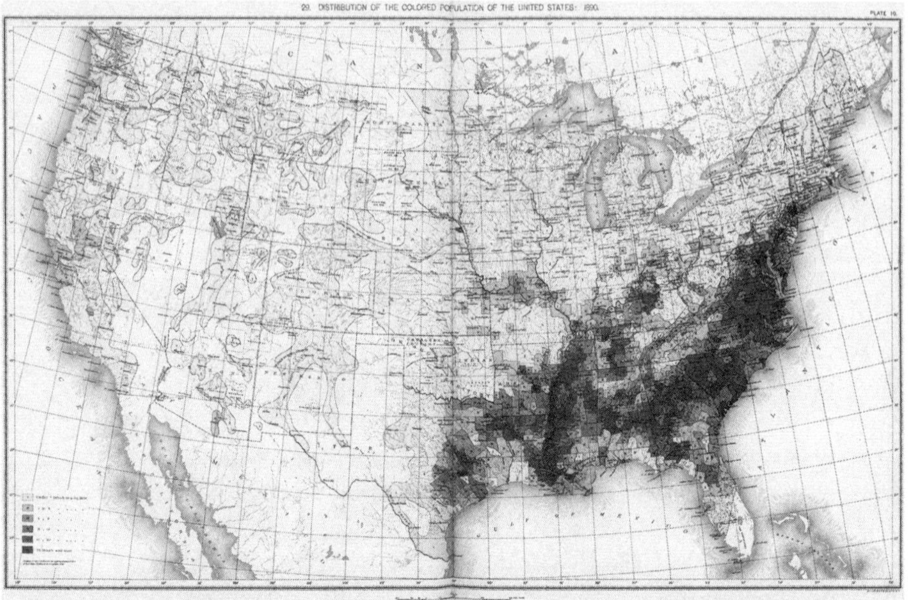

FIGURE 10.2. Distribution of the colored population of the United States, 1890.

numbers of African Americans in many of the country's most populous and rapidly growing cities. For instance, Chicago, San Francisco, Detroit, Cleveland, Buffalo, Rochester, Milwaukee, Omaha, Minneapolis, and St. Paul—all among the nation's twenty-five largest cities—had Black populations falling in the lowest statistical category, less than one inhabitant to a square mile (fig. 10.2). And as a percentage of their total population (fig. 10.3), each of these ten cities, plus nine others—New York, Brooklyn, Boston, Philadelphia, Pittsburgh, Providence, Newark, Jersey City, and Cincinnati—had "colored" populations of less than 7 percent. Even remote portions of Michigan's Upper Peninsula and northernmost Wisconsin had higher "colored" percentages—most likely Native people not living in tribal communities—than the burgeoning city of Milwaukee three hundred miles to the south.[17]

To put it bluntly, the racial distribution of the U.S. population in 1890 remained sharply segregated by region. The overwhelming majority of

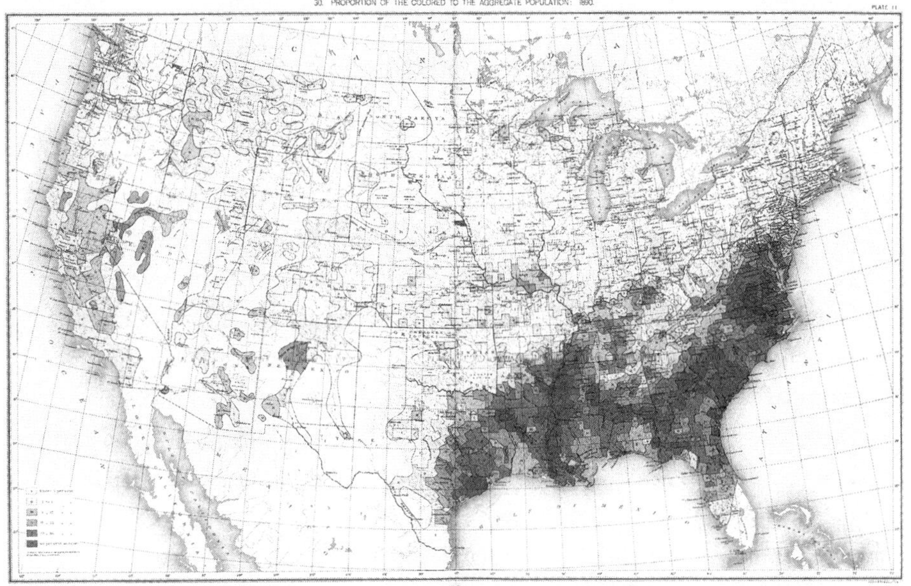

FIGURE 10.3. Proportion of the colored to the aggregate population, 1890. Although they appear to be quite similar, this map differs from Figure 10.2 in showing the relative proportion of "colored" Americans to the overall population. This accounts for the high percentage in surprising places like central Nevada (where the overall population was very small) and reveals the low percentage of African Americans in major cities of the urban Northeast like Chicago, Cleveland, New York, and Boston.

the Black population still lived in what had been the slave states before 1865. The urban Northeast was overwhelmingly White, and its population was growing much faster than that of the South. Nevertheless, the White South remained overrepresented in the national legislature. The Civil War amendments abolished the three-fifths clause, so African Americans were now counted in full for the apportioning of each state's representation (and any potential direct taxation, although that prospect would soon come to an end). But the collapse of Reconstruction in 1877 and the rise of Jim Crow meant that Black Americans' voting rights had been suppressed. The augmented political power of the Southern states now lay entirely in the hands of Southern Whites. Despite the abolition of slavery through civil war and constitutional amendment, the political nation in 1890 looked remarkably similar to the way it did thirty years earlier, with near-universal suffrage for white males but Black males and all female citizens still excluded from the franchise.[18]

Statistically speaking, Northern cities like Milwaukee had almost no Black residents in 1890—less than 1 percent of its population was "colored." But these cities were epicenters of the ethnic "hyphenated American," their populations expanded by waves of European immigration in the decades since the Civil War. Immigration further differentiated the nation's distinctive geographical zones. For example, Milwaukee grew from twenty thousand inhabitants in 1850 to two hundred thousand in 1890, nearly doubling every decade. Among all American cities, Milwaukee had the smallest percentage of people whose parents had been born in the United States—barely over 10 percent. Nine in ten of Milwaukee's inhabitants were either European immigrants or their children. As Figure 10.4 shows, Milwaukee was only the most extreme example of a pattern common to all the large cities in the American Northeast, where immigrants and their children outnumbered the children of native-born by more than two to one.

The South differed from the North in this regard as well. Maps of the distribution of immigrants in the United States (figs. 10.5 and 10.6) look like photo negatives of the distributional maps of African Americans in 1890 (figs. 10.2 and 10.3). The former Confederacy essentially had no significant immigrant presence, as the foreign-born population amounted to less than one person per square mile, and less than 1 percent of the aggregate population. On first glance at the bar graphs in Figure 10.4, which show the "Constituents of the Population of Great Cities" in 1890, Southern cities such as New Orleans, Washington, Baltimore, and Louisville seem to resemble their Northern counterparts in having large immigrant populations. But this impression is distorted by the inclusion in the census of the word "white" in the categories for immigrants or children of immigrants, and by the decision to place the "colored" population's contribution to the total on the far-right side of each bar in the graph. This arrangement deliberately emphasizes the alien nature of the combined colored and

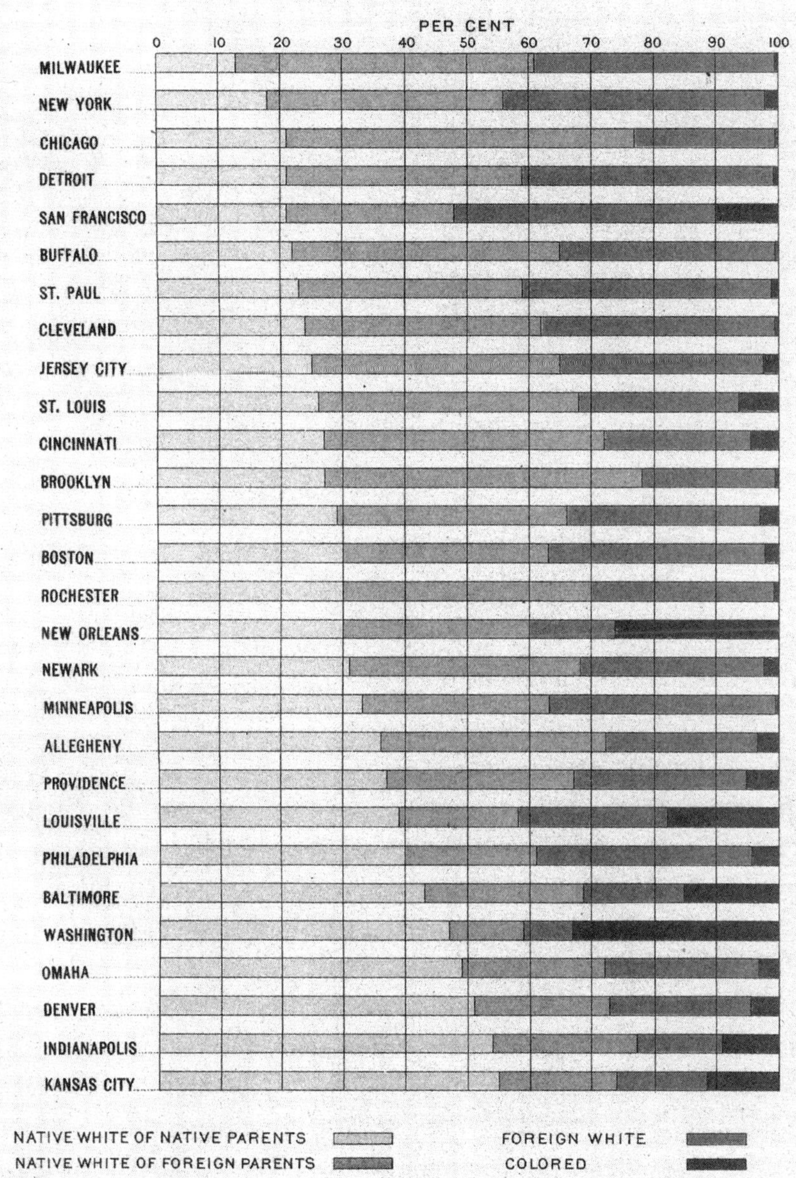

FIGURE 10.4. Constituents of the population of great cities, 1890. Note that in large Southern cities such as New Orleans, Louisville, Baltimore, and Washington, DC, the graph maker's decision to place the bar showing the "colored" population, almost all of whom were native-born U.S. citizens, to the right of the bars for immigrants and immigrants' children, makes these Southern cities appear demographically more similar to the immigrant-heavy cities of the urban Northeast than they actually were.

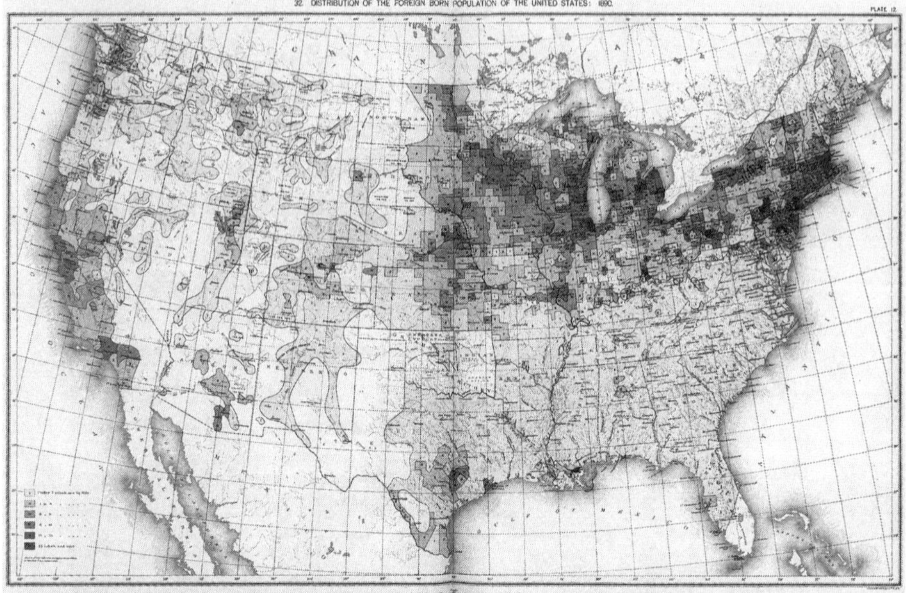

FIGURE 10.5. Distribution of the foreign-born population of the United States, 1890. The darker the color, the more foreign-born people per square mile.

immigrant populations against a normative "native white of native parents" category displayed on the far left of each bar. Given that the international slave trade had ended in 1808, the overwhelming majority of the African American population also had parents who were born in the United States. Therefore, in these Southern cities, children of the native-born, White or Black, far outnumbered the foreign-born and their children. This clearly differentiated Southern cities from the Northern cities where immigrant populations were numerically dominant.

The West differed from both the North and the South regarding immigration. Note how in Figure 10.5, most of the settled parts of the United States that lie west of the 100th meridian closely resemble the South in terms of foreign-born population—very few immigrants. Yet in Figure 10.6, the West seems similar to the urbanizing North—a high percentage of immigrants. The explanation for this apparent

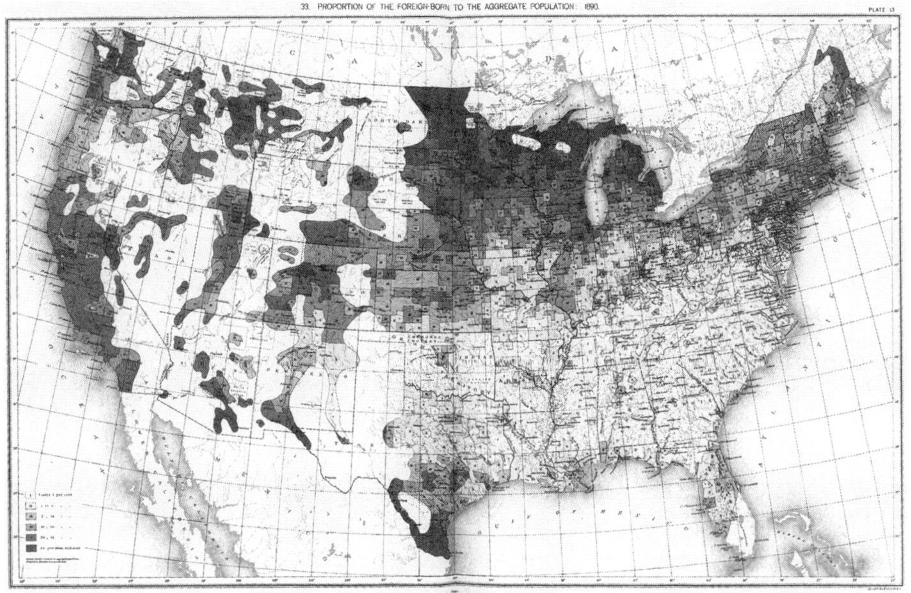

FIGURE 10.6. Proportion of the foreign-born to the aggregate population, 1890. The darker the color, the higher the proportion of foreign-born within the total population.

contradiction is that the population of the West was so small that in raw numbers there were few immigrants (fig. 10.5), just as in the South. But at the same time the characteristics of that small population more closely resembled the old North; a high proportion, however few in number, were foreign born (fig. 10.6).

Taken together, these population tables and maps from 1890 paint a clear portrait of the United States divided into three distinct sub-nations. The South, which had been the dominant U.S. region in wealth and power until the Civil War, was now a starkly isolated and still extremely rural region. Its majority White and large minority Black populations were seemingly frozen in place, growing slowly but with virtually no influence from the immense numbers of European immigrants sweeping the rest of the country. The Northeast, stretching from the Atlantic seaboard across the Mississippi River toward the 100th meridian, was rapidly changing, increasingly dominated by recent migrants and by galloping urbanization. The arid West, by contrast to both, remained sparsely populated by settler colonists, many of them immigrants (including most of the nation's East Asian immigrants) but very few of them African Americans. The West was home to most of the tribal Indigenous nations living within U.S. bounds. And the West was predominantly male compared to the East's higher female population. The meaning of these divisions, and their significance for national government under the Constitution, comes into focus with additional data from the census and beyond.

Late nineteenth-century interstate migration and the nation's industrial and commercial networks reinforced the South's isolation. Like foreign immigrants, few native-born Americans chose to move to the South after the Civil War; among Southern states only Arkansas was among the top ten states receiving native-born migrants from other states. Although high numbers of native-born people left the New England states, for example, the number who moved to the old South was statistically insignificant. A census survey in 1900 placed nine of the eleven Confederate states at the top of a list of states with the highest percentage of native-born state residents, averaging roughly 90 percent (South Carolina was the highest at 95 percent). By contrast, the states ranging from the Northeast through the Great Lakes averaged around 60 percent native-born residents (with Minnesota, Massachusetts, and Rhode Island closer to 50 percent); the rest were migrants from other states or from abroad.[19]

The South also had the nation's lowest literacy rates. In Louisiana, Alabama, Mississippi, South Carolina, and Georgia in 1890, two out of every five people aged ten years and older could not read. Illiteracy among their white populations averaged around one in five. The nationwide illiteracy rate was 13.3 percent. In Massachusetts the rate was 5 percent, in New York 4.4 percent, and in Illinois 3.9 percent, and in these states the large majority of illiterate people were immigrants who had not been educated in the states' public schools.[20] In terms of religious affiliation, the South was an island dominated by traditional Protestant denominations such as Baptists and Methodists (and to a lesser extent Episcopalians and Presbyterians), but with very few Roman Catholics (save for southern Louisiana and southern Texas, where ethnic migrant groups who had arrived before the Civil War remained a presence). The South had none of the offshoots of the colonial religious traditions developed in the Northeast (Congregationalists, Unitarians, Quakers, Latter-day Saints) and very few members of the German-dominated Lutheran or Reformed churches. The South had almost no Jews.[21] In other words, while the rest of the nation was experiencing intense contact, mixing, and sometimes conflict among varied ethnic and religious traditions, the South clung to pre–Civil War ethnic and religious patterns.

Varying conditions of employment, labor, industry, and trade profoundly differentiated the nation's regional economies as well. Plate 42 (fig. 10.7) from the 1890 census atlas shows the distribution of wage earners in American industries; as of 1890, about a third of all Americans worked for wages of some kind. Wage earners in industry and manufacturing were heavily concentrated in the region stretching from Ohio through Pennsylvania and New York to New England. They were least concentrated in the Cotton Belt of the South, from North Carolina to Texas. By contrast, wage earners in agriculture—farm hands of one kind or another—were heavily concentrated in the former Confederacy. Henry Grady, editor of the *Atlanta Constitution,* conveyed these stark regional economic differences in an 1889 speech at the Bay State Club of Boston in which he described the funeral of a poor man from Georgia: "The South didn't furnish a thing on earth for that funeral but the corpse and the hole in the ground. There they put him away and the clods rattled down on his coffin, and they buried him in a New York coat and a Boston pair of shoes and a pair of breeches from Chicago and a shirt from Cincinnati, leaving him nothing to carry into the next world with him to remind him of the country in which he lived, and for which he fought for four years, but the chill of blood in his veins and the marrow in his bones."[22]

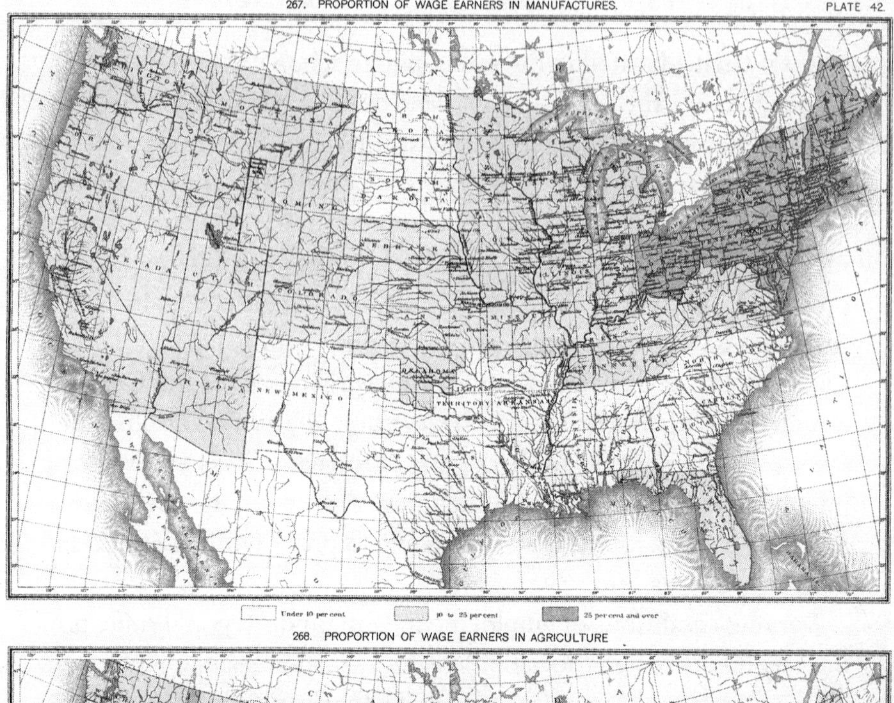

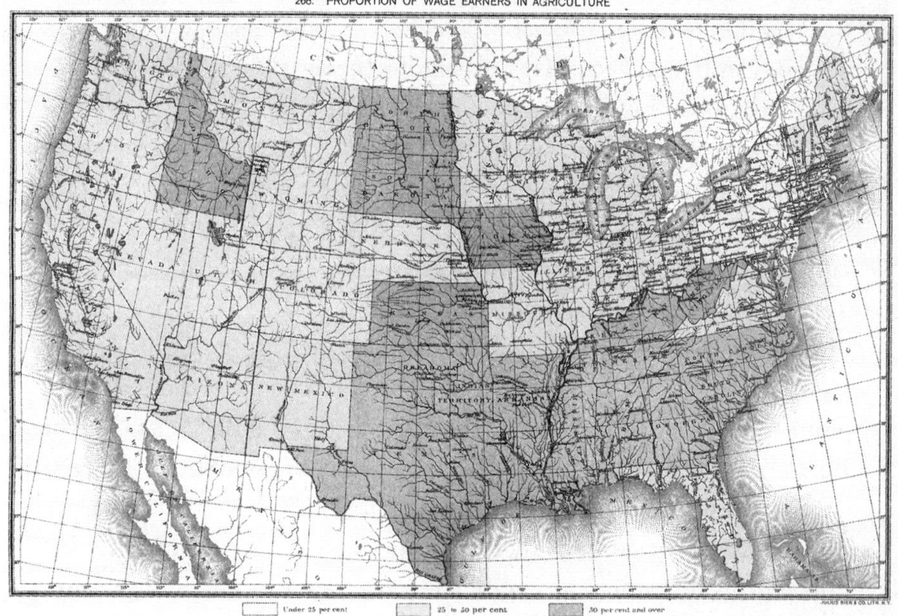

FIGURE 10.7. Proportion of wage earners in manufacturing and agriculture. The upper map depicts wage earners in manufacturing, and the lower map depicts wage earners in agriculture, but the scales on the two maps differ. In the *upper* map, the darkest color shows states where greater than 25 percent of wage earners work in manufacturing. In the *lower* map, the darkest color shows states where greater than 50 percent of wage earners work in agriculture.

Nationwide, the categories of "farmer" or "farm laborer" remained the most common for males in 1890 by an enormous margin—over 8 million American men listed these as their principal occupation, along with another 2 million unspecified "laborers." The next largest group, at about 1.3 million, was the female-dominated "servants" category. After that the numbers dropped off sharply: "Iron and steel workers," a predominantly male occupation, employed fewer than 200,000 Americans.[23] The total number of Americans working in "manufactures" of all kinds came to 4 million, less than half the number in farming.[24] Furthermore, many American farmers did not work for wages at all, but owned, rented, or worked as sharecroppers on farms and received their compensation at harvest time when they sold their crops. In sharecropping, the former Confederacy predominated. South Carolina, Georgia, Mississippi, and Alabama, where more than half of all farms were rented or farmed on shares, headed the list. In the Northeast, which had the highest values of farm products per acre of improved land, sharecropping was virtually nonexistent.[25] The cumulative effects of all these social conditions are evident in the map showing the "True Valuation of Real and Personal Property per Capita, 1890" (fig. 10.8), in which the former Confederate states are at the lowest levels—below $500 per capita. The immense destruction brought on by the Southern states' violent rebellion was responsible for the South's poverty, for in 1860 Southern states had been among the wealthiest in the nation, with Mississippi atop the list in per capita wealth.[26] Making matters worse, the Southern states now had the nation's highest state debt per capita. Even the patterns of national commerce in 1890 worked to exclude the South. Interstate flows of goods, payments, and credit all strongly connected the Northeast with the expanding West but excluded the former Confederacy.[27]

In 1892, the Christian socialist clergyman Francis Bellamy composed the "Pledge of Allegiance" as part of his campaign to put an American flag in every public schoolhouse in the United States. His cousin, Edward Bellamy, author of the wildly popular utopian novel *Looking Backward* (1888), was the celebrated inspiration of Nationalist political clubs and *The Nationalist* monthly magazine. But at the

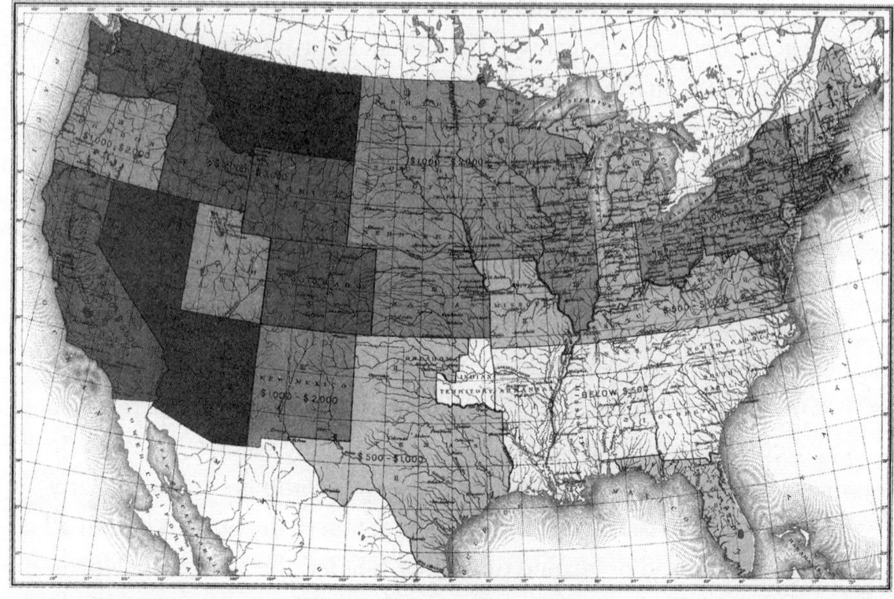

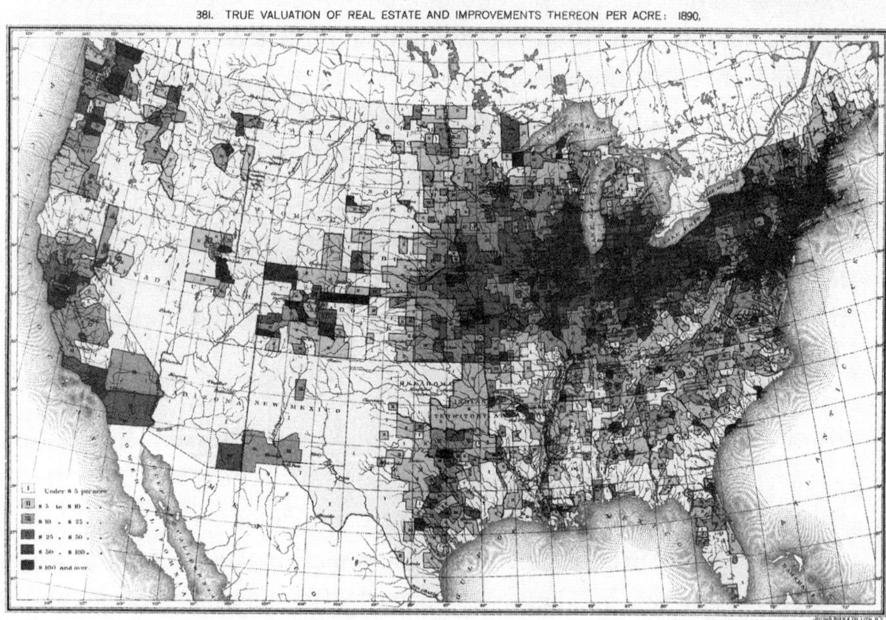

FIGURE 10.8. True valuation of real and personal property per capita, 1890. The lighter the color, the lower the property per capita ratio. States such as Montana, Nevada, and Arizona have very high ratios because of their very low populations. The bottom map, showing the value of real estate and improvements on a per acre basis for every U.S. county, reinforces the stark divide in wealth between the North and the South, twenty-five years after the Civil War ended.

end of the republic's first century under the Philadelphia Constitution, the "one Nation indivisible" that the Bellamy cousins dreamed of remained wholly aspirational.

The census affords us this social portrait of a tripartite American nation in 1890, but what did the *government* of the United States look like after the first century under the Constitution? With the admission of six new states (Washington, Montana, North and South Dakota, Idaho, and Wyoming) in 1889–90, the continental state-making project, a major focus of national government effort since 1790, was nearly complete. So what was left for it to do?

During the nation's first century, the bulk of revenue collection and governmental expenditure took place at the local and state levels, much as the Constitution's framers had expected. In the social and political circumstances of the 1780s, this made good sense. The individual states were already large by eighteenth-century standards. Communication across great distances was difficult. As the colonists had complained in the revolt against British rule, a central government located thousands of miles away could not be expected to know the interests of local populations. States and counties, cities and towns, were the appropriate institutions to carry out most government functions.[28]

The "police power" lay with state and local governments—they had by far the most direct involvement with quotidian issues of governance. They spent money on education, health care, poor relief, police and fire departments, sanitation, prisons, transportation, and governmental operations. By contrast, the federal government spent money in only three categories: military forces, the Post Office, and "general public services." The last (and least costly) of these involved maintaining the basic operations of government, including the federal court system and the other (non–Post Office) cabinet departments (State, Treasury, Justice, Interior, Agriculture), which included the Customs Service (for revenue collection), and the Bureau of Indian Affairs.[29] During the Civil War, massive military expenditures temporarily disrupted this traditional pattern. In 1865, the federal government outspent combined state and local governments by a ratio of eight to one. But by 1890, the older pattern had been restored; state and local governments spent more than half again as much as the federal government.

In 1890, the United States government collected $464 million in revenue. Just over $400 million (86 percent of the total) came from taxation in two forms: customs duties on foreign imported goods and excise taxes on domestically produced alcohol and tobacco products. These were the *only* taxes levied by the national government. The remaining $60 million came from the operations of the U.S. Post Office—customers paying for postage. By comparison, the nation's largest single railroad, the Pennsylvania Railroad, had more revenue and employed more workers than the Post Office. The nation's railroads collectively took in and spent three times as much money as the federal government did.[30] The entire federal government was funded by small taxes on American consumers' purchases of imported goods and domestic nonessentials plus the fees charged for communications, mostly paid by the business community which relied heavily on efficient mail service.[31]

These simple forms of taxation yielded revenue some $80 million in excess of federal expenditures in 1890, which amounted to $384 million. About three-quarters of that spending went to three areas: $173 million for defense, $66 million for operating the Post Office, and $36 million for interest on the national debt, still left over from the massive government borrowing during the Civil War. Federal spending was so limited in part because state and local governments were the locus of the police power. The legislatures of the states took on the functions of their colonial predecessors, administering the internal development of each new state as its population grew and their needs expanded. Local governments were the largest source of government expenditure in 1890, outspending the states by a ratio of almost seven to one. Local governments collectively spent $488 million compared to the federal government's $384 million.

In 1890, it was difficult to conceive of *national* programs of government action involving extensive expenditures that would be widely useful and could be administered equitably across the three extraordinarily different sub-nations of the United States. Continental state making and Indigenous displacement were largely complete—there was little more for the federal government to do to realize its founding project. But with the recent admission of a large number of Western states with small populations, the West was now significantly overrepresented in the U.S. Senate. In the South, Reconstruction had failed, rejected by Southern white supremacists in their quest for power within their states.[32] By suppressing the vote of African Americans and many poor whites as well, a Southern white minority controlled the region's politics and was disproportionately represented in the House. This left the nation's most populous region, the Northeast, in an embattled position in both House and Senate, pursuing very different interests from its Western and Southern regional competitors. So what kind of legislative programs could the national government pursue under these conditions?

In the 51st Congress, from March 1889 to March 1891, the Republican Party held majorities in both houses. This was the first time since 1875 that a single party controlled the presidency and both houses, which meant that it could be an activist Congress by nineteenth-century standards. Critics called it the "Billion Dollar Congress" because of the new spending measures it introduced (although annual federal budgets remained far short of the billion-dollar figure until World War I). But the specific programs this Congress enacted, ambitious as they seemed at the time, highlight the *limits* of the national government's reach in the nineteenth century. The big-ticket item the 51st Congress passed was the Dependent and Disability Pension Act, providing pensions for all Union military veterans who were unable to work, regardless of how they became disabled. This was the Republican Party's way, now that it was in power again, of rewarding aging Civil War veterans for their service. By 1893, the $159 million devoted to disabled veterans' pensions would be the single largest item on the national budget, more than a third of the total.[33]

The remainder of the major legislation in the 51st Congress was devoted to using the federal government's regulatory power to balance the demands of different interest groups across the nation's regions. Although it did not create major programs involving extensive spending, regulatory authority is one area where the federal government extended its influence over society.[34] The McKinley Tariff Act, sponsored by the Ohio congressman and future president, raised duties on foreign imports to very high rates to protect U.S. industry from foreign competition; this favored the industrial Northeast. The McKinley Tariff's revenues were meant to fund the new pensions for disabled Civil War veterans. At the same time, Congress passed the Sherman Anti-Trust Act, designed to prevent American industries from forming monopolies, as well as the Sherman Silver Purchase Act, which expanded the money supply to appease America's agricultural and mining sectors in compensation for the McKinley Tariff.[35] The Immigration Act of 1891 extended the federal government's power over who could enter the country, excluding potential immigrants with criminal histories or dangerous diseases, as well as those likely to become public charges. It also developed a federal bureaucracy that included the opening of Ellis Island in New York. The Forest Reserve Act gave the president power to set aside forests as part of the public domain in order to prevent large corporations from exploiting the nation's timber resources. In 1890, lumber products, valued at over $600 million (nearly twice the national government's overall expenditures), were the nation's largest single category of manufactures, exceeding flour, textiles, iron, and steel. Yet the limits of the country's biological resources were becoming apparent as the continental expansion project reached its end.

The Forest Reserve Act was a measure that William the Conqueror, King John, or any other medieval English king would easily have understood: the need to keep a country's limited strategic resources from being wasted by excessive consumption.[36] But the Forest Reserve Act and other legislation of the 51st Congress indicated the government's emerging understanding that the *scale* of production and consumption was rapidly changing. The change was driven by organized corporate forces of industrial production and distribution that far surpassed the medieval imagination. The new scale already exceeded the capacities of an eighteenth-century federal government's structure to contain or regulate it. Edward Bellamy's 1888 novel, *Looking Backward,* imagined that by the year 2000, a solution to the problems of the industrial era would be achieved. But in Bellamy's imagination, it was not government in its current form that solved these problems, but rather the consolidation of ever-larger industrial and commercial monopolies into a single mega-corporation, run collectively by the people. The future lay in a business that essentially became the state: "a single syndicate representing the people . . . [;] the nation . . . organized as the one great business corporation in which all other corporations were absorbed."[37] The problems *Looking Backward* lamented were of a scale that surpassed the capacities of the current federal government to solve under the terms of its 1787 Constitution.

The stark regional disparities and economic inequalities of the Gilded Age, the divide between urban-industrial and rural-agrarian America, the concentrated power of corporations, and the widespread perception of corruption in state and urban political machines generated new political movements. Starting in the 1890s, members of the Populist and Progressive movements promoted structural reforms in national government that ultimately led to four new amendments to the Constitution: the Sixteenth Amendment (1913), allowing the creation of a federal income tax; the Seventeenth Amendment (1913), mandating the direct popular election of U.S. Senators; the Eighteenth Amendment (1919), prohibiting the production, sale, or transportation of intoxicating liquors in the United States; and the Nineteenth Amendment (1920), granting women citizens the right to vote.

The Eighteenth Amendment, promoted by temperance activists for decades as a solution to chronic social problems, stands out from every other constitutional amendment in having little bearing on the functioning of the national government itself, though its enforcement created new additions to national policing powers. Resistance and social unrest caused by widespread evasion led to Prohibition's repeal in 1933, though agencies such as the Federal Bureau of Investigation that it had spawned remained.[38]

By contrast, the Nineteenth Amendment's prohibition of the denial of the right to vote on the basis of sex is in line with earlier and subsequent amendments, especially the post–Civil War Fifteenth Amendment. Although women's suffrage expanded Americans' eligibility to participate in national governance, it did not address concerns about the structure and functions of the national government itself. It did, however, acknowledge the dramatic social changes since the nation's founding, when voting rights were premised on the household as the fundamental unit of economic production. In the premodern agrarian world, it was assumed that a male head of household would be the voice of the dependents under his authority: women, children, servants, apprentices, or slaves. The Nineteenth Amendment recognized that for large and ever-increasing portions of the nation, these older social conventions no longer reflected the reality of women's lives and could not represent their interests.[39]

The Sixteenth and Seventeenth Amendments, both ratified in 1913, did more to alter the basic premises of what the United States government represented and how it functioned than any other formal amendments in the nation's history. The Sixteenth Amendment, allowing for a federal income tax, aimed to provide expanded revenue for the nation's growing needs and make the federal tax system less regressive. Value-added taxes, such as the customs and excise duties that had funded the federal government over its first century, are based on consumption, which is usually a larger portion of the income of the poor than of the rich. The income tax was designed to require the rich to pay more than the poor, and to avoid the regional political conflicts that the tariff system had long engendered.[40] The Seventeenth Amendment called for the direct popular election of senators in response to fears that the Senate was being corrupted, either by millionaires buying the votes of state legislators who selected the senators or by dysfunctional state legislatures incapable of filling vacant Senate seats. In the 1890s, the People's (or Populist) Party, an insurgent movement representing farmers and laborers in opposition to corporate interests, endorsed both a graduated income tax and the direct popular election of senators.[41] By 1908, many individual states had passed laws to elect their senators by popular vote. It's not merely coincidental that Charles A. Beard published his *Economic Interpretation of the Constitution of the United States* (1913) in the same year these two amendments were finally ratified. Beard thrust into the national conversation a powerful argument that the Constitution was originally designed to protect the economic interests of the nation's wealthy elites. Surely the new amendments would help to rectify these deep-seated flaws.

Yet in attempting to do so, each of these amendments undermined the logic of representative government hammered out in Philadelphia in the summer of 1787. In order to avoid the Supreme Court challenges that had struck down earlier income tax legislation, the Sixteenth Amendment eliminated the clause in Article I, Section 2 of the Constitution that linked the number of representatives each state received to the amount of direct taxes it would have to pay to the national government, determined by each state's population.[42] The idea behind this clause, perhaps the strongest inheritance of the colonies' rebellion against Britain and an Anglo-American constitutional principle reaching back to Magna Carta, was that representation and taxation must be tightly connected. If the government demands payment directly from the people, then the people must have a say in approving such decisions and in fairly distributing the amounts to be paid.

The apportionment of direct taxes by states according to their population was an indispensable component of the central compromise at the Philadelphia Convention. The compromise created a popular representative system that was national in scope without doing away with the existence and significance of the states themselves—the entities coming together to create the national constitution. In 1787, smaller and poorer states had argued that the large, rich states would use the power granted them by proportional representation in the national legislature to run roughshod over the small states. The fear was that large states with many votes in Congress would devise systems of taxation that shifted heavy financial burdens onto smaller, less populous states while benefitting larger ones. By pegging the apportionment of direct taxation amounts to representation levels, the compromise guaranteed that any governmental schemes the large states made would have to be paid for proportionally by the large states as well.[43]

The other essential compromise that had allowed the convention to move past the impasse over the Virginia Plan was the agreement that all the states would have equal votes in the Senate, despite the obvious fact that the states were far from equal in size, population, wealth, and power. The 1787 Constitution's provision for state legislatures (rather than popular election) to choose the senators emphasized the power of this fiction of the equality of the states. By this logic, the size of a state's population was irrelevant because the Senate was not representing people, it was representing states as constitutional entities, as bodies politic. This compromise—maintaining the equality of states in the Senate—was intended to give small states an additional measure of safety against the power of states with large populations and plentiful land.

Together, the two amendments of 1913 quietly dismantled the ancient logic of representation embodied in the 1787 Constitution. The fundamental concept of representation in the agrarian age when the constitution was framed assumed that x amount of land + y numbers of people = z amount of wealth and power. The Sixteenth Amendment forcefully declared that this logic no longer applied to the process of apportioning taxation in the United States. Congress could now introduce measures that would tax income wherever in the union that income happened to be, regardless of state boundaries, heedless of the need to apportion national taxation evenly across states by population. It could, in the words of historian Robin Einhorn, "tax in proportion to the distribution of income rather than the distribution of population."[44] Supporters of the Sixteenth Amendment knew this full well. It was eagerly ratified by Southern and Western state legislatures because they knew that the burden of the income tax would not fall heavily upon their states and that their overrepresentation in Congress would give them additional control over how—and where—the income tax revenue would be spent.

In 1916, the first year with recorded statistics, 60 percent of all the national income tax revenue came from just three states—New York, Pennsylvania, and Illinois—where five of the nation's ten largest cities were located, and where America's industry, banking, and finance were centered. New York alone contributed 45 percent of the nation's income tax, though it had only 11 percent of the nation's population. New Yorkers paid nearly seven dollars per capita in income tax; people from Alabama paid ten cents per capita. In South Carolina it was six cents, while in the Dakotas, South and North, it was eight and nine cents, respectively. Citizens of Illinois paid ten times as much as citizens of Georgia.[45] Although these extreme differences diminished over time as taxable wage income increased nationwide, the disparities have not disappeared.[46] In constitutional terms, the Sixteenth Amendment weakened the tight link between representation and taxation at the federal level, subtly but decisively undermining the rationale of the compromise in 1787 that apportioned each state's delegation in the House of Representatives according to its population.

In its own, more subtle way, the Seventeenth Amendment had a similar effect. The Philadelphia Convention delegates agreed to create the Senate as a body where all the states were equal even though this was obviously not the case, in either population or land area. The size of their populations was irrelevant to the representation the states received in the upper chamber of Congress. The convention therefore placed the choice of senators in the hands of the state legislatures—small numbers of men already elected by the state's voters ostensibly to advance the best interests of their states. These legislators were presumed to have the wisdom and knowledge to select the state's best men for the Senate.[47] Senators had to be older (and presumably more mature) than members of the House. Senators served longer terms than House members, faced reelection less frequently, and could take the long view on national issues. All in all, the Senate was meant to be a more august deliberative body than the House, at a remove from shifting winds of popular sentiments.

By changing the selection process to direct popular election, the Seventeenth Amendment further muddled the logic of representation. It suggested that now U.S. Senators *did* represent the people of their states (just as members of the House of Representatives represented the people of the districts within their states). Candidates for the Senate would now appeal directly to the people in order to garner a victorious majority of voters. But why, if they were popularly elected, was the size of the population of each state still irrelevant? Why should eighty thousand people in Nevada get to choose two senators just like New York, which in the 1910 US Census had more than one hundred times as many people? The nineteenth-century process for admitting new states under the National Ratio—requiring that a territory had at least the population represented on average by each member of Congress before it could apply for statehood—had been intended to equalize the population of the states. It had worked well through the 1850s, but it had failed in the West. Since the admission of Nevada in 1864, inequality among state populations had been growing. By allowing the direct election of senators without allocating senators to the states by population, the Seventeenth Amendment made the failure to sustain equality among the states all the more obvious, as minority rule via the upper chamber of Congress became all the more likely. The late-nineteenth century influx of new states with tiny populations meant that majorities in the Senate could readily be formed by Senators who represented very few people, outvoting Senators who represented large populations.

In the century since the Seventeenth Amendment, this problem has grown worse. The U.S. population at the 2020 US Census was 331 million; the average population of the fifty states is about 6.6 million. That would be the Senate's equivalent of a "National Ratio" for each state. Today only seventeen of the nation's states are above that population figure; thirty-three are below it. In 2020, twenty-one of the fifty states had populations of *less than half* of 6.6 million—barely qualifying for even a single senator if the Senate were a representative body. Six states had more than twice the 6.6 million average (deserving at least four Senators). In the 1910 census, only sixteen of the forty-six states had less than half the national average population, and only four states had more than twice the national average. In 1910, twenty of the forty-six states had populations above the mean, with only twenty-six below the mean. No matter how you measure it, the nation's population was more evenly distributed across the states in the 1910s than it is in the 2020s. The polarization between populous and sparse states continues to grow.

These formal constitutional changes in the Sixteenth and Seventeenth Amendments, together with the nearly contemporaneous decision by Congress in 1911 not to increase the number of members of the House of Representatives beyond 435, have pushed the nation back in the direction of the "virtual representation" characteristic of Britain's Parliament in the eighteenth century, the very position that the

American rebellion and the early state constitutions had repudiated. Recall that British members of Parliament did not consider themselves to be the representatives merely of the voters from their home districts. In some cases—the notorious "rotten boroughs"—there were districts with no voters at all. Instead, each member of Parliament was meant to act for the good of the entire realm, to represent "virtually" all the common people in the kingdom (i.e., not the aristocrats), whether or not they were entitled to vote (most were not) or lived in a district that sent someone to Westminster. This was the basis on which the British government could claim that the colonies were represented in Parliament—virtually—despite the fact they could send no one there to speak for them: neither could Birmingham, a booming English industrial city larger than any city in America at the time of the Revolution.

With their successful rebellion, Americans had decisively rejected virtual representation. They insisted on the close relationship between direct taxation and popular representation determined by fixed geographical districts where equity would be carefully maintained across time. The two amendments of 1913, together with the fixing of the House of Representatives at 435 members, loosened that tight conceptual link between taxation and representation. By the late nineteenth century, it had already become clear that the original plan of admitting new states of relatively similar area to equalize the disparities among the original thirteen was faltering. The huge new states in the arid West were not attracting sufficient population to make them comparable to the older agricultural states east of the 100th meridian. Further growth in these states would require resources far beyond the means of their small populations, resources only the federal government could provide. Here too, the link between direct taxation and popular representation would be undermined by the advent of the federal income tax.

If the 1913 amendments had been only the beginning of the formal retooling of the U.S. Constitution for the twentieth century—with further amendments to deal with new practices of representation and taxation, new powers of Congress and the executive, and new procedures for administering a larger and more active federal government—then the widening gap between the constitutional theory that gave birth to the United States and the evolving practice of government might well have been resolved. But that is not what happened. Instead, the formal constitutional amendment process ground to a halt.

Yes, there have been ten additional amendments in the century since the Sixteenth and Seventeenth were passed. But two of these were the passage and then repeal of Prohibition—a wash. Four of the other eight focused on removing voting barriers for citizens—women's suffrage (Nineteenth), Electoral College votes for the District of Columbia (Twenty-Third), elimination of poll taxes (Twenty-Fourth), establishing eighteen as the voting age (Twenty-Sixth). The other four made technical adjustments to existing constitutional provisions, such as the date of the president's inauguration (Twentieth), presidential term limits and line of succession (Twenty-Second and Twenty-Fifth), and lastly, a rule prohibiting the current Congress from changing its own salaries (Twenty-Seventh)—an amendment originally proposed in 1789. While the expansion of the franchise broadened individual rights, none of these later amendments contained substantive reforms to adapt the national government's fundamental powers and functions to the new conditions of twentieth-century society. This project, barely begun with the Sixteenth and Seventeenth Amendments, remains unfinished.

11

The Great Transformation

THE MAKING OF A NATIONAL GOVERNMENT AND A NATIONAL SOCIETY

> Our economy is not agricultural any longer.
> Our economy is the Federal Government.
> We no longer farm in Mississippi cotton-fields.
> We farm now in Washington corridors
> and Congressional committee-rooms.
>
> —WILLIAM FAULKNER, 1956

IN THE 1780S, inequality among the thirteen states in land and population presented a difficult challenge to the American confederation. The constitutional reforms of that decade provided the national government with tools to address the problem. By 1848, when Wisconsin, the last of the nation's original territory, was admitted to statehood, the thirty states in the union were far more equal in population and land than the original thirteen had been sixty years earlier. The constitutional plan was working.

By 1890, the problem of the 1780s was returning, as Congress began to admit new states in the arid West that would fail to gain much of a settler population, states that would be wildly overrepresented in Congress. But the nation's challenges of inequality were no longer exclusively or even primarily at the state level. As we have seen in the previous chapter, at the end of the nation's first century there were three distinct regional sub-nations within the United States: the populous and prosperous Northeast; the impoverished South, stagnant in the aftermath of civil war; and the arid West, where the expansionist methods devised at the founding had foundered. The older constitutional system—the nineteenth-century Domesday Machine—was not designed to meet these new challenges. Over the next century, the nation would devise new methods to transform the land and people—the body of society—in even more startling ways than in its first century. Using new powers and resources, and taking advantage of opportunities afforded by the emergencies of economic depression and war, the federal government would promote the internal migration of the nation's population and the redistribution of its wealth in ways that would reduce the sharp differences among the nation's three regions that the nineteenth century had produced.

New political movements of the late nineteenth century had already pressed for constitutional change. In certain respects, the decade of the 1910s, which saw four new amendments to the constitution, resembled the 1780s, a decade of incremental progress toward constitutional reform to meet the nation's challenges. But unlike in the 1780s, there was no culminating moment, no constitutional convention to propose sweeping changes—progress stalled out around 1920 with the Nineteenth Amendment. However, with the income tax amendment in place by 1913, and with a developing pattern of government intervention in economic development, especially in the West, the federal government was amassing sufficient power and resources to launch major transformations in the social order and remake the body of American society.

The huge land grants that the federal government awarded to transcontinental railroad companies during the Civil War marked the start of a trend in which Congress distributed the nation's resources to promote settlement and commercial activity in underpopulated or impoverished regions. The subsequent movement to regulate the nation's railroads as public utilities, ensuring fair prices and access to the nation's transport system, culminated in the creation of the Interstate Commerce Commission in 1887. This sequence would, in many ways, be a pattern for the twentieth century. The federal government would recognize a challenge in the lives of citizens, often directed to the problem (or opportunity) by wealthy and powerful individuals. The government's intervention would inaugurate social change on a large scale, with widespread public engagement in new endeavors. As these new endeavors developed, their scale and significance for the lives of many Americans would require federal government regulation and support. By the end of the nineteenth century, as the national government expanded its regulatory capacities across an array of social issues from public health and safety to markets and commerce, the police power was, in the words of historian William Novak, "going national" and was being used to reshape the nation.[1]

Often associated with the New Deal, the expansion of the size, power, and reach of the federal government experienced a slow run-up that the Great Depression and World War II then accelerated. Long before the New Deal, the growing scale of American corporations, along with the continental reach of American railroads, communications, retail organizations, food distribution systems, and other essentials of daily life, exceeded the regulatory capacities of individual states. The national government stepped into the breach, shifting the assumptions of the founding era that the states would be the locus of the police power. But beyond merely regulating existing systems, the national government would also take up the challenge of addressing the disparities across the republic's three great sub-nations.

This wholesale transformation of American society required a comparable remaking of the United States government, an explosive growth in the size and complexity of the state to develop and administer the necessary programs. Once again, we can turn to the U.S. census and its sophisticated measurement tools as a way to simplify and visualize this transformation, to get a visceral feel for an impossibly complicated subject. We begin, as in the previous chapter, with a Domesday assessment of the nation in 1990, but then turn to the story of a single place in the arid West—Phoenix, Arizona—for a dynamic view of a city, one among many, that exemplifies the transformation of land, people, and government across the twentieth century.

———

In 1990, at the end of the second century under the Philadelphia Constitution, the U.S. Census Bureau employed more than half a million enumerators, an elevenfold increase from 1890, to tally the nation's population. The 1890 census had published twenty-six thousand pages of information. The 1990 census published fifteen times as much data.[2] The number of Americans quadrupled across this century, from 62 million in 1890 to 250 million in 1990. Because the land area possessed by the United States did not change significantly, population density quadrupled as well (just as it had in the nation's first century).

While the explosive population growth that characterized the nineteenth century slowed somewhat across the twentieth, territorial expansion within North America ceased altogether. Without new land to occupy, the nation's growing population continued its trend toward urbanization. But the enormous expansion of America's suburbs set twentieth-century urbanization apart. The nation's metropolitan areas ballooned away from the central city. The rise of the automobile as a dominant force in America's economy and culture generated rapid movement of urban workers to the suburbs, especially after World War II. By 1990, more than half of the nation's urban population lived in suburbs rather than central cities.[3]

In the nineteenth century, urbanization had been a major factor dividing the United States into distinct sub-nations—the heavily urban Northeast versus the rural South and the lightly populated West. In the twentieth century, the continuing growth of cities and suburbs told radically different stories. One was the rise not just of urbanization but of "metropolitanization." In the nineteenth century, much of the nation's urban population had dwelled in relatively small towns; with "urban" defined by the census as places with more than eight thousand residents. Many of these towns were scattered across the countryside, the county seats and market towns that served as islands of commerce, government, and culture in the endless sea of rural America. But in the twentieth century, the Census Bureau introduced a new concept: the "metropolitan area" consisting of a "core area containing a substantial population nucleus together with adjacent counties having a high degree of social and economic integration with that core."[4] At the beginning of the twentieth century, less than three in ten people lived in these "metropolitan areas." By the end of the century, eight out of every ten Americans did.

The United States became an overwhelmingly metropolitan country by virtue of the tremendous expansion of cities and their suburbs in the American South and West. In 1890, there was only one city in the former Confederacy, New Orleans, with more than one hundred thousand residents. Only two such cities, Denver and San Francisco, were in the Western half of the nation. All the rest, twenty-one others, were in the Northeast (fig. 11.1). By 1990, this pattern had been completely altered. Dozens of large cities now stretched across the old Confederacy and into the far West. In the 1990 census, thirty of the nation's fifty largest cities were now in the South or the West, with California, Texas, and Florida accounting for more than half of these. In 1890, only one of the nation's ten largest cities, San Francisco, had been in the South or West. In 1990, six of the ten were in the South or West—Los Angeles, Houston, San Diego, Dallas, Phoenix, and San Antonio. This profound redistribution of the American population southward and westward was brought about by many forces, some of them long-standing—a continuation of nineteenth-century processes of immigration, industrialization, and urbanization. But other forces, in which a rapidly expanding federal government took a leading part, were radically new.

We can glimpse this dual transformation of society and government through one particular example: the rise of Phoenix, Arizona. Phoenix was founded in the aftermath of the Civil War in the Arizona Territory's Salt River Valley. Phoenix had a population of 3,152 in 1890, less than half the number to qualify as urban by the census standards at the time. Hundreds of years earlier the Hohokam people of this region had developed an irrigated farming system, digging more than one hundred

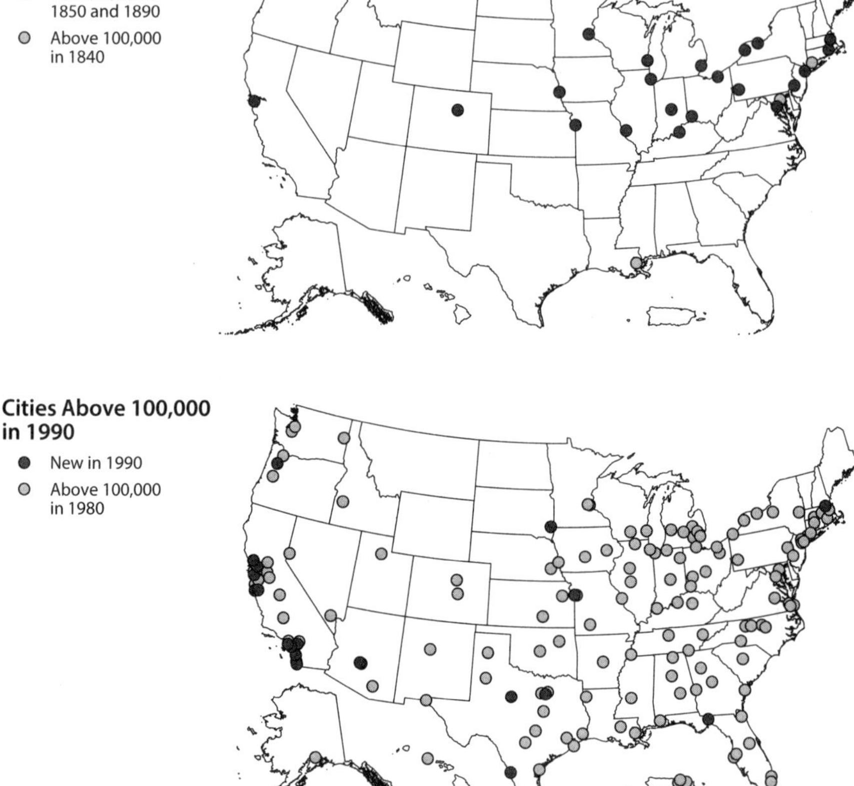

FIGURE 11.1. Cities above 100,000, 1890 versus 1990. Note that almost all of the "new" cities above 100,000 in 1990 are in the West and South; only one is located in the Northeast.

miles of canals that had supported one of the largest population concentrations north of Mexico. The Hohokam civilization dissipated around the year 1400, possibly due to drought or excessive irrigation.[5] The modern "Phoenix" was built on the dream of bringing an ancient civilization back to life, resuscitating the region's agricultural past through renewed irrigation. In 1867, a Confederate veteran named Jack Swilling formed the Swilling Irrigating and Canal Company, reusing and extending the ancient Hohokam canals to irrigate the region's fertile soil. Phoenix grew up around this renewed irrigation system, eventually becoming the seat of Maricopa County and the territorial capital of Arizona.[6]

Private irrigation ventures stimulated local agriculture with some success. But unlike urban areas in the well-watered East, Phoenix would never have grown beyond its modest nineteenth-century population without an infusion of capital, resources, and infrastructure. For these purposes, the federal government was indispensable. Early Phoenix was isolated, with no navigable water routes to the Pacific or Gulf coasts. The Southern Pacific Railroad connecting Los Angeles to New Orleans was built in the 1870s, but it ran well to the south of the Salt River Valley. A branch line connecting Phoenix to Maricopa on the Southern Pacific line was completed in 1887. It was subsidized by railroad bonds approved by the Arizona Territorial legislature and operated by a subsidiary of the Southern Pacific Railroad, itself the recipient of eighteen million acres in federal land grants as well as bonds and loans from the federal government.[7] The branch line connected Phoenix to distant markets for the alfalfa, grain, cotton, and citrus fruits grown on its irrigated lands. But for Phoenix to expand agricultural production to supply these new markets, it required more and better regulated water than the Salt River and its canals supplied.

Intermittent droughts and floods plagued Phoenix in the 1890s and reduced the region's cultivated acreage. In response, the federal government granted the first major project under the National Reclamation Act of 1902 to Phoenix. This act, described by historian Donald Worster as "the most important single piece of legislation in the history of the West," was designed to "reclaim" land for agriculture across the arid West by building dams and irrigation systems.[8] As John Wesley Powell had earlier observed in his geological survey of the West, rivers ran high in spring when the winter's snow melted, but by summer and fall water was scarce. Dams and reservoirs could preserve the water to distribute for year-round agricultural use. Private efforts at large-scale dam building across the West in the late nineteenth century had failed for lack of funds and engineering capacities. With the Reclamation Act, the federal government stepped in; money from the sale of public lands in arid regions would be set aside to pay for reclamation projects. After dams were built, the now-irrigated adjacent public lands would be sold for higher prices, creating a revolving fund to finance future reclamation.[9] The aim was much the same as that of nineteenth-century land grants to railroads; the future value of public lands would be increased by the investment in the railroad's transportation benefits. But dam building required greater and more direct government involvement than railroad grants.

The Bureau of Reclamation built the Roosevelt Dam in the Salt River sixty miles east of Phoenix. When completed in 1911 it was the world's largest masonry dam and formed the world's largest artificial lake, the first in a series of ever-larger hydraulic projects throughout the West. The Roosevelt Dam provided storage and flood control during wet years, distributed water during droughts, and generated cheap hydroelectric power for Phoenix as well. The reclamation project tripled the amount of irrigated farmland in the area as Phoenix's population grew from three thousand to nearly fifty thousand by 1930.[10] While dramatic rates of urban growth were familiar from nineteenth-century cities such as Chicago, the massive investment by the federal government in irrigation and electricity to promote this growth was utterly new.

The climate of Phoenix, with average rainfall of only seven inches per year and intense heat through the summer months, further limited the area's population growth until the advent of air conditioning. In the 1920s and '30s, Phoenix became a national center of the air-conditioning industry, and by 1940 it led the nation in home air-conditioning units. By 1960, one-quarter of all Phoenix homes had central air conditioning, half of all homes in Arizona had some form of air conditioning, and government buildings, schools, and universities were routinely built with it. Beginning in 1950, the federal government subsidized air conditioning: the Internal Revenue Service (IRS) offered tax deductions and credits for homeowners who installed it, and the Federal Housing Administration (FHA) encouraged lending institutions to penalize mortgagees in hot climates who did not install it. With more people moving to Phoenix and taking advantage of these new technologies, the region's demand for electricity grew.[11]

The growing demand was initially met by New Deal hydroelectric power projects. Well before the Depression, the Bureau of Reclamation had planned a gigantic dam on the Colorado River at the Arizona-Nevada border, equidistant from Phoenix and Los Angeles. Completed in 1935, the Hoover Dam and the reservoir it created at Lake Mead would supply water and energy on a colossal scale. But the New Deal marked a transition; subsequent Bureau of Reclamation projects, rather than being paid for by purchasers of the newly irrigated land, would now receive ever-larger budgets directly from congressional appropriations. Taxes paid by citizens across the nation would fund these projects, effectively transferring the nation's wealth to places deemed worthy by Congress.

The value of the crops produced on "reclaimed" Western farmland seldom justified the expense of dam building, but expected sales of hydroelectric power offset some of the costs. These energy-generating projects were called "cash register" dams by the Bureau of Reclamation. For the dams to earn that cash, large numbers of new customers for the energy had to migrate to the region. And for this growing population, Phoenix required ever-larger supplies of water. To that end, the federal government financed municipal pipelines in Phoenix and the pumping of ground water from the region's aquifers. Ground water pumping became so extensive that parts of the city began to sink. In the 1960s, a long-standing lawsuit between Arizona and California over Colorado River water rights was resolved. This allowed Congress to pass a new act spending billions of dollars to create the Central Arizona Project, a pipeline to deliver water to Phoenix from Lake Havasu, yet another reservoir on the Colorado River created by the Bureau of Reclamation.[12]

Phoenix grew exponentially, its population doubling in the 1940s and quadrupling in the 1950s (the fastest growth rate of any U.S. city that decade) to reach 439,000 by 1960. It was now the largest city in the Southwest, and the federal government fostered employment for the newcomers. World War II and the subsequent Cold War spawned the expansion of nearby military bases, along with defense, aviation, and technology industries. The reliable weather of its desert climate made this an ideal region for building and testing aircraft. Manufacturing plants built by the government during World War II were afterwards sold to private companies, often at a fraction of the original cost.[13] The jobs in these technical industries required an educated workforce; here too, the federal government's postwar promotion of higher education through programs like the GI Bill and grants from the National Science Foundation and NASA helped Phoenix to grow.[14] The small teachers college in neighboring Tempe founded by the territorial legislature in 1885 grew into Arizona State College by 1945. Renamed Arizona State University in 1958, it became one of the largest universities in the United States. In addition, Maricopa County developed one of the largest community college systems in the nation.[15] Once again, while the overall pattern of urban growth might seem familiar from older American cities, massive federal spending and government involvement in this expansion through environmental manipulation was unlike anything in the nineteenth century.

From 1945 to 1970, electricity consumption in Phoenix grew by 2,000 percent. The source of this energy shifted from the prewar hydroelectric dams, which could not keep pace with explosive demand, to new coal-fired power plants. These plants were built four hundred miles away on Navajo Indian territory on the Colorado Plateau and fueled by enormous strip mines run by private companies on federal land. With high-capacity power lines capable of transmitting electricity across great distances, Phoenix's sprawling metropolitan area now transformed the desert ecology and the lives of Indigenous peoples in northwestern New Mexico, hundreds of miles away from the city. Coal companies pumped millions of gallons of groundwater to wash coal and transport it to the Four Corners Power Station, depleting the aquifer on which the Hopi and Navajo Nations relied.[16]

Tourism became a major draw in postwar Phoenix. The city received federal funding to expand its airport and take a leading part in the air travel boom. The creation of the Social Security Administration by the New Deal and Congress's expansion of its benefits in the 1950s and '60s gave older Americans greater freedom to travel, along with financial security in retirement. With the arrival of "snowbirds" from Illinois, Indiana, Michigan, Ohio, Wisconsin, and Minnesota—the old Northwest

Territory—came the rise of planned retirement communities. Sun City, which opened in 1960 fifteen miles northwest of downtown Phoenix, was the first of a series of five such developments in Maricopa County. These unincorporated retirement communities became the model for other planned communities, a major factor in the postwar suburbanization of Phoenix. The federal government's mortgage loan guarantees through the GI Bill and the FHA, as well as the Interstate Highway System that poured federal revenues into road construction, fostered suburban growth away from the center city. By annexing neighboring property and merging with sprawling nearby suburbs, Phoenix became one of the nation's major metropolitan areas (fig. 11.2).[17] A century after the 1890 census, the village of 3,152 people in the Sonoran Desert had grown to a city just shy of 1 million. Today, with more than 1.7 million people, Phoenix is America's fifth largest city, the position held by St. Louis a century earlier. The Phoenix metropolitan area has 5 million residents, more than two-thirds of Arizona's total population.

Phoenix's history is illustrative but not unique. Variations of this story could be told for dozens of places across the American South and West over the twentieth century. Before the days of air conditioning, Southern Florida was mostly uninhabited. At its founding in 1896, Miami had a population of 300. Today it is the center of a metropolitan area of more than 6 million, and Florida has gone from thirty-second to third in the ranking of states by population. Four cities in Texas—Houston, San Antonio, Dallas, and Austin—each had fewer than 40,000 people in 1890. Their combined metro areas in 1990 were home to 7.8 million people. In 1890, California had one large city, San Francisco, ranked eighth in the nation, and two smaller ones, Los Angeles and Oakland, ranked fifty-seventh and sixtieth. In 1990, a century later, four of the nation's fifteen largest cities were in California, and fifteen of the top one hundred. Collectively, seventy of the one hundred largest cities in 1990 were located in the West or the South, both now heavily urbanized, a complete reversal of the situation in 1890. Some of the country's most rural regions at the start of the twentieth century had become its most urbanized by the beginning of the twenty-first (fig. 11.3).[18]

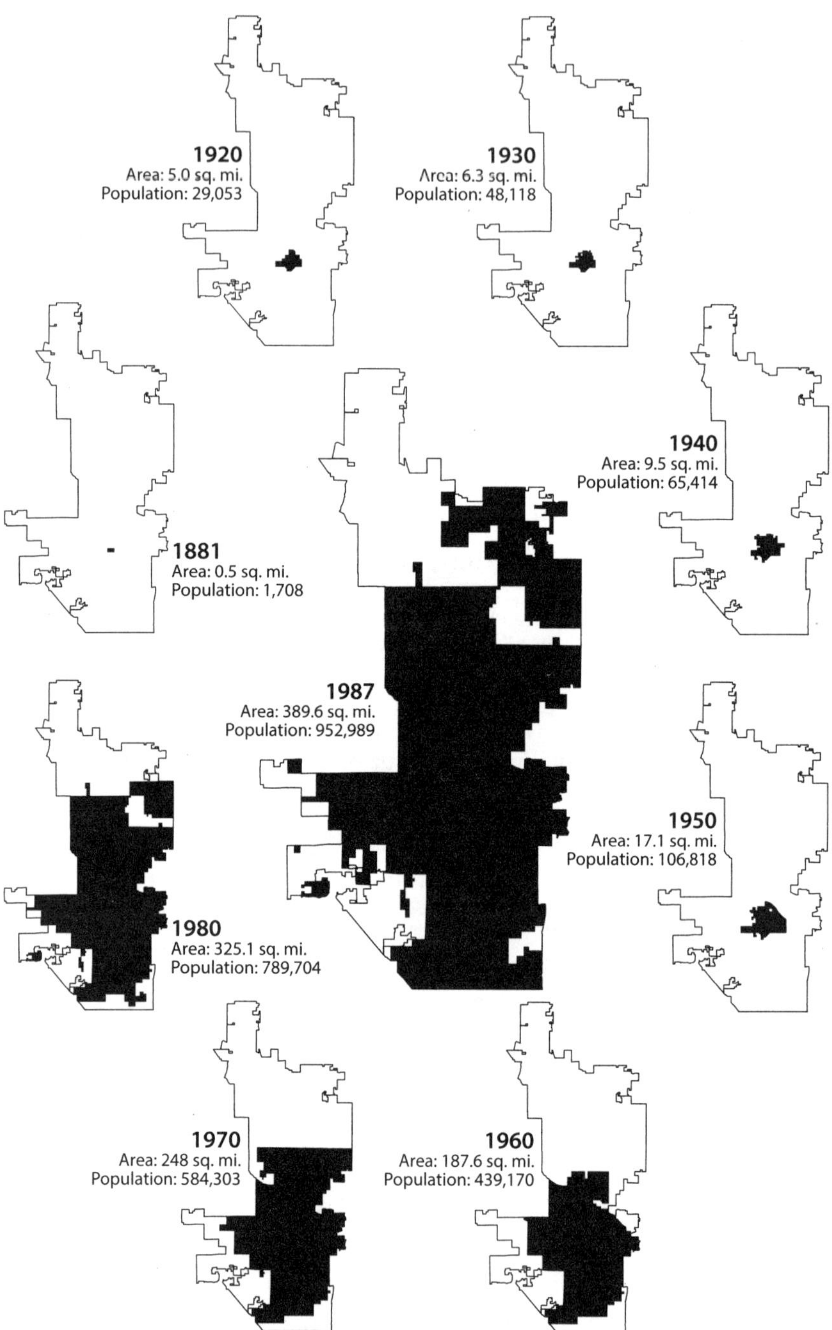

FIGURE 11.2. City of Phoenix Planning Department illustration of the city's spatial and population growth, 1881–1987. What this assemblage of maps cannot depict is the far wider geographical range of Phoenix's ecological footprint, its spatial reach for the vital water and energy resources necessary to make the urban space depicted here livable for large concentrations of human residents.

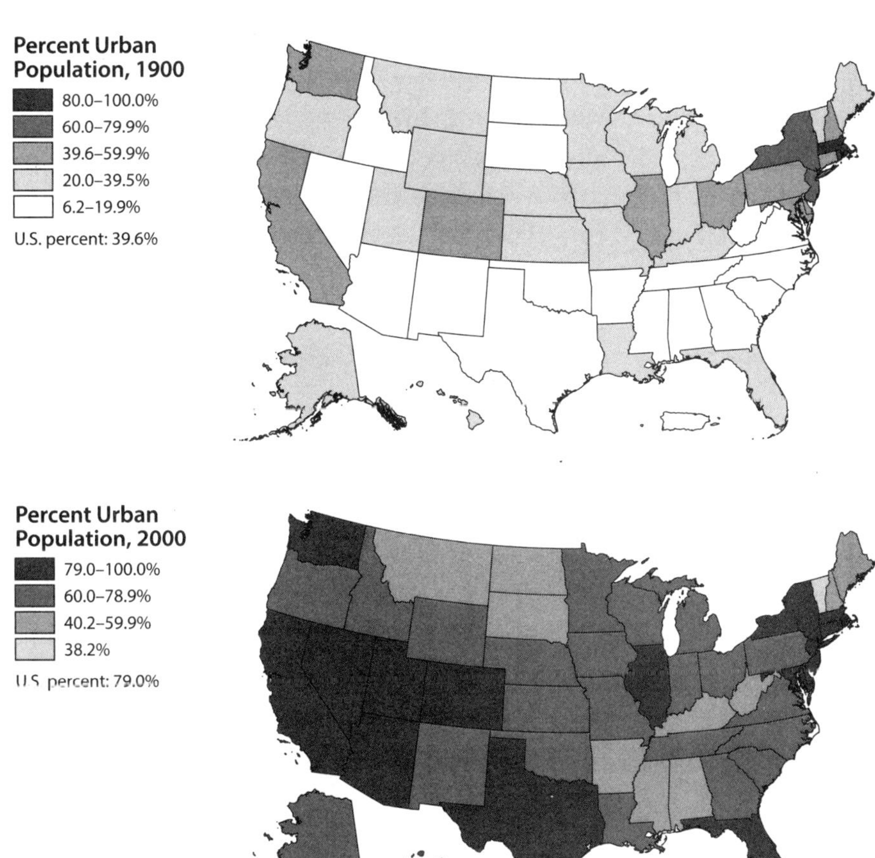

FIGURE 11.3. Percentage of urban population by state, 1900 and 2000. In 1900, states and territories such as Hawai'i, Nevada, Arizona, Texas, and Florida were all below the national average of 39.6 percent for urban populations; by 2000 they were all in the highest category, above 79 percent.

These changes came at a cost to some of the nation's most prominent urban places of the nineteenth century. The federal government's massive investment in the South and West, especially with the New Deal and the rise of "military Keynesianism" in World War II and the Cold War, was essentially a disinvestment in the Northeast as well, a geographical wealth transfer.[19] The policy choices of diverting federal resources to supply water, energy, and infrastructure to the West and South, and moving military installations and defense industries there as well, encouraged depopulation and stagnation in America's older cities. Differential aspects of other federal government policies, such as the exemption of agricultural and domestic workers from the New Deal's Wagner Act, which affirmed collective bargaining rights for labor, mitigated against the development of strong labor unions in the South. Cheap and non-union labor in the South and West encouraged factory owners in the Northeast to move operations to those regions.[20] St. Louis, Missouri, might be seen as Phoenix's counterpart in this process. America's fifth largest city in 1890, with 450,000 residents, St. Louis had shrunk to 400,000 by 1990, fallen to thirty-fourth place, and lost its National Football League franchise . . . to Phoenix. Of many similar examples, Detroit's story is perhaps the most dramatic. Already the nation's fifteenth largest city in 1890, Detroit was transformed by the automobile industry. By 1950, it was the nation's fifth largest city, with nearly 2 million residents. Since then it has lost 1.2 million residents and fallen to twenty-seventh place. Pittsburgh has likewise lost more than half of its residents since 1950, and dozens of smaller cities like Rochester, New York, and Worcester, Massachusetts, have experienced similar declines.[21]

Across the twentieth century, no other nation in the world experienced such a massive redistribution of its population. This extraordinary transformation in the urban character and regional distribution of the United States' population was accompanied by changes in every other category measured by the census—sex, race, ethnicity, immigration, internal migration, employment, education, poverty. By 1990, the country no longer consisted of three clear and distinct sub-nations; the increasing influence of the federal government in every sphere of American life served as a national homogenization project as well.

To see this transformation, we can begin with the racial and ethnic redistribution of the American population. Recall that in 1890, African Americans, the nation's largest racial minority at 11.9 percent of the population, continued to live mainly where they had lived before the Civil

War, in a band of territory running from Virginia to East Texas. A century later, while this region remained a center of Black population, the national distribution had changed dramatically. Beginning with the Great Migration of the 1910s and '20s and continuing through the World War II economic boom and the civil rights movement, African Americans left the South in large numbers. In 1890, most of America's largest cities were in the Northeast and had very small Black populations. By 1990, African Americans made up roughly the same percentage of the national population (12.1 percent) as in 1890, but every major city across the United States had significant Black populations. And by the year 2000 in Northern states such as Illinois, Michigan, and New York, the percentage of the population identifying as African American was similar to that in Alabama, Georgia, and South Carolina, while the percentage in Washington State and Minnesota resembled that in Kentucky and Texas (fig. 11.4).

Racial and ethnic categories that had barely registered in the 1890 census became significant elements in the late twentieth-century American population. Starting in the late nineteenth century and culminating in 1924, a series of congressional laws restricted immigration, freezing the racial and ethnic composition of the U.S. population where it had been as of the 1890 census. The immigration freeze would remain in place for nearly half a century. But after the Immigration and Nationality Act of 1965 eased these restrictions, immigrants from Asia, Africa, and southern and eastern Europe began to arrive in larger numbers. In 1920, foreign-born Americans made up 18 percent of the U.S. labor force. Immigration restriction reduced that number to 5 percent by 1970. By 2015, it was back to 17 percent, close to the traditional figures from the nineteenth century.[22] In 1890, the very small Asian population of the United States lived almost exclusively in the far West—only California, Oregon, and Nevada had Asian populations above 2.5 percent. In 2000, California remained a center of Asian population, but Asian-descended people had spread across the country; Virginia, New York, and Massachusetts were similar to Washington and Nevada in numbers of Asian residents.

The U.S. Census Bureau considers "race" (including "Asian") separately from "ethnicity." The census did not include a specific question about Hispanic ethnicity (regardless of race) until 1980. But the

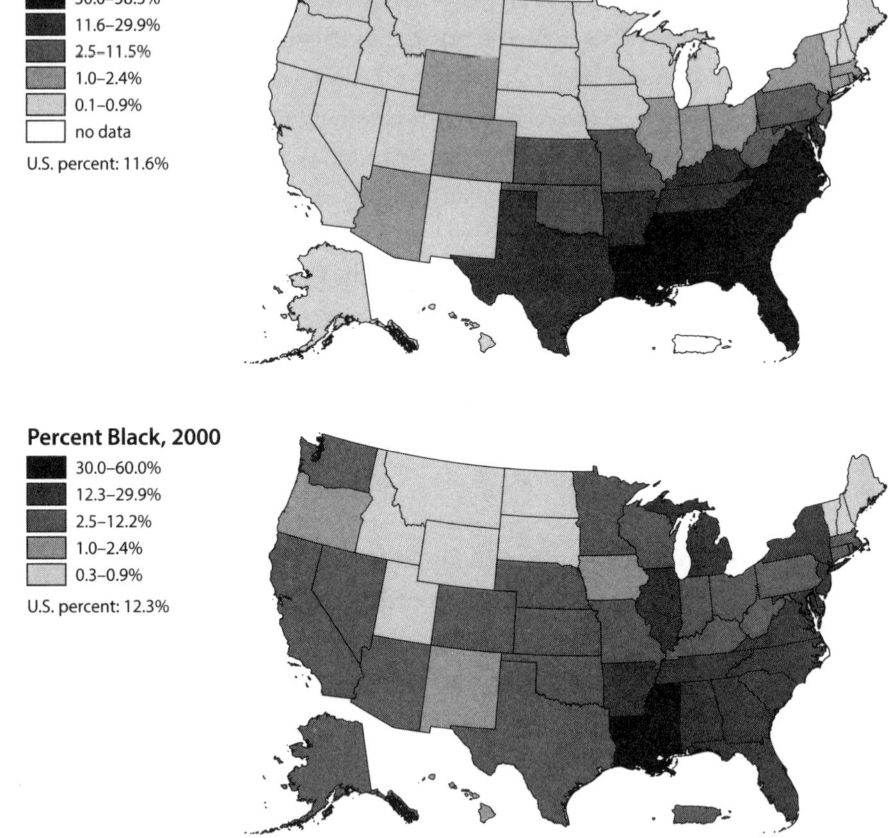

FIGURE 11.4. Percentage of Black population by state, 1900 and 2000.

Hispanic-identifying population of the United States, whether native-born or immigrant, although concentrated in the Southwestern states bordering Mexico, has also spread widely across the nation, with large numbers in every major city from the Northeast to the Southwest.[23] The same can be said for the immigrant population in the United States as a whole. In 1890, the vast majority of immigrants were concentrated in the Northeast and Midwest, especially in their fast-growing cities. At the end of the twentieth century this was no longer the case. Immigrants from Mexico constituted the largest number of foreign-born residents from any single nation, but collectively immigrants from Germany, El Salvador, Canada, Cuba, Korea, Vietnam, India, the Philippines, and China equaled those from Mexico. These newcomers were widely dispersed across the nation, including in states where very few immigrants had lived in 1890, such as Georgia, Florida, North Carolina, and Virginia. Immigrants continued to be heavily concentrated in cities, but by the end of the twentieth century the American population as a whole was concentrated in cities, and these cities were now spread widely across all regions of the nation. In 1890, if you knew the ethnic and racial makeup of an American city, then you would know where in the country it was likely to be located. By the beginning of the twenty-first century this was no longer the case (fig. 11.5).

Given these dramatic shifts in the geography of the nation's population, it should come as no surprise that interstate mobility patterns looked completely different in the 1990s from what they had been in the 1890s. No longer was the South isolated and stagnant. In the period from 1995 to 2000, the South was the *most* mobile region of the United States, receiving nearly twice as many migrants from other parts of the United States as the other regions—Northeast, Midwest, or West. (The South had more out-migrants than these regions as well.) The South had become the region that immigrants from abroad were *most* likely to move to. In 1890, Wisconsin was among the states with the lowest percentage of native-born residents, and South Carolina had the highest percentage (95 percent). In 2000, Wisconsin was among the states with the highest percentage of native-born residents, while South Carolina (now 64 percent) was barely above the national average.[24]

Immigration and population mobility also undermined the regional differences in religious affiliation that had characterized the United States in 1890. This is not to say that the trend toward homogenization eradicated all regional differences—the South remains a bastion of Southern Baptists, and in the northern plains Lutherans still predominate. But by the late twentieth century, Roman Catholics could be found in significant numbers in every region. The same was true of Jews and of more recent religious immigrant groups such as Muslims, who were as likely to live in urban Texas as in Illinois or Pennsylvania.[25]

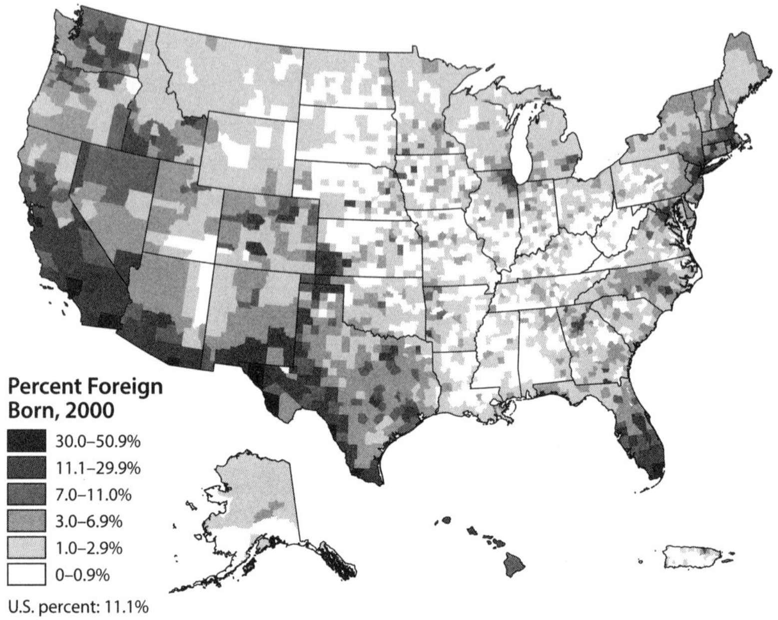

FIGURE 11.5. Percentage foreign-born population by county, U.S. Census, 2000. Counties with some of the highest percentages of foreign-born population in 2000, including southwestern Kansas, western Oklahoma, and southwestern Idaho, were places that had had almost no foreign-born population a century earlier; compare with Figure 10.5.

The transformation in education at all levels, fostered by the federal government's growing support, also helped to erase differences across the regions. By the early twenty-first century, illiteracy rates remained slightly higher in the South, but no longer radically different from the North. High school enrollment is now uniformly high across the nation for fourteen- to seventeen-year-olds. An adult in North Carolina is as likely to have earned a bachelor's degree as an adult in Massachusetts.[26] Across the second half of the twentieth century, the South had the greatest increases in students attending school and graduating from high school (fig. 11.6).

These improvements in education have reduced regional poverty and transformed patterns of employment across the nation. The South and parts of the West (including many Indigenous reservations)

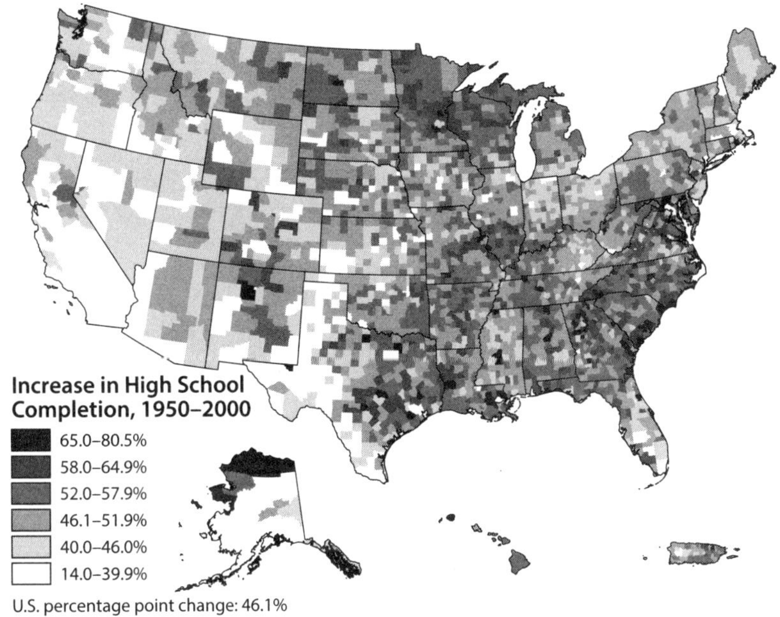

FIGURE 11.6. Increase in high school completion by county, 1950 to 2000, U.S. Census, 2000.

remained the most impoverished parts of the nation at the end of the twentieth century. But since 1938, when Franklin Roosevelt declared Southern poverty to be the country's major economic problem, the federal government has worked to alleviate it with considerable success. Southern poverty levels have fallen decade by decade (fig. 11.7). The expansion of higher education in the South raised median income levels and brought about parity with other regions (fig. 11.8).

Perhaps the most striking transformation from 1890 to 1990 can be seen in patterns of work and employment. In 1890, 70 percent of Americans still lived in rural areas. Farm work was the normative occupation across the nation. Even in 1950, at the height of America's postwar industrial supremacy, farming and farm labor remained the most prevalent occupations across huge stretches of the country, especially the Great Plains, Midwest, and South. At midcentury, manufacturing remained concentrated in the Northeast, although the New Deal and the

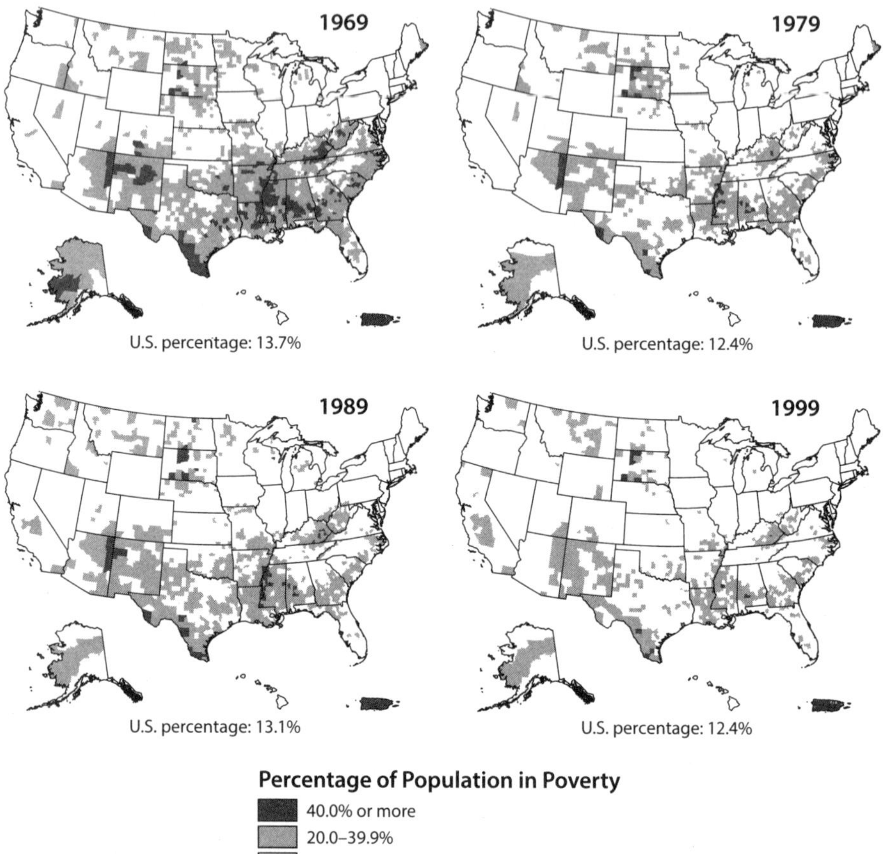

FIGURE 11.7. Percentage of U.S. population in poverty, 1969 to 1999, U.S. Census, 2020.

immense military/industrial expansion that began during World War II had brought more of it to the West and South (fig. 11.9).

By 2000, all this had changed. As mechanization of agriculture reduced labor demands, farming as the prevalent occupation had disappeared from all but a handful of counties across the United States (fig. 11.10). In many counties across the South in 1950, from 70 to 92 percent of the population had worked in agriculture. In 2000, agricultural workers in these counties were less than 5 percent of the population, even when the category of "farming" was made more capacious by

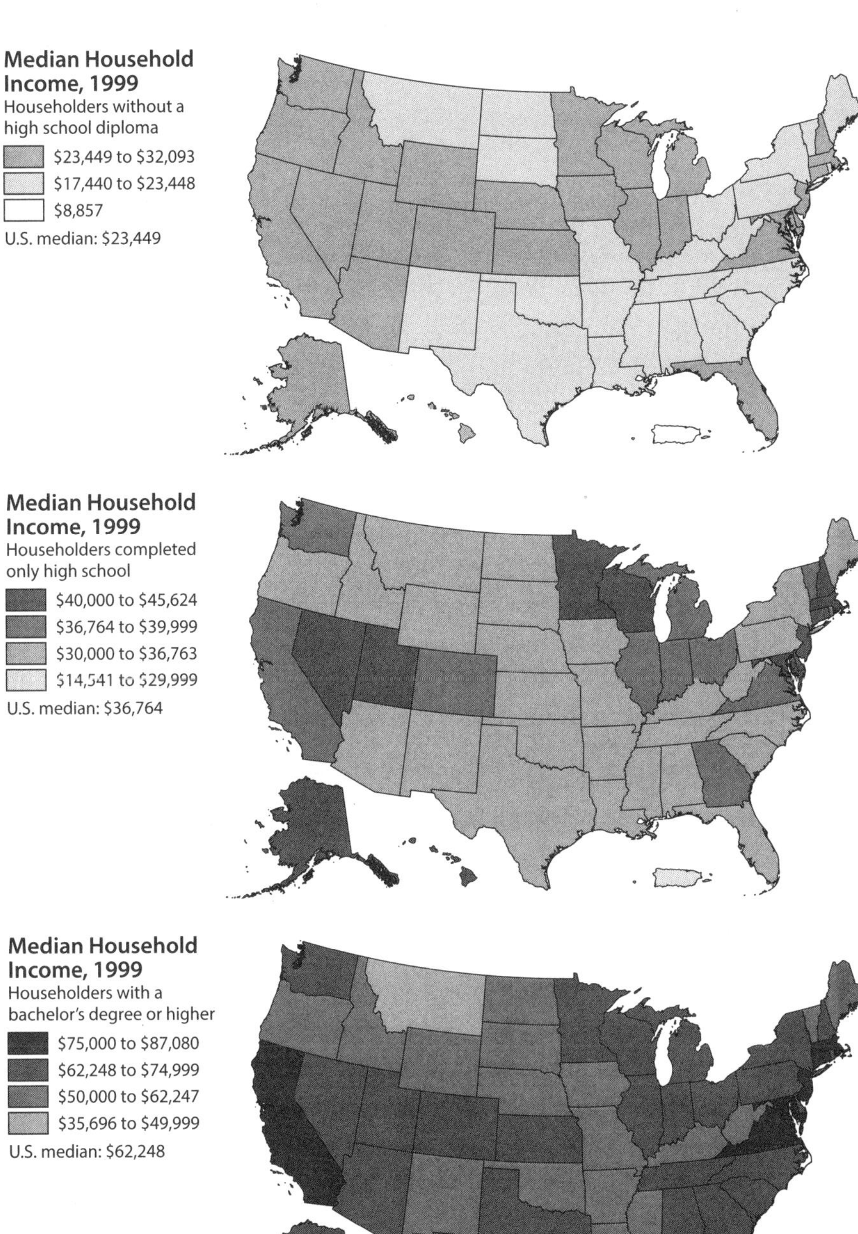

FIGURE 11.8. Median household income levels with differing educational achievement, 1999, U.S. Census.

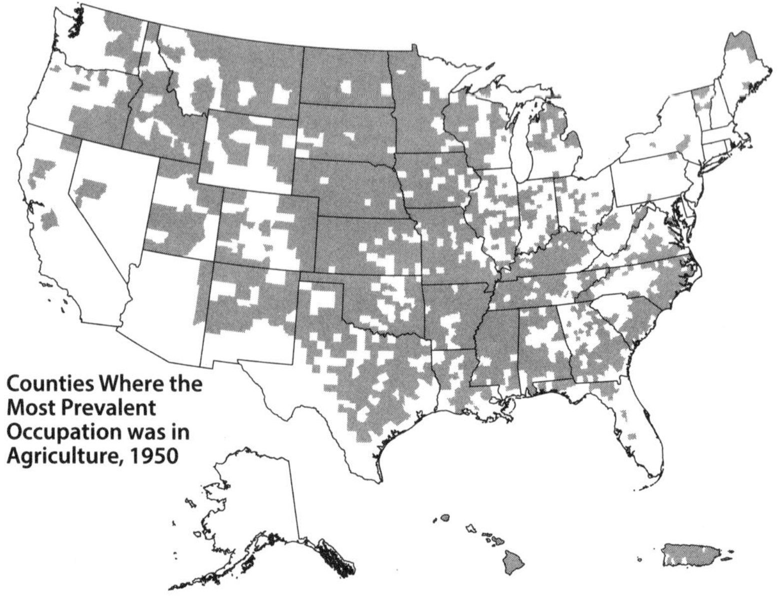

FIGURE 11.9. Most common occupational category in each U.S. county, 1950. In 1950, "farmer," "farm manager," or "wage farm labor" was the prevalent occupation in a majority of the counties in the U.S., stretching from coast to coast and from the northern to the southern border.

the Census Bureau to include fishing and forestry (fig. 11.11). At midcentury, Mississippi was as pervasively agricultural as any state in the union, but by 1956, its preeminent novelist was sensing the change. William Faulkner observed that ever since the New Deal's farm subsidies, "Our economy is not agricultural any longer. Our economy is the federal government. We no longer farm in Mississippi cotton-fields. We farm now in Washington corridors and congressional committee-rooms."[27]

Manufacturing, which had mainly been confined to the Northeast in 1890 and had been largely absent from the South, was evenly spread across both regions by 2000 (fig. 11.12). All across the nation, the most prevalent occupations were now in sales and office work, production and transportation, management, services, and the professions. The political economy of the United States had been fundamentally transformed in the century after 1890. And the most significant force in bringing about

FIGURE 11.10. Most common occupational category in each U.S. county, 2000. In 2000, the census map shows only a handful of counties—one in Washington State, one in western Nebraska, and three in south central Florida—where farming, fishing, and forestry occupations are the prevalent occupation.

this change, the federal government, can be seen on the map as well. Figure 11.13 shows the distribution of civilian employment by the federal government; the West and the South clearly predominate.

How did the government of the United States change over the course of this century, both to foster and to cope with these radical transformations in the land and people, the body of American society? This is, of course, an enormous historical question. What follows is a brief attempt to sketch the government's structural changes in terms consistent with the history of American constitutionalism told here. As the example of Phoenix shows, at every step a symbiotic relationship emerged between

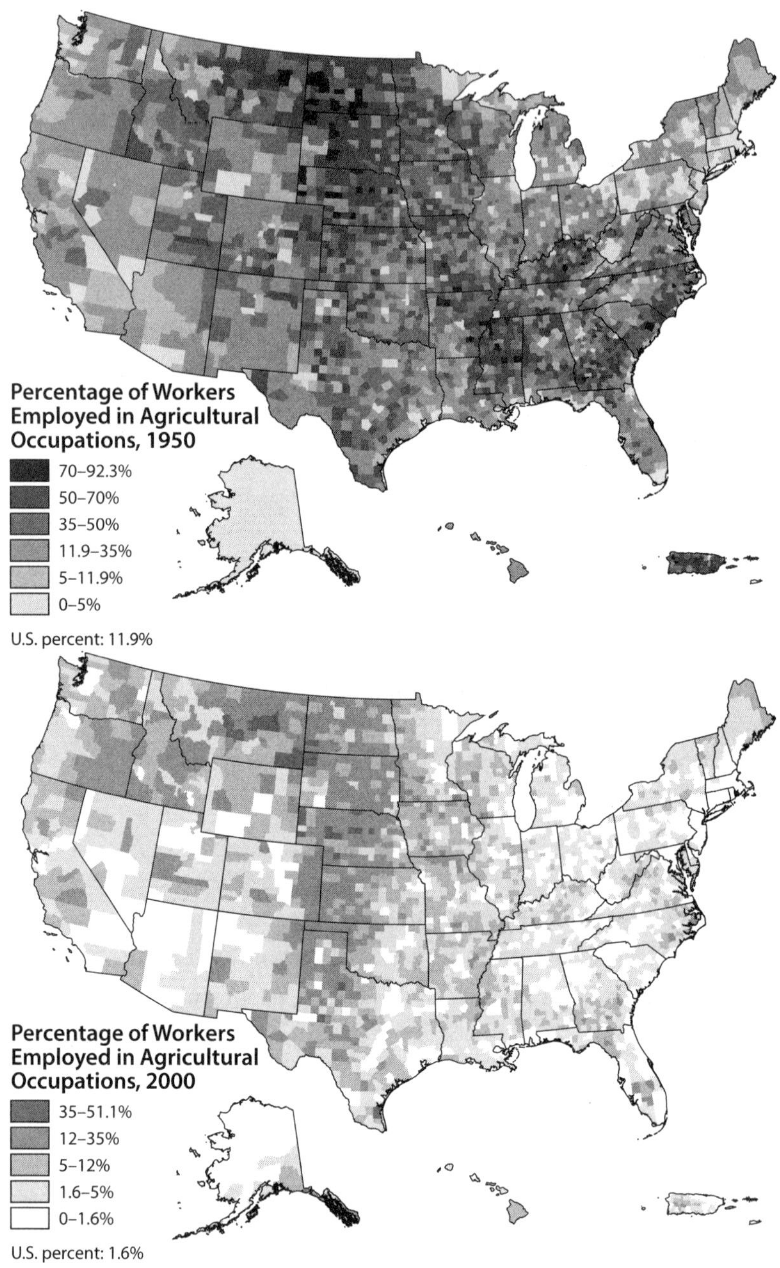

FIGURE 11.11. Percentage of U.S. population working in agricultural occupations, 1950 versus 2000. Over this half century, the percentage of Americans working in agriculture dropped from 11.9 percent to 1.6 percent; the decline in the South was especially precipitous, as these maps reveal.

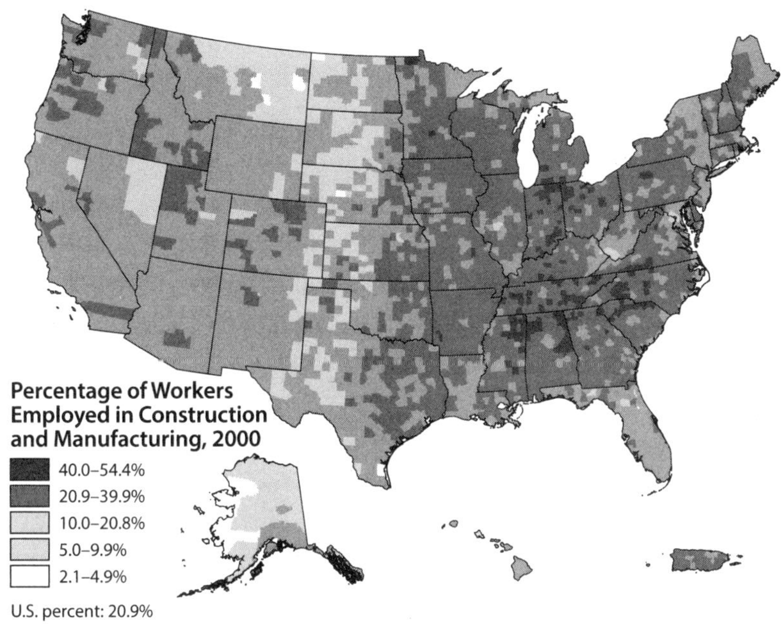

FIGURE 11.12. Percentage of population working in construction and manufacturing, 2000. By 2000, construction and manufacturing employment was as common in the South as in the North; for comparison, see Figure 10.7.

the needs of American citizens and the creation of government programs to address them. The same had been true in the nineteenth century, but in the more complex economy of the twentieth century, the nature and scale of government's responses were different. The 1787 Constitution was designed to accommodate the challenges familiar to an agrarian world. But it could not have foreseen the problems faced by an urban, industrial nation numbering in the hundreds of millions.

In the century from 1890 to 1990, the United States added only six additional states to the union: Utah, Oklahoma, New Mexico, Arizona, Alaska, and Hawai'i, notably fewer and at a far slower rate than the thirty-one states added in the previous century. When the United States annexed Texas in 1845, it was offered statehood within the year. It took California only two years from its acquisition in the Mexican War to achieve statehood. By contrast, Arizona and New Mexico (also acquired in the 1848 treaty with Mexico) waited sixty-four years for statehood.

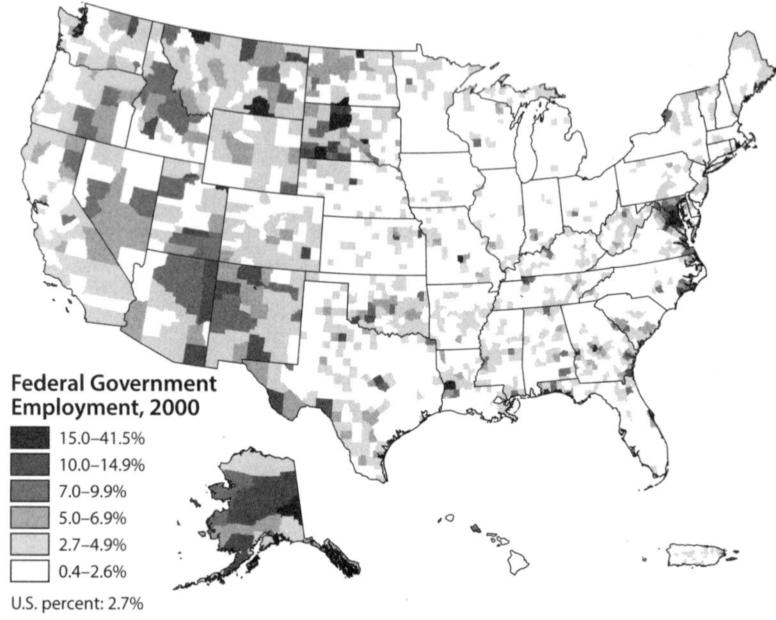

FIGURE 11.13. Percentage of civilian population in federal government employment, 2000. Outside of the region around the national capital in Washington, DC, the arid West beyond the 100th meridian has the highest concentrations of the civilian population working for the federal government.

Oklahoma, part of the 1803 Louisiana Purchase, waited more than a century. Alaska remained a territory for nearly a century from its purchase in 1867 to statehood in 1959. Hawai'i, although not formally annexed until 1898 in the Spanish-American War, had been colonized by American missionaries and corporations decades before this, also waited until 1959 for statehood.

What these states shared that kept them in territorial status so long were large Indigenous and/or non-Anglo-Protestant populations (Japanese in Hawai'i, Catholic/Hispanic in New Mexico and Arizona); Protestant Anglo-whites were minorities. Despite having much larger populations than Nevada, Wyoming, or Montana, they remained in territorial limbo decade after decade. The influx of large white populations—brought about in Oklahoma when the federal government opened "the Strip" in 1889 and with the subsequent discovery of oil in the territory, and in Hawai'i and Alaska with the military expansion that World War II brought—seemed to be required for Congress to grant them statehood.[28] Indeed, the federal government rejected a 1905 proposal for an Indigenous state of Sequoyah within what became Oklahoma. Whites quickly came to outnumber Indigenous people in the two decades following the Land Rush of 1889, when Oklahoma's population grew sixfold.[29]

If state making slowed to a crawl during the nation's second century (we are currently in the longest period without a new state in the nation's history, at sixty-seven years and counting), congressional representation of the nation's growing population ground to a complete halt. Following the 1910 census, the Apportionment Act of 1911 expanded the House of Representatives to 433, plus 2 more for the anticipated admission of New Mexico and Arizona to statehood, bringing the number to 435. But after the 1920 census, which spurred the immigration restriction legislation of the next few years, Congress failed for the first time to expand the nation's representation. Instead, in 1929, the Reapportionment Act kept the number of representatives at 435 despite two decades of rapid population growth from 92 million to 123 million, a 33 percent increase. The 1929 act mandated that future census results would merely redistribute this arbitrarily fixed number—435—according to shifts in the distribution of the nation's population rather than increase the number of representatives as the nation's population grew. When Alaska and Hawai'i were admitted to statehood, the number briefly increased to 437 (adding 1 representative for each new state) but then reverted to 435 after the 1960 census. Sixteen states lost representatives in the 1960 reapportionment, but Arkansas and Maine experienced the most dramatic losses in representatives per population—both states now had more than twice as many people per representative as Alaska.

Congress offered no rationale for why two long-existing states should lose representation because two new states were admitted to the union; this demonstrated the truth of the concern that went back to 1803—that admission of new states from foreign territory diminished the power of existing states. And while each member of Congress represented about 210,000 people when the number was fixed at 435 in 1911, by 1990 that ratio had grown to one representative for 570,000 people. As of 2020, it was one for every 760,000.[30]

By 1990, those 435 representatives presided over the collection of tax revenues incomparably larger than their predecessors of 1890, and they authorized expenditures across a dizzying array of government initiatives, assembled piecemeal over the century. Recall that in 1890, the U.S. government collected $464 million in revenue and spent $384 million. Adjusted for inflation, the 1890 amounts in 1990 dollars would be $6.7 billion in revenue, $5.5 billion in spending.[31] By comparison, in 1990, the federal government collected just over $1 trillion in revenue (although the "just over" amount rounded off here is four times as much as all the federal revenue a century earlier) and spent $1.252 trillion, more than two hundred times as much as a century earlier, adjusted for inflation.[32]

The scale and range of the federal government's activities changed so dramatically over the century that direct comparisons are virtually impossible. Nor is there space here to describe the vast array of projects the late twentieth-century federal government pursued. But the following broad strokes sketch the general character and magnitude of a century's changes.

In 1890, more than 86 percent of the federal government's revenue came from ad valorem taxation—tariffs and excise taxes. In 1990, this form of taxation had shrunk to about 6 percent of federal revenue. What replaced ad valorem taxes as the primary source of federal revenue were two forms of taxation that did not exist in 1890—income taxes (on both individuals and corporations) and social insurance taxes initiated by the Social Security Act of 1935. Both of these taxes were often collected by prior withholding from the wages of millions of Americans who now worked for regular paychecks, making them easy for the government to collect and creating a steady stream of income. Together, these two categories of taxation generated $940 billion in federal revenue in 1990, more than 90 percent of the nation's total direct revenue. Income taxes accounted for 60 percent and social insurance taxes for 40 percent of this amount.[33]

During the Civil War, Congress had introduced an income tax to help fund the war effort (though the vast majority of war expenses were financed through government borrowing). But the Civil War income tax had applied to relatively few people and raised far less revenue than the simultaneous increase in excise taxes. The income tax was reduced shortly after the Civil War and then repealed altogether.

In 1894, Congress reintroduced an income tax on a small scale, a 2 percent tax on incomes above four thousand dollars, as an addition to a tariff bill, to help pay for the generous veterans' pensions it had recently authorized. But the Supreme Court struck it down, arguing that an income tax was a direct tax and therefore had to be apportioned across the states according to their populations, not levied at uniform rates on all income earners regardless of where they lived.[34] The subsequent movement to reintroduce an income tax—in part to replace the politically divisive tariff as a source of revenue, in part to fund the veterans' pensions the 1890 Congress had enacted—required an amendment to the Constitution. As the previous chapter discussed, the Sixteenth Amendment, ratified in 1913, authorized a new way of collecting taxes that would revolutionize the federal government's revenue and spending capacities.[35] In terms of the federal government's operations, the Sixteenth Amendment was the most dramatic change in the written constitution in the nation's second century.

In practical terms, the revenue from the income tax would eventually make it possible for the federal government to outspend state and local governments as it took over a wider range of the police powers, reversing the dominant trend that went back to 1789. Shortly after the Sixteenth Amendment was ratified, U.S. entry into World War I dramatically increased federal spending on military matters. After the war, the traditional pattern briefly returned; state and local governments once again spent more than the federal government. But the federal initiatives spurred by the Great Depression and then World War II permanently reversed the pattern. Beginning in 1935, as New Deal programs such as old-age pensions, unemployment insurance, and Aid to Families with Dependent Children were launched, the federal government for the first time outspent state and local governments during peacetime.[36]

The extraordinary demands of World War II would ratchet up federal spending even further. In 1945, federal spending reached $92 billion, as compared to a collective $12 billion for all state and local spending. But the usual postwar reversion to the traditional spending pattern failed to emerge. U.S. spending patterns generated in World War II never really ended; they simply morphed into the Cold War. Federal spending would henceforth always dwarf state and local expenditures. In 1987, during the Reagan administration's military buildup, federal spending topped the $1 trillion mark for the first time. In 1990, the federal government spent $1.25 trillion (and transferred an additional $142 billion to state and local governments).

Defense was the largest single category of federal spending in 1990, as it always had been.[37] But defense represented only a little over one-quarter of the 1990 total, a much smaller percentage than in 1890, when defense constituted 45 percent of all federal spending. The reason for the change is not that the American military had shrunk—far from it. Rather, the proportion of spending on defense decreased because the federal government invested so heavily in so many other aspects of national life, made possible by income and social insurance tax revenues. Major categories in which federal spending had been zero in 1890—pensions for the elderly and disabled, health care, education, welfare payments (including unemployment benefits, aid to families and children, and housing), federal policing and prisons, and transportation—in 1990 collectively amounted to $595 billion, plus an additional $119 billion transferred by the federal government to state and local governments to spend in these categories. Altogether, the federal government spent more than twice as much on this array of programs affecting people's daily lives as it did on defense. This shift reversed the assumptions of 1787 about the responsibilities of different levels of government in the American federal system.[38]

In 1890, states and local governments spent more than half again as much as the federal government. In 1990, this was reversed as well, with federal spending half again more than state and local spending. In 1890, the spending categories of the different levels of government were highly differentiated—defense and communications were handled by the national government, everything else by state and local. In 1990, "everything else" had become an intricate partnership among federal, state, and local governments, with large amounts of state and local spending financed by federal transfers. These programs and institutions played critical roles in building populous new cities in the South and West (like Phoenix), alleviating poverty, making education at every level available to a wide array of Americans, transforming the nature and distribution of health care, creating a nationwide highway system and air travel infrastructure, building the world's largest and most sophisticated military forces, and countless other endeavors. The functions and practices of the national government had utterly changed over the course of the twentieth century, with the rise of truly national programs designed to promote the health, education, and general welfare of a much more integrated and homogenized population across the entire nation, paid for by direct taxes on the incomes of the nation's people.

In 1890, the U.S. government's executive branch was organized in eight cabinet departments: State, Treasury, War, and Justice (all present since the Constitution's inauguration in 1789) plus the Department of the Navy (separated from the War Department in 1798), the Postmaster General (made a cabinet position in 1829), and the Departments of the Interior and Agriculture (created in 1849 and 1862, respectively). By 1990, there were fourteen cabinet departments. Commerce, Labor, Health and Human Services, Housing and Urban Development, Transportation, Energy, Education, and Veteran's Affairs were added to the earlier eight. The Navy and War Departments were consolidated into a single Department of Defense, and the U.S. Postal Service was eliminated from the cabinet. Of the eight new cabinet departments of the twentieth century (compared with the two created in the nineteenth), six were created after World War II. The titles of these new departments provide an overview of the range of aspects of governance now addressed at the federal level.

Under the umbrella of each of these departments, Congress created numerous agencies to manage and regulate the nation's interests. For example, the Department of Transportation, created in 1966, oversees the Federal Aviation Administration, the Federal Highway Administration, the Pipeline and Hazardous Materials Safety Administration, the Federal Transit Administration, and numerous others. These national transportation systems were beyond the capacity of individual states to control and therefore required federal regulation. Many of these interstate activities were fostered by federal government expenditures, from the railroad land grants of the 1860s to the interstate highway system of the 1950s. In addition, there are several dozen independent or semi-independent federal agencies that fall outside the cabinet structure, including the Environmental Protection Agency, the Federal Reserve System, the Federal Election Commission, the Nuclear Regulatory Commission, the Social Security Administration, and many more. There are dozens more government-owned or -sponsored enterprises such as Amtrak, the mortgage companies popularly known as Fannie Mae and Freddie Mac, the Federal Deposit Insurance Corporation, and the Smithsonian Institution.[39] Each of them plays a critical part in making the United States what it is today.

With the growth of these departments and agencies, the number of employees of the federal government expanded exponentially. In 1901, roughly 231,000 civilians worked for the federal government, with an additional 136,000 employed by the Postal Service. In 1990, the number was nearly tenfold greater, at 2.25 million (with an additional 843,000 employed by the Postal Service).[40] An additional 2 million people were members of the U.S. military in 1990, including active-duty service and reserves.[41] However, these figures mask the true size of the modern federal workforce. Over the latter decades of the twentieth century, the government increasingly relied on private contractors and grant-based labor rather than employees on the federal payroll to do its work. In 1990, contract and grant-based employees of the federal government made up another 4.8 million workers, bringing the total (civilian, postal, military, contract, and grant) to roughly 9 million. Of the roughly 125 million people in the American workforce in 1990, more than 7 percent of them worked, directly or indirectly, for the federal government.[42] Three times as many Americans worked for the federal government in 1990 as worked in farming, once the nation's predominant occupation.[43]

No account of the transformation of the United States government across its second century could be complete without acknowledging the tremendous expansion of its overseas footprint, the twentieth century's counterpart to the expansion across North America in the nineteenth century. Beginning with the Spanish-American War in 1898, the United States acquired a series of overseas colonies for which eventual U.S. statehood in the nineteenth-century pattern was extremely unlikely—Hawai'i being the exception that proves the rule. Although the United States gave up direct governance of the most populous of these acquisitions, the Philippines, in 1946, the idea of developing overseas military bases to project U.S. power everywhere around the globe became a permanent feature of American government. By the end of the twentieth century, the Department of Defense acknowledged the existence of more than seven hundred military bases on foreign soil, in addition to roughly six thousand bases in the United States and its territories. However, scholars have demonstrated that seven hundred was an undercount. The real number of overseas bases was closer to a thousand, though impossible to determine precisely.[44] These military installations house hundreds of thousands of soldiers and contractors, and they employ many more local workers—not U.S. citizens on the federal payroll, but people working in the service of U.S. global power nonetheless. Nearly all of this enormously expanded federal government apparatus, the administrative state, falls under the authority of the executive branch.

The twentieth century thus witnessed the great unbalancing of the federal government. In modern times, the three coequal branches created by the 1787 Constitution do not seem remotely coequal when it comes to their personnel and their direct influence over American society. By 1990, when the executive branch oversaw more than 4.5 million employees (including military personnel) and millions more contract workers, the combined total for the legislative and judicial branches was just over 60,000, about 30,000 each (that number remains about the same today).[45]

This outcome was not dictated by the Constitution; its text makes scant mention of the president's cabinet and has no express language to support an administrative state under executive branch control.[46] Executive control was not foretold by the Anglo-American constitutional tradition. Britain's administrative state is overseen by elected members of

Parliament who serve as ministers in charge of government departments staffed by a permanent and apolitical civil service. Prior to independence, the legislatures of Britain's North American colonies conducted a great deal of administrative work in the development of colonial society.[47] Under the Articles of Confederation, the administrative work of the national government—military affairs, finance, and diplomacy—was managed by committees of members of the Confederation Congress.[48] During the Constitutional Convention, several proposals made by delegates to create a formal council or cabinet for the president were voted down, largely over fears that it would encourage the replication of Britain's monarchical government, where corrupt ministers were thought to have undue influence over the king. Instead, the Constitutional Convention opted for vague language allowing the president to seek "advice" from the Senate on diplomacy and appointments, and request the "written opinions" of executive officers.[49] However, the Constitution's text also suggests the possibility that Congress would have major administrative functions, much like the colonial legislatures. The very first of its enumerated powers in Article I, Section 8 states that Congress "shall have the Power to lay *and collect* Taxes, Duties, Imposts, and Excises" (emphasis added). As the list of congressional powers goes on, terms and phrases like "regulate," "establish," "promote," "provide and maintain a Navy," and "raise and support Armies" all project an active administrative role for Congress.

In short, the specific terms of the twentieth century's enormous expansion and restructuring of the federal government were neither dictated by the original structure of the Philadelphia Constitution nor accompanied by amendments to the written text. How this happened and the implications for constitutional government in the United States today are the questions we turn to next.

12

The Long Crisis of the Constitution

GOVERNMENTAL CHANGE AND INSTRUMENTAL STASIS IN THE TWENTIETH CENTURY

> No amendment which any powerful economic interests or the leaders of any powerful political party have had reason to oppose has ever been ratified within anything like a reasonable time. And thirteen States which contain only five percent of the voting population can block ratification even though the thirty-five States with ninety-five percent of the population are in favor of it.
>
> —FRANKLIN DELANO ROOSEVELT, MARCH 9, 1937

WHAT WAS THE most dramatic change to the constitution of the United States over its first century from 1790 to 1890? Quite obviously, it was the addition of more than thirty new states to the original thirteen, along with approximately 2.7 million square miles of additional territory and fifty-eight million more people. These additions utterly remade the United States, altering the fundamental conditions of the land and people that constituted the nation. Especially transformative were those new states carved out of territory that had not been part of the original United States, territory acquired from foreign countries without a clear mandate in the text of the Constitution. The speed and scale of expansion was significantly advanced when Congress usurped the power to make new states out of foreign territory, assuming for itself the sovereign power that the people had jealously guarded during the constitution-making process. In 1811, during debates over the admission of Louisiana to statehood, Thomas Jefferson failed to speak out in defense of the people's authority over this constitutional power, despite his own sympathy with this position and calls in Congress for formal amendments. The subsequent transformation of America's land and people was as consequential for the Western Hemisphere as Napoleon's ambitions for the Old World would have been if France had succeeded in taking over all of Great Britain, Spain, Germany, Italy, the Low Countries, and Austria, creating a single imperial nation over Western Europe. The United States became the hegemonic power of the Americas, reversing the trend of the entire period of human occupation of the Western Hemisphere up to about 1800, when Central and South America were dominant.

Dramatic changes to America's fundamental constitutional order stemming from "acts beyond the constitution"—the phrase Jefferson used to describe the Louisiana Purchase—were thus not new to the twentieth century.[1] Yet these changes would take new forms and directions in the nation's second century under the Philadelphia Constitution. First of all, the role of land in constitutional change would be different. The United States continued to acquire new territories, beginning with the Spanish-American War in 1898, during which the Philippines, Puerto Rico, Guam, and Hawai'i were formally annexed. But the implicit promise that began with Louisiana, the promise that newly acquired foreign territory would be on a path to statehood, was abandoned in the twentieth century. As the agrarian assumptions of 1787 gave way to a more complex industrial economy, and as the Domesday Machine failed to transform the arid West as it had the eastern half of North America, "more land and more states" was no longer a plausible solution to the nation's challenges.

Instead, the federal government would take on new powers and amass ever-larger resources, both financial and administrative, to influence the lives of its citizens. In the twentieth century, the national government reshaped the body of society by intervening in the political economy of the United States (and the world) in ways the founding generation never imagined. The assumption at the founding was that the states would retain the great majority of the police power over citizens' lives, and the federal government would be outward facing; the twentieth century would see the overthrow of these principles. The national government assumed an extensive role in internal police powers, acting in partnership with the states. And while continuing to engage in traditional treaty making and diplomacy, the federal government enormously expanded its overseas capacities, especially in military and "security" terms, to become a global hegemon whose interests knew no geographical limits.

In these pursuits, the United States government has grown into what is perhaps the largest enterprise the world has ever known. Today it spends more money on military matters than the next nine largest countries combined, more than 40 percent of the world's total. Yet defense spending constitutes less than half the total of the U.S. government's discretionary spending.[2] The society it governs, while comprising less than 5 percent of the world's population, consumes more than 25 percent of the world's resources and generates 30 percent of the world's waste.[3] These conditions too are part of the nation's constitution, elements of an "American Way of Life" that has been fostered by the nation's government across the twentieth century. Yet the modern nation is barely comprehensible from the point of view of the written constitution generated in Philadelphia in 1787. No one reading the Constitution alone could have any idea what sort of country the United States is today or how its government works. The eighteen clauses of Article I, Section 8, defining the powers allocated to Congress describe almost none of what modern congressional legislation addresses. The executive power and judicial power allocated in Articles II and III are essentially undefined. The nation's vast administrative structure is invisible within the confines of its written constitution.

In the early twentieth century, new political movements generated amendments meant to adapt the constitution to the changing conditions of the modern nation. One of these, the Sixteenth Amendment, gave Congress the power to lay and collect income taxes without apportionment among the states according to population. This laid the foundation for the immense expansion of the federal government and redistribution of the nation's wealth described in chapter 11. But the structural amendment process stalled out in 1920. The written instrument has remained remarkably static ever since, despite the wholesale transformation of the body of society and its government over the past century. Over the modern period, constitutional change has essentially involved the nation and its government being pulled ever further away from the instrument written to describe and delimit the powers of government.

The nineteenth century's most significant unwritten constitutional changes stemmed from President Jefferson's decision to remain silent in the face of an issue in which the consent of the sovereign people through a constitutional amendment seemed necessary. The twentieth-century constitution, by contrast, was remade in the opposite way: A president with even greater power and popularity than Jefferson, supported by an overwhelmingly dominant party in Congress, chose openly to forgo the amendment process. Franklin Roosevelt and the Democratic Party abandoned the effort to adapt the written instrument to the massive changes their administration was making in the structure and functions of the government. Unlike Jefferson, Roosevelt believed that the open-ended qualities of the written instrument allowed fundamental constitutional change without the need for formal amendments, a process no longer viable for a modern industrial society in the face of global emergencies.

There was another key difference. The power Congress assumed in the nineteenth century over territorial acquisition and state making, while itself unsupported by constitutional amendments, generated permanent transformations of the nation by producing new entities—new states—unassailably supported by the written constitution. Once admitted to the union, a state is forever. But beginning with the New Deal, many of the new powers assumed by the president and Congress and the institutions they generated lack specific support in the written constitution and therefore, no matter how much they may have changed the basic character of the nation and government, are perpetually subject to the vicissitudes of politics in every branch of government—the legislature, the executive, and the courts. The ever-widening gaps between the nation, the government, and the written instrument—and the lastingly bitter politics these gaps have engendered—have produced the long constitutional crisis of the past century that is now coming to a head.

The Spanish-American War precipitated the first dramatic reversal of a nineteenth-century constitutional tradition. Overseas expansion itself was not new. The conquest of Mexico in the 1840s had been accomplished by U.S. naval and military forces sending troops by ship to Veracruz on the Gulf coast and around Cape Horn to California. By using military force in similar fashion to seize control over the Philippines, Guam, and Puerto Rico, the United States gained valuable new territory; sugar rather than cotton was now the prized commodity. In 1848, the vast territory of conquered Mexico had been divided in the treaty that ended the war. This division allowed the United States to command the more sparsely populated parts of Mexico north of the Rio Grande and west to Alta California, while keeping heavily populated central Mexico out of the United States.[4] By contrast, the new island possessions were densely populated—together the Philippines and Puerto Rico had eight million people in 1898, more than 10 percent of the total U.S. population at the time. (New York, then the largest state, had about seven million people). In addition, much of this population was seen as "alien" to the United States by its White and Protestant political leaders: Hispanic and Catholic in Puerto Rico, and Indigenous, Catholic, and Muslim in the Philippines. The nineteenth-century practice implemented by Congress in 1803–11 (despite Jefferson's reservations) that newly acquired territory would be eligible for statehood on the same terms as the original 1783 territory no longer seemed so appealing to U.S. leaders if the new citizens might be Indigenous or "alien" rather than White American colonizers. Furthermore, if these islands were treated as territories and potential states, trade with them would not be subject to tariffs. Article I, Section 8, of the Constitution insists that all taxes, duties, imposts, and excises be uniform within the United States. And tariffs were at the center of the fiscal policies of the Republican Party in power at the time.[5]

In this context, the U.S. Supreme Court issued a series of decisions that upended the expansionist pattern prevalent since the Louisiana Purchase. In the first of these so-called Insular Cases, *Downes v. Bidwell* (1901), the court invented a new doctrine of incorporation to distinguish "incorporated" territories from "unincorporated" territories. The former would include the Hawai'ian Islands, annexed by the United States in July 1898 and dominated politically by White American landowners and sugar interests. Hawai'i already conformed to the mold of nineteenth-century U.S. settler colonies on the mainland—since 1887 it had been under a treaty arrangement that allowed Hawai'ian sugar to be shipped to the United States duty-free. But by the newly invented doctrine the Philippines, Guam, and Puerto Rico would be declared "unincorporated" territories, meaning they were essentially permanent colonies. Although they belonged to the United States, these islands would be subject to foreign tariffs (much as Britain had imposed on its American colonies in the 1760s and '70s). Their residents would not be under the Constitution's protection regarding individual rights, and they would not enjoy the path to statehood that U.S. territories since the Northwest Ordinance had anticipated.[6] Coming fifty years after the Mexican War, these court decisions opened the possibility that territory conquered by the United States in war (as the region from Texas to California had been) could be disposed of as readily as it had been acquired, simply by congressional action. The Philippines experienced this process, interrupted by World War II, from 1934 to 1946.[7]

With the continental expansion project complete, and with the diminishing prospect of extensive uninhabited spaces becoming open to American colonization, the Insular Cases reversed the previous century's practice of altering the constitution by the admission of states from new territories. These Supreme Court decisions offered a new vision of a bifurcated nation, different from the precedent of 1787, and reminiscent of the old British Empire. Unincorporated acquired territories would never become fully part of the nation, and their residents would always be treated as colonial subjects, second-class citizens of the United States. Despite the blatantly racist language of these Supreme Court decisions, in which the peoples of the newly acquired islands were described as "savages" and "alien races," subsequent attempts to overturn them in the courts have failed, most recently in October 2022.[8]

In both the Civil War and World War I, the size and power of the United States government rapidly expanded to unprecedented levels, but in each case the war's aftermath brought rapid demobilization and a return to earlier norms. The extraordinary and *permanent* change in the size and functions of the United States government began with the global crisis of the Great Depression in the 1930s.

The scale of the suffering and misery across all regions of the country—urban and rural, North and South, East and West—and all sectors of the American economy, from agriculture to industry to finance, was unprecedented. As stock markets plummeted and banks closed by the thousands, enormous reserves of wealth disappeared. Investment in the economy ground to a halt. Unemployment levels in the United States reached 25 percent of the workforce, with upwards of twelve million people out of work. The new administration of President Franklin Roosevelt, with large Democratic majorities in both houses of Congress, concluded that "the Federal Government is the only governmental body with sufficient power and credit to meet this situation. We have assumed this task and we shall not shrink from it in the future."[9]

The only precedent even slightly resembling what FDR proposed was the wartime footing of the Union during the emergency of the Civil War. For the federal government to tackle the challenge of the Depression, it would require unprecedented powers in the executive and legislative branches, powers not expressly delegated in the Constitution. In Europe, democratic nations turned to dictators such as Mussolini and Hitler to lead them out of the Depression. Mussolini had asserted that "the liberal state is destined to perish" because constitutional democracies lacked the force, direction, and decisiveness to manage this emergency in modern industrial society. There were those in the United States, from both ends of the political spectrum, who sympathized with this idea. They saw the need for "strong medicine" in the form of "extraordinary powers" granted to the incoming President Roosevelt that would require adjustments in the country's constitutional balance.[10]

For some of the dire economic problems of the 1930s, such as the collapse of markets for agricultural products, the federal government could build on older legislative and administrative precedents. The U.S. Department of Agriculture (USDA), founded in 1862 during the Civil War, was the third largest non-military department of the federal government (after the Post Office and the Treasury). The USDA already had a history of supporting the nation's farmers through agricultural experiment stations—scientific research centers connected to the nation's land grant universities. Among the first measures of Roosevelt's New Deal was the Agricultural Adjustment Act (AAA), devised by economists like Rexford G. Tugwell of Columbia University, part of the Brain Trust brought in to address the economic crisis. It authorized the USDA to extend credit to farmers and to negotiate trade treaties to find foreign markets for American produce. Most significantly, the AAA subsidized farmers directly by paying them to take acreage out of production and reduce the number of livestock they raised; reduced production would raise prices on the more limited volume of crops and animal products.

Given the millions of Americans engaged in farming across the continent, the AAA required an enormous expansion of the USDA bureaucracy to handle the intricate details of these programs. The USDA built new headquarters in Washington, DC, that became, for a time, the largest office building in the world. There were 3.6 million farm owners in the United States, and millions more tenants, sharecroppers, wage laborers, and unpaid family members who worked in the agricultural sector. The activities of all these had to be coordinated for the agency's "adjustments" to succeed.[11] The nineteenth-century United States had developed a welfare system of a sort, what might anachronistically be called "social security," by using the government's power to make immense amounts of land available cheaply to American farmers. Now the twentieth-century state was managing the resulting system through the Agricultural Adjustment Act by paying farmers not to farm their lands. In the modern, globally interconnected economic system, given the risk that farming had always entailed, organized responses were now required on a scale that only the federal government could provide.

Unlike the situation in the agricultural sector, federal government intervention in America's industrial economy did not have large and long-established bureaucracies and institutions to build on. Earlier efforts by Congress or individual states to regulate industry had been struck down by the U.S. Supreme Court as violations of the contract-making rights of America's businesses. In 1905, the Supreme Court in *Lochner v. New York* invalidated a New York State law setting maximum hours (ten hours per day, six days per week) for bakery employees. This was the beginning of the Lochner Court and its infamous protection of the economic rights of "persons" (including incorporated businesses) under Section 1 of the Fourteenth Amendment.[12] To the extent that Congress before the New Deal had been allowed by the court to regulate business, its power generally came from the commerce clause in Article I, Section 8, of the Constitution, which grants Congress the power "to regulate commerce with foreign nations, among states, and with the Indian tribes."[13] Under what was known as the doctrine of surrogacy, Congress could extend this express power to other powers not named. For instance, Congress had passed laws to prohibit or restrict prostitution, the use of narcotics, and pornography, all unmentioned in the Constitution. But the laws were based on Congress's powers to regulate interstate commerce and the Post Office, and the court upheld this interpretation. There were limits to this doctrine, as when the Supreme Court in 1918 struck down the Keating–Owen Child Labor Act, which used the commerce clause to ban child labor. The court considered this a matter of manufacturing and labor relations, not commercial regulation, and thus beyond Congress's express authority.[14]

In the famous "First 100 Days" of the Roosevelt Administration in 1933, Congress's signature intervention in the industrial economy, the counterpart of the AAA's regulation of the agricultural sector, was the National Industrial Recovery Act (NIRA). Like the AAA, the NIRA was drafted by a team of experts chosen by Roosevelt, and then sent to Congress. Congress passed it with very little debate, effectively ceding law-making authority to the president. The NIRA was an omnibus bill that created a Public Works Administration to spend $3.3 billion in government funds on national infrastructure projects. The NIRA authorized the president to play an unprecedented role in controlling the nation's money supply and to regulate industry to stimulate the economy. It created the National Recovery Administration, an agency designed to coordinate activity among industries, much as the AAA coordinated farm production, and to help industries write codes of fair competition practices. Title I, Section 7, of the NIRA guaranteed labor the right to organize unions and engage in collective bargaining. It also set standards for maximum working hours, minimum wages, safe working conditions (including the elimination of child labor), and production targets. The NIRA was a clear break with constitutional tradition and the Supreme Court's interpretive position of the previous half century.[15]

Within two years, the Supreme Court had declared both the AAA and the NIRA to be unconstitutional. Regarding the NIRA, the court's unanimous decision in *Schechter v. United States* found that Congress had acted improperly in delegating its authority to the president and to corporations charged with drafting regulatory codes. The court also held that the centralization of national authority over business regulation violated the rights of states; the federal government lacked the authority to regulate wages and working hours or prohibit child labor. Regarding the AAA, the court in another decision in 1936 described it as "a statutory plan to regulate and control agricultural production, a matter beyond the powers delegated to the federal government."[16]

These decisions, and others like them, were not utterly surprising to New Deal supporters. Many in Roosevelt's circle believed that radical changes in the power of the executive and legislative branches to regulate and stimulate the American economy would best be secured by constitutional amendments that expressly granted these powers. As far back as 1920, Progressive political scientist Robert Cushman had argued that in matters such as the national regulation of child labor, a constitutional amendment transferring some of the states' police powers to Congress would be a better solution than relying on the doctrine of surrogacy.[17]

This moment bears comparison to the one faced by Jefferson and his Democratic-Republican colleagues at the time of the Louisiana Purchase. In 1803, President Jefferson expressed caution when colleagues in his party, like Senator Nicholas of Virginia, pushed to bypass the formal amendment process by asserting Congress's power over foreign expansion and state making. In the midst of the New Deal, the roles were reversed; members of Congress favored the amendment process, while the president opposed it. Senator Burton Wheeler of Montana—a Democrat, a strong supporter of Roosevelt's programs, and a critic of the Supreme Court's decisions—favored amending the Constitution to achieve the New Deal's goals. Wheeler proposed an amendment that would give Congress the power to overturn a decision by the Supreme Court that declared an act of a previous Congress to be unconstitutional. It would require a two-thirds majority in both houses, much like Congress's power to override a presidential veto.[18] The fact that the Democrats enjoyed supermajorities in both houses of Congress made Wheeler's amendment seem plausible as a way to sustain the New Deal. Similarly, Roosevelt's secretary of the interior, Harold Ickes, recommended "trying to put through a number of amendments to the Constitution to meet the various situations" that the court's opposition had stymied. Other Roosevelt staffers, Ben Cohen and Tom Corcoran, drafted versions of a formal amendment similar to Wheeler's proposal.[19]

Roosevelt chose ordinary politics rather than constitutional amendment, the same choice Jefferson made. But Roosevelt was much more open about the dilemma than Jefferson—he did not instruct his friends in Congress to keep quiet about the constitutional issue. Instead, he went public, using his radio "fireside chats" to address a national audience of millions and to engage in open debate with Senator Wheeler and others. In a radio address on February 5, 1937, Roosevelt outlined his famous "court-packing" bill to remake the structure of the Supreme Court, dominated at the time by the so-called Nine Old Men, conservative holdovers from the Lochner era. Roosevelt proposed the appointment of six additional justices who would be more amenable to the New Deal's amalgamation of powers in the hands of the president and Congress. Senator Wheeler and other members of Congress gave radio presentations in rebuttal. The question of whether constitutional amendment was the more appropriate way to expand the powers of Congress and the president was debated at length in the Senate.[20]

This was not merely an abstract or isolated discussion. Sixty-six proposals for amendments were submitted during this session of Congress. Some of these were quite specific proposals to grant the federal government authority over working hours, wages, and conditions. Others were more general, giving Congress the authority "to regulate agriculture, commerce, industry, and labor," or even to legislate for the "general welfare" where the states were incapable of doing so.[21] Still others proposed variations on Roosevelt's court-packing scheme or Wheeler's amendment allowing congressional supermajorities to override the court. But in another radio address a month later, on March 9, Roosevelt rejected these amendment plans. He explained to the national audience his view that the amendment process would take too long, given the national emergency: "It would take months or years to get substantial agreement upon the type and language of an amendment. It would take months and years thereafter to get a two-thirds majority in favor of that amendment in *both* Houses of the Congress." In addition, Roosevelt worried that even a congressionally approved amendment would fail to be ratified by the states: "No amendment which any powerful economic interests or the leaders of any powerful political party have had reason to oppose has ever been ratified within anything like a reasonable time. And thirteen States which contain only five percent of the voting population can block ratification even though the thirty-five States with ninety-five percent of the population are in favor of it."[22]

Roosevelt explained to the American public that in a global emergency in a complex industrial economy, the nation no longer had the luxury of using a cumbersome process that suited the slow-moving agrarian society of the eighteenth century.[23] This was public recognition by the nation's highest officer that the *method* devised in the 1780s for determining the sovereign will of the people, the special conventions for drafting and ratifying constitutional changes, could no longer function in modern industrial society. Instead, FDR and his supporters in Congress justified the constitutionality of their new powers by the large supermajorities the Democrats won in the 1932, 1934, and 1936 national elections. In 1936, after four years of experimental New Deal measures, Roosevelt carried forty-six of the forty-eight states, and Democrats won more than 75 percent of all seats in the House and the Senate, and three-quarters of the states' governorships as well. The size of their mandate seemed sufficient to justify the New Deal as the will of the people.

In the end, neither Roosevelt's court-packing bill nor the amendment process prevailed. Faced with Roosevelt's challenge, the Supreme Court performed its "switch in time." As Congress passed new measures to achieve New Deal goals—such as the Social Security Act providing old age pensions, aid to dependent children, and unemployment insurance; and the Wagner Act that created the National Labor Relations Board and guaranteed workers' rights to form unions (labor's "Magna Carta")—the Supreme Court, reversing its earlier positions regarding the AAA and the NIRA, upheld their constitutionality.[24] Roosevelt withdrew his court-packing scheme, and the pressure for constitutional amendments diminished as well. The new powers asserted by Congress and the president, and the privileges and rights that these new laws protected, went forward as a revision to the "higher law" of the constitution. That is, the court endorsed the federal government's power to provide for the security and well-being of the body of society in new ways, but without any formal changes to the written instrument itself—merely a new interpretive stance on the part of the judiciary.

The federal government's accretion of new constitutional powers in the New Deal resembled what happened with respect to the Louisiana Purchase, when Congress bypassed the amendment process as it assumed new powers not delegated by the Constitution. But there is a critical difference. In the nineteenth century, once Congress created new states, from Louisiana to Wyoming, these states had permanent status in the formal written constitution. Articles IV and V guarantee that a state cannot be altered against its will or deprived of its equal representation in the Senate. States stand in a constitutional class by themselves as permanent entities wielding enormous power. By contrast, none of the new powers that the president or Congress gained during the New Deal, or the rights and entitlements that its legislation generated—collective bargaining, old age pensions, farmers' subsidies, unemployment insurance—were supported or guaranteed by formal changes in the text of the Constitution. As the court's "switch in time" demonstrated, a shift in the interpretive strategies among nine appointed individuals could overturn established constitutional traditions. Just as readily, future Congresses and presidents could alter these changes to the nation's "higher law," much as nineteenth-century Congresses had upended the non-statehood parts of earlier compromises, like the Missouri Compromise line that divided U.S. territories into slave and free regions.

Among the many other amendments proposed in the Seventy-Fifth Congress, one was directed not at the economic crisis of the Great Depression, but at another looming danger of the 1930s. Germany's rearmament under Hitler, Italy's overseas aggressions in Ethiopia, Spain's civil war, Stalin's arms buildup in the Soviet Union, and Japan's military expansion in the Pacific all foretold the return of global warfare. Strong antiwar sentiment in the United States had encouraged Congress to pass the Neutrality Act of 1935, which prohibited the sale of arms to any belligerent nations. In 1938, Louis Ludlow, a Democratic congressman from Indiana, went a step further and proposed a constitutional amendment to require a national popular referendum before Congress could declare war. According to Ludlow's proposal, the international events that had drawn the United States into war with Spain in 1898 and Germany in 1917 would no longer be sufficient for a congressional declaration of war unless first backed by a popular referendum.[25]

A war referendum had been a Progressive idea since the 1920s; public opinion polls of the mid-1930s showed approval rates above 70 percent. Ludlow and his supporters were not isolationists aiming to avoid any and all "foreign entanglements." Rather, they wanted the United States to lead by example. They believed that requiring popular referendums before declarations of war, if copied by other nations, would bring about the end of war as a means to resolve conflict. Following an incident in China in December 1937, when a Japanese warplane bombed a U.S. gunboat (reminiscent of the *USS Maine* explosion in Havana in 1898 that led to the Spanish-American War), Congress voted on the Ludlow Amendment. It received nearly 50 percent approval despite a direct appeal from President Roosevelt to Democrats in Congress to reject it.[26]

In retrospect, the failed Ludlow Amendment of 1938 was a last gasp, a final attempt to use the Article V process to shape how the United States deployed its growing military power. In the wake of its failure, the trend has been entirely in the opposite direction: away from control by the American people and their representatives in Congress (despite the fact that the power to declare war belongs exclusively to Congress under the Constitution), and ever more into the hands of the executive branch and the enormous military enterprise it oversees. Over the next seven years, the relationship between the U.S. Constitution and the nation's war-making capacities would undergo a revolutionary transformation. This military revolution ran parallel to but was far more extensive than the remaking of the federal government's role in the American economy. Underlying both these transformations was the emerging concept of "national security." A growing belief among government leaders, Franklin Roosevelt foremost among them, postulated that the risks and uncertainties of an increasingly interconnected world required the national government to create proactive systems to guard the security of its people. In both economic and military terms, anticipated but unpredictable threats could now come from anywhere around the globe.[27]

On December 8, 1941, a day after Japanese forces attacked the U.S. territories of Hawai'i and the Philippines, Congress declared war against Japan and, three days later, against Germany and Italy. (Although formally neutral, the United States had been supporting the Allied war effort against the German-Italian Axis since Germany had invaded Poland in 1939.) These World War II declarations would be the last time that Congress would ever exercise its exclusive power from Article I,

Section 8, to declare war.[28] By 1945, when the Senate voted to ratify the charter of the United Nations, a resolution by the UN Security Council was sufficient to authorize the president to commit U.S. forces to foreign wars, as President Truman did in Korea starting in 1950. Every president since Truman has authorized the use of military force overseas without declarations of war by Congress.

By World War II's end, sixteen million Americans had been in military service—12 percent of the nation's 1940 population. The war effort generated a raft of government programs to develop a gigantic armaments industry, producing ships, planes, tanks, guns, ammunition, and everything else required by American soldiers and sailors fighting around the world, while rationing consumption by American civilians. Building on institutions created during the New Deal but accelerated by the War Powers Acts of December 1941 and March 1942, the federal government reached into nearly every aspect of American life. It regulated and coordinated industry, and set wages, prices, and working hours. It created the U.S. Employment Service to get the right workers in the right jobs. It built factories for some wartime needs and contracted with private companies for others. And it invested in scientific research by universities and corporations to generate innovations—most significantly, if secretively, the Manhattan Project for building an atomic bomb.

By the end of the war, the federal government owned 40 percent of the nation's capital assets. Military spending (or "defense" spending, as the new postwar terminology would have it) soared. During the 1930s, it had averaged less than 10 percent of the federal budget; it grew from 21 percent in fiscal year 1941 to 90 percent in fiscal year 1945 (and defense spending after the war remained at high levels, roughly 50 percent through the 1950s and '60s).[29] In 1941, the federal government spent $1.6 billion (1.7 percent of gross domestic product) on national defense; in 1945, this figure reached $83 billion (38 percent of GDP). By 1950, the amount of land controlled by the U.S. Atomic Energy Commission, newly created to oversee nuclear projects, was greater than the area of Delaware and Rhode Island combined. To administer all this new activity, Congress created a multitude of federal agencies to which it delegated its legislative authority, deferring to the expertise or the need for secrecy that war demanded.[30]

To pay for all this, the federal government expanded the taxation system, especially the income tax, as never before. Before World War II, relatively few Americans—only about 4 to 8 percent of the working population—paid any federal income tax. By the end of the war, two-thirds of wage-earning Americans were paying federal income and social security taxes. The nation's personal income tax revenues rose twentyfold, from $892 million in 1939 to $18.4 billion in 1945. Corporate income taxes rose from $1.2 billion to $16 billion. After a decade of Depression, the American economy had grown rapidly during the war, as GDP rose from $92 billion in 1939 to $223 billion in 1945. After the war, with Europe and Japan in ruins, more than 50 percent of the world's manufacturing now took place in the United States.[31] This surge in economic growth massively expanded the federal government's discretionary revenue.

The social and political implications of federal income taxes quickly became clear. Representatives of states with little wage or investment income—generally poorer agrarian states—could vote for federal programs that would benefit their communities, knowing that their own citizens would not be heavily taxed to pay for these benefits. This change undergirded the enormous transfer of resources and population from the industrial Northeast to the West and South over the twentieth century. The map in Figure 12.1, from W. E. B. Du Bois's introduction to the NAACP pamphlet *An Appeal to the World!* (1947), offers a graphic depiction of how this worked.

Since the imposition of Jim Crow poll taxes and literacy tests in the late nineteenth-century South, the voting rights of Southern Blacks and poor whites had been suppressed. Voting was restricted to a minority of whites. Southern congressmen were elected by tiny numbers of disproportionately powerful white voters, even though the allocation of congressional seats was based on the entire population of the state. In the Deep South, each member of Congress was elected by, on average, only about fifteen thousand voters, while those in the North and West were elected by about one hundred thousand voters. Southern

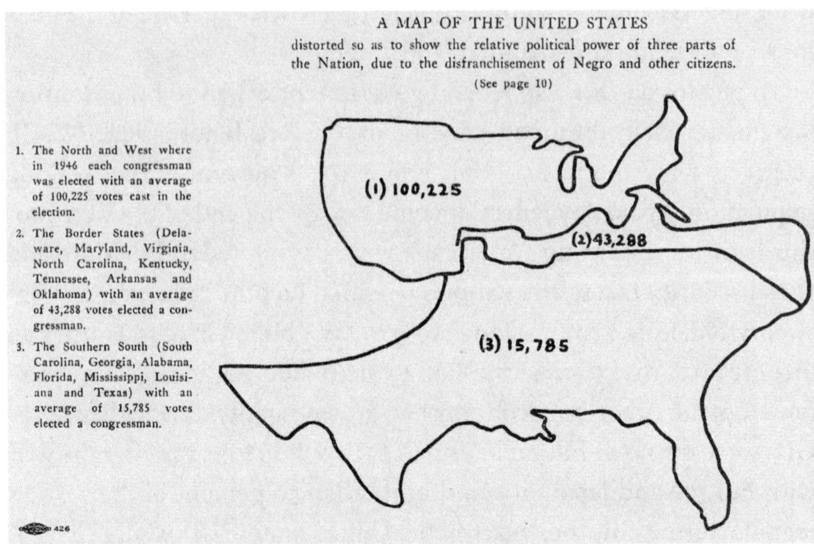

FIGURE 12.1. A map of the United States distorted so as to show the relative political power of three parts of the Nation, due to the disenfranchisement of Negro and other citizens. This hand-drawn map is remarkably effective at showing the exaggerated political power of enfranchised whites in the Deep South, a consequence of voter suppression affecting African Americans and poor whites.

congressmen could steer national resources raised via income taxes paid mainly by the Northeast to their own region, while ensuring through local control of politics that the benefits of these resources were distributed in discriminatory and segregated ways.[32] Such a massive national redistribution project would not have been possible before the Sixteenth Amendment, when direct taxation was still linked to population distribution.

The decisions made by Congress to implement these massive economic interventions, and the congressional politics that shaped these decisions, had a profound effect on the lives of millions of Americans. The Democratic Party coalition that Roosevelt commanded needed the votes of its Southern wing to sustain its congressional majority. This gave the federal government a strong incentive to invest the nation's tax revenues, paid in large part by the citizens and corporations of the North and East, in military production and bases located in the South and West, as chapter 11 described.[33] Southern members who headed major congressional committees were happy to support this legislation. Just as in the New Deal, many federal programs during the war (including conscription) were administered at the state and local level, which allowed racial prejudice and discriminatory laws to guide their administration. This included the federal government's enormous investment in veterans as a reward for military service. The GI Bill (the Servicemen's Readjustment Act of 1944) offered money for college tuition, low-interest home mortgages and loans to start businesses, and unemployment compensation for veterans returning home. A decade after the war ended, some 8.7 million veterans had taken advantage of the GI Bill, but its benefits were denied to most Black veterans. Of the sixty-seven thousand mortgages in the New York City suburbs insured by the GI Bill, for example, fewer than one hundred went to non-whites.[34]

Unlike in the aftermath of the Civil War and World War I, at the end of World War II the federal government did not scale back its massive new expenditures and endeavors. There was a brief demobilization period as World War II ended, resulting in a decline in military spending. But the emerging threat of the Soviet Union, which consolidated its control over eastern and central Europe in the postwar years, the Chinese Communist Party's takeover of China in 1949, the proliferation of nuclear weapons, and the outbreak of the Korean War in 1950 quickly ramped up the fiscal-military state. Atomic warfare, with its capacity to rain down inconceivable destruction from a distance, made it possible to fear that any conflict or crisis, anywhere in the world, could become a dire threat to the nation's survival. The notion that a time-consuming process of deliberation in the House and Senate was required for a declaration of war seemed untenable in the permanent state of emergency brought on by the nuclear era.[35]

Instead of a post-war return to a traditional role for the federal government—scaling back spending and abandoning emergency powers like Cincinnatus returning to the plow—the executive branch extended its power to control all matters having to do with the new and far-reaching concept of national security. In the words of historian Daniel Yergin, national security "postulates the interrelatedness of so many different political, economic, and military factors that developments halfway around the globe are seen to have automatic and direct impact on America's core interests. Virtually every development in the world is perceived to be potentially crucial. An adverse turn of events anywhere endangers the United States."[36] In these circumstances, the Cold War became what historian Mary Dudziak describes as "a period of state-building akin to the New Deal Era. During both periods, the United States embraced a new logic of governance. New institutional structures and economic relations flowed from these shifts in government."[37]

In 1947, Congress passed the National Security Act, which Andrew Preston argues was "one of the single most important pieces of congressional legislation in American history, one that changed not only the character of US foreign and military policies but of American society itself."[38] The act reorganized the command structure of the armed services, created the National Security Council as an advisory board to the president, and established the Central Intelligence Agency. For the first time, the United States had a permanent foreign intelligence agency capable of conducting covert and paramilitary operations, with a secretive and classified budget, answerable directly to the president. In parallel to the CIA, its domestic counterpart the Federal Bureau of Investigation expanded by leaps and bounds during World War II and the Cold War (its employee numbers grew from 1,912 in 1939 to 13,984 in 1953), providing a national police force and an internal civilian surveillance system.[39] The cluster of new or expanded federal agencies and departments, each with its own acronym, became the foreign policy equivalent of the New Deal's "alphabet agencies," with the federal government now overseeing the twin realms of security, social and national. In conceptual terms, national security offered a "New Deal for the world" with programs such as the Marshall Plan to rebuild the postwar economies of Europe and fend off the threat of Soviet communism, extending the new definition of security that emerged in the Great Depression to address U.S. interests around the globe.[40]

Some of the Cold War agencies, such as the CIA and the expanded FBI, were utterly alien to the 1787 Constitution. They were products of emergencies that seemed to demand executive policing authority and secretive powers beyond anything the founding generation could have imagined. The emerging concept of national security, when applied to worrisome events around the globe, ensured that this state of emergency had no foreseeable end. In 1950, the National Security Council published a paper, NSC-68, which famously predicted "an indefinite period of tension and danger" going forward. Later that year President Truman declared a state of emergency in response to the Korean conflict, the first of many such declarations that would characterize the Cold War. In the two decades after 1950, Congress passed more than four hundred statutes empowering the executive branch to act under emergency powers.[41] In January 1961, at the end of his two terms as president, Dwight D. Eisenhower warned the nation in his farewell address that the United States "has been compelled to create a permanent armaments industry of vast proportions," and that its "total influence—economic, political, and even spiritual—is felt in every city, every statehouse, every office of the federal government." Eisenhower decried "the acquisition of unwarranted influence by the military industrial complex" and its potential for the "disastrous rise of misplaced power."[42] The immense U.S. military buildup that had led to victory in World War II and left America as the world's only superpower had an ironic, not to say tragic, outcome. As historian Andrew Preston argues, it generated an ideological commitment to the belief that the values and commitments of the United States were less secure than ever before and required constant militaristic vigilance—a garrison state—to defend the "American Way of Life."[43]

What did *not* happen in these postwar decades was any formal adjustment to the written text of the U.S. Constitution. No amendments were passed to recognize these dramatic changes in the scale of federal powers and their redistribution across the branches of government. New powers were never affirmed by the written constitution, nor new fetters put in place to restrain them from abuse. During his four terms in office, President Roosevelt nominated eight new justices to the Supreme Court. As the elderly justices who had resisted federal expansion during the early years of the New Deal retired, Roosevelt replaced them with justices more sympathetic to the centralization of federal power. Unlike in the early years of the New Deal, there was little pushback from the court against the Cold War's expansion and reorganization of the national security state. The occasional exception, as when the court struck down President Truman's attempt during the Korean War to take over steel mills to resolve a strike that was threatening war production, proved the general rule.[44] A specific action by the president might be restricted by the court's interpretation of the Constitution. But the dramatic expansion of the federal government's powers, increasingly under the control of the executive branch, went on unabated.

In effect, both the court and Congress seemed to acknowledge the truth of Franklin Roosevelt's 1937 radio address. The formal process for amending the Constitution was obsolete in the era of permanent emergency first heralded by the worldwide economic depression and then sealed by the advent of the nuclear age.[45] In 1803, Jefferson had imagined that without constitutional amendments clarifying the federal government's authority to expand into overseas territory, the reach of the United States might expand ad absurdum, even to the annexation of the very empire from which it had won its independence. Jefferson's concern came to a weird fruition in the global spread of American economic and military power in the name of national security.[46]

During the subsequent decades of the seemingly endless Cold War, the unprecedented new powers of the national security state were offset, to a degree, by victories through legislation and the courts in favor of individual rights and liberties. In many cases these victories were achieved through political and social action by America's minority groups, who gained a measure of protection after suffering long histories of discrimination and abuse. The repressive powers of the state and its surveillance agencies were painfully evident in the Red Scare of the 1950s. But at the same time, pressure generated by competition with the Soviet Union for international influence made politicians and judges more amenable to addressing the worst aspects of America's racist, discriminatory, and colonial history. The African American civil rights movement won significant victories in Supreme Court decisions such as *Brown v. Board of Education* (1954) and *Loving v. Virginia* (1967). Legislative transformations such as the Civil Rights Act of 1964 and the

Voting Rights Act of 1965 built on these decisions. Congress designed administrative programs to promote equality in employment and education that attempted to fulfill the promise, deferred for a century, of the Fourteenth Amendment.[47]

In similar fashion, Indigenous Americans worked to gain federal recognition as Indian nations and protection against eliminationist and assimilationist programs. The Indian Citizenship Act of 1924 preserved tribal rights while granting U.S. citizenship to Indians born within U.S. territory. The Indian Child Welfare Act of 1978 ended decades of oppressive policies removing Indian children from their families and tribal cultures. Victories for Indigenous forms of self-government and tribal sovereignty were won through the courts as well.[48]

Immigrant Americans also gained new support from congressional legislation. After forty years of highly discriminatory immigration regulations based on the "National Origins Formula," which largely restricted immigration to people from northern and western Europe, the Immigration and Nationality Act of 1965 opened migration to the United States to a far wider range of the world's peoples.

After decades of activism for equal rights and opportunities for women, neglected by the Philadelphia Constitution in 1787 and deliberately omitted from the Fourteenth Amendment in 1868, progress for women's rights was made through the Equal Pay Act of 1963 and the Civil Rights Act of 1964, which included sex among the categories protected against discrimination in employment. Supreme Court decisions including *Griswold v. Connecticut* (1965) and *Roe v. Wade* (1973) asserted a right to privacy and, under its umbrella, the protection of reproductive freedoms. Spurred by these advances, gay and gender rights activists would use legislation and the courts to win protection from criminalization and eventually marriage and adoption rights and medical protection.

The combined effect of these advances in Congress and the courts has been to extend the protections of the Bill of Rights to the states and to develop explicit protection for rights not enumerated in the Constitution, making good on the implicit promise of the Ninth Amendment. In the words of historian Gary Gerstle, "Because Progressives—and their liberal successors—wanted the courts to embrace rights not enumerated in the Constitution, such as the right to privacy, they had no choice but to adopt a jurisprudential philosophy similar to that of their laissez-faire antagonists."[49] Collectively, these changes to the nation's "higher law" represented what liberal legal scholars referred to as the "living constitution"—a counterbalance in the realm of civil and personal rights to the expansion of government powers over matters of security.

In 1972, the Equal Rights Amendment, stating that "equality of rights under the law shall not be denied or abridged by the United States or by any State on account of sex," was passed by Congress after half a century of similar proposals following the 1920 passage of the Nineteenth Amendment, which guaranteed women's right to vote. But the ERA failed to secure ratification by the necessary thirty-eight states, despite its simple proposal that was utterly consistent with the "creedal constitutionalism" that emerged in the wake of World War II. FDR's warning in the March 1937 fireside chat had been all too prescient. The failure of the ERA to be ratified was an ominous sign of the vulnerability of post–New Deal forms of "higher law" making.[50] The liberal achievements of the Warren Court and the Cold War political consensus, which balanced the demands of America's overseas military commitments and ambitions against the need for domestic reforms of the nation's discriminatory history, were precariously dependent on political circumstances. The powers, rights, and achievements they promoted lacked the permanent foundation of formal Article V constitutional amendments. They were as subject to change by shifting political coalitions and court interpretations—a new "switch in time"—as the Lochner Court's rulings had been.

And the politics came. The promotion of a civil rights agenda by the Democrats under Lyndon Johnson's leadership inaugurated a radical shift among white Southerners from the Democratic to the Republican Party. This political party migration was fueled by racial resentment over federal efforts to ameliorate centuries of discrimination against African Americans. Many of the strongest supporters of this partisan shift came from exactly those places, the Deep South and the arid West, that had benefitted the most from the federal government's geographical redistribution of the nation's taxpayer investments.[51] Long-standing ideological and practical opposition to New Deal social programs among conservatives gained strength from the nation's economic downturn beginning in the 1970s, when global industrial competitors began to catch up to the American juggernaut. These forces coalesced in the election of Ronald Reagan to the presidency in 1980.[52]

The Reagan administration attempted to roll back many of the previous half century's transformations that had seemingly acquired "higher law" status. Reagan appointed administrators who promised to dismantle the regulatory state, attacked labor's right to collective bargaining, and nominated to federal courts judges who would challenge the judicial logic that had supported the Warren Court's expansion of individual rights and protection of the rights of minorities. The new form of jurisprudence designed to attack the living constitution model was known as "originalism." In its invocation of "original intent," it partook of a venerable tradition in Anglo-American constitutionalism: pretending that answers to radically new problems could be found in the way things had been done in the distant past. Originalism also had deep roots in Protestant ways of thinking about historical change, akin to the sixteenth-century Reformers' claim that sacred scripture had been corrupted by centuries of interpretive error. For originalists, the 1787 Constitution and *The Federalist Papers* were the sacred scripture.[53] The Constitution's true meaning could be recovered only by a "return" to strict devotion to the written instrument, and by carefully constructing the canon of sources from which to decide what counts as original to the nation's constitution. Originalism's appeal was buttressed by the bicentennial celebrations of the Declaration of Independence in 1976 and the Constitution in 1987, accompanied by a wave of Founding Fathers hero worship. With the aid of Attorney General Ed Meese, an early supporter of the movement, the Reagan administration promoted the appointment of originalists at every level of the federal judiciary.[54]

As an interpretive doctrine on the federal bench, originalism and its variations (including "original public meaning," "textualism," and a proliferation of other varieties in the legal academy) became the courtroom tool of choice to attack the welfare and administrative state and the expansion of individual liberties and minority rights endorsed by the previous generation's legislatures and courts. A split between the social security and the national security sides of the New Deal–to–Cold War transformation had begun to appear as early as the 1950s, when the Truman administration's Fair Deal social programs, including provisions for universal health care, failed to achieve the support that the national security state gained.[55] While originalism built upon the veneration of the Constitution promoted by World War II and the Cold War, it left the national security state largely untouched. But originalists attacked the New Deal's social security programs through their professed devotion to the sanctity of the original text and the world of the Founders. In its obsession with the literal meaning of particular words found (or not) in the Philadelphia text, originalism lacks a historical sensibility capable of seeing, for instance, that the written Constitution of 1787 did in fact promote social welfare in the agrarian terms of the eighteenth century—by empowering the government to provide cheap land to American citizens.

Originalism can also be seen as the culmination of a trend that began with the court's central role in first rejecting and then confirming the legislative transformations of the New Deal era. With the abandonment of the Article V amendment process, the ownership of all matters "constitutional" now lay with the high priests of the court and their supporters in the legal academy.[56] Using originalism's radical new interpretive strategy, the Rehnquist Court (1985–2005) transformed the written Constitution of 1787 from a blueprint for a nation in the making to a kind of prison or cage. Hewing to a narrow interpretation of the written text as the entire embodiment of "the Constitution" became a way to prevent the nation from becoming anything other than what it was at its birth, despite the obvious fact that after two centuries, the nation the United States had become was unrecognizable from the viewpoint of 1787.[57]

The one aspect of the New Deal–to–Cold War transformation that the conservative backlash did not seek to roll back was the national security state. Instead, the Reagan administration dramatically increased spending on defense. Congress supported expensive new programs such as the B-1 and B-2 bombers, Trident submarines, and the Strategic Defense Initiative (or "Star Wars") while simultaneously cutting taxes and attacking the social and non-military administrative state. The Reagan military buildup expanded the process of deliberately embedding valuable, job-producing military contracts, factories, and bases in every state and congressional district, enhancing bipartisan support for the military-industrial complex.[58] President Eisenhower's warning at his farewell address in 1961 had proven prophetic; the "total influence—economic, political, and even spiritual" of the military-industrial complex was now apparent even in the way American politicians spoke about the traditional problems of society. In December 1943, when Franklin Roosevelt described his administration's policies from the Great Depression to World War II, he reached for a medical metaphor: Dr. New Deal had become Dr. Win-the-War.[59] But from the 1960s onward, warfare became the predominant metaphor used by both parties in managing the nation's social problems: the War on Poverty, the War on Drugs, the War on Crime, the War on Cancer, the War on AIDS, even the culture wars.[60] In the wake of Al Qaeda's 2001 attacks on the World Trade Center and the Pentagon, the George W. Bush administration expanded the military language even further to encompass a Global War on Terror, recognizing no spatial or temporal limits to the permanent state of emergency—the "forever wars"—addressed by the national security state.[61] This trend in language has been accompanied by the increasing militarization of other aspects of the state and public life. Civilian police forces with special weapons and tactics (SWAT) teams use military weapons supplied by the federal government to "fight" crime. The nation's prison system and incarcerated population expanded enormously, creating a pipeline connecting service in the military to civilian policing to private security to prison employment.[62] In the Global War on Terror, this trend was manifested in the U.S. government's willingness to violate constitutional and human rights with the "extraordinary rendition" of terrorist suspects to foreign prisons for secretive interrogations, sometimes using torture. In recent years, the militarized language has been turned against immigrants, whose presence in the country is described as an invasion, occupation, or insurrection—language carefully chosen to justify a militarized response by the federal government.[63]

As the nation's second century under the Constitution came to an end, the Cold War structure that had stabilized the nation's politics for four decades ended as well, first with the breach of the Berlin Wall on November 9, 1989, then with the Soviet Union's dissolution in 1991. The end of the Cold War exposed a fundamental asymmetry in American government. The military-industrial complex and national security state remained and continued to expand, even though the emergency conditions through which it had been created had seemingly come to an end. The lack of formal constitutional amendments to support the overgrown defense establishment did not make it vulnerable to radical reduction; congressional politics, corporate power, and the defense industry had embedded it in every corner of American life, as Eisenhower had warned. But the expansion of the state in every other realm, the myriad ways in which the national government had become directly involved in supporting and managing the growth and well-being of the body of society—the social security of the nation's land and people—remained political footballs to be kicked around in partisan conflicts.

These conflicts are played out in a political arena that itself has been badly distorted by the nation's failure to adapt its governmental institutions to changing populations and technologies, a system corrupted by the overrepresentation of depopulated areas, gerrymandering of voting districts, and the corrosive influence of unlimited money in electoral politics. The political contest is driven not simply by differing policy positions on specific matters but by the more fundamental question of whether the federal government should have the authority to address these matters at all, despite how essential it has been in creating and sustaining the body of the nation as we know it today. And this question is fueled by a lingering fantasy that the nation could somehow return to being what it was at some unspecified moment in the distant past.

Since the Cold War ended at the close of the nation's second century, the United States has been constitutionally adrift. The purpose that dominated the nation's first century, the end for which the Constitution was written in 1787, had been completed by 1890, when the Census Bureau declared the "frontier" to be closed. The "creedal constitution" of the nation's second century, crafted to meet the emergencies of a dangerous world, to defend the "American Way of Life," and to address the nation's shortcomings in living up to the ideals of equality and liberty enunciated at its founding, has come apart amid unremitting partisan bitterness.[64] With it has come a dramatic loss of faith in the prospect that collective democratic self-government, as embodied in the nation's traditional institutions defined by the Constitution, can meet the urgent challenges of the twenty-first century.

Epilogue

TOWARD 2090: RETHINKING THE PURPOSE OF THE UNITED STATES

IT MAY SEEM like a peculiar question to ask: What is the *purpose* of a country or nation? Especially if we turn to a country with an ancient history, rooted in a specific place, occupied by a distinctive people with their own language and culture—Japan, or Peru, or Egypt, to name just a few of many possible examples around the globe—why should it have a purpose? When William, Duke of Normandy, invaded England and defeated its Anglo-Saxon king, he had no grander purpose beyond expanding his own power over a neighboring Christian kingdom. Is it not enough to say that a country simply exists, and that all the purpose it, or its government, needs is to secure the well-being of its people?

And yet the question of purpose is never far from the surface when it comes to thinking about the United States of America, a nation that was consciously crafted out of constituent parts and then deliberately went on to expand itself out of new "material," as Willa Cather might have put it. The question looms large in the nation's founding documents. The Declaration of Independence begins by explaining why it is *necessary* to form a new country, a new people, breaking apart an older one. It goes on to define the philosophical principles and describe the historical events that justify this radical act of self-creation. But it never quite answers the implicit question of why these particular thirteen of Britain's twenty-six American colonies now constitute a distinct people and an incipient nation, and why it is that the colonies of Nova Scotia, East Florida, Jamaica, or Barbados are not part of this new people who have the right to be independent states and the duty to form a new nation.

The Articles of Confederation offered an initial take on the purpose of a "League of Friendship" among these newly sovereign states. The confederation was "*for* their common defence, the security of their Liberties, and their mutual and general welfare." This was pretty generic, just what any country's government might be for. But the Treaty of Paris in 1783 that recognized the sovereign autonomy of the United States also highlighted defects in this initial union. By granting to the sovereign states extensive land claims over which they had no actual authority, the treaty revealed the inadequacy of the Articles to meet the challenge of expansion necessary to make these claims real. Subsequent efforts to amend the Articles, ultimately yielding a new written constitution in 1787, aimed to make the union more perfect. In so doing, the Constitutional Convention imbued the revised nation with a new set of structures and powers that would allow it to resume the colonizing project that Britain had begun two centuries earlier.

When colonization comes into view, the question of *purpose* in the making and governing of new societies becomes inescapable. In this sense, the formation of the United States was neither new nor exceptional in world historical terms. From the time humans began to record their history and states began to form empires, intent on extending their authority over new and distant territories, the expression of purpose—the claim that a colonizing society has superior gods, more just laws, or better economic practices than the colonized—became a justification for imperial expansion. All the Abrahamic religions expressed versions of such claims as they expanded and built ruling authorities in new lands. The children of Israel in their conquest of Canaan, as well as the followers of Jesus and Muhammad who inherited the Hebraic tradition, justified expansion and state building as bringing true religion and just laws to pagans and infidels.

Europe's encounter with the Americas in the late fifteenth century, accompanied and spurred on by early modern utopian thought, opened vast new realms for colonization. New worlds offered opportunities to rethink old traditions and raised the prospect of endless abundance, for the planet was not as cramped and crowded as it had seemed. Spain led the way, but Britain's colonization of North America and the Caribbean partook of this tradition in a distinctive fashion. As latecomers to American colonization, and as a newly Protestant nation, the English critiqued their Spanish imperial predecessors—they were too autocratic, violent, and oppressive of the Indigenous people and taught them a false version of Christianity. English colonists would bring true Christianity to Native peoples, along with their free and fair laws and effective forms of agriculture.

But even among the English colonies, differing purposes were expressed in their settlements. Early Virginians envisioned a place where England's poor and unemployed, its "masterless men," would find work and abundant land, restoring social harmony while expanding the realm. Whereas Virginians were happy to replicate the established church in their colony, Massachusetts Puritans wanted radical reform to the Church of England and pursued a more egalitarian social vision of self-governing churches and towns. Maryland's founders dreamed of a refuge for English Catholics and a return to pre-Reformation ways. Pennsylvania's Quakers rejected the exclusivity of New England's churches and offered a new model for peaceable relations with Indigenous peoples. Even Georgia, founded in the 1730s, began (at least initially) as an experiment, an attempt to create a colony without the noxious institution of chattel slavery that earlier colonies had developed.

In that sense, the idea that these colonial societies should have a *purpose*, a design for improving the world, was already baked into the histories of the states that created the United States. But to make their confederation more perfect, allowing these very different societies to act in a concerted fashion, the states had to compromise, to strip down their distinctive features, to arrive at something like a common purpose. A single national religion among these thirteen diverse and coequal states was impossible. The different traditions of the various states were embedded too deeply for any single one to predominate. By eschewing a national religion, the United States discarded the one locus of "purpose" that even premodern, traditional countries shared—the site where a collective set of values, a cosmology, or the trajectory of a nation's sacred history might be expressed.

Without a national religion, what remained to frame a purpose for the United States were two things: (1) the civic values inherited from the British tradition, as refined and reshaped by the resistance movement against British rule and the War of Independence, the practices of representative self-government, the common law, and the rights and liberties of the British constitution stretching back to Magna Carta and beyond; and (2) the continuing commitment to colonization, the persistent belief that America's Indigenous owners were inadequately civilized and were misusing the resources of a vast continent. By taking possession, Americans would transform the continent into a land of limitless abundance for its own citizens. With just a few phrases, the Constitution of 1787 excluded the continent's Indigenous populations ("Indians not taxed") from any claim to these benefits and reserved them for the nation's white male citizens and their dependents. At the time, this dependent population included some eight hundred thousand enslaved Africans, whose condition was regulated by the sovereign states, not the national confederation. Thus was born the Domesday Machine.

For its first century, this is what the United States was *for*. The main purpose of the framework of government at the federal level was to carry out the revised American version of the colonization project Britain had initiated. By acquiring land from Indigenous people and extinguishing their claims to it, the federal government engaged in a project to create social and national security for its own privileged citizens. It provided for their material well-being and eliminated any threat to their enjoyment of the land from either Indigenous owners or foreign competitors. In the process, American colonists transformed the environmental conditions of the continent, turning forests and prairies into farmland, cities, and factories. In so doing, Americans generated the material abundance that utopian writers had dreamed of. Over the nineteenth century, the United States became the world's largest economy and its people developed habits and expectations of material consumption unprecedented in world history.

The civic values built into America's colonization project meant that its purpose differed from other colonizing empires. The constitutional promise to make territories into states fully incorporated in the self-governing republic came to mean that the United States rejected the colonization of foreign peoples deemed undesirable for inclusion in the national realm. Britain, for example, ruled over millions of people in India who were racially, ethnically, and religiously distinct. But with the conquest of Mexico, the United States refused to consider a similar colonial arrangement. It chose instead to annex only Mexico's sparsely populated northern regions that it could transform into states dominated by European-descended settlers. In other words, people in acquired foreign territories who were seen as similar to "Indians not taxed" were kept outside of the civic promise of U.S. colonial expansion. When, with the Spanish-American War, the United States gained foreign territories in the Philippines and Puerto Rico, where the exclusion of alien peoples from the land was impossible, the promise of civic incorporation for U.S. territories was revoked, affirmed by the Supreme Court's Insular Cases and their ironically named "doctrine of incorporation."

At the turn of the twentieth century, the completion of the continental expansion project and the beginnings of overseas colonization on a new model signaled that the purpose of the United States defined by the 1787 Constitution was coming to an end as well. But the idea of a purpose for the United States did not come to an end. The Domesday Machine had done its work; now what would the United States be *for*? The Civil War had tested the civic values of the union, inherited from Britain and revised by the American Revolution, by way of a breakaway movement in favor of a cause unthinkable in 1776. If, as the British anthem claimed, Britons never will be slaves, the Southern Confederates argued that slavery (for some) was a positive good and Jefferson's claim for human equality in the Declaration was mistaken. Abraham Lincoln's eloquent rhetoric reaffirmed the civic values of the founding by framing the insurrection as a test of the "proposition that all men are created equal." This proposition, the belief that America was an experiment "conceived in liberty," became a template for American ideas of purpose in the twentieth century, played out as much on a global as on a national scale.

In the nineteenth century, the American democratic republic had consciously avoided intervening in overseas conflicts, even when colonized peoples were fighting for their own independence from tyrannical rule. The United States steered clear of Haiti's revolution, the Spanish American colonial wars of independence, and the Greek revolution against the Ottoman Empire, to cite just a few examples from the republic's early years. The United States would not help other nations carry out the experiment or test the propositions Lincoln described, despite having been assisted by France in its own war for independence. In the twentieth century, the United States took on an ever-larger role in overseas affairs. Woodrow Wilson's slogan as the nation entered the Great War (despite his campaign promise to maintain neutrality)—that Americans were joining the conflict to "make the world *safe* for democracy"—enunciated a new purpose for the United States—to extend the civic values and forms of security it had built for its own citizens to a wider world. But as the Great War turned out not to be the war that ended war, future conflicts modified and refined this purpose.

Making the world safe for democracy meant defending the "American Way of Life" all around the world, and this included the nation's productive capacities and consumption habits. The corporations that organized the twentieth-century industrial economy required access to resources around the globe. As Dwight Eisenhower, the general who organized the American assault on the Nazis' European fortress, would write, "The purpose of America is to defend a way of life rather than merely to defend property, homes, or lives."[1] The United States proceeded to build the largest military arsenal in history, prepared to address threats anywhere in the world to its interests, while expanding the scope of its domestic government to promote this security at home. The nation's record of using this power to defend liberty and equality in its interventions around the globe has been spotty at best. And while a corollary of the Cold War project to defend the "American Way" included efforts to extend the promise of the nation's founding values to all Americans, to remedy the suffering of the nation's internally colonized peoples, these efforts too remain fraught, opposed by many who continue to insist that not everyone is entitled to the "American Way of Life."

The Cold War came to an end just as the United States completed its second century under the Philadelphia Constitution; whatever coherence remained of the United States' purpose in the twentieth century crumbled with it. The triumphalism of Americans' response to this Pyrrhic victory meant that there was little reckoning with the damage that a century of government driven by emergency—government "beyond the constitution," as Jefferson might have put it—had done to the relationship between the land and people, the government, and the written constitution of the United States. It was little noticed that the garment no longer fit the body. And given that much of the American purpose had been played out around the globe, there was little reckoning with the damage American power had inflicted overseas.

Since that time the United States has been constitutionally adrift, lacking in purpose. Its overseas military ventures have been decidedly ineffective and difficult to justify to a skeptical public. Its internal politics have become bitterly divided, even in the absence of a starkly differentiating national issue akin to what slavery was in the nineteenth century. Threats to the commitments to liberty and equality declared in the nation's founding come from authoritarian sources that are as much internal to the national culture as they are "out there" in a dangerous world. And the grave planetary challenges all nations face—a rapidly warming climate, soil degradation, alarming rates of species extinction and loss of biodiversity, increasing threats of epidemic disease, and grotesque inequalities in the consumption of the world's resources—are ignored by a sclerotic political system in which moneyed interests dominate.

What, then, might become the purpose of the United States as we look ahead toward the end of its third century? Will there be a United States in 2090, and if so, what will it be *for*?

Any historian with a long view of the past would be foolish to imagine that an immense, confederated nation or an empire built up through conquest and colonization is destined to endure forever. At the time the United States came into being, the Venetian-born artist Giovanni

Battista Piranesi was producing prints and engravings of the ruins of ancient Rome, its contemporary human inhabitants looking like insects crawling amid the rubble of monumental arches, fountains, temples, columns, and baths.[2] Spain's sixteenth-century monarchs believed they had surpassed their ancient Roman ancestors by building a truly global empire, but Spain lost most of its American possessions within a few decades of U.S. independence. Britain's empire continued to expand after the loss of its American colonies but came apart across the twentieth century, the "American Century." The Ottoman Empire failed to survive the Great War after centuries of rule over much of what Rome had once conquered. The list could go on. The United States differs from each of these empires, but they each differed one from the other—there is no reason to assume that the American empire is exempt from the entropic forces that other great states have faced. Nor is it necessarily a bad thing for overgrown polities to come apart, especially if the rewards of great size benefit the few at the expense of the many.

There is, of course, justifiable concern that the breakdown of the United States' constitution would mean the loss of the freedoms, rights, and protections it provides, the very things that Americans have long venerated, the civic values proclaimed at the nation's founding. They are currently under assault, though not for the first time. Lincoln described the Slave Power's insurrection as a test of these propositions, but they are always being tested because they are hard to sustain. These values exist above and beyond the written Constitution of 1787 and its Bill of Rights. They can survive its demise if people rededicate themselves to these propositions in a new alignment of constitutional principles, just as former British Americans did in framing their independent state and national constitutions.

In the legislatures, conventions, pamphlets, newspapers, town meetings, and county courthouses where Americans debated constitution making in the 1770s and '80s, differences of opinion were widespread and profound. But there was one idea, one principle of action, on which every participant in the process agreed: that a free and sovereign people have the power to frame a government that protects their rights and meets the challenges of the world they live in, that they should not be imprisoned by their own constitutional history. The idea was expressed in the Declaration of Independence: It argued that when an existing government becomes persistently destructive of "unalienable Rights" such as "Life, Liberty and the pursuit of happiness," then "it is the Right of the People to alter or to abolish it, and to institute new Government, laying its foundation on such principles and organizing its powers in such form, as to them shall seem most likely to effect their Safety and Happiness." The Massachusetts Constitution of 1780, like those of many other states, offered a version of this sentiment, claiming that the purpose of government is to furnish its people "with the power of enjoying, in safety and tranquility, their natural rights, and the blessings of life: And whenever these great objects are not obtained, the people have a right to alter the government, and to take measures necessary for their safety, prosperity and happiness." The preamble to the Constitution of the United States drafted in Philadelphia in 1787 expanded on the purposes for which such actions might be taken: "to form a more perfect Union, establish Justice, insure domestic Tranquility, provide for the common defence, promote the general Welfare, and secure the Blessings of Liberty to ourselves and our Posterity."

The safety and happiness of the people of the United States are now intricately entwined with the safety and happiness of the rest of the world. What it means today, and will mean in the future, to promote the general welfare or secure the blessings of liberty to ourselves and our posterity is quite different from what it meant in the 1780s. We can think about this by reviewing, for a moment, the long time span that this book has crossed, from the Norman Conquest of England in the eleventh century to our present moment in the twenty-first.

As the series of graphs in Figure E.1 depicts with striking regularity, the independence of the United States and the making of its first constitutions occurred at the end of a very long period, at least eight centuries, of relative stability in an agrarian world. Three basic indicators of human welfare—global population, average global life expectancy, and economic productivity—remained largely unchanged across these centuries. Similarly, three basic indicators of environmental conditions relevant to human welfare—global industrial production of

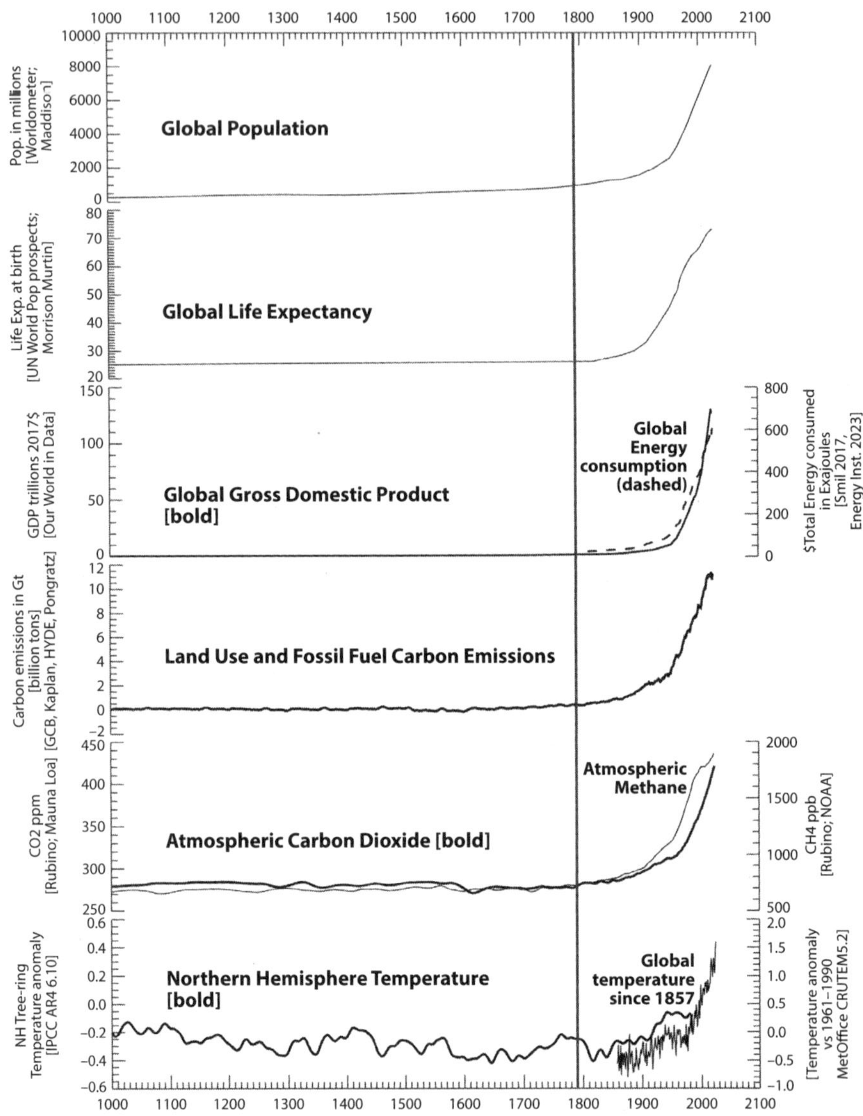

FIGURE E.1. Population, economy, and climate change, 1000–present. The vertical line drawn across these graphs marks the year of the Philadelphia Constitutional Convention, 1787. It neatly divides the long agrarian era of stability in population, human lifespan, economic productivity, industrial carbon dioxide emissions, atmospheric carbon dioxide, and ambient temperature from the subsequent era of rapid acceleration across all these categories.

carbon dioxide, atmospheric carbon dioxide levels, and temperature—were relatively stable across these centuries as well. Temperatures in the Northern Hemisphere went through long cycles of fluctuation but were no higher in 1800 than in 1000.

Then, starting around 1800, all this changed. The now-familiar "hockey stick" graph shows a sharp and continuous rise across all these categories—human population and life expectancy, economic productivity, industrial carbon production, atmospheric carbon dioxide, and global temperatures—with no sign of leveling off, let alone turning downward. And while the longer lifespans and greater wealth of the world's people are undoubted benefits of the past two centuries, they have also been intimately tied to industrial production of atmospheric carbon and rapidly rising global temperatures. The extraordinary growth of modern industrial production and consumption now pose threats to societies around the globe. If the rest of the world were to adopt the levels of material consumption that have historically come to define the "American Way of Life," it would require the resources of five planet Earths to sustain it. None of these developments, or the challenges they present to our general welfare and that of our posterity, were thinkable in 1787. They are urgent and inescapable now.

In 1787, faced with the challenges of a rapidly growing population, insecure claims to Western land, and a national debt without any means to collect revenue, the Philadelphia Convention altered the nation's constitution, providing structures and powers to the national government to address these problems. But nothing in that document or its subsequent amendments provides the national government with the capacity to meet the most urgent challenges our nation and our planet face in the twenty-first century. In fact, to say as much is already old news.

More than half a century ago, Rexford G. Tugwell, a former member of Franklin Roosevelt's New Deal Brain Trust, addressed this problem. Tugwell, an economist recruited from Columbia University, played a major part in designing the Agricultural Adjustment Act but left the federal government after the act was struck down by the Supreme Court. He later served as the last appointed governor of Puerto Rico, assisting in the island's transition to electing its own executive. Afterwards he returned to academia, where he led the Center for the Study of Democratic Institutions, researching problems in American government and its relationship to the constitution. In 1974, he assembled the group's findings in a seven-hundred-page book, *The Emerging Constitution.*[3]

Across thirteen chapters, Tugwell's book assesses the challenge of constitutional government in modern society, addressing defects in the three government branches under the current constitution. He also devotes chapters to aspects of modern governance for which the eighteenth-century text had no provisions: the role of party systems in a mass-communication society, the assessment of government operations at modern scale and complexity, and the need for an administrative apparatus within the state. Along the way, he explores constitutional approaches to problems that were unimaginable in 1787—for instance, "the duty of framers to achieve consonance with their environment." He puts this problem at the forefront of contemporary constitutional challenges: "Natural rights were in the framers' minds, but not natural duties. The obligation to learn nature's imperatives and to obey them had no recognition. For the putative framers of a new constitution this should be the first of all considerations."[4] In a concluding chapter Tugwell offers a draft of a way forward, "A Proposed Constitutional Model for the Newstates of America."[5]

As the title suggests, one of Tugwell's proposals is something that was briefly contemplated at the Philadelphia Convention: a remodeling of the states in the interest of equality. Under this proposed constitution, there would be a smaller number of states, at most twenty, each with at least 5 percent of the nation's population. The proposal further recommends changes in the legislative branch by remaking the Senate as a national body, with members drawn from former presidents, vice presidents, state governors, and other high offices. The presidency is redefined as a single nine-year term, and a judicial assembly is created to regularly review the nation's legal system.

Beyond reforms of existing elements, Tugwell's model proposes new institutions and powers that are absent from the 1787 Constitution. It endows the House of Representatives with new powers to address issues of a modern society: the power to establish a civil service to administer laws; to work with international agencies to "assist in the maintenance of world order," including the regulation of outer space and the world's oceans; to establish social insurance; to promote education for all; and to protect natural resources. Tugwell's model adds entirely new branches of government: a nonpartisan electoral branch to guarantee fair election procedures; a planning branch to assess long-term budgetary needs and investment opportunities; and a regulatory branch to oversee the rules of conduct for the nation's economy, including a uniform national system for chartering corporations. It proposes a new procedure for constitutional amendments and provides for a national referendum every twenty-five years on whether a new constitution is needed. While this new constitutional model begins with a Bill of Rights, it adds a Bill of Responsibilities as well, listing thirteen duties citizens owe to the nation, such as "Each citizen shall participate in the processes of democracy, assisting in the selection of officials and the monitoring of their conduct in office" and "Each shall assist in preserving the endowments of nature and enlarging the inheritance of future generations."

Needless to say, Tugwell's model did not transform America's constitution any more than John Wesley Powell's 1879 model for the future organization of the arid West changed the way Congress went about the creation of new states. Nor am I endorsing Tugwell's model as the right way forward in our twenty-first-century predicament. Tugwell himself prefaced his book by saying "Coming generations ought not to be precluded from making their own basic law. This offering is for now and for the immediate—not the far—future." Two of Tugwell's proposed twenty-five-year cycles for considering constitutional renewal have already passed since his model was published—a fifth of the republic's history has gone by. The written constitution remains unamended over that time, even as the body of society and the structure of our government drift farther away from it. As a veteran government official, Tugwell recognized the dangers of this constitutional misalignment even before the rise of the judicial movement that aims to constrict the capacities of government to the written framework of 1787. He expressed this concern with respect to environmental issues:

> In considering how much is now known about these matters that was not known in 1787, it becomes very strange indeed that this knowledge has not worked its way into the Constitution. Because it is not there, but is applied only in extraconstitutional regulation, it is always half-hearted and ineffective. Legislators cannot say to lobbyists that what predators want they cannot have because the Constitution will not permit it. So unwittingly, or under pressure, they give way. The public lands are overgrazed; the water tables are lowered; the minerals are used up; the forests are cut—and all the other resources similarly are given away.[6]

What was, and is, true for environmental matters is also the case for countless other forms of "extraconstitutional" legislation, regulation, and administration: the practices necessary to sustain a modern state with governmental responsibilities over a society of a third of a billion people and with commitments and interests that influence and encircle the globe.

I conclude with this discussion of a serious but unrealized effort to rethink the American constitution because I agree with its author, and also with the framers of all the American constitutions created in the revolutionary era: "coming generations ought not to be precluded from making their own basic law." To paraphrase the Massachusetts Constitution of 1780, whenever "the great objects of government" are not obtained, "the people have a right to alter it, and to take measures necessary for their safety, prosperity and happiness."

It is Americans' great and continuing misfortune that the most radical and forceful effort to alter the nation's fundamental law resulted in civil war. This effort was led by oligarchic rulers in pursuit of the worst possible cause: a commitment to permanent human inequality, oppression, and subordination. It was conducted in the worst possible way, by an unprovoked military insurrection that brought on the bloodiest and most destructive war in the history of the Western Hemisphere. The nation feels its scars to this day. But that catastrophe should not prevent future generations from reclaiming the vision of the nation's founders—the belief that the present generation has it in its power, as a sovereign people, to realign the strongest and most enduring values of our constitutional history with new frameworks of government well designed to meet the challenges of *our* world, to promote the general welfare of *our*selves and *our* posterity.

How will this happen? The skill set of a historian is not particularly conducive to predicting the future. But I will lean on history to risk the assertion that a radical realignment of the American constitution is unlikely to happen in "constitutional" fashion, by the mechanisms endorsed in the written instrument of 1787. This is in part an assessment of the historic weakness of the amendment process laid out in Article V; Franklin Roosevelt's diagnosis of its futility as a tool for making major changes has not been contradicted by subsequent events. But it is also a historical observation that major constitutional interventions in the Anglo-American tradition, including the Philadelphia Constitution itself, tend not to be constitutional—they are more likely to bend or break the existing rules than they are to follow them. This historical pattern makes it all the more important to think carefully and systematically now—after the example of a John Adams or a James Madison, who arrived at constitutional conventions with plans in mind—about what a better frame of government for the people of the United States and for their relationship to the world would look like. If we are fortunate, we may find opportunities for constructive change while avoiding violence of the sort that the leaders of the Confederacy released upon the nation in 1861, or that broke the British Empire apart in 1775. We do not know when or how a moment of plasticity for a new constitutional realignment might occur. But it would be good to have a plan for when it does.

ACKNOWLEDGMENTS

THIS BOOK IS a product of the Covid-19 years. 2019 was the year my previous book, *The City-State of Boston*, was published. In March 2020 I was presenting a talk about it at Oxford University's Rothermere American Institute when the pandemic swept across the earth and froze us all in our socially distanced cells. Shortly thereafter, a small group of early Americanists of a certain generation, friends for decades, began a regular Sunday afternoon Zoom meeting. We wanted to sustain the conversation and comradery that bolsters the scholarly enterprise, which even in the best of times necessitates a certain amount of social isolation. In the five years since we began, two of our members have died tragically young, each of them cut off in the prime of their careers. This book is dedicated to their memory. To the surviving members of our virtual pub, I offer my undying gratitude—the weekly conversations in our electronic treehouse have inspired and shaped this work in countless ways.

This book began to emerge in Berkeley, California, where I taught a course on the deep history of the formation of the United States Constitution. It took concrete form with the help of two friends, Tom Laqueur and Daniel Sargent, who kindly read a misshapen and overly long op-ed essay I had written and convinced me that it was not an op-ed but a book proposal. They were right. Within weeks it was under contract, thanks to my agent, Geri Thoma, and to Brigitta van Rheinberg and Eric Crahan at Princeton University Press, who were keen on the project from the get-go. Other Berkeley friends helped to shepherd it along, most notably Jonathan Sheehan, who read and commented on big chunks of undercooked text. Jonathan also organized a departmental seminar in the spring of 2025 to discuss the book's central section; Beth Berry, Brian Delay, Carla Hesse, David and Joan Hollinger, Trevor

Jackson, Danny Kelly, Tom Laqueur, and Ethan Shagan offered the sharp but congenial criticism for which Berkeley's department is justly renowned. Berkeley graduate students from that era, some of whom took the aforementioned course, were also instrumental in shaping my thoughts on constitutions and frames of government, especially Hannah Farber, Anthony Gregory, Bobby Lee, Derek O'Leary, Franklin Sammons, and Russ Weber.

The contents of this book span a very long time period and include many subjects on which I am by no means an expert. I have relied on the guidance and generosity of colleagues and friends who are experts and have tried to steer me away from trouble. Their aid has been indispensable, but the remaining errors and misjudgments are mine alone. Thanks go to Phil Withington, Caroline Winterer, Phil Stern, Andrew Preston, Ariel Ron and Noam Maggor and their online US Political Economy Lab, and Richard John and his study group at Columbia University. Richard John gave the manuscript a thorough and incisive reading for which I'm very grateful.

The bulk of the research and writing on this book was done at Yale, made possible by sabbatical leaves in 2019–2020 and again in spring 2024. The work has been supported by conversation and collaboration with a wonderful set of colleagues in many contexts, including Lauren Benton, Ned Blackhawk, David Blight, Rohit De, Maura Dykstra, David Engerman, Hussein Fancy, Beverly Gage, Bruce Gordon, Isaac Nakhimovsky, Bill Rankin, Paul Sabin, Stuart Schwartz, and Arne Westad. Isaac Nakhimovsky and Giulia Oskian organized a timely workshop at Yale on "Constitutional Promises" in the spring of 2025, where I presented a chapter of the book, and I'm grateful to the participants for their comments.

The Yale Early American History seminar (yeah, YEAH) brings together graduate students and faculty to discuss each others' ongoing work in the field. I thank YEAH's stalwart members for allowing me to present drafts of chapters and for sharing their collective wisdom: Kaelyn Apple, Lauren Benton, Zach Brown, Elliott Cramer, Jane Coppock, Teddy Delwiche, Nathaniel Donahue, Joanne Freeman, Winston

Hill, Henry Ishitani, Eva Landsberg, Jay Mehta, Oliver Riskin-Kutz, Ed Rugemer, Wulf Scouller, River Sell, Tisa Wenger, and Emily Yankowitz. And I much appreciate Eric Areklett's assistance in cleaning up the endnotes. Thanks too to Jordan Peccia, head of Yale's Benjamin Franklin College, for inviting me to discuss Franklin's constitutionalism at one of the college's Fellows Seminars.

It has been hugely advantageous, though not a little intimidating, for a historian of the constitution with no formal legal training to work across the street from Yale Law School and its extraordinary collection of legal historians and constitutional experts. When I was mid-way through drafting the manuscript I had the benefit of an informal workshop organized at YLS, where Nick Parillo, Claire Priest, Arne Westad, John Witt, and Maggie Blackhawk (of NYU Law School) read the manuscript and offered encouragement; I'm particularly grateful to Maggie for her comments and critiques during numerous runs up and down East Rock. As I was finishing the manuscript, a symposium at Yale Law School organized by the *Yale Journal of Law and the Humanities* on Jonathan Gienapp's book, *Against Constitutional Originalism*, offered me another opportunity to present and discuss my own work. Thanks to Zach Brown for the invitation and to the symposium's many participants for engaging with the work of an interloper.

It has once again been an unalloyed pleasure to work with Princeton University Press in bringing this book into being. Three external readers for the Press, Max Edling, Lige Gould, and an anonymous reader, offered thorough, careful, and critical reports that collectively helped me to focus the argument and clarify the organization. Along the way I have enjoyed editorial advice from Bridget Flannery-McCoy and Priya Nelson; Priya's close reading of the text at a critical moment made a huge difference. Emma Wagh's steady guidance through the production process has been immensely helpful and reassuring. Dimitri Karetnikov deserves credit for managing the illustrations, and Rob McCaleb for cartography. Thanks also to the people at Westchester Publishing Services, Elizabeth Ploski, for assisting with the technical production, and Christina Nichols for assiduous copyediting.

Mary Woolsey has always been my best reader, editor, and interlocutor as well as my best friend; I depend on her love and support to do this work. Our children, Rowan and Thomas, are doing the kind of work that inspires me and brings me hope for our collective future. And our very ancient dog, Cricket, now seventeen years old, has offered faithful if noisy companionship throughout.

NOTES

Introduction. "Like a Garment to the Bodie"

1. On American "creedal constitutionalism," see Aziz Rana, *The Constitutional Bind: How Americans Came to Idolize a Document That Fails Them* (University of Chicago Press, 2024), 1–38; and Michael Kammen, *A Machine That Would Go of Itself: The Constitution in American Culture* (Alfred A. Knopf, 1986).

2. "How the National Archives Became Home to the US Constitution, Declaration of Independence, and Bill of Rights," National Park Service, https://www.nps.gov/articles/000/how-the-national-archives-became-home-to-the-us-constitution-declaration-of-independence-and-bill-of-rights.htm.

3. "On the Constitution of England," in *The Freeholders Magazine* 1 (London, 1769), 60, quoted in John Brewer, *Party Ideology and Popular Politics at the Accession of George III* (Cambridge University Press, 1976), 243.

4. George III, quoted in John Brooke, *King George III* (McGraw Hill, 1972), 56.

5. "Monthly Miscellany," *New American Magazine* (Woodbridge, NJ) 1, no. 13, January 1759, 320.

6. [John Adams], "III. The Earl of Clarendon to William Pym, 27 January 1766," *Founders Online*, National Archives, https://founders.archives.gov/documents/Adams/06-01-02-0063-0004.

7. James Otis, *The Rights of the British Colonies Asserted and Proved* (Boston, 1764), 13, 21. North Americans sometimes referred to the Seven Years' War as "The French War" or the "French and Indian War." The initial fighting broke out in 1754 in North America, two years before the more general conflagration began in Europe and beyond.

8. Brunswick-Lüneburg was the German duchy of which George I, the first Hanoverian king, had been duke; Frederick was the Prince of Wales, son of George II and father of George III, who died before he could inherit the throne; Charlotte was the queen consort of George III.

9. "Second Petition from Congress to the King, 8 July 1775," *Founders Online*, National Archives, https://founders.archives.gov/documents/Jefferson/01-01-02-0114.

10. King George III, *A Proclamation for Suppressing Rebellion and Sedition*, August 23, 1775 (London, 1775).

11. Thomas Smith, *De Republica Anglorum: The Maner of Governement or Policie of the Realm of England* (London: Henrie Midleton, 1584), 17. Smith composed this treatise in the 1560s, but it was not published until 1583.

12. Smith, *De Republica Anglorum*, 17.

13. Benjamin Rush, "On Patriotism," *Pennsylvania Journal,* October 20, 1773, in Lyman Butterfield, ed., *The Letters of Benjamin Rush* (Princeton University Press, 1951), I:84 Emphasis added.

14. Historian Jack Rakove makes a similar argument about the constitutional "garment" when he writes, "Since 1789 Americans have always possessed two constitutions, not one: the formal document adopted in 1787–88, with its amendments, and the working constitution, comprising the body of precedents, habits, understandings, and attitudes that shape how the federal system operates at any given moment." Rakove, *Original Meanings: Politics and Ideas in the Making of the Constitution* (Knopf, 1996), 339–40. At the time Smith composed *De Republica Anglorum,* no stark distinctions were made—none were needed—between written instruments of government and other forms by which its authority was defined and expressed, such as ritual, custom, and historical memory; all were equally valid elements in defining the "garment" of government.

15. This book makes a distinction between the document crafted in Philadelphia in 1787 and subsequently amended some twenty-seven times, and the wider constitutional history and tradition of the United States, which began long before the Philadelphia Convention. The document produced by the Philadelphia Convention, titled "The Constitution of the United States," does not completely encompass the constitution of the nation as a whole. That document has been amended twenty-seven times, and there are now fifty state constitutions, several territorial constitutions, and other documents such as the Land Ordinance of 1785, the Northwest Ordinance of 1787, and the Judiciary Act of 1789 that are fully part of the constitution, as well as customs and institutions such as the common law not encompassed in any document. In other words, the American constitution is much more capacious than the Philadelphia text. To maintain this distinction, the word "Constitution" will be capitalized when it refers to the document; lowercase constitution will be used for the more capacious version of the tradition.

16. On the significance of distinguishing written instruments from constitutions as systems or frames of government, see Mary Sarah Bilder, "The Emerging Genre of *The Constitution*: Kent Newmyer and the Heroic Age," *Connecticut Law Review* 52, no. 4 (2021): 1264–79.

17. Shakespeare's usage of the term tends to follow this definition, as in *Twelfth Night,* act 1, sc. 3, line 127, when Sir Toby Belch refers to the "excellent constitution" of Sir Andrew Aguecheek's leg, or in *The Merchant of Venice,* act 3, sc. 2, line 256, when Portia marvels at how bad news "could turn so much the constitution of any constant man."

18. Smith was by no means singular in this use of bodily metaphors for "constitution." For instance, John Adams, in the same essay in which he praised the British constitution's devotion to liberty (cited in note 6), offers an extended discussion of "the constitution of the human body" and compares the "fundamentals" of a human constitution to those of a political constitution. And during the French Revolution a satirical cartoon, "Fashion Before Ease," by James Gilray depicts Thomas Paine trying to force Britannia into a formal constitutional corset much too tight for her body. For a general discussion, see Eric Slauter, *The State as a Work of Art: The Cultural Origins of the Constitution* (University of Chicago Press, 2009), 39–55, Gilray image reproduced on p. 40.

19. *Oxford English Dictionary Online,* "constitution," definitions 5 and 6, https://www.oed.com/dictionary/constitution_n?tab=meaning_and_use#8393697.

20. The latter point is demonstrated eloquently, ad absurdum, by Jorge Luis Borges's brief story "Of Exactitude in Science," in *A Universal History of Infamy* (Penguin Books, 1975), 131.

21. For these important documents, which will be cited again in subsequent chapters, see Magna Carta (1215), UK National Archives, https://www.nationalarchives.gov.uk/education/resources/magna-carta/british-library-magna-carta-1215-runnymede/; Bill of Rights (1688), Acts of English Parliament, https://www.legislation.gov.uk/aep/WillandMarSess2/1/2/introduction; Constitution of Pennsylvania, September 28, 1776, *Avalon Project*, Yale Law School, https://avalon.law.yale.edu/18th_century/pa08.asp; The Constitution of Virginia (1776), Encyclopedia Virginia, https://encyclopediavirginia.org/primary-documents/the-constitution-of-virginia-1776/; Northwest Ordinance (1787), National Archives, https://www.archives.gov/milestone-documents/northwest-ordinance; Articles of Confederation (1777), National Archives, https://www.archives.gov/milestone-documents/articles-of-confederation.

Chapter 1. Land, Conquest, and the Substance of Constitutions

1. Thomas Paine, *Common Sense* (Philadelphia: W. and T. Bradford, 1776), 26.

2. David Howarth, *1066: The Year of the Conquest* (Viking, 1977); Hugh M. Thomas, *The Norman Conquest: England After William the Conqueror* (Rowman and Littlefield, 2007); George Garnett, "England After the Conquest," in *The Cambridge Constitutional History of the United Kingdom*, 2 vols., ed. Peter Cane and H. Kumarasingham (Cambridge University Press, 2023), 2:30–62.

3. From Richard FitzNeal, *The Ancient Dialogue Concerning the Exchequer*, trans. John Rayner (London, 1758), 31. Latin original published c. 1179.

4. F. W. Maitland, *The Constitutional History of England* (Cambridge University Press, 1908), 538.

5. In medieval England, a hundred was a taxation and governance district, larger than the village but smaller than the county or shire. Its name may have derived from the concept that one hundred hides, the hide being the amount of land thought sufficient to sustain a peasant household, constituted a reasonable unit of local government. Each hundred held a monthly court, where disputes were decided by customary law, with all dwellers in the hundred expected to attend. The term was still in use in the early days of English colonization in North America.

6. Garnett, "England After the Conquest," 2:31–33, argues that while William's consecration oath and writ to the city of London "emphasized that nothing, legally speaking, was to change under the new king," nonetheless his insistence on being the sole allodial holder of all the land in the realm (allodial means holding land with complete independence, without any obligations to a superior lord) was a constitutional innovation that made his "powers as lord" vastly greater than those of prior Anglo-Saxon kings.

7. Christopher Dyer, *Making a Living in the Middle Ages: The People of Britain, 850–1520* (Yale University Press, 2002), 207.

8. Anna Powell-Smith, "Groton," *Open Domesday*, https://opendomesday.org/place/TL9541/groton/; G. H. Martin and Ann Williams, *Domesday Book: A Complete Translation* (Penguin Books, 2003), 1191.

9. Powell-Smith, "Groton"; Martin and Williams, *Domesday Book*, 1239.

10. Powell-Smith, "Groton"; Martin and Williams, *Domesday Book*, 1300.

11. Centuries earlier, the Roman Empire had conducted censuses, and in some of its richest provinces, such as Egypt, it had enumerated landholdings and values, but there is no evidence

that anything like the Domesday Book had ever been produced in Britain or northern Europe before; see W. Graham Claytor and Roger S. Bagnall, "The Beginnings of the Roman Provincial Census: A New Declaration from 3 BCE," *Greek, Roman, and Byzantine Studies* 55 (2015): 637–53.

12. Christine Desan, *Making Money: Coin, Currency, and the Coming of Capitalism* (Oxford University Press, 2014), 37–69; Michael Dolley, *The Norman Conquest and the English Coinage* (Spink, 1966).

13. A recent translation of Domesday, tightly printed in double columns in small typeface, runs to 1,456 pages; see Martin and Williams, *Domesday Book*. In its original physical form, Domesday was actually two books, "Great" and "Little" Domesday.

14. Frederic W. Maitland, *The Constitutional History of England* (Cambridge University Press, 1908), 1–10.

15. In his writ issued to the citizens of London in 1066, William assured them that they would enjoy "all the law which you had in King Edward's day." Garnett, "England After the Conquest," 2:30.

16. Maitland, *Constitutional History*, 14–17; J. C. Holt, *Magna Carta* (Cambridge University Press, 1965), 1–19, 149–200.

17. Magna Carta was written in medieval Latin. The translation used here is from "Magna Carta, 1215," [UK] National Archives, https://www.nationalarchives.gov.uk/education/resources/magna-carta/british-library-magna-carta-1215-runnymede/.

18. Although it may seem absurd for a mere mortal, even a king, to make a "grant" to an omnipotent supernatural divinity, this opening article of Magna Carta reflects the profoundly institutional structure of medieval English constitutionalism—the institutional form that "God" took in the world was the Roman Catholic Church, and its place in England's pyramid of sovereign authority was below the king.

19. The phrase "free man" in Magna Carta could have multiple meanings, ranging from the more restrictive sense of lords who had the privilege of holding manorial courts to the much broader sense of all social grades that held land by free tenure, so that an undertenant of a lord could also be a free man. In other words, "Magna Carta assumed legal parity among all free men to an exceptional degree" in the context of other medieval European charters of law or liberty, which tended to restrict the privileges of free people to individuals of a particular, narrow status. Holt, *Magna Carta*, 184–85.

20. See the Constitute Project, an online effort to make accessible the current status of national constitutions around the world: "United Kingdom 1215 (rev. 2013)," Constitute Project, https://www.constituteproject.org/constitution/United_Kingdom_2013.

21. Holt, *Magna Carta*, 218–23; Paul Brand, "England in the Thirteenth Century," in Cane and Kumarasingham, *Cambridge Constitutional History*, 2:73–81.

22. This rhetorical pattern was consistent with a belief that the best sources of authority are ancient, as in Christianity's foundation in scriptural revelations of the distant past. The passage of time was more likely to cause decay from original truth than progress toward a better version. The ruptures of the Protestant Reformation were justified as a return to original biblical authority from which Roman Catholicism had drifted.

23. David Chan Smith, "England in the Sixteenth Century," in Cane and Kumarasingham, *Cambridge Constitutional History*, 2:142–43.

24. G. R. Elton, *The Tudor Constitution: Documents and Commentary* (Cambridge University Press, 1972), 344, 355 (Act for Restraint of Appeals, 1533) and 39–58 (Act of Supremacy, 1534); on the dissolution of the monasteries, see Diarmaid MacCulloch, *Thomas Cromwell: A Revolutionary Life* (Viking, 2018), 193–204, 319–22, 430–42, 488–92.

25. J. G. A. Pocock, *The Ancient Constitution and the Feudal Law: English Historical Thought in the Seventeenth Century* (W. W. Norton, 1967), 44–49; see "Petition of Right (1628)," Online Library of Liberty, https://oll.libertyfund.org/pages/1628-petition-of-right.

26. "The Petition of Right," Acts of the English Parliament, https://www.legislation.gov.uk/aep/Cha1/3/1.

27. "Bill of Rights," chap. 2, Acts of the English Parliament, https://www.legislation.gov.uk/aep/WillandMarSess2/1/2/introduction; Glenn Burgess, "The English Constitution in the Seventeenth Century: Crises of Inadequacy," in Cane and Kumarasingham, *Cambridge Constitutional History*, 2:160–87.

28. The most authoritative account of the chartering of England's American colonies is Charles McLean Andrews, *The Colonial Period of American History*, 4 vols. (Yale University Press, 1934–38), vols. 1–2, "The Settlements."

29. There is, of course, a rich historiography on the founding and constitutional development of British colonies in the West Indies and throughout the world. The West Indies in particular played a major role in the American Revolution, as did the continental colonies that did not join the rebellion. But as this book is ultimately a history of constitutionalism in the United States, attention to these other parts of the empire will be necessarily limited.

30. Charter of Massachusetts Bay, 1629, *Avalon Project*, Yale Law School, https://avalon.law.yale.edu/17th_century/mass03.asp.

31. In fact, by 1660, after the English Civil Wars, Interregnum, and Restoration of Charles II to the crown, Parliament would pass the Abolition of Tenures Act, which eliminated all but free and common socage for future forms of landholding in England as well. B. H. McPherson, "Revisiting the Manor of East Greenwich," *American Journal of Legal History* 42, no. 1 (1998): 35–56. On the utility of less restrictive land tenure to colonization, see Karen Ordahl Kupperman, *Providence Island: The Other Puritan Colony* (Cambridge University Press, 1993), 139–47, 247–56, 346–47.

32. The initial settlement of the "Pilgrims" of Plymouth in 1620 was on farmland of the Patuxet Indians, most of whom had died in an epidemic between 1616 and 1619 caused by the introduction of new diseases from Europe; see John S. Marr and John T. Cathey, "New Hypothesis for Cause of Epidemic Among Native Americans, New England, 1616–1619," *Emerging Infectious Diseases* 16, no. 2 (2010): 281–86.

33. Philip J. Stern, *Empire, Incorporated: The Corporations That Built British Colonialism* (Belknap Press of Harvard University Press, 2023), 16–93; Stern, "Bundles of Hyphens: Corporations as Legal Communities in the Early Modern British Empire," in *Legal Pluralism and Empires, 1500–1850*, ed. Lauren Benton and Richard J. Ross (New York University Press, 2013), 21–47, quotation from Blackstone, *Commentaries*, at 25.

34. Francis J. Bremer, *John Winthrop: America's Forgotten Founding Father* (Oxford University Press, 2005), 29–70.

35. John Winthrop, *The History of New England from 1630 to 1649*, 2 vols., ed. James Savage (Boston: Little, Brown, 1853), 1:84; Herbert L. Osgood, "The Corporation as a Form of Colonial

Government, II." *Political Science Quarterly,* 11, no. 3 (1896): 515, cited in Stern, "Bundles of Hyphens," 31; Bremer, *John Winthrop,* 203–28; Andrews, *Colonial Period,* 1:430–61.

36. Allan Greer, *Property and Dispossession: Natives, Empires, and Land in Early Modern North America* (Cambridge University Press, 2018), chap. 2, esp. 36–64. On the richness of the land, see Edmund S. Morgan, *American Slavery, America Freedom: The Ordeal of Colonial Virginia* (W. W. Norton, 1975), 44–70; and William Cronon, *Changes in the Land: Indians, Colonists, and the Ecology of New England* (Hill and Wang, 1983), 34–53.

37. See Winthrop, "General Observations," 2:111–17; David Armitage, *The Ideological Origins of the British Empire* (Cambridge University Press, 2000), 92–99.

38. Arthur Bousfield and Garry Toffoli, *Royal Spring: The Royal Tour of 1939 and the Queen Mother in Canada* (Dundurn Press, 1989).

39. Ken MacMillan, *Sovereignty and Possession in the English New World: The Legal Foundations of Empire, 1576–1640* (Cambridge University Press), 84, and in general chap. 3, 79–120.

40. MacMillan, *Sovereignty and Possession,* 50–78; Robert J. Miller, Jacinta Ruru, Larissa Behrendt, and Tracey Lindberg, *Discovering Indigenous Lands: The Doctrine of Discovery in the English Colonies* (Oxford University Press, 2010), chap. 1, "The Doctrine of Discovery."

41. First Charter of Virginia, 1606, *Avalon Project,* Yale Law School, https://avalon.law.yale.edu/17th_century/va01.asp; https://avalon.law.yale.edu/17th_century/va02.asp; Andrews, *Colonial Period,* vol. 1.

42. Charter of Connecticut, 1662, *Avalon Project,* Yale Law School, https://avalon.law.yale.edu/17th_century/ct03.asp.

43. Nicholas Canny, *Making Ireland British, 1580–1650* (Oxford University Press, 2001); Canny, "The Origins of Empire: An Introduction," in *The Oxford History of the British Empire,* ed. Nicholas Canny, vol. 1, *The Origins of Empire* (Oxford University Press, 1998), 1–33.

Chapter 2. Colonies and Constitutions from Charter to Independence

1. Karen Ordahl Kupperman, *Indians and English: Facing Off in Early America* (Cornell University Press, 2000); Sam White, *A Cold Welcome: The Little Ice Age and Europe's Encounter with North America* (Harvard University Press, 2017), 122–23, 148, 157, 253–54.

2. This is in no way meant to diminish the violence of the Spanish conquest of Mexico; see Camilla Townsend, *Fifth Sun: A New History of the Aztecs* (Oxford University Press, 2019). The same applies to the Norman Conquest: where resistance to the Normans was strong, as exemplified by the Yorkshire-Northumberland rebellions of 1069, William's forces suppressed this dissent with extreme violence, destroying villages and killing thousands of people, leaving much of this territory to be listed as "waste" in Domesday; see Ann Williams, *The English and the Norman Conquest* (Boydell Press, 1995), 24–44.

3. For examples, see Harry Andrew Wright, ed., *Indian Deeds of Hampden County* (Springfield, MA, 1905), or Jeremy Dupertuis Bangs, *Indian Deeds: Land Transactions of Plymouth Colony, 1620–1691* (New England Historic Genealogical Society, 2002). Although I use Massachusetts as an example here, similar transactions took place across all the English colonies in North America; see Allan Greer, *Property and Dispossession: Natives, Empires, and Land in Early Modern North America* (Cambridge University Press, 2018).

4. Virginia DeJohn Anderson, *New England's Generation: Great Migration and the Formation of Society and Culture in the Seventeenth Century* (Cambridge University Press, 1991); Robert Charles Anderson, *The Great Migration Begins: Immigrants to New England, 1620–1633*, vols. 1–3 (New England Historic Genealogical Society, 1995); David D. Hall, *A Reforming People: Puritanism and the Transformation of Public Life in New England* (Alfred A. Knopf, 2011); Greer, *Property and Dispossession*, 202–20.

5. William Bradford, *Of Plimoth Plantation*, 400th anniv. ed., ed. Kenneth P. Minkema, Francis J. Bremer, and Jeremy D. Bangs (Colonial Society of Massachusetts, 2020), 30–31, 188–93; Greer, *Property and Dispossession*; Stuart Banner, *How the Indians Lost Their Land: Law and Power on the Frontier* (Harvard University Press, 2005).

6. Edmund S. Morgan, *American Slavery, America Freedom: The Ordeal of Colonial Virginia* (W. W. Norton, 1975), 94; Susan M. Kingsbury, ed., *The Records of the Virginia Company of London*, vol. 3 (U.S. Government Printing Office, 1906), 98–101, https://www.loc.gov/item/06035006/; Greer, *Property and Dispossession*, 220–27; Hall, *Reforming People*, 53–95.

7. Stephen Innes, *Labor in a New Land: Economy and Society in Seventeenth-Century Springfield* (Princeton University Press, 1983); Joseph Smith, ed., *Colonial Justice in Western Massachusetts: The Pynchon Court Record* (Harvard University Press, 1961); John Frederick Martin, *Profits in the Wilderness: Entrepreneurship and the Founding of New England Towns in the Seventeenth Century* (University of North Carolina Press, 1991), 129–254; Greer, *Property and Dispossession*, 220–23.

8. Hall, *Reforming People*, 22–52; Michael Winship, *Godly Republicanism: Puritans, Pilgrims, and a City on a Hill* (Harvard University Press, 2012), 183–205.

9. Jack P. Greene, *The Quest for Power: The Lower Houses of Assembly in the Southern Royal Colonies, 1689–1776* (University of North Carolina Press, 1963), 3–18; Edmund S. Morgan, *Inventing the People: The Rise of Popular Sovereignty in England and America* (W. W. Norton, 1988), 122–48.

10. Lewis Namier and John Brooke, *The House of Commons, 1754-1790*, 3 vols., (History of Parliament Trust, 1964), 184, cited in Bernard Bailyn, *The Origins of American Politics* (Knopf, 1968), 26; Richard Pares, *King George III and the Politicians* (Oxford, 1953), 3–5.

11. Budget data drawn from "UK Public Spending Details for 1730," *UK Public Spending*, https://www.ukpublicspending.co.uk/year_spending_1730UKmn_17mc1n#ukgs302.

12. Budget data drawn from "UK Public Spending Details for 1762," and "UK Public Spending Details for 1750," *UK Public Spending*, https://www.ukpublicspending.co.uk/uk_year1762_UK.html; https://www.ukpublicspending.co.uk/uk_year1750_UK.html.

13. Julian Hoppit, *Britain's Political Economies: Parliament and Economic Life, 1660–1800* (Cambridge University Press, 2017), argues for a "legislative revolution" in Parliament, especially after 1760, as the imperial crisis began, but also notes that "private" legislation that was "local and specific in scope" occurred at a "much larger volume" than the more familiar legislation relating to public finances and overseas trade. Indeed, between 1660 and 1800, the success rate of parliamentary bills for specific or private legislation was roughly three times as great as it was for general or public acts; see table 2.1, p. 54, and pp. 34–37.

14. Bailyn, *Origins of American Politics*, 103–4.

15. In 1696, Parliament passed "An Act for Remedying the Ill State of the Coinage of the Kingdom," known as the "Great Recoinage" to replace England's highly debased silver money supply; it would not take a similar action again until 1816.

16. Curtis P. Nettels, *The Money Supply of the American Colonies Before 1720* (University of Wisconsin Press, 1934): Jeffrey Sklansky, *Sovereign of the Market: The Money Question in Early America* (University of Chicago Press, 2017).

17. Mark Peterson, *The City-State of Boston: The Rise and Fall of an Atlantic Power, 1630–1865* (Princeton University Press, 2019), 85–138; Jeffrey Sklansky, *Sovereign of the Market*, 56–92; Simon Middleton, "William Fishbourn's 'Misfortune': Public Accounting and Paper Money in Early Pennsylvania," *Early American Studies: An Interdisciplinary Journal* 19, no. 1 (2021): 64–99; The Currency Act, April 19, 1764, *Avalon Project*, Yale Law School, https://avalon.law.yale.edu/18th_century/curency_act_1764.asp.

18. Mark Peterson, "Demography," in *The Oxford Handbook of the Seven Years War*, ed. Trevor Burnard, Emma Hart, and Marie Houllemaire (Oxford University Press, 2024), 633–652. Indeed, the present State of North Carolina is larger in land area than England.

19. Bernard Bailyn, *The Peopling of British North America: An Introduction* (Knopf, 1986), 89–131.

20. Philip S. Haffenden, *New England in the English Nation, 1689–1713* (Clarendon Press, 1974); Richard R. Johnson, *Adjustment to Empire: The New England Colonies, 1675–1715* (Rutgers University Press, 1981).

21. Fred Anderson, *Crucible of War: The Seven Years' War and the Fate of Empire in British North America, 1754–1766* (Knopf, 2000), 5–7.

22. Gregory Evans Dowd, *War Under Heaven: Pontiac, the Indian Nations, and the British Empire* (Johns Hopkins University Press, 2004); Colin Calloway, *The Scratch of a Pen: 1763 and the Transformation of North America* (Oxford University Press, 2007).

23. Banner, *How the Indians Lost*, 85–95; Calloway, *Scratch of a Pen*, 92–111; Great Britain, King George III, *The Royal Proclamation of 1763*, Government of Canada, https://www.rcaanc-cirnac.gc.ca/eng/1370355181092/1607905122267.

24. The specific plan for land distribution laid out in the proclamation was strikingly hierarchical. Field officers (colonels and higher, most of whom were aristocrats) would receive grants of five thousand acres; ordinary enlisted men would receive fifty acres. This was reminiscent of the Norman Conquest, ran counter to colonial traditions of land distribution (especially in egalitarian New England), and inspired fears of a reversion to feudal patterns that led John Adams to write his *Dissertation on the Canon and Feudal Law* (1765).

25. Greer, *Property and Dispossession*, 381–86.

26. Edmund S. Morgan and Helen M. Morgan, *The Stamp Act Crisis: Prologue to Revolution*, 3rd ed. (University of North Carolina Press, 2011), 54–74; Anderson, *Crucible of War*, 641–708; Great Britain, Parliament, *The Stamp Act*, March 22, 1765, Avalon Project, Yale Law School, https://avalon.law.yale.edu/18th_century/stamp_act_1765.asp.

27. Morgan and Morgan, *Stamp Act Crisis*, 92–101; for Patrick Henry's resolutions, see "Patrick Henry's Stamp Act Resolves," 30 May 1765, *Founders Online*, National Archives, https://founders.archives.gov/documents/Jefferson/03-07-02-0369-0002; "Thomas Jefferson to William Wirt, 14 August 1814," *Founders Online*, National Archives, https://founders.archives.gov/documents/Jefferson/03-07-02-0403.

28. Allodial landholding meant owning land with no superior landlord of any kind, essentially by finding, occupying, and defending vacant land or conquering someone else's land.

29. John Adams, "A Dissertation on the Canon and the Feudal Law," No. 3, 30 September 1765, *Founders Online,* National Archives, https://founders.archives.gov/documents/Adams/06-01-02-0052-0006.

30. John Adams, "A Dissertation on the Canon and the Feudal Law," No. 4, 21 October 1765," *Founders Online,* National Archives, https://founders.archives.gov/documents/Adams/06-01-02-0052-0007; C. F. Adams, ed., *The Works of John Adams,* 10 vols. (Boston: Little, Brown, 1850-56), 2:466–67; James P. Muldoon, *John Adams and the Constitutional History of the Medieval British Empire* (Palgrave Macmillan, 2018).

31. Andrew David Edwards, "Grenville's Silver Hammer: The Problem of Money in the Stamp Act Crisis," *Journal of American History* 104, no. 2 (2017): 337–62; Morgan and Morgan, *Stamp Act Crisis,* 286–87; *The Examination of Doctor Benjamin Franklin Before an August Assembly, Relating to the Repeal of the Stamp-Act, &c.* (Boston: Edes and Gill, 1766), https://www.masshist.org/database/viewer.php?item_id=251&pid=2.

32. The Declaratory Act, March 18, 1766, *Avalon Project,* Yale Law School, https://avalon.law.yale.edu/18th_century/declaratory_act_1766.asp.

33. In *Federalist* no. 17, Publius (Alexander Hamilton) makes a similar analogy between the former colonies and feudal baronies. He writes in late 1787: "The separate governments in a confederacy may aptly be compared with the feudal baronies; with this advantage in their favor, that from the reasons already explained, they will generally possess the confidence and goodwill of the people, and with so important a support, will be able effectually to oppose all encroachments of the national government." Alexander Hamilton, *The Federalist,* no. 17, in *The Federalist,* ed. Jacob E. Cooke (Wesleyan University Press, 1961).

34. The phrase "Novus Ordo Seclorum" appeared on the Great Seal of the United States, undergirding a pyramid meant to represent the states united in strength and overseen by the favorable eye of a watchful providence—a pyramid without an earthly king at the top. The seal was designed in 1782 by Charles Thompson, Secretary of Congress. Richard S. Patterson and Richardson Dougall, *The Eagle and the Shield: A History of the Great Seal of the United States* (U.S. Department of State, 1976).

35. Willi Paul Adams, *The First American Constitutions: Republican Ideology and the Making of State Constitutions in the Revolutionary Era* (University of North Carolina Press, 1980), 49–90; Gordon S. Wood, *The Creation of the American Republic, 1776–1787* (University of North Carolina Press, 2011), 127–61.

36. There is a rather lazy tradition in popular history of saying that the British constitution is "unwritten" in contrast to the "written" constitution of the United States. But it should be quite obvious by now that Britain's constitution was a mixture of customs, traditions, and ancient institutions along with written legal instruments. The same is true of the United States, as subsequent discussion will show.

37. Wood, *Creation,* 344–54; Adams, *First American Constitutions,* 126–46.

38. This problem was widely understood across the colonies and was eloquently expressed in 1777 by Thomas Jefferson in his draft of "A Bill for Establishing Religious Freedom," presented to the Virginia Assembly in 1779, which reads: "We well know that this Assembly, elected by the people for the ordinary purposes of legislation only, have no power to restrain the acts of succeeding Assemblies, constituted with powers equal to our own, and that therefore to declare

this act irrevocable would be of no effect in law." *National Constitution Center*, https://constitutioncenter.org/the-constitution/historic-document-library/detail/thomas-jefferson-a-bill-for-establishing-religious-freedom.

39. Wood, *Creation*, 306–43; Oscar and Mary Handlin, eds., *The Popular Sources of Political Authority: Documents on the Massachusetts Constitution of 1780* (Harvard University Press, 1961).

40. Wood, *Creation*, 438–53; Richard Tuck, *The Sleeping Sovereign: The Invention of Modern Democracy* (Cambridge University Press, 2016), 181–248.

41. Jack Rakove, *The Beginnings of National Politics: An Interpretive History of the Continental Congress* (Johns Hopkins University Press, 1982), 135–91; Merrill Jensen, *The Articles of Confederation: An Interpretation of the Social-Constitutional History of the American Revolution, 1774–1781* (University of Wisconsin Press, 1976), 107–224. The Articles of Confederation can be accessed at *Milestone Documents*, National Archives, https://www.archives.gov/milestone-documents/articles-of-confederation.

42. The Treaty of Paris, 1783, *Milestone Documents*, National Archives, https://www.archives.gov/milestone-documents/treaty-of-paris.

43. All the parties represented at the Paris peace talks, that is. Just as in the diplomacy that ended the Seven Years' War, Indian nations that had made formal alliances with Britain were not included in the treaty negotiations.

44. Richard B. Morris, *The Peacemakers: The Great Powers and American Independence* (Harper and Row, 1965), 341–85; Jonathan Dull, *The Diplomatic History of the American Revolution* (Yale University Press, 1985), 137–64; Thomas Perkins Abernethy, *Western Lands and the American Revolution* (Russell and Russell, 1959), 274–83; Andrew Stockley, *Britain and France at the Birth of America: The European Powers and the Peace Negotiations of 1782–1783* (University of Exeter Press, 2001), 60.

45. Morris, *Peacemakers*; Paul Mapp, "The Revolutionary War and Europe's Great Powers," in *The Oxford Handbook of the American Revolution*, ed. Edward G. Gray and Jane Kamensky (Oxford University Press, 2013), 311–26; Leonard Sadosky, *Revolutionary Negotiations: Indians, Empires, and Diplomats in the Founding of America* (University of Virginia Press, 2010), 115–18.

46. Calloway, *Scratch of a Pen*, 165–71.

47. Eric Hinderaker, *Elusive Empires: Constructing Colonialism in the Ohio Valley, 1673–1800* (Cambridge University Press, 1997), 187–267.

48. During the War of Independence, the United States signed two formal treaties with Indigenous allies: the 1776 Treaty of Watertown with Mi'kmaq and St. John Indians, and the 1778 Treaty of Fort Pitt with Lenape Indians.

Chapter 3. Independent States and the Challenge of the West

1. Thomas Sargent and Francois Velde, "Macroeconomic Features of the French Revolution," *Journal of Political Economy* 103, no. 3 (1995): 474–518, http://www.jstor.org/stable/2138696; Simon Schama, *Citizens: A Chronicle of the French Revolution* (Knopf, 1989), 60–69.

2. By comparison, Britain spent roughly £80 million on the American War and also ended the war with a total national debt of around £250 million. But eighteenth-century Britain had made great strides in developing efficient means to raise revenue and service debt in the interest

of state power. Britain's debts from the Seven Years' War and American Revolution were similar to France's but did not bring about a revolutionary crisis in the metropole. See John Brewer, *The Sinews of Power: War, Money, and the English State, 1688–1783* (Harvard University Press, 1990), 114–15.

3. See Rafe Blaufarb, *The Great Demarcation: The French Revolution and the Invention of Modern Property* (Oxford University Press, 2016), 1–14; and Rebecca Spang, *Stuff and Money in the Time of the French Revolution* (Harvard University Press, 2015), 19–57.

4. During the war, the U.S. Navy built a handful of frigates (smaller and lighter warships suitable for capturing enemy merchant ships), and converted existing merchant ships for similar purposes. But these were no match for the dozens of large and powerful "ships of the line" that the French and British fleets maintained, which played decisive roles in major battles such as the Battle of the Capes near the mouth of the Chesapeake Bay, where the French victory sealed the fate of General Cornwallis's army at Yorktown; see William M. Fowler, *Rebels Under Sail: The American Navy During the Revolution* (Scribners, 1976), 212–33.

5. It is not uncommon for American historians of the constitutional era to describe the American war debt as enormous, but they seldom bother to compare it with that of the war's other combatants. Contemporaries such as Yale President Ezra Stiles knew better; Stiles pointed out that the entire principal of the U.S. debt was smaller than the annual interest Britain owed on its debt. See Ezra Stiles, *The United States Elevated to Glory and Honor* (New Haven, CT: Thomas and Samuel Green, 1783), 27; Stephen Mihm, "Funding the Revolution: Monetary and Fiscal Policy in Eighteenth-Century America," in *The Oxford Handbook of the American Revolution*, ed. Edward G. Gray and Jane Kamensky (Oxford University Press, 2013), 327–51; E. James Ferguson, *The Power of the Purse: A History of American Public Finance, 1776–1790* (University of North Carolina Press, 1961), 179–219; and Thomas K. McCraw, *The Founders and Finance: How Hamilton, Gallatin, and Other Immigrants Forged a New Economy* (Harvard University Press, 2012), 87–96.

6. Mihm, "Funding the Revolution"; McCraw, *Founders and Finance*, 56–73.

7. Robin Einhorn, *American Taxation, American Slavery* (University of Chicago Press, 2006), 53–78.

8. George William Van Cleve, *We Have Not a Government: The Articles of Confederation and the Road to the Constitution* (University of Chicago Press, 2017), 48–73; McCraw, *Founders and Finance*, 61–73; Jack Rakove, *The Beginnings of National Politics: An Interpretive History of the Continental Congress* (Alfred A. Knopf, 1979), 205–15; Ferguson, *Power of the Purse*, 3–69.

9. Alan Kulikoff, "'Such Things Ought Not to Be': The American Revolution and the First National Great Depression," in *The World of the Revolutionary American Republic*, ed. Andrew Shankman (Routledge, 2014), 134–164.

10. Benjamin Rush, "Address to the People of the United States," *American Museum* (January, 1787): 8–11.

11. Gregory Evans Dowd, *War Under Heaven: Pontiac, the Indian Nations, and the British Empire* (Johns Hopkins University Press, 2002), 54–89; Colin Calloway, *The Scratch of a Pen: 1763 and the Transformation of North America* (Oxford University Press, 2007), 47–65.

12. Mark Peterson, "Demography," in *The Oxford Handbook of the Seven Years War*, ed. Trevor Burnard, Emma Hart, and Marie Houllemaire (Oxford University Press, 2024), 633–652.

13. Thomas Perkins Abernethy, *Western Lands and the American Revolution* (Russell and Russell, 1959); Peter S. Onuf, *The Origins of the Federal Republic: Jurisdictional Controversies in the United States, 1775–1787* (University of Pennsylvania Press, 1983), 3–20.

14. Ian K. Steele, *The English Atlantic, 1675–1740: An Exploration of Communication and Community* (Oxford University Press, 1986), 207–8.

15. Isaac Nakhimovsky, *The Closed Commercial State: Perpetual Peace and Commercial Society from Rousseau to Fichte* (Princeton University Press, 2011).

16. Rufus King, quoted in Peter S. Onuf, *Statehood and Union: A History of the Northwest Ordinance* (University of Notre Dame Press, 2019), 16.

17. Colin Calloway, *The Indian World of George Washington: The First President, the First Americans, and the Birth of the Nation* (Oxford University Press, 2018), chap. 13.

18. On the frenzy of land speculation these conditions generated, see Michael Blaakman, *Speculation Nation: Land Mania in the Revolutionary Republic* (University of Pennsylvania Press, 2023).

19. Malyn Newitt, *A History of Portuguese Overseas Expansion, 1400–1688* (Routledge, 2005).

20. J. H. Elliott, *Empires of the Atlantic World: Britain and Spain in America, 1492–1830* (Yale University Press, 2006).

21. Edmund S. Morgan, *American Slavery, American Freedom: The Ordeal of Colonial Virginia* (Norton, 1975), 83–107.

22. Charles McLean Andrews, *The Colonial Period of American History*, 4 vols. (Yale University Press, 1934–38), 1:41–45.

23. Morgan, *American Slavery, American Freedom*; Karen Kupperman, *The Jamestown Project* (Harvard University Press, 2008); and Bernard Bailyn, *The Barbarous Years* (Knopf, 2012), all offer variations on this story.

24. This range of climatic variation across this distance is among the most dramatic in the world; see D. W. Meinig, *The Shaping of America*, vol. 1, *Atlantic America, 1492–1800* (Yale University Press, 1986), 248–50.

25. The harsh years of the "Little Ice Age," which coincided with many of the early European colonization ventures in North America, tended to reduce the availability of Indian food surpluses, heightening the tensions and violence that the arrival of Europeans generated; see Sam White, *A Cold Welcome: The Little Ice Age and Europe's Encounter with North America* (Harvard University Press, 2020).

26. Allan Greer, *Dispossessing America: Natives, Empires, and Land in Early America* (Cambridge University Press, 2018); Stuart Banner, *How the Indians Lost Their Land: Law and Power on the Frontier* (Harvard University Press, 2005), 10–84.

27. Bernard Bailyn, *The Origins of American Politics* (Knopf, 1968).

28. An exception to this general rule can be found in what I have called "The City-State of Boston," where the Massachusetts Bay Company had the distinct early advantage of bringing large numbers of colonists with substantial resources at the beginning of their enterprise, combined with religious and political reasons for pursuing autonomy from the English crown; see Mark Peterson, *The City-State of Boston: The Rise and Fall of an Atlantic Power, 1630–1865* (Princeton University Press, 2019), 25–188.

29. Bernard Bailyn, *Voyagers to the West: A Passage in the Peopling of British North America on the Eve of the American Revolution* (Knopf, 1986); Van Cleve, *We Have Not*, 133–60.

30. Brian DeLay, "The Arms Trade and American Revolutions," *American Historical Review* 128, no. 3 (2023): 1144–81; Holger Hoock, *Scars of Independence: America's Violent Birth* (Broadway Books, 2017).

31. Colin Calloway, *The American Revolution in Indian Country: Crisis and Diversity in Native American Communities* (Cambridge University Press, 1995); Calloway, *Indian World.*

32. Note that I am using "small" in the eighteenth-century sense, referring to land area. Maryland was the sixth largest state in population, trailing Virginia, Massachusetts, Pennsylvania, North Carolina, and New York; see Rosemarie Zagarri, *The Politics of Size: Representation in the United States, 1776–1850* (Cornell University Press, 1987). New Hampshire did lay claim to the territory that eventually became the state of Vermont, but did not have charter-based claims extending to the Pacific Ocean as neighboring Massachusetts did.

33. Charter of Connecticut, 1662, *Avalon Project,* Yale Law School, https://avalon.law.yale.edu/17th_century/ct03.asp; Charter of Massachusetts Bay, 1629, *Avalon Project,* Yale Law School, https://avalon.law.yale.edu/17th_century/mass03.asp.

34. Constitution of Pennsylvania, September 28, 1776, *Avalon Project,* Yale Law School, https://avalon.law.yale.edu/18th_century/pa08.asp; Constitution of New York, April 20, 1777, *Avalon Project,* Yale Law School, https://avalon.law.yale.edu/18th_century/ny01.asp.

35. This included the territory that became the present states of Kentucky, Ohio, Indiana, Illinois, Michigan, and Wisconsin, with a combined land area of over 340,000 square miles. The 1774 Quebec Act had seized most of this territory from Virginia's control. The total land area of France is about 250,000 square miles. The combined area of the thirteen original states within today's boundaries, much of which had not yet been occupied by settler colonists in 1776, is about 365,000 square miles. Virginia's constitution was insisting on the state's right to control territory larger than the rest of the United States combined.

36. Virginia Constitution, June 29, 1776, *Founders Online,* National Archives, https://founders.archives.gov/documents/Jefferson/01-01-02-0161-0008.

37. Constitution of North Carolina, December 18, 1776, *Avalon Project,* Yale Law School, https://avalon.law.yale.edu/18th_century/nc07.asp; Constitution of Georgia, February 5, 1777, *Avalon Project,* Yale Law School, https://avalon.law.yale.edu/18th_century/ga02.asp; Constitution of South Carolina, March 26, 1776, *Avalon Project,* Yale Law School, https://avalon.law.yale.edu/18th_century/sc01.asp.

38. In fact, the standard scholarly work on the subject, Willi Paul Adams, *The First American Constitutions: Republican Ideology and the Making of State Constitutions in the Revolutionary Era* (Chapel Hill: University of North Carolina Press, 1980), has no entry in its index for "land," "territory" or "Western lands."

39. See Articles of Confederation, art. 9, § 2, *Milestone Documents,* National Archives, https://www.archives.gov/milestone-documents/articles-of-confederation#transcript.

40. Articles of Confederation, art. 11. Note how curious this provision is. It excludes the automatic admission of Britain's other North American colonies—Nova Scotia, East and West Florida—colonies where there was little to no overlap with the land claims of the thirteen states. And it automatically admits the enormous mega-colony of Quebec, defined by Parliament as stretching down to the Ohio River—exactly the territory that Virginia's 1776 constitution claimed for itself. Had Quebec joined the confederation, it would instantly have created an enormous boundary dispute with Virginia, and with Connecticut, Massachusetts, and New

York as well, over the question of which state owned this vast region. Yet Virginia was the first of the states to ratify the Articles, in December 1777. All this suggests that at this time the Canada prospect seemed so unlikely as not to cause Virginia's legislature any concern, but also that the beleaguered states assembled in Congress were not yet closely attending to the challenge and opportunity of the West.

41. Articles of Confederation, art. 3.

42. Merrill Jensen, *The Articles of Confederation: An Interpretation of the Social-Constitutional History of the American Revolution, 1774–1781* (University of Wisconsin Press, 1976), 211–38.

43. Rakove, *Beginnings of National Politics*, 157. On the prevalent desire among the states and the Continental Congress in the 1780s to sell undeveloped land to raise revenue, see Blaakman, *Speculation Nation*, 58–98.

44. Peter S. Onuf, "From Colony to Territory: Changing Concepts of Statehood in Revolutionary America," *Political Science Quarterly* 97, no. 3 (1982): 448–53. This was quite obviously the case for Connecticut and Rhode Island, as they continued to govern themselves under their colonial charters after independence.

45. Jonathan Jackson to Benjamin Lincoln, April 19, 1783, Fogg Collection, vol. 19, Maine Historical Society, quoted in Rakove, *Beginnings of National Politics*, 326; *Falmouth Gazette and Weekly Advertiser* (Falmouth, Maine) vol. 1, no. 21, May 21, 1785, quoted in Onuf, *Origins*, 34.

46. Abernethy, *Western Lands*, 217–57; Blaakman, *Speculation Nation*, 67–72; Zagarri, *Politics of Size*, 64; Onuf, *Origins*, 13.

47. Such had been the case in 1782, when Congress's adjudication system defended Pennsylvania's right to control its northeastern corner against Connecticut's charter claims to this territory; see Onuf, *Origins*, 49–74.

48. *The Last Official Address of His Excellency, George Washington, to the Legislatures of the United States* (Hartford: Hudson and Goodwin, 1783).

Chapter 4. Constitutional Solutions Before the Constitution

1. Catherine Drinker Bowen, *Miracle at Philadelphia: The Story of the Constitutional Convention, May–September 1787* (Little, Brown, 1966). The veneration of *The Federalist Papers*, as if they offered the key to constitutional interpretation rather than being the partisan pamphlets that they were (see, for example, Hamilton's reference to the "imbecility of our government" under the Articles in *Federalist* no. 15), adds to this common misunderstanding; see *The Federalist*, ed. Jacob E. Cooke (Wesleyan University Press, 1961).

2. For example, see "Amendments to the Articles of Confederation Proposed by a Grand Committee of Congress, 7 August 1786," in *The Documentary History of the Ratification of the Constitution*, vol. 1, *Constitutional Documents and Records, 1776–1787*, ed. Merrill Jensen (Wisconsin Historical Society Press, 1976), 163–68.

3. Jack Rakove, *Original Meanings: Politics and Ideas in the Making of the Constitution* (Knopf, 1996), 23–35, offers an account of the connections among these national issues.

4. Andro Linklater, *An Artist in Treason: The Extraordinary Double Life of General James Wilkinson* (Walker, 2009); David E. Narrett, "Geopolitics and Intrigue: James Wilkinson, the Spanish Borderlands, and Mexican Independence," *William and Mary Quarterly* 69, no. 1 (2012): 101–46.

5. Drew McCoy, *The Elusive Republic: Political Economy in Jeffersonian America* (UNC Press, 1980), 123–24; George William Van Cleve, *We Have Not a Government: The Articles of Confederation and the Road to the Constitution* (University of Chicago Press, 2017), 161–87.

6. Note North Carolina's fluid language regarding constitutional documents: its "Constitution" is not a single written text that describes a whole system or frame of government, but rather part of a larger whole (the Bill of Rights is another part) described in multiple texts.

7. Gregory Ablavsky, "The Savage Constitution," *Duke Law Journal* 63, no. 5 (2014): 1029–30; New York raised similar objections when congressional representatives attempted to negotiate an Indian treaty at Fort Stanwix in 1784; see Colin Calloway, *The Indian World of George Washington* (Oxford University Press, 2018), 301–4.

8. James Madison, "Vices of the Political System of the United States, April 1787," *Founders Online*, National Archives, https://founders.archives.gov/documents/Madison/01-09-02-0187.

9. Alexander Hamilton, June 18, 1787, quoted in Max Farrand, *Records of the Federal Convention of 1787* (Yale University Press, 1966), 1:297.

10. William Ellery, quoted in Paul H. Smith and Ronald M. Gephart, eds., *Letters of the Delegates of the Continental Congress* (Library of Congress, 1994), 21:177. Other delegates, including Arthur Lee of Virginia, made similar suggestions; see 21:606–7.

11. Van Cleve, *We Have Not*, 84–101.

12. Calloway, *Indian World*, 291, 356.

13. The European Union, a league of sovereign states designed for economic cooperation, has managed to frame collective customs regimes for its diverse nations.

14. In that sense, the 1787 Constitution did not really solve the problem that arose with the unratified Jay–Gardoqui Treaty negotiations. The states as represented by the Senate have rejected other treaties negotiated by the executive branch—notably the Treaty of Versailles proposed by President Woodrow Wilson at the end of World War I.

15. Willard Sterne Randall, *Ethan Allen: His Life and Times* (W. W. Norton, 2011), 441–45; Vermont State Constitution, 1777, Vermont State Archives and Record Administration, https://sos.vermont.gov/vsara/learn/constitution/1777-constitution.

16. Peter S. Onuf, *The Origins of the Federal Republic: Jurisdictional Controversies in the United States, 1775–1787* (University of Pennsylvania Press, 1983), 33–41.

17. The Ordinance of 1784, April 23, 1784, *Founders Online*, National Archives, https://founders.archives.gov/documents/Jefferson/01-06-02-0420-0006.

18. Though no more than coincidence, this was exactly the original size of the township of Concord, Massachusetts, where the Revolutionary War began with the "shot heard 'round the world."

19. Michael Blaakman, *Speculation Nation: Land Mania in the Revolutionary Republic* (University of Pennsylvania Press, 2023), 188, 257.

20. Land Ordinance of 1785, May 20, 1785, Gilder Lehrman Institute of American History, https://www.gilderlehrman.org/sites/default/files/inline-pdfs/Land%20Ordinance%201785.pdf.

21. *Return of the Whole Number of Persons Within the Several Districts of the United States* (Philadelphia, 1793), in Publications of the Bureau of the Census: 1790 Census, Printed Schedules, National Archives Catalog, https://catalog.archives.gov/id/231287860.

22. Northwest Ordinance (1787), *Milestone Documents*, National Archives, https://www.archives.gov/milestone-documents/northwest-ordinance.

23. At this time, slavery was still legal and in force in both of the Northwest Territory's neighboring states, Pennsylvania and Virginia. Pennsylvania had passed a gradual emancipation law in 1780, but it took decades to implement; many individuals in Pennsylvania remained enslaved. An Act for the Gradual Abolition of Slavery, March 1, 1780, Pennsylvania Historical and Museum Commission, https://www.phmc.state.pa.us/portal/communities/documents/1776-1865/abolition-slavery.html.

24. On the Northwest Ordinance, see Peter S. Onuf, *Statehood and Union: A History of the Northwest Ordinance* (University of Notre Dame Press, 2019).

25. David Andrew Nichols, *Red Gentlemen and White Savages: Indians, Federalists, and the Search for Order on the American Frontier* (University of Virginia Press, 2008), 58.

26. Calloway, *Indian World*, 292.

27. James Drake, *The Nation's Nature: How Continental Presumptions Gave Rise to the United States of America* (University of Virginia Press, 2011), 272; Andrew Cayton, *The Frontier Republic: Ideology and Politics in the Ohio Country, 1780–1825* (Kent State University Press, 1986), 7.

28. Calloway, *Indian World*, 294–99.

29. *Virginia Journal and Alexandria Advertiser* (Alexandria, Virginia) vol. 1, no. 43, November 25, 1784: [1], *Readex: America's Historical Newspapers*. https://infoweb-newsbank-com.yale.idm.oclc.org/apps/readex/doc?p=EANX&docref=image/v2%3A10CBAA5E454916A0%40EANX-10F337335FB391F0%402372982-10F337336539C518%400.

30. Calloway, *Indian World*, 294–99; quotation in Calloway, *The World Turned Upside Down: Indian Voices from Early America* (Bedford Books, 1994), 170.

31. Calloway, *Indian World*, 299; Fred Anderson and Andrew Cayton, *The Dominion of War: Empire and Liberty in North America, 1500–2000* (Penguin Books, 2005), 180–84. Note the way "right" and "left" are used here, suggesting that the trans-Appalachian settlers would be facing eastward. The great fear was that they would face westward and be lost to the original thirteen Atlantic seaboard states.

32. The Society of the Cincinnati was founded in 1783 by officers who had served in the Continental Army, with membership restricted to officers and their descendants. It received criticism at the time for its quasi-aristocratic aspirations.

33. Calloway, *Indian World*, 295; Blaakman, *Speculation Nation*, 179–89.

34. Rufus King to Elbridge Gerry, 30 April 1786, in *Letters of the Members of the Continental Congress*, ed. Edmund C. Burnett (Carnegie Institution, 1936), 8:345–47. See also Ablavsky, "Savage Constitution," 1088.

35. Ablavsky, "Savage Constitution," 1067–71; Calloway, *Indian World*, 350–51.

Chapter 5. From Convention to Ratification

1. Important exceptions include the work of Greg Ablavsky, Peter Onuf, Colin Calloway, and Leonard Sadosky, cited elsewhere in this book. See also Maggie Blackhawk, "Foreword: The Constitution of American Colonialism," *Harvard Law Review* 137, no. 1 (2023): 1–152.

2. Although the Confederation Congress that passed the Northwest Ordinance met in New York while the convention delegates met in secret session in Philadelphia, there was

communication between the two bodies; Alexander Hamilton was a member of the New York state legislature and traveled back and forth between New York and Philadelphia during the convention. Staughton Lynd, "The Compromise of 1787," in *Class Conflict, Slavery, and the U.S. Constitution* (Cambridge University Press, 2009), 185–216.

3. Historical accounts of the role of slavery in the making of the Constitution began with the abolitionist movement: see Wendell Phillips, *The Constitution a Pro-Slavery Compact* (New York: American Anti-Slavery Society, 1856). Modern scholarly studies include Staughton Lynd, *Class Conflict, Slavery, and the United States Constitution* (Cambridge University Press, 2009); David Waldstreicher, *Slavery's Constitution: From Revolution to Ratification* (Hill and Wang, 2009); George Van Cleve, *A Slaveholder's Union: Slavery, Politics, and the Constitution in the Early American Republic* (University of Chicago Press, 2010); Sean Wilentz, *No Property in Man: Slavery and Anti-Slavery at the Nation's Founding* (Harvard University Press, 2018); Matthew Mason, *Slavery and Politics in the Early American Republic* (University of North Carolina Press, 2006); and Michael Klarman, *The Framers' Coup: The Making of the United States Constitution* (Oxford University Press, 2016), 257–304.

4. For a recent and provocative argument on the motive force of modern constitutionalism, see Linda Colley, *The Gun, the Ship, and the Pen: Warfare, Constitutions, and the Making of the Modern World* (Livewright, 2021). Colley argues that the emergence of modern warfare and its cost to the state was the major force behind the proliferation of written constitution making starting in the late eighteenth century. This argument is not inconsistent with my own, but in its reach for generalization it ignores the particular conditions that generated dramatic differences in the constitutional challenges faced by varied nations, such as the immense but as yet unrealized land claims of the early United States. Differing nations had different challenges to address when remaking their fundamental frameworks of government.

5. See, for instance, Ablavsky, "Savage Constitution," which differentiates between "Madisonian" and "Hamiltonian" views on Indians and expansion in the making of the Constitution.

6. The events of the Philadelphia Convention have been narrated countless times. A useful and strictly chronological version, assembled from the extant notes of several delegates, can be found in Edward J. Larson and Michael Winship, *The Constitutional Convention: A Narrative History from the Notes of James Madison* (Modern Library, 2005). The most complete record can be found in Max Farrand, ed., *The Records of the Federal Convention of 1787*, 3 vols. (Yale University Press, 1911); along with James H. Hutson, ed., *Supplement to Max Farrand's* "The Records of the Federal Convention of 1787" (Yale University Press, 1987). But note the work of Mary Sarah Bilder, *Madison's Hand: Revising the Constitutional Convention* (Harvard University Press, 2015), which demonstrates convincingly that James Madison doctored his notes from the convention in later years as his political positions shifted with the times.

7. Proceedings of the Commissioners to Remedy the Defects of Government, Annapolis, MD, September 11, 1786, *Avalon Project*, Yale Law School, https://avalon.law.yale.edu/18th_century/annapoli.asp; Report of Proceedings in Congress, February 21, 1787, *Avalon Project*, Yale Law School, https://avalon.law.yale.edu/18th_century/const04.asp.

8. New Jersey was the only other state to send its sitting governor, William Livingston, as a delegate to the Constitutional Convention.

9. On the significance of Washington's presence, see Colin Calloway, *The Indian World of George Washington* (Oxford University Press, 2018), 314ff; after declining to be considered as a

Virginia delegate to the convention for much of the preceding year, Washington changed his mind in March 1787; see Van Cleve, *Slaveholder's Union*, xviii–xix.

10. Variant Texts of the Virginia Plan, Presented by Edmund Randolph to the Federal Convention, May 29, 1787—Text A, *Avalon Project*, Yale Law School, https://avalon.law.yale.edu/18th_century/vatexta.asp.

11. At Virginia's ratifying convention in 1788, Patrick Henry, who opposed the new Constitution, would make this point repeatedly, echoing the stand he had taken in the 1760s; see Patrick Henry, *Documentary History of the Ratification of the Constitution*, ed. John P. Kaminski and Gaspare J. Saladino (State Historical Society of Wisconsin, 1993), 9:957. On Henry's significance at the Virginia ratifying convention, see Pauline Maier, *Ratification: The People Debate the Constitution, 1787–1788* (Simon and Schuster, 2010), 255–91.

12. Variant Texts of the Plan Presented by William Patterson—Text A, *Avalon Project*, Yale Law School, https://avalon.law.yale.edu/18th_century/patexta.asp.

13. Much as the *Virginia Journal* in 1784 had encouraged in its promotion of canal building schemes, *Virginia Journal and Alexandria Advertiser* (Alexandria, Virginia) vol 1, no. 43, November 25, 1784.

14. Max Edling, *A Revolution in Favor of Government: Origins of the U.S. Constitution and the Making of the American State* (Oxford University Press, 2003), describes how the Constitution generated an American variation on Britain's "fiscal-military state"; Eliga Gould, *Among the Powers of the Earth: The American Revolution and the Making of a New World Empire* (Harvard University Press, 2012), focuses on "treaty-worthiness" as an essential goal of the new republic's relationships with its neighbors and competitors; see especially pp. 11–13, 130–34. Michael Klarman describes this enhancement of national power as the "Framers' Coup." Klarman, *Framers' Coup*. See also Isaac Kramnick, "The 'Great National Discussion': The Discourse of Politics in 1787," *William and Mary Quarterly* 45, no. 1 (1988): 23–31.

15. Thomas Jefferson, First Annual Message to Congress, December 8, 1801, quoted in Gould, *Among the Powers*, 12.

16. Blackhawk, "Foreword," 26–52; Greg Ablavsky, *Federal Ground: Governing Property and Violence in the First U.S. Territories* (Oxford University Press, 2021), 1–15.

17. This remains the case today for federal territories such as Puerto Rico and the District of Columbia, even though they easily meet the population requirements for statehood.

18. Temporary could be quite a long time. Wisconsin remained under territorial government until gaining statehood in 1848, sixty years after the Constitution's ratification, longer than Georgia was a British colony. Oklahoma, part of the territory acquired by the United States in the Louisiana Purchase of 1803, waited until 1907 for statehood. Alaska, purchased from Russia in 1867, waited nearly a century, gaining statehood in 1959.

19. Ablavsky, "Savage Constitution," offers among the clearest expositions of this subject, and the following paragraphs are indebted to his work, especially pp. 1038–50. See also Colin Calloway, *Indian World*, 322–23.

20. Ablavsky, "Savage Constitution," 1043.

21. Article IV, Section 3, adds a curious clause regarding territorial claims: that "nothing in this Constitution shall be so construed as to Prejudice any Claims of the United States, or of any particular State." This acknowledges that there are fully constitutional claims that predate

the Constitution. As of the time of its drafting, neither Georgia nor North Carolina had ceded their Western lands to Congress, and the delegates from these two states insisted on this clause so that their claims to this territory would remain valid. Nevertheless, Article IV's property clause provided the national government with clear authority over Western lands within the national domain.

22. In this sense, the U.S. federal government was adopting the same policy that Britain's Royal Proclamation of 1763 had imposed; on the deep continuities between the British and U.S. colonizing projects, see Robert Lee, "The Indian Boundary Line and the Imperialization of U.S. Indian Affairs," in *The Early Imperial Republic: From the American Revolution to the U.S.–Mexican War*, ed. Michael A. Blaakman, Emily Conroy Krutz, and Noelani Arista (University of Pennsylvania Press, 2023), 27–44.

23. Washington accurately predicted the future—he discouraged his agent from selling the land at two dollars per acre, and would later sell it at seven dollars per acre; Calloway, *Indian World*, 317; John E. Ferling, *The First of Men: A Life of George Washington* (University of Tennessee Press, 1988), 364.

24. Other scholars have done this work brilliantly, including Jack Rakove, *Original Meanings: Politics and Ideas in the Making of the Constitution* (Knopf, 1996); Akhil Reed Amar, *America's Constitution: A Biography* (Random House, 2005); Richard Beeman, *Plain Honest Men: The Making of the American Constitution* (Random House, 2009); and Klarman, *Framers' Coup*.

25. Woody Holton, *Unruly Americans and the Origins of the Constitution* (Hill and Wang, 2007), ix–xi, makes a similar argument, though Holton offers a different account from my own of "the most compelling motive of the Constitution."

26. *Return of the Whole Number of Persons Within the Several Districts of the United States* (Philadelphia: Childs and Swaine, 1791), https://www2.census.gov/library/publications/decennial/1790/number-of-persons.pdf.

27. Drew R. McCoy, *The Elusive Republic: Political Economy in Jeffersonian America* (University of North Carolina Press, 1980), offers the best account of the prevailing belief that agrarian societies were best suited to republican self-government; for Jefferson's vision, see his *Notes on the State of Virginia*, published in 1785, the same year he drafted the land ordinance.

28. Articles of Confederation, art. 8, *Milestone Documents*, National Archives, https://www.archives.gov/milestone-documents/articles-of-confederation. It's telling, however, that only *improved* land counted; no state would be assessed for claimed but as yet undeveloped land—everyone understood that commodified, revenue-producing property was what mattered.

29. Robin L. Einhorn, *American Taxation, American Slavery* (University of Chicago Press, 2006), 117–56, provides a definitive account of the origins of national taxation policies.

30. Samuel Chase of Maryland argued this in July 1776, when the first decisions about revenue were being debated, the same month Congress declared that "all men are created equal." In fact, the initial plan in 1776 to assess the value of real estate rather than using a simpler population count was a means to avoid controversy over slavery in wartime; see Einhorn, *American Taxation, American Slavery*, 120–21; Waldstreicher, *Slavery's Constitution*, 51.

31. Einhorn, *American Taxation, American Slavery*, 121, 142–45.

32. Charles Pinckney, July 12, 1787, quoted in Farrand, *Records of the Federal Convention*, 1:596; Einhorn, *American Taxation, American Slavery*, 164.

33. Most of the state constitutions of the 1770s and '80s had some provision for this; Massachusetts apportioned representation in its upper house by the amount of taxes paid by each district in the state, while other states used high property qualifications for upper house members to ensure that wealth would be represented; see Willi Paul Adams, *The First American Constitutions: Republican Ideology and the Making of the State Constitutions in the Revolutionary Era* (Rowman & Littlefield, 2001).

34. Nathaniel Gorham, July 11, 1787, quoted in Farrand, *Records of the Federal Convention,* 1:580.

35. James Wilson, July 11, 1787, quoted in Farrand, *Records of the Federal Convention,* 1:587; Einhorn, *American Taxation, American Slavery,* 164.

36. Gouverneur Morris, July 12, 1787, quoted in Farrand, *Records of the Federal Convention,* 1:591–92.

37. Alexander Hamilton, *Federalist* nos. 21, 17; in Jacob E. Cooke, ed., *The Federalist* (Wesleyan University Press, 1961).

38. Gordon S. Wood, *The Creation of the American Republic, 1776–1787* (University of North Carolina Press, 2011), 547–49.

39. On June 9, 1787, during debates over how to fairly allocate representation under the Virginia Plan, David Brearley of New Jersey, who said little else in the convention, argued that the only solution was "that a map of the U.S. be spread out, that all the existing boundaries be erased, and that a new partition of the whole be made into 13 equal parts." David Brearley, June 9, 1787, quoted in Farrand, *Records of the Federal Convention,* 1:177. His suggestion went nowhere.

40. Calloway, *Indian World,* 325.

41. For example, Ohio, the first state admitted from the Northwest Territory, measures forty-five thousand square miles, nearly identical to Pennsylvania's forty-six thousand square miles.

42. James Madison, June 28, 1787, quoted in Farrand, *Records of the Federal Convention,* 1:449.

43. Peter S. Onuf, *The Origins of the Federal Republic: Jurisdictional Controversies in the United States, 1775–1787* (University of Pennsylvania Press, 1983), 153, 195.

44. As recorded in the first U.S. Census, 1790; see *Return of the Whole Number.*

45. The most thorough account can be found in Maier, *Ratification.* Maier's work builds on the remarkable archive of primary source materials produced by the University of Wisconsin's *Documentary History of the Ratification of the Constitution,* which can be accessed at https://search.library.wisc.edu/digital/AConstitution. An important selection of these sources can be found in Bernard Bailyn, ed., *The Debate on the Constitution,* 2 vols. (Library of America, 1993). Ablavsky, "Savage Constitution," 1050–75, offers the best account of the significance of Western lands and Indian affairs in the ratification process; the following section is indebted to his scholarship.

46. Maier, *Ratification,* 122–24.

47. Van Cleve, *Slaveholder's Union,* 63; Jack Rakove, *The Beginnings of National Politics: An Interpretive History of the Continental Congress* (Alfred A. Knopf, 1979), 338.

48. Kathleen DuVal, *Independence Lost: Lives on the Edge of the American Revolution* (Penguin Random House, 2016), 259.

49. George Washington to Samuel Powel, 18 January 1788, National Archives, *Founders Online,* https://founders.archives.gov/documents/Washington/04-06-02-0034; Holton, *Unruly*

Americans, 244–46; Calloway, *Indian World*, 350–51; Ablavsky, "Savage Constitution," 1067–71, quotations at 1032, 1068.

50. Ablavsky, "Savage Constitution," 1039; George William Van Cleve, *We Have Not a Government: The Articles of Confederation and the Road to the Constitution* (University of Chicago Press, 2017), 134–60.

51. Leonard Richards, *Shays' Rebellion: The American Revolution's Final Battle* (University of Pennsylvania Press, 2002), 118–25; Mark Peterson, *The City-State of Boston: The Rise and Fall of an Atlantic Power, 1630–1865* (Princeton University Press, 2019), 356–63.

52. This was another of Patrick Henry's major critiques at the Virginia Ratifying Convention; see Maier, *Ratification*, 285; and Bailyn, *Debate on the Constitution*, 2:676–79.

53. Edling, *Revolution in Favor of Government*, 122.

54. Ablavsky, "Savage Constitution," 1059; Saul Cornell, "Aristocracy Assailed: The Ideology of Backcountry Anti-Federalism," *Journal of American History* 76, no. 4 (1990): 1156–68.

55. Ablavsky, "Savage Constitution," 1060–62.

56. Hamilton, *Federalist*, no. 24, 155–57; no. 25, 158.

57. Maier, *Ratification*, 316–19.

58. Ratification of the Constitution by the State of Virginia, June 26, 1788, *Avalon Project*, Yale Law School, https://avalon.law.yale.edu/18th_century/ratva.asp.

59. Fred Anderson and Andrew Cayton, *The Dominion of War: Empire and Liberty in North America, 1500–2000* (Penguin Books, 2005), 189, who argue that this was a critical element of what they call the "American Revolutionary Settlement," the American equivalent to Britain's Glorious Revolution Settlement of 1689; Brian Balogh, *A Government Out of Sight: The Mystery of National Authority in Nineteenth-Century America* (Cambridge University Press, 2009).

60. Anderson and Cayton, *Dominion of War*, 193; Andrew J. Birtle, "The Origins of the Legion of the United States," *Journal of Military History* 67, no. 4 (2003): 1250–51.

61. Ablavsky, "Savage Constitution," 1071–72.

62. Richard Sylla, "Financial Foundations: Public Credit, the National Bank, and Securities Markets," in *Founding Choices: American Economic Policy in the 1790s*, ed. Douglas A. Irwin and Richard Sylla (University of Chicago Press, 2011); McCraw, *Founders and Finance*, 99–109; Gautham Rao, *National Duties: Custom Houses and the Making of the American State* (University of Chicago Press, 2016), 1–4.

63. Ablavsky, "Savage Constitution," 1083; Patrick Henry, Speech in Virginia Ratifying Convention, 5 June 1788, *Documentary History*, 9:959.

64. James Wilson, Speech in Pennsylvania Ratifying Convention, 4 Dec 1787, *Documentary History*, 2:477.

Chapter 6. Two Paths to Westward Expansion, North and South

1. Eric Hinderaker, *Elusive Empires: Constructing Colonialism in the Ohio Valley, 1673–1800* (Cambridge University Press, 1999); Gregory Evans Dowd, *A Spirited Resistance: The North American Indian Struggle for Unity, 1745–1815* (Johns Hopkins University Press, 1993).

2. Ohio was not the original homeland of the Delaware, or Lenape, people. But it was Neolin, a Lenape prophet, who inspired the resistance movement in the Ohio country that generated

Pontiac's rebellion against British rule in 1763 and continued to inspire the Ohio confederation's resistance to U.S. settlement in the 1790s.

3. Colin Calloway, *The Indian World of George Washington* (Oxford University Press, 2018), 321–45.

4. David Andrew Nichols, *Red Gentlemen and White Savages: Indians, Federalists, and the Search for Order on the American Frontier* (University of Virginia Press, 2008), 116–18; John P. Bowes, *Land Too Good for Indians: Northern Indian Removal* (University of Oklahoma Press, 2016), 18–31.

5. Nichols, *Red Gentlemen*, 128–59; Andrew R. L. Cayton, *The Frontier Republic: Ideology and Politics in the Ohio Country, 1780–1825* (Kent State University Press, 1986), chap. 3; Colin Calloway, *The Victory with No Name: The Native American Defeat of the First American Army* (Oxford University Press, 2015).

6. Calloway, *Indian World*, 397–421; Nichols, *Red Gentlemen*, 140–51, quotation at 149.

7. Figures drawn from *Historical Statistics of the United States*, Series P 99–108, Federal Government Finances—Treasury Expenditures, 1789–1945 (Bureau of the Census, 1975), 301, https://www2.census.gov/library/publications/1949/compendia/hist_stats_1789-1945/hist_stats_1789-1945-chP.pdf; Act Making Appropriations for the Support of the Military Establishment, March 21, 1794, in *Statutes at Large of the United States* (Little, Brown, 1845), 1:346–47. https://www.loc.gov/law/help/statutes-at-large/3rd-congress/session-1/c3s1ch10.pdf.

8. Jeffrey Ostler, *Surviving Genocide: Native Nations and the United States from the American Revolution to Bleeding Kansas* (Yale University Press, 2019), 82–122; William H. Bergmann, *The American National State and the Early West* (Cambridge University Press, 2012), 42–93; Wiley Sword, *President Washington's Indian War: The Struggle for the Old Northwest, 1790–1795* (University of Oklahoma Press, 1985); Calloway, *Indian World*, 378–98.

9. Richard Bland Lee, *Annals of Congress*, 3rd Congress, 262, https://www.congress.gov/annals-of-congress/page-headings/3rd-congress/commerce-of-the-united-states/20901, quoted in Michael Kammen, *A Machine That Would Go of Itself: The Constitution in American Culture* (Alfred A. Knopf, 1986), 15.

10. Although formal ratification was complete by the summer of 1788 with nine states' approval, North Carolina did not ratify until November 1789; see Pauline Maier, *Ratification: The People Debate the Constitution, 1787–1788* (Simon and Schuster, 2010), 408–25, 457–58.

11. My account of expansion in the Southwest relies on the following: Calloway, *Indian World*, 346–76; Nichols, *Red Gentlemen*; Ostler, *Surviving Genocide*, 112–38; Thomas Abernethy, *The South in the New Nation, 1789–1819* (Louisiana State University Press, 1961), 74–102; Arthur Preston Whitaker, *The Spanish-American Frontier, 1783–1795: The Westward Movement and the Spanish Retreat in the Mississippi Valley* (Houghton Mifflin, 1927); and Franklin Sammons, "Yazoo's Settlement: Finance, Law, and Dispossession in the Southeastern Borderlands, 1783–1820" (PhD diss., University of California, Berkeley, 2021). I am grateful to Professor Sammons for introducing me to the complicated world of expansion and dispossession in the Southwest.

12. Nichols, *Red Gentlemen*, 118–24; Sammons, "Yazoo's Settlement," chap. 1.

13. Sammons, "Yazoo's Settlement," chap. 3–4.

14. Ostler, *Surviving Genocide*, 135.

15. Franklin Sammons, "'The Fruit of the Yazoo Compromise': Mississippi Stock and the Panic of 1819," *Journal of the Early Republic* 40, no. 4 (2020): 671–76, https://doi.org/10.1353/jer.2020.0094.

16. Robert A. Williams, Jr., *The American Indian in Western Legal Thought: The Discourses of Conquest* (Oxford University Press, 1990), 307–17; Stuart Banner, *How the Indians Lost Their Land: Law and Power on the Frontier* (Harvard University Press, 2005), 171–76; Sammons, "Yazoo's Settlement," chap. 5. In this sense, *Fletcher v. Peck* was to Indian land rights what *Dred Scott* in 1857 was to African American personal rights: a judicial declaration of prevailing social practices that categorically denied legal protection for colonized peoples.

17. Johnson & Graham's Lessee v. McIntosh, 21 U.S. 543 (1823).

18. Banner, *How the Indians Lost*, 187.

19. Banner, *How the Indians Lost*, 178–88.

20. Sammons, "Yazoo's Settlement," chap. 5.

21. R. Kent Newmyer, *John Marshall and the Heroic Age of the Supreme Court* (LSU Press, 2007); James W. Ely, *The Contract Clause: A Constitutional History* (University Press of Kansas, 2016).

22. Robert V. Haynes, "From Province to Territory," in *The Mississippi Territory and the Southwest Frontier, 1795–1817* (University Press of Kentucky, 2010), 6–26.

23. Ostler, *Surviving Genocide*, 123–50; Fred Anderson and Andrew Cayton, *The Dominion of War: Empire and Liberty in North America, 1500–2000* (Penguin Books, 2005), 207–34; Bergmann, *American National State*, 213–52; Bowes, *Land Too Good for Indians*, 18–50.

24. Adam Rothman, *Slave Country: American Expansion and the Origins of the Deep South* (Harvard University Press, 2005), 119–62.

25. Ostler, *Surviving Genocide*, 168.

26. Ostler, *Surviving Genocide*, 164–75; Rothman, *Slave Country*, 119–39. Jackson insisted that even Creeks who opposed the Red Sticks and joined his forces nonetheless deserved this punishment for having failed to reject Tecumseh's diplomatic overtures or turn him over to U.S. authorities for his treasonous plotting against the United States.

27. *Population of States and Counties of the United States, 1790–1990*, ed. Richard L. Forstall (U.S. Bureau of the Census, 1996); *Historical Statistics of the United States, Colonial Times to 1970* (U.S. Bureau of the Census, 1975).

28. Rothman, *Slave Country*, 1–35; Jefferson's draft for an independent constitution for Virginia in June 1776 included a clause that "no person hereafter coming into this country shall be held in slavery under any pretext whatever." Second Draft by Jefferson [before June 13, 1776], *Founders Online*, National Archives, https://founders.archives.gov/documents/Jefferson/01-01-02-0161-0003. In his draft for Congress's Land Ordinance of 1784, Jefferson recommended that after the year 1800, slavery would be outlawed in all the new trans-Appalachian states (with fanciful names such as Metropotamia and Polypotamia) proposed in the ordinance; see Report of the Committee, 1 March 1784, *Founders Online*, National Archives, https://founders.archives.gov/documents/Jefferson/01-06-02-0420-0004. Needless to say, neither of Jefferson's suggestions withstood opposition from other slave owners.

29. David Rice, *Slavery Inconsistent with Justice and Good Policy: Proved by a Speech Delivered in the Convention, Held at Danville, Kentucky* (Philadelphia, 1793).

30. Georgia allowed for continued slave imports from 1783 onward, while South Carolina banned the trade in 1787 but resumed it in 1804 because of intensifying demand from the expansion of cotton; see David Eltis and David Richardson, *Atlas of the Transatlantic Slave Trade* (Yale University Press, 2010), maps 140, 144, 145, 210–18.

31. Sven Beckert, *Empire of Cotton: A Global History* (Knopf, 2014), 98–120; Adam Rothman, *Slave Country: American Expansion and the Origins of the Deep South* (Harvard University Press, 2005), 37–70; Claudio Saunt, *Unworthy Republic: The Dispossession of Native Americans and the Road to Indian Territory* (W. W. Norton, 2020), 303–22.

32. That said, each individual white voter in the expanding slave South would be hyper-represented in Congress. With slave and free populations in the South being more or less equal in size, each Southern white voter's representation was increased by the three-fifths addition for each slave. To put it another way, a single plantation owner of one hundred slaves received the same amount of congressional representation as sixty-one non–slave owners.

33. Population figures drawn from *Population of States and Counties*, 4; those regarding land area from *Historical Statistics of the United States, Colonial Times to 1970*, 39.

Chapter 7. The President Who Failed to Bark

1. Peter J. Kastor, *The Nation's Crucible: The Louisiana Purchase and the Creation of America* (Yale University Press, 2004), 25–34; Ashli White, "The Impact of the Haitian Revolution on the United States," in *The Cambridge History of the Age of Atlantic Revolutions*, 3 vols., ed. Wim Klooster (Cambridge University Press, 2023), 2:739–60.

2. Thomas Jefferson to Wilson Cary Nicholas, 7 September 1803, *Founders Online*, National Archives, https://founders.archives.gov/documents/Jefferson/01-41-02-0255.

3. Thomas Jefferson to John Breckinridge, 12 August 1803, *Founders Online*, National Archives, https://founders.archives.gov/documents/Jefferson/01-41-02-0139.

4. Thomas Jefferson to Levi Lincoln, 30 August 1803, *Founders Online*, National Archives, https://founders.archives.gov/documents/Jefferson/01-41-02-0225.

5. Under terms such as these, the written constitution today would have to include at least twenty-four additional amendments to accommodate all the new states formed beyond the original territory of the United States, unless a future amendment made a blanket provision for future state admission in acquired territory by Congressional authority.

6. Jefferson to Breckenridge, 12 August 1803.

7. Thomas Jefferson to Adamantios Coray, 31 October 1823, *Founders Online*, National Archives, https://founders.archives.gov/documents/Jefferson/98-01-02-3837. Here, Jefferson was giving advice to a Greek author during the Greek Revolution, advising him and his countrymen to form a constitution with great deliberation that was suitable to the needs of their own nation.

8. Jefferson made this argument eloquently in *A summary view of the rights of British America: set forth in some resolutions intended for the inspection of the present delegates of the people of Virginia, now in convention.* (Williamsburg, Va.: Printed by Clementina Rind, 1774), Pdf. https://www.loc.gov/item/08016823/, where he cited many instances of "unwarrantable encroachments and usurpations" made by Parliament on the colonies.

9. Keeping in mind, of course, that the volitional aspect was confined to white men. It expressly excluded the enslaved and "Indians not taxed," and implicitly excluded women and

dependents under then-common assumptions about patriarchal authority and political representation.

10. If territorial acquisition required a treaty, then a two-thirds vote in the Senate would be necessary for its ratification. But even this rule could be subverted, as when President James Polk requested that Congress bypass the treaty process by way of a joint resolution of both houses in favor of the annexation of Texas in 1845; see "Joint Resolution of the Congress of Texas, June 23, 1845," in Hunter Miller, ed., *Treaties and Other International Acts of the United States of America* (U.S. Government Printing Office, 1934), 4:689–90, quoted in Emily A. Yankowitz, "Who Is a Citizen? Negotiating American Citizenship Before the Fourteenth Amendment" (PhD diss., Yale University, 2025), 215.

11. Jefferson to Nicholas, 7 September 1803.

12. Mark Peterson, *The City-State of Boston: The Rise and Fall of an Atlantic Power, 1630–1865* (Princeton University Press, 2019), chap. 8.

13. By 1810, over nine thousand migrants from Haiti had come to Louisiana, two-thirds of them enslaved or free people of color, collectively comprising 12 percent of the population of the Territory of Orleans; see Kastor, *Nation's Crucible*, 64–65, 115–17; and Adam Rothman, *Slave Country: American Expansion and the Origins of the Deep South* (Harvard University Press, 2005), 75–76, 104–5.

14. Quincy's speech was frequently republished in schoolbooks and textbooks of the era.

15. *Speech of the Hon. Josiah Quincy, in the House of Representatives of the U.S., January 14, 1811: On the Passage of the Bill to Enable the People of the Territory of Orleans, to Form a Constitution and State Government: And for the Admission of Such State into the Union* (Baltimore: B. Edes, 1811), 16–17.

16. Daniel Rasmussen, *American Uprising: The Untold Story of America's Largest Slave Revolt* (Harper Collins, 2011), 97–114; Rothman, *Slave Country*.

17. *Speech of Josiah Quincy*, 19; Peterson, *City-State of Boston*, 422–29.

18. *Speech of Josiah Quincy*, 14, 16.

19. Edmund Quincy, *Life of Josiah Quincy of Massachusetts* (Ticknor and Fields, 1867), 260–61.

20. Lillie Richardson, "The Admission of Louisiana into the Union," *Louisiana Historical Quarterly* 1, no. 4 (1917–18): 333–52, quotation at 346–47.

21. The latter understanding is what allowed Chief Justice John Roberts, in his confirmation hearings before the Senate, to describe the work of a Supreme Court justice as simply "calling balls and strikes," as if the complex and shifting life of the nation and its laws were somehow equivalent to a game of baseball; see Charles Fried, "Balls and Strikes," *Emory Law Journal* 61, no. 4 (2012): 641–62.

22. Jefferson to Breckenridge, 12 August 1803.

Chapter 8. The Machine Runs Amok

1. Robert Lee's work on the St. Louis Superintendency of Indian Affairs has been enormously influential for my understanding of the process of expansion in the Louisiana Territory; see Robert Lee, "The Boon's Lick Land Rush and the Coming of the Missouri Crisis," in *A Fire Bell in the Past: The Missouri Crisis at 200*, ed. John Craig Hammond and Jeffrey L. Pasley, vol. 1,

Western Slavery, National Impasse (University of Missouri Press, 2021), 77–112; Lee, "'A Better View of the Country': A Missouri Settlement Map by William Clark," *William and Mary Quarterly* 79, no. 1 (2022): 89–119; Lee, "The Indian Boundary Line and the Imperialization of U.S.–Indian Affairs," in *The Early Imperial Republic: From the American Revolution to the U.S.–Mexican War*, ed. Michael A. Blaakman, Emily Conroy Krutz, and Noelani Arista (University of Pennsylvania Press, 2023), 27–44.

2. Robert Pierce Forbes, *The Missouri Compromise and Its Aftermath: Slavery and the Meaning of America* (University of North Carolina Press, 2007), 69–120.

3. Thomas Jefferson to John Holmes, 22 April 1820, *Founders Online*, National Archives, https://founders.archives.gov/documents/Jefferson/03-15-02-051898-01-02-1234. John Holmes, to whom Jefferson wrote the letter, was one of the architects of the Missouri Compromise and one of Maine's first two U.S. senators.

4. For example, the Netherlands, upon winning its independence from Spain in the Eighty Years' War, maintained for many generations a republic divided between a Protestant majority and a Catholic minority—inveterate enemies in the religious wars of the preceding century—by guaranteeing religious toleration. Canada has endured for more than a century and a half with a large and populous Francophone province in the heart of an otherwise mostly Anglophone nation.

5. Philip C. Brooks, *Diplomacy and the Borderlands: The Adams-Onís Treaty of 1819* (University of California Press, 1939); Adam Rothman, *Slave Country: American Expansion and the Origins of the Deep South* (Harvard University Press, 2005), 167–68.

6. Iowa has roughly the same land area as Arkansas and Louisiana, while Missouri, Florida, and Texas are all far larger.

7. Soil exhaustion also pushed the U.S. government to begin claiming Pacific Ocean islands with large deposits of bird guano, a valuable fertilizer, in order to control the supply and price of this valuable commodity in high demand among planters; see Daniel Immerwahr, *How to Hide an Empire: A History of the Greater United States* (Farrar, Straus and Giroux, 2019), 46–58.

8. "Number of Documented Migrants That Came to the United States Between 1820 and 1957 by Decade," *Statista*, https://www.statista.com/statistics/1045043/total-documented-migration-to-us-1820-1957-decade/. For comparative population numbers in the new trans-Appalachian states, see chapter 6.

9. Erin Stewart Mauldin, *Unredeemed Land: An Environmental History of Civil War and Emancipation in the Cotton South* (Oxford University Press, 2018), 11–41; Matthew Karp, *This Vast Southern Empire: Slaveholders at the Helm of American Foreign Policy* (Harvard University Press, 2016); Leonard L. Richards, *The Slave Power: The Free North and Southern Domination, 1780–1860* (LSU Press, 2000); Don Fehrenbacher, *The Slaveholding Republic*, comp. and ed. Ward M. McAfee (Oxford University Press, 2002), 89–133, 253–94.

10. Karp, *Vast Southern Empire*, 199–225; Amy S. Greenberg, *A Wicked War: Polk, Clay, Lincoln, and the 1846 U.S. Invasion of Mexico* (Knopf, 2012); Brian DeLay, *War of a Thousand Deserts: Indian Raids and the U.S.-Mexican War* (Yale University Press, 2008).

11. The Utah Territory was already primarily the settlement of Latter-day Saints emigrants. It had relatively few enslaved people, but the Mormons' strained relationships with the United States and mainstream U.S. culture, especially because of their practice of polygamy, meant that statehood there was unlikely any time soon; it would be forty-six years before Utah gained statehood.

12. United States Department of State, Pierre Soulé, John Y. Mason, and James Buchanan, *The Ostend Manifesto, 1854* (New York: A. Lovell, 1892).

13. Michel Gobat, *Empire by Invitation: William Walker and Manifest Destiny in Central America* (Harvard University Press, 2018); Karp, *Vast Southern Empire*, 172–98, 229–31; Gregory Downs, *The Second American Revolution: The Civil War Era Struggle over Cuba and the Rebirth of the American Republic* (University of North Carolina Press, 2019), 77–87.

14. Albert von Frank, *The Trials of Anthony Burns: Freedom and Slavery in Emerson's Boston* (Harvard University Press, 1999); Mark Peterson, *The City-State of Boston: The Rise and Fall of an Atlantic Power, 1630–1865* (Princeton University Press, 2019), 605–22.

15. Republican Party Platform of 1856, *American Presidency Project*, https://www.presidency.ucsb.edu/documents/republican-party-platform-1856; William E. Gienapp, *The Origins of the Republican Party, 1852–1856* (Oxford University Press, 1987), 335.

16. David Potter, *The Impending Crisis, 1848–1861* (Harper and Row, 1976); Dred Scott v. Sandford, (1857), National Archives, *Milestone Documents*, https://www.archives.gov/milestone-documents/dred-scott-v-sandford.

17. Technically, before the introduction of the secret ballot in the 1880s, there was no general "ballot" that listed all candidates—rather, candidates' supporters made paper ballots with slates of electors pledged to their candidate available for voters to choose. Lincoln was so unpopular in these states that no ballots with electors pledged to him were produced and hence no votes were cast for him at all. In Virginia, the one exception in the future Confederacy, nearly all of the paltry number of votes for Lincoln were cast in the part of the state that would become West Virginia during the Civil War; see Christian McWhirter, "Was Lincoln 'Removed' from Southern Presidential Ballots?" Abraham Lincoln Presidential Library and Museum, https://presidentlincoln.illinois.gov/Blog/Posts/181/Abraham-Lincoln/2024/1/Was-Lincoln-removed-from-Southern-presidential-ballots/blog-post/.

18. Confederate States of America—Declaration of the Immediate Causes Which Induce and Justify the Secession of South Carolina from the Federal Union, *Avalon Project*, Yale Law School, https://avalon.law.yale.edu/19th_century/csa_scarsec.asp.

19. Not to mention that when Josiah Quincy argued in 1811 that the constitutional compact was broken by the national legislative act that admitted Louisiana to statehood, and that Massachusetts was therefore released from its obligations, his argument was utterly denigrated by Southerners in Congress.

20. Confederate States of America—Mississippi Secession, *Avalon Project*, Yale Law School, https://avalon.law.yale.edu/19th_century/csa_missec.asp.

21. See 1860 U.S. Census, *Statistics of the United States*, United States Census Bureau (U.S. Government Printing Office, 1866), https://www.census.gov/library/publications/1866/dec/1860d.html.

22. Confederate States of America—Mississippi Secession, *Avalon Project*, Yale Law School, https://avalon.law.yale.edu/19th_century/csa_missec.asp, emphasis added.

23. John Quincy Adams received only 30 percent of the popular vote in 1824, but he did not win an Electoral College majority, or even a plurality of electoral votes. His election was decided by the House of Representatives.

24. Constitution of the Confederate States, March 11, 1861, *Avalon Project*, Yale Law School, https://avalon.law.yale.edu/19th_century/csa_csa.asp, emphasis added. This was a brutally

ironic place to attach a clause protecting property in persons. A bill of attainder was an ancient English legal practice whereby the legislature (Parliament) could convict and punish a person for a crime without a trial; nullify their rights, including the right to own property; deny their heirs any right to their property; and even execute them. Thus in the very same sentence of its constitution, the Confederacy denies its Congress the power to enact bills of attainder, while at the same time guaranteeing the power of white citizens to punish their slaves without trial and rob them of all rights including property, inheritance, and self-ownership.

25. Constitution of the Confederate States, March 11, 1861, *Avalon Project*, Yale Law School, https://avalon.law.yale.edu/19th_century/csa_csa.asp.

26. The Twelfth Amendment (1804) merely tweaked the Electoral College's procedure for casting presidential votes to avoid a repeat of the Electoral College tie that had derailed the 1800 presidential election. The Sixteenth Amendment, which empowered Congress to levy national income taxes, was not passed by Congress until 1909 and was only ratified in 1913.

27. As with all other aspects of the Civil War, the scholarly literature on its legal dimensions is formidable; I rely here on Eric Foner, *The Second Founding* (W. W. Norton, 2019); and Michael Vorenberg, *Final Freedom: The Civil War, the Abolition of Slavery, and the Thirteenth Amendment* (Cambridge University Press, 2001). For sources, see Kurt T. Lash, *The Reconstruction Amendments: The Essential Documents*, 2 vols. (University of Chicago Press, 2021).

28. In fact, this language predated the Northwest Ordinance. In 1784, Jefferson included a similar phrase in his draft of a land ordinance that proposed a ban on slavery west of the Appalachians; see Thomas Jefferson, Report of the Committee, 1 March 1784, *Founders Online*, National Archives, https://founders.archives.gov/documents/Jefferson/01-06-02-0420-0004.

29. For the text of the Civil War Amendments, see The Constitution: Amendments 11–27, *America's Founding Documents*, National Archives, https://www.archives.gov/founding-docs/amendments-11-27.

30. Richard White, *The Republic for Which It Stands: The United States During Reconstruction and the Gilded Age* (Oxford University Press, 2017), 622.

31. Eric Foner, *The Second Founding* (W. W. Norton, 2019).

Chapter 9. The Machine Stalls Out

1. The Territory of Nevada's population in the 1860 U.S. census was only 6,857, about one-twentieth the size of the "ratio of representation." New Mexico, the most populous of the U.S. territories at the time, had a population of 93,516, three-fourths of the ratio of representation and well above the original Northwest Ordinance standard. 1860 Census, Population of the United States, United States Census Bureau, https://www.census.gov/library/publications/1864/dec/1860a.html.

2. Charles Stewart III and Barry R. Weingast, "Stacking the Senate, Changing the Nation: Republican Rotten Boroughs, Statehood Politics, and American Political Development," *Studies in American Political Development* 6, no. 2 (1992): 223–71; James Bryce, *The American Commonwealth*, 3 vols. (Macmillan, 1888), 2:219, quote. See also Gilman Marston Ostrander, *Nevada: The Great Rotten Borough* (Knopf, 1966).

3. On California statehood and its role in the sectional conflict over slavery, see Leonard Richards, *The California Gold Rush and the Coming of the Civil War* (Alfred A. Knopf, 2007).

4. This map was produced by the U.S. Census in 1870, showing the "Constitutional Population" in shades of gray, with "Indians not taxed" depicted in shades of brown on Western reservations. A population density map of the United States in 2020 would look strikingly similar, when adjusted for the invention of air conditioning and air travel, which have made south Florida and Arizona habitable for far more people. The raw numbers have obviously grown, but the pattern of settlement is nearly identical today to what it was in 1870.

5. Malcolm J. Rohrbough, *Days of Gold: The California Gold Rush and the American Nation* (University of California Press, 1997); Leonard Richards, *California Gold Rush*, 91–118.

6. Harvey Leifert, "Dividing Line: The Past, Present, and Future of the 100th Meridian," *Earth Magazine*, January 2018, https://www.earthmagazine.org/article/dividing-line-past-present-and-future-100th-meridian.

7. Eric Foner, *Free Soil, Free Labor, Free Men: The Ideology of the Republic Party before the Civil War* (Oxford University Press, 1970/1995), 74–79; Ariel Ron, *Grassroots Leviathan: Agricultural Reform and the Rural North in the Slaveholding Republic* (Johns Hopkins University Press, 2020), 219–20.

8. Richard White, *The Republic for Which It Stands: The United States During Reconstruction and the Gilded Age* (Oxford University Press, 2017), 807. A predecessor to the Homestead Act, the Preemption Act of 1841, had allowed squatters on public land who could prove that they had been residing on or improving the land to purchase it at very low prices; see The Preemption Act of 1841, 27th Congress, Ch. 16, 5 Stat. 453 (1841), http://www.minnesotalegalhistoryproject.org/assets/Microsoft%20Word%20-%20Preemption%20Act%20of%201841.pdf.

9. Two years later, Congress chartered a third railroad corporation, the Northern Pacific, with a grant for an additional forty million acres.

10. Remember, there are 640 acres to a square mile, so this was a grant of ten square miles of adjacent land for every mile of railroad track.

11. Heather C. Richardson, *Greatest Nation on Earth: Republican Economic Policies During the Civil War* (Harvard University Press, 1997), 172–87; William Cronon, *Nature's Metropolis: Chicago and the Great West* (W. W. Norton, 1991); Richard White, *Railroaded: The Transcontinentals and the Making of Modern America* (W. W. Norton, 2011).

12. For remarkable work on the Morrill Act's foundation in land expropriated from Indigenous Americans and given to the new public universities, see Robert Lee et al., *Land-Grab Universities: A "High Country News" Investigation*, https://www.landgrabu.org/; Tristan Ahtone and Robert Lee, "Looking Forward from *Land-Grab Universities*," *Native American and Indigenous Studies* 8, no. 1 (2021): 176–82; and Tristan Ahtone et al., "Misplaced Trust," *Grist*, February 7, 2024, https://grist.org/project/equity/land-grant-universities-indigenous-lands-fossil-fuels/.

13. Henry George, "What Railroads Will Bring Us," *Overland Monthly* 1, no. 4 (1868), 297–306; Christopher William England, *Land and Liberty: Henry George and the Crafting of Modern Liberalism* (Johns Hopkins University Press, 2023), chap. 2. On nineteenth-century boosterism, see Cronon, *Nature's Metropolis*, 31–40.

14. Henry George, *Our Land and Land Policy: Speeches, Lectures, and Miscellaneous Writings*, ed. Kenneth C. Wenzer (Michigan State University Press, 1999).

15. Thomas Paine, *Agrarian Justice, Opposed to Agrarian Law, and to Agrarian Monopoly* (Paris: W. Adlard; repr. London: T. Williams, 1797), 6–7, emphasis in original. On the sources of George's ideas on the land tax, see England, *Land and Liberty*, 10–15.

16. Even the Land Ordinance of 1785, a far more orderly approach to land distribution than the speculative frenzy that had emerged in the late colonial period and in the Georgia-Yazoo scandals, set the minimum purchase amount at 640 acres, equal to a square mile, which was beyond the means of most families to use.

17. George, *Our Land and Land Policy*, 24–25.

18. George, *Our Land and Land Policy*, 57–58.

19. Investment in the stock of a railroad company or a manufacturing enterprise encouraged economic development by putting capital in the hands of an active business, while investment in land speculation inhibited economic development by keeping land out of production or charging unwarranted prices for its use.

20. George, *Our Land and Land Policy*, 72–73.

21. George, *Our Land and Land Policy*, 91. According to the Roman historian Livy's *History of Rome*, the farm of Cincinnatus measured exactly four *iugera*, or 2.68 acres; Livy 3.26.7. My thanks to Carlos Norena for the reference.

22. "Growth of Mount Vernon," George Washington's Mount Vernon, https://www.mountvernon.org/library/digitalhistory/digital-encyclopedia/article/growth-of-mount-vernon; Colin Calloway, *The Indian World of George Washington: The First President, the First Americans, and the Birth of the Nation* (Oxford University Press, 2018).

23. Paine, *Agrarian Justice*, 7.

24. George, *Our Land and Land Policy*, 89, 68.

25. Donald Worster, *A River Running West: The Life of John Wesley Powell* (Oxford University Press, 2002).

26. J. W. Powell, *Report on the Lands of the Arid Regions of the United States*, 2nd ed. (Washington: Government Printing Office, 1879), 1.

27. John Wesley Powell, "Institutions for the Arid Lands," *Century Magazine*, May 1890, 113.

28. See, for example, Richard B. Morris, *The Peacemakers: The Great Powers and American Independence* (Harper and Row, 1965), "Metes and Bounds," 341–85.

29. Powell, "Institutions for the Arid Lands," 114; Donald Worster, *Rivers of Empire: Water, Aridity, and the Growth of the American West* (Random House, 1985), 131–43.

30. Powell made this declaration at the second International Irrigation Congress, held in Los Angeles in 1893; Worster, *Rivers of Empire*, 132.

31. Powell, *Report on the Lands*, 112.

32. Heather Cox Richardson, *Wounded Knee: Party Politics and the Road to an American Massacre* (Basic Books, 2010), 100–102.

33. Stewart and Weingast, "Stacking the Senate," 236–42.

34. 50 Cong. Rec. H1907 (daily ed. Feb. 14, 1889); Stewart and Weingast, "Stacking the Senate," 240.

35. White, *Republic for Which It Stands*, 593–601, 607–12.

36. White, *Railroaded*, 17–36, 118–33; Cronon, *Nature's Metropolis*, 81–93, 207–24.

37. Carey McWilliams, *Factories in the Field: The Story of Migrant Farm Labor in California* (University of California Press, 1939).

38. Julie Guthman, *Agrarian Dreams: The Paradox of Organic Farming in California* (University of California Press, 2004), chap. 4, "California's Agro-Industrial Legacy," 96–124.

39. Claudio Saunt, *Unworthy Republic: The Dispossession of Native Americans and the Road to Indian Territory* (W. W. Norton, 2023), 53–82.

40. Saunt, *Unworthy Republic*, 84–142; Jeffrey Ostler, *Surviving Genocide: Native Nations and the United States from the American Revolution to Bleeding Kansas* (Yale University Press, 2019), 327–58.

41. Robert Lee, "The Indian Boundary Line and the Imperialization of U.S. Indian Affairs," in *The Early Imperial Republic: From the American Revolution to the U.S.–Mexican War*, ed. Michael A. Blaakman, Emily Conroy Krutz, and Noelani Arista (University of Pennsylvania Press, 2023), 27–44; Stuart Banner, *How the Indians Lost Their Land: Law and Power on the Frontier* (Harvard University Press, 2005), 230–36.

42. White, *Republic for Which It Stands*, 297–305, 635–49; Pekka Hämäläinen, *Lakota America: A New History of Indigenous Power* (Yale University Press, 2019), 337–79.

Chapter 10. A Union of Three Distinct Sub-Nations and the Beginnings of Constitutional Reform

1. *The Anglo-Saxon Chronicle: A Revised Translation*, ed. Dorothy Whitelock (London, 1961), 161–62. A "hide" was a unit of land for tax assessment purposes, the amount of land that could support a household, roughly 120 acres; see Hull Domesday Project, Weights and Measures, "Hides," https://www.domesdaybook.net/domesday-book/data-terminology/weights-measures/hides.

2. Christopher Dyer, *Making a Living in the Middle Ages: The People of Britain, 850-1250* (Yale University Press, 2002), 94–95; *1790 Census: Return of the Whole Number of Persons Within the Several Districts of the United States* (Philadelphia, 1793), https://www.census.gov/library/publications/1793/dec/number-of-persons.html.

3. As early as 1751, Benjamin Franklin was making bold predictions about the demographic growth of British America's population. A generation later Ezra Stiles, president of Yale College, had a similar vision for the future growth of the United States. See Benjamin Franklin, "Observations Concerning the Increase of Mankind," 1751, *Founders Online*, National Archives, https://founders.archives.gov/documents/Franklin/01-04-02-0080; Ezra Stiles, *The United States Elevated to Glory and Honor . . .* (New Haven, CT: Thomas and Samuel Green, 1783), 8–9; and Mark Peterson, "Demography," in *The Oxford Handbook of the Seven Years' War*, ed. Trevor Burnard, Emma Hart, and Marie Houllemare (Oxford University Press, 2024).

4. Margo J. Anderson, *The American Census: A Social History*, 2nd ed. (Yale University Press, 2015), 7–39.

5. Robin Einhorn, *American Taxation, American Slavery* (University of Chicago Press, 2006), 184–99. During the War of 1812, the New England states gathered at the Hartford Convention protested that exempting the enslaved population from military service violated the three-fifths clause because military service could be regarded as a direct tax on the labor of each state that only the free states where slavery had been abolished were paying in full; see Mark Peterson, *The City-State of Boston: The Rise and Fall of an Atlantic Power, 1630–1865* (Princeton University Press, 2019), 438.

6. Information drawn from U.S. House of Representatives, History, Art, and Archives, Congress Profiles, https://history.house.gov/Congressional-Overview/Profiles/1st/.

7. Anderson, *American Census*, 106–9; Carroll D. Wright, *The History and Growth of the United States Census* (U.S. Government Printing Office, 1900), 72.

8. The 1890 census figure was strikingly close to Benjamin Franklin's 1751 prediction—he imagined that British North America would reach 64 million by 1900.

9. Wright, *History and Growth*, 84–88.

10. From its beginnings at 869,735 square miles after the Treaty of Paris, the United States grew to something over 3 million square miles by 1890 (the exact size of the Alaska Territory remained unknown). Franklin K. Van Zandt, *Boundaries of the United States and the Several States: With Miscellaneous Geographical Information Concerning Areas, Altitudes, and Geographical Centers* (U.S. Government Printing Office, 1976), 168. Of course, it should be remembered that in 1790, the majority of this 869,735 square miles was owned and occupied by Indian nations; less than half was in the form of states controlled by U.S. citizens.

11. Indeed, there were only six such places in the United States in 1790: New York, Philadelphia, Boston, Charleston, Baltimore, and the "Northern Liberties" township which would eventually become part of Philadelphia; these six had an aggregate population just under 120,000. Salem, Massachusetts, fell 79 persons shy of the 8,000 threshold. In the 1790 census, "urban" had been defined as those places with more than 2,500 people. Henry Gannett, *Statistical Atlas of the United States, Based upon Results of the Eleventh Census* (Washington, DC: U.S. Government Printing Office, 1898), 15–16.

12. New Orleans, the largest southern city, was ranked number twelve, and the next four largest southern cities ranged from number thirty-four to number forty-three. Population figures here and in the following paragraphs are drawn from Gannett, *Statistical Atlas of the United States*, (1898), and Robert P. Porter, *Compendium of the Eleventh Census: Part 1, Population* (U.S. Government Printing Office, 1892).

13. Gannett, *Statistical Atlas*, 15–16, plate 7, Porter, *Compendium*, lxxi–lxxvi.

14. Gannett, *Statistical Atlas*, plate 9, Porter, *Compendium*, lxxvii–lxxxv.

15. Porter, *Compendium*, xcviii–cviii.

16. Gannett, *Statistical Atlas*, plate 29.

17. For U.S. urban populations in 1890, see Gannett, *Statistical Atlas* (1890), plate 7; Porter, *Compendium*, lxxi–lxxvi.

18. Eric Foner, *Reconstruction: America's Unfinished Revolution, 1863–1877* (Harper and Row, 1988), 604–9; W. E. B. Du Bois, *Black Reconstruction in America* (Library of America, 2021), 805–51.

19. Gannett, *Statistical Atlas*, plates 23–31; see also Henry Gannett, *Statistical Atlas of the Twelfth Census of the United States (1900)* (U.S. Census Office, 1903), plates 47, 53.

20. Gannett, *Statistical Atlas* (1890), tables 140–43, 32–33.

21. Gannett, *Statistical Atlas* (1890), plate 40, before 35. By 1890, Roman Catholicism was the single largest denomination (or "sect," as the 1890 census described it) in the United States; see plate 33.

22. Henry Grady, "Before the Bay State Club," in *The Speeches of Henry Grady* (Atlanta: Charles F. Byrd, 1895), 94–95.

23. Gannett, *Statistical Atlas* (1890), figs. 270, 50.

24. Gannett, *Statistical Atlas* (1890), figs. 334, 58.

25. Gannett, *Statistical Atlas* (1890), figs. 283, 284, 53.

26. The GOP-dominated politics of the postwar era, especially its tariff policies that favored Northern manufacturing interests, further served to redistribute the nation's wealth from the South to the Northeast; see Douglas Irwin, "Tariff Incidence in America's Gilded Age," *Journal of Economic History* 67, no. 3 (2007): 582–607.

27. On the geography of the nation's credit relationships in the late nineteenth century, see William Cronon, *Nature's Metropolis: Chicago and the Great West* (W. W. Norton, 1991), 269–309, especially the map on p. 306 showing the South's exclusion from national banking networks.

28. Max Edling, *Perfecting the Union: National and State Authority in the U.S. Constitution* (Oxford University Press, 2020), 75–104.

29. For data on government spending at the federal, state, and local levels, see "Government Spending Details for 1890," USGovernmentSpending.com. This website aggregates data from the federal, state, and local levels, drawn from *Bicentennial Edition: Historical Statistics of the United States* (U.S. Government Printing Office, 1975) and *Historical Statistics of the United States, 1789–1945* (U.S. Government Printing Office, 1949).

30. In 1890, the Pennsylvania Railroad had $71 million in revenue and 110,000 employees, compared to the Post Office's 95,000; Alfred D. Chandler Jr., *The Visible Hand: The Managerial Revolution in American Business* (Harvard University Press, 1977), 204–5.

31. State and local taxation was far more intrusive than federal taxation. The great bulk of state and local revenue came from property taxes that required the assessment and valuation of individual property holdings—in other words "direct taxes" of the sort which Congress also had the constitutional power to levy but had not exercised since the War of 1812. For 1890 government revenue data, see "Government Revenue Details for 1890," USGovernmentSpending.com, https://www.usgovernmentrevenue.com/year_revenue_1890USmn_24ms1n_00102025304050607080 90E0G0H0J0.

32. But for a recent argument for the longer legacy of Reconstruction, see Manisha Sinha, *The Rise and Fall of the Second American Republic: Reconstruction, 1860–1920* (Liveright, 2024).

33. "Government Revenue Details for 1893," USGovernmentSpending.com, https://www.usgovernmentspending.com/year_spending_1893USmn_26ms2n_30#usgs302.

34. William J. Novak, *New Democracy: The Creation of the Modern American State* (Harvard University Press, 2022).

35. Douglas A. Irwin, *Clashing over Commerce: A History of US Trade Policy* (University of Chicago Press, 2017), 263–69.

36. Keith Pluymers, *No Wood, No Kingdom: Political Ecology in the English Atlantic* (University of Pennsylvania Press, 2021)

37. Edward Bellamy, *Looking Backward: 2000–1887* (Boston: Ticknor, 1888), 70–79, quotation at 77. As Bellamy put it,

> The people of the United States concluded to assume the conduct of their own business, just as one hundred odd years before they had assumed the conduct of their own government, organizing now for industrial purposes on precisely the same grounds that they had then organized for political purposes. At last, strangely late in the world's history, the obvious fact was perceived that no business is so essentially the public business as the industry and commerce on which the people's livelihood depends, and that to

> entrust it to private persons to be managed for private profit, is a folly similar in kind, though vastly greater in magnitude, to that of surrendering the functions of political government to kings and nobles to be conducted for their personal glorification. (78–79)

38. Anthony Gregory, *New Deal Law and Order: How the War on Crime Built the Modern Liberal State* (Harvard University Press, 2024), 55–71.

39. Linda K. Kerber, *No Constitutional Right to Be Ladies: Women and the Obligations of Citizenship* (Hill and Wang, 1998), 3–46, 81–123. The 1920 Census included a monograph describing the increase in women's "gainful employment" outside the home, with the largest increases founded in the most heavily industrial states of the Northeast; see *1920 Census Monograph 9: Women in Gainful Occupations, 1870 to 1920*, United States Census Bureau, https://www.census.gov/library/publications/1929/dec/monograph-9.html.

40. The "Tariff of Abominations" enacted in 1828 had caused the Nullification Crisis, when South Carolina threatened to nullify federal law over a tariff that favored Northern industrial interests at the expense of Southern cotton planters.

41. Charles Postel, *The Populist Vision* (Oxford University Press, 2007), 274; Richard White, *The Republic for Which It Stands: The United States During Reconstruction and the Gilded Age* (Oxford University Press, 2017), 836–46.

42. The Sixteenth Amendment reads: "The Congress shall have power to lay and collect taxes on incomes, from whatever source derived, without apportionment among the several States, and without regard to any census or enumeration."

43. Einhorn, *American Taxation, American Slavery*, 157–73. Again, if we think of the states as "artificial barons," the equivalent of the subordinate lords of the king in the medieval constitution, then of course the richer and more powerful barons were expected to contribute more to the king's military adventures than the poorer and less powerful ones. Pairing representation with the apportionment of direct taxation was designed to defend this principle.

44. Robin L. Einhorn, "Look Away, Dixieland: The South and the Federal Income Tax," *Northwestern University Law Review* 8, no. 3 (2014): 773.

45. Einhorn, "Look Away, Dixieland," 773, 783.

46. A 1974 study by the Tax Foundation calculated that the citizens of New York and New Jersey paid roughly twice as much per capita ($1510 and $1548) as the citizens of Mississippi and Arkansas ($728 and $814); see *Federal Tax Burdens in States and Metropolitan Areas*, Research Aid No. 5 (Tax Foundation, 1974), table 5, "Allocation of Tax Burden by State," https://files.taxfoundation.org/legacy/docs/ra5.pdf?_gl=1*1f6rn9l*_ga*MTM2MDAzNTMwNy4xNjkyNzQxMTE4*_ga_FP7KWDV08V*MTY5MjcoMTExOC4xLjEuMTY5MjcoMjUyMi42MC4wLjA, 14. For the current disparities in state contributions to and receipts from federal revenue, see Rockefeller Institute of Government, "Who Gives and Who Gets: Explore the Balance of Payments between States and the Federal Government," https://rockinst.org/issue-areas/fiscal-analysis/balance-of-payments-portal/.

47. At the time of the Constitution, state legislatures on average consisted of roughly 100 members. The average size of a U.S. state legislature today, House plus Senate, is 148 members, even though the country is now nearly one hundred times as populous as it was then; see Peverill Squire, *The Evolution of American Legislatures: Colonies, Territories, and States, 1619–2009* (University of Michigan Press, 2012), 84.

Chapter 11. The Great Transformation

1. William J. Novak, *New Democracy: The Creation of the Modern American State* (Harvard University Press, 2022), 95, 108–45.

2. See Margo J. Anderson, *The American Census: A Social History*, 2nd ed. (Yale University Press, 2015).

3. Trudy Suchan, Marc J. Perry, James D. Fitzsimmons, Anika E. Juhn, Alexander M. Tait, and Cynthia A. Brewer, *Census Atlas of the United States*, Series CENST-29 (U.S. Census Bureau, 2007), see fig. 2-2, chaps. 2, 9.

4. Suchan et al., *Census Atlas*, chaps. 2, 9.

5. On the deep history of the Hohokam, or Huhugam, see Kathleen DuVal, *Native Nations: A Millennium in North America* (Random House, 2024), 18–25.

6. Bradford Luckingham, *Phoenix: The History of a Southwestern Metropolis* (University of Arizona Press, 2016), 12–39; Philip VanderMeer, *Desert Visions and the Making of Phoenix, 1860–2009* (University of New Mexico Press, 2010), 11–27; Elizabeth Tandy Shermer, *Sunbelt Capitalism: Phoenix and the Transformation of American Politics* (University of Pennsylvania Press, 2013).

7. Luckingham, *Phoenix*, 29–30; Richard White, *Railroaded: The Transcontinentals and the Making of Modern America* (W. W. Norton, 2011), 94.

8. Donald Worster, *Rivers of Empire: Water, Aridity, and the Growth of the American West* (Random House, 1985), 130.

9. Marc Reisner, *Cadillac Desert: The American West and Its Disappearing Water*, rev. ed. (Penguin, 1993), 111–19; Mission of the Bureau of Reclamation, National Park Service, U.S. Department of the Interior, https://www.nps.gov/articles/3-mission-of-the-bureau-of-reclamation.htm.

10. Gerald D. Nash, *The Federal Landscape: An Economic History of the Twentieth-Century West* (University of Arizona Press, 1999), 58–59; VanderMeer, *Desert Visions*, 19, 29–32. Irrigated farmland in the Phoenix area grew from 120,000 to 360,000 acres between 1890 and 1930. For comparison's sake, 360,000 acres is roughly the same amount of land as a single farming county in Iowa, such as Marshall County, which today has a population of roughly 40,000, of whom 27,000 live in the county's largest town, Marshalltown: U.S. Census Bureau, State and County Quick Facts, Marshall County, Iowa, https://web.archive.org/web/20110607071809/http://quickfacts.census.gov/qfd/states/19/19127.html.

11. Luckingham, *Phoenix*, 106–7; VanderMeer, *Desert Visions*, 112–14.

12. Worster, *Rivers of Empire*, 264–79; Luckingham, *Phoenix*, 109–10; Reisner, *Cadillac Desert*, 260. In subsequent decades, ever-increasing population in the Southwest, conflicting claims on water, and the warming climate have created a crisis—the Colorado River is running dry.

13. Nash, *Federal Landscape*, 56–58; VanderMeer, *Desert Visions*, 95–123; Luckingham, *Phoenix*, 136–76.

14. Gary Gerstle, *Liberty and Coercion: The Paradox of American Government from the Founding to the Present* (Princeton University Press, 2015), 267.

15. Luckingham, *Phoenix*, 166–67, 249–50.

16. Andrew Needham, *Power Lines: Phoenix and the Making of the Modern Southwest* (Princeton University Press, 2014), 11, 123–58.

17. VanderMeer, *Desert Visions*, 187–223.

18. Campbell Gibson, "Population of the 100 Largest Cities and Other Urban Places in the United States: 1790 to 1990," U.S. Census Bureau, https://www.census.gov/library/working-papers/1998/demo/POP-twps0027.html.

19. On military Keynesianism and its impact on the South, see Bruce J. Schulman, *From Cotton Belt to Sun Belt: Federal Policy, Economic Development, and the Transformation of the South, 1938–1980* (Oxford University Press, 1991), 135–73.

20. See, for example, Tami J. Friedman, "Exploiting the North-South Differential: Corporate Power, Southern Politics, and the Decline of Organized Labor After World War II," *Journal of American History* 95, no. 2 (2008): 323–48.

21. See Schulman, *Cotton Belt to Sun Belt*, fig. 5.1, p. 119, which depicts federal payments to state and local governments as a percent of all state and local government revenue in 1959. It clearly shows that the old industrial states of the Northeast, from Illinois and Wisconsin east through the Great Lakes region to New England, received the lowest percentage of federal payments, and the South and West received the highest. New Jersey received the lowest percentage at 6.4 percent, with Wyoming and Alaska receiving the highest at 32.3 percent. For the South's growing share of national defense contracts, from 7.6 percent in 1951 to 24.2 percent in 1980, see Schulman, *Cotton Belt to Sun Belt*, table 6.1, p. 140.

22. Eric Newburger and Thomas Gryn, "The Foreign-Born Labor Force in the United States, 2007," *American Community Survey Reports* (U.S. Census Bureau, 2007).

23. Suchan et al., *Census Atlas*, 44–47.

24. Bonny Berkner and Carol S. Faber, *Geographical Mobility: 1995–2000*, Census 2000 Brief, September 2003, https://usa.ipums.org/usa/resources/voliii/pubdocs/2000/c2kbr-28.pdf.

25. U.S. Religion Census, "Maps from the 2000 Study," Glenmary Research Center, https://www.usreligioncensus.org/maps2000_study.

26. Jaleh Soroui, *New Tools Map Literacy and Numeracy Skills Across U.S. States and Counties (2020)*, American Institutes for Research, https://www.air.org/resource/qa/new-tool-maps-literacy-and-numeracy-skills-across-us-states-and-counties; "120 Years of Literacy," *National Assessment of Adult Literacy*, National Center for Education Statistics, https://nces.ed.gov/naal/lit_history.asp.

27. William Faulkner, "On Fear: Deep South in Labor: Mississippi," in *Essays, Speeches, and Public Letters by William Faulkner*, ed. James B. Meriwether (Random House, 1965), 98.

28. Although the United States endorsed Philippine independence in 1946, Puerto Rico remains under territorial status 125 years after U.S. annexation, despite having a population larger than twenty of the fifty states.

29. Linda D. Wilson, "Statehood Movement," *Encyclopedia of Oklahoma History and Culture*, https://www.okhistory.org/publications/enc/entry.php?entry=ST025.

30. Historical Apportionment Data, 1910–2020, United States Census Bureau, https://www.census.gov/data/tables/time-series/dec/apportionment-data-text.html.

31. Consumer Price Index Inflation Calculator, https://www.in2013dollars.com/us/inflation/1890?endYear=1990&amount=464000000.

32. "Government Spending Details for 1990," USGovernmentSpending.com, https://www.usgovernmentspending.com/year_spending_1990USbn_24bs2n_0010202530405060708090E0G0H0J0#usgs302.

33. The vast majority of 1990's income tax, 83 percent, was paid by individuals, and only 17 percent came from corporations. By 2020, 88 percent came from individuals, 12 percent from corporations; see US Government Revenue, Government Revenue Details for 1990, https://www.usgovernmentrevenue.com/year_revenue_1990USmn_24ms1n_00102025304050607080 90E0G0H0.

34. Pollock v. Farmers' Loan & Trust Co., 157 U.S. 429, 573–74, 582–83, modified on reh'g, 158 U.S. 601 (1895). In particular, it was the tax on income that investors earned on stocks and bonds and the like that the Supreme Court viewed as a direct tax.

35. Robin L. Einhorn, "Look Away, Dixieland: The South and the Federal Income Tax," *Northwestern University Law Review* 8, no. 3 (2014), 773–98; see also Monica Prasad, *The Land of Too Much: American Abundance and the Paradox of Poverty* (Harvard University Press, 2012), 123–29.

36. Historical information on federal spending in this and the following paragraphs is drawn from US Government Spending History from 1900, USGovernmentSpending.com, https://www.usgovernmentspending.com/past_spending.

37. This was the case from 1789 all the way until 1994, when federal pensions and then soon after federal health care spending began to surpass annual defense spending, which remains the case today.

38. Although in 1990 the federal government ran a deficit and had to borrow extensively to pay for all this, the interest payments on the debt did not differ all that significantly from 1890 as a percentage of overall expenditures: 9 percent in 1890, 14 percent in 1990. By 2020, interest payments were down to 5 percent of total federal spending.

39. For useful charts of the structure of the U.S. government, see U.S. General Services Administration, Government Organization Chart, https://www.usgovernmentmanual.gov/ReadLibraryItem.ashx?SFN=Myz95sTyO4rJRM/nhIRwSw==&SF=VHhnJrOeEAnGaa/rtk/JOg==; "Structure of the United States Federal Government," *Simple Legal Guides*, January 20, 2021, https://cdn.shopify.com/s/files/1/2724/8374/files/SLG.Federal.Government.Org.Chart.png?v=1611121483.

40. "Federal Government—Employment: 1901–2002," *Statistical Abstract of the United States: 2003*, No. HS-50, U.S. Census Bureau, https://www2.census.gov/library/publications/2004/compendia/statab/123ed/hist/hs-50.pdf.

41. By comparison, in 1898, on the eve of the Spanish-American War, the U.S. Army consisted of 28,000 officers and enlisted men, with another 12,000 in the U.S. Navy, for a total of 40,000, one-fiftieth of the 1990 figure; see "The U.S. Army in the 1890s," U.S. Army Center of Military History, https://history.army.mil/Unit-History/Force-Structure-Support/The-US-Army-in-the-1890s/; and "U.S. Navy Personnel Strength, 1775 to Present," Naval History and Heritage Command, https://www.history.navy.mil/research/library/online-reading-room/title-list-alphabetically/u/usn-personnel-strength.html.

42. Paul C. Light, "The True Size of Government is Nearing a Record High," Brookings Institution, https://www.brookings.edu/articles/the-true-size-of-government-is-nearing-a-record-high/. See also Light, *The Government-Industrial Complex: Tracking the True Size of Government, 1984–2018* (Oxford University Press, 2019). However, it should be noted that the percentage of American workers in the public sector is not particularly high by world standards. Among the thirty-eight nations in the Organization for Economic Co-operation and

Development measured in 2021, the United States, at 15 percent, was well below the average (18.6 percent) of overall public sector employment (which in the United States would include state and local government as well as federal); see "Government at a Glance 2023: United States," OECD, https://www.oecd.org/en/publications/government-at-a-glance-2023_c4200b14-en/united-states_015a6beb-en.html.

43. Marcello Castillo, "Family and Hired Workers on U.S. Farms, 1950–2000," USDA Economic Research Service, November 21, 2024, https://www.ers.usda.gov/data-products/chart-gallery/chart-detail?chartId=63450.

44. Daniel Immerwahr, *How to Hide an Empire: A History of the Greater United States* (Farrar, Straus, and Giroux, 2019); Chalmers Johnson, *The Sorrows of Empire: Militarism, Secrecy, and the End of the Republic* (Henry Holt, 2004), 4–5; David Vine, *Base Nation: How U.S. Military Bases Abroad Harm America and the World* (Metropolitan Books, 2015), 3–5.

45. David Coleman, "How Many People are Employed by the U.S. Federal Government? The Numbers Since 1962," History in Pieces, Research, https://historyinpieces.com/research/federal-personnel-numbers-1962; Executive Branch Civilian Employment Since 1940, U.S. Office of Personnel Management, https://www.opm.gov/policy-data-oversight/data-analysis-documentation/federal-employment-reports/historical-tables/executive-branch-civilian-employment-since-1940/.

46. Lindsay Chervinsky, *The Cabinet: George Washington and the Creation of an American Institution* (Harvard University Press, 2020).

47. Bernard Bailyn, *The Origins of American Politics* (Vintage Books, 1968), 102–4; Novak, *New Democracy*, 222.

48. Jack Rakove, *The Beginnings of National Government: An Interpretive History of the Continental Congress* (Johns Hopkins University Press, 1982).

49. Chervinsky, *Cabinet*, 4–5, 112–17.

Chapter 12. The Long Crisis of the Constitution

1. Thomas Jefferson to John Breckinridge, 12 August 1803, *Founders Online*, National Archives, https://founders.archives.gov/documents/Jefferson/01-41-02-0139.

2. "Chart Pack: Defense Spending," Peter G. Peterson Foundation, https://www.pgpf.org/article/chart-pack-defense-spending/.

3. "Consumer Spending by Country," World Population Review, https://worldpopulationreview.com/country-rankings/consumer-spending-by-country.

4. Matthew Karp, *This Vast Southern Empire: Slaveholders at the Helm of American Foreign Policy* (Harvard University Press, 2016), 118–22; Amy S. Greenberg, *A Wicked War: Polk, Clay, Lincoln and the 1846 U.S. Invasion of Mexico* (Knopf, 2012), 243–60.

5. Daniel Immerwahr, *How to Hide an Empire: A History of the Greater United States* (Farrar, Straus and Giroux, 2019); Chalmers Johnson, *The Sorrows of Empire: Militarism, Secrecy, and the End of the Republic* (Henry Holt, 2004), 84; Bartholomew H. Sparrow, *The "Insular Cases" and the Emergence of an American Empire* (University of Kansas Press, 2006), 111–22.

6. Sparrow, *Insular Cases*, 79–110.

7. Legal historian Maggie Blackhawk argues that the administrators of these permanent U.S. overseas colonies went on to play significant roles in shaping the colonial aspects of modern

American constitutionalism, including the continued holding of the governments of Indigenous nations in subordination; Blackhawk, "Foreword: The Constitution of American Colonialism," *Harvard Law Review* 137, no. 1 (2023): 2–152.

8. A. G. Hopkins, *American Empire: A Global History* (Princeton University Press, 2018), 515–16; Immerwahr, *How to Hide an Empire*, 85–87. On the continuity from the Mexican War to the Spanish-American War of the racist assumptions of the new U.S. territorial regime, see Juan E. Perea, "Fulfilling Manifest Destiny: Conquest, Race, and the *Insular Cases*," in *Foreign in a Domestic Sense: Puerto Rico, American Expansion, and the Constitution*, ed. Christina Duffy Burnett and Burke Marshall (Duke University Press, 2001), 140–66. On recent efforts to overturn the Insular Cases, see Amy Howe, "Court Declines to Take Up Petition Seeking to Overturn Insular Cases," *SCOTUS Blog*, October 17, 2022, https://www.scotusblog.com/2022/10/court-declines-to-take-up-petition-seeking-to-overturn-insular-cases/.

9. Franklin Roosevelt, quoted in Gary Gerstle, *Liberty and Coercion: The Paradox of American Government from the Founding to the Present* (Princeton University Press, 2015), 186.

10. Ira Katznelson, *Fear Itself: The New Deal and the Origins of Our Time* (W. W. Norton, 2013), 5 (quoting Mussolini), 108–19 (citing Walter Lippman, who urged the idea of offering President Roosevelt enhanced powers for a year while the ordinary functions of both houses of Congress would be suspended).

11. Gerstle, *Liberty and Coercion*, 188–206.

12. The Lochner Court introduced the doctrine of "substantive due process" as a way to offer protections for individual liberties—in this case the "freedom of contract"—that were not expressly named in the Fourteenth Amendment, Section 1, which prevents the states from making laws that abridge the "privileges and immunities" of U.S. citizens or deprive them of "life, liberty, or property, without due process of law." Although the early twentieth-century court used this doctrine in conservative, pro-business ways, it would later be used to identify and protect civil rights and individual liberties across a wide range of progressive causes.

13. William J. Novak, *New Democracy: The Creation of the Modern American State* (Harvard University Press, 2022), 108–45, argues that the influence of the Lochner Court has been overstated by legal scholars, and that a robust regulatory regime built around the concept of the "public utility" of corporations providing transportation, communications, energy, water, and the shipping and storage of agricultural products predated the New Deal. But at the federal level, prior to the New Deal there was no bureaucratic equivalent in industry to the USDA's influence over agriculture.

14. Gerstle, *Liberty and Coercion*, 100–6; Bruce Ackerman, *We the People 2: Transformations* (Harvard University Press, 1998), 257.

15. Ackerman, *We the People 2*, 286–89; Katznelson, *Fear Itself*, 227–32.

16. United States v. Butler, 297 U.S. 1 (1936).

17. Gerstle, *Liberty and Coercion*, 106.

18. Wheeler and other Progressives had been promoting similar amendments as far back as 1924.

19. Ackerman, *We the People 2*, 312–24.

20. *The Public Papers and Addresses of Franklin D. Roosevelt (1938–1950)*, compiled by Samuel I. Rosenman, 13 vols. (Macmillan, 1950), 1937 vol. (1941); 35–65; Ackerman, *We the People 2*, 317–333.

21. For a full list of the amendments proposed during the Seventy-Fifth Congress (1937–39), see Harvard's *Amendments Project*, https://amendmentsproject.org/search?view=None&search_any_field=&summary=&amendment_text=&type=&date_before=&date_after=&congress=cdf8f894-6a15-4657-950d-f6f14c612ca3&sort=relevance&size=25&page=1.

22. Rosenman, *Public Papers and Addresses*, (1937 vol.), 122–132, quoted in Ackerman, *We the People* 2, 326. In 1930, the smallest thirteen states had 5.1 percent of the population. In 2026, thirteen states are still sufficient to block the ratification of any constitutional amendment, but now the smallest thirteen states comprise only 4.4 percent of the nation's population, as the degree of inequality between the most and least populous states continues to widen.

23. Ackerman, *We the People* 2, 324–40.

24. Gerstle, *Liberty and Coercion*, 230; likewise in *West Coast Hotel v. Parrish* (1937) the Supreme Court upheld the power of states to enforce minimum wage regulations and held that the "liberty of contract" emphasized by the Lochner Court could be restricted when the protection of the community, health and safety, or the welfare of vulnerable groups was at stake. On the significance of the "switch in time" for cementing a new vision of "creedal constitutionalism," a New Deal version of faith in the Constitution as adequate to the needs of modern American society, see Aziz Rana, *The Constitutional Bind: How Americans Came to Idolize a Document That Fails Them* (University of Chicago Press, 2024), 329–51.

25. Andrew Preston, *Total Defense: The New Deal and the Invention of National Security* (Harvard University Press, 2025), 156–157.

26. Katznelson, *Fear Itself*, 291; Stephen Wertheim, *Tomorrow, the World: The Birth of U.S. Global Supremacy* (Harvard University Press, 2020), 46.

27. Preston, *Total Defense*, 138–172.

28. Technically speaking, Congress also issued declarations of war against Rumania, Bulgaria, and Hungary in June 1942, at the insistence of FDR, who believed it was wrong to wage war against these minor Axis powers without a congressional declaration. His rejection of the amendment process during the New Deal did not mean FDR ignored constitutional checks and balances.

29. *The Budget of the United States Government for the Fiscal Year Ending June 30, 1941* (U.S. Government Printing Office, 1940), General Budget Summary, xix, https://fraser.stlouisfed.org/files/docs/publications/usbudget/bus_1941.pdf?utm_source=direct_download; *The Budget of the United States Government for the Fiscal Year Ending June 30, 1945* (U.S. Government Printing Office, 1944), table 1, https://fraser.stlouisfed.org/files/docs/publications/usbudget/bus_1945.pdf?utm_source=direct_download.

30. James T. Sparrow, *Warfare State: World War II Americans and the Age of Big Government* (Oxford University Press, 2011); Katznelson, *Fear Itself*, 342–51, 430–36; Gerstle, *Liberty and Coercion*, 251–74.

31. Gerstle, *Liberty and Coercion*, 270–71; Sheldon Pollack, *War, Revenue, and State Building: Financing the Development of the American State* (Cornell University Press, 2009), 260–69.

32. In the text of his *Appeal*, Du Bois points out that one South Carolina congressman was elected in 1946 with a total of 3,527 votes (out of 3,530 votes cast altogether in the district), while a Black congressman from Illinois was elected with a total of 38,040 votes (out of 66,885 cast altogether); W. E. B Du Bois, introduction to *An Appeal to the World!*, ed. W. E. B Du Bois (National Association for the Advancement of Colored People, 1947), 9.

33. See Bruce J. Schulman, *From Cotton Belt to Sun Belt: Federal Policy, Economic Development, and the Transformation of the South, 1938–1980* (Oxford University Press, 1991); and Heather Cox Richardson, *How the South Won the Civil War* (Oxford University Press, 2020), 156–57.

34. Ira Katznelson, *When Affirmative Action Was White* (W. W. Norton, 2006); Glenn Altschuler and Stuart Blumin, *The GI Bill: A New Deal for Veterans* (Oxford University Press, 2009); Kathleen Frydl, *The GI Bill* (Cambridge University Press, 2009). Similarly, veterans who were given an undesirable discharge "issued because of homosexual acts or tendencies" were also routinely denied GI Bill benefits; see Margot Canaday, "Building a Straight State: Sexuality and Social Citizenship under the 1944 G.I. Bill," *Journal of American History* 90, no. 3 (2003): 935–57.

35. In 1948, the political scientist Clinton Rossiter published *Constitutional Dictatorship: Crisis Government in Modern Democracies*, along with a series of articles focusing on the need for emergency powers in the nuclear era; see Joel Isaac, "Constitutional Dictatorship in Twentieth-Century American Political Thought," in *States of Exception in American History*, ed. Gary Gerstle and Joel Isaac (University of Chicago Press, 2020), 225–33.

36. Daniel Yergin, *Shattered Peace: The Origins of the Cold War and the National Security State* (Houghton Mifflin, 1977), 196; Harold Koh, *The National Security Constitution: Sharing Power After the Iran-Contra Affair* (Yale University Press, 1990), 67–100; Preston, *Total Defense*, 192–217.

37. Mary L. Dudziak, *WarTime: An Idea, Its History, Its Consequences* (Oxford University Press, 2012), 91. See also Gerstle, *Liberty and Coercion*, 262–70.

38. Preston, *Total Defense*, 214.

39. Gerstle, *Liberty and Coercion*, 254–58; Beverly Gage, *G-Man: J. Edgar Hoover and the Making of the American Century* (Viking, 2022), 103–4, 238–40.

40. Preston, *Total Defense*, 205–6, 214–16; Douglas Stuart, *Creating the National Security State: A History of the Law that Transformed America* (Princeton University Press, 2008), 230–73.

41. Kim Lane Scheppele, "Law in a Time of Emergency: States of Exception and the Temptations of 9/11," *University of Pennsylvania Journal of Constitutional Law* 6, no. 5 (2004): 1015–19; Jules Lobel, "Emergency Power and the Decline of Liberalism," *Yale Law Journal* 98, no. 7 (1989): 1400–1408, quotation at 1401.

42. President Dwight D. Eisenhower's Farewell Address (1961), National Archives, *Milestone Documents*, https://www.archives.gov/milestone-documents/president-dwight-d-eisenhowers-farewell-address; Dudziak, *WarTime*, 91–92; James Ledbetter, *Unwarranted Influence: Dwight D. Eisenhower and the Military-Industrial Complex* (Yale University Press, 2011), 211–20.

43. Preston, *Total Defense*, 173–91.

44. Maeve Marcus, *Truman and the Steel Seizure Case* (Duke University Press, 1994); Lobel, "Emergency Power," 1408; Dudziak, *WarTime*, 88–89.

45. Tellingly, Stuart's *Creating the National Security State*, cited above, has no entry in its index for "Constitution," "amendments," or "Supreme Court." This lack of attention to constitutional formalism is common to other works on the Cold War state, and very different from the scholarship on the New Deal. W. E. B. Du Bois made a similar point about the impossibility of Article V amendments in his introduction to *An Appeal to the World!* (9–10), but not because of the permanent emergency of the nuclear age. Rather, Du Bois cited the Jim Crow disenfranchisement

of Black voters and the consequent empowerment of tiny numbers of Southern whites, who could block otherwise popular amendments at both the congressional passage and the state ratification stages.

46. See Rana, *Constitutional Bind*, 389–445, on the adaptations of creedal constitutionalism to the new U.S. role as international police power.

47. On the importance of the connections among court decisions, legislation, and administrative support in bringing about social change, see Linda Greenhouse, "Social Progress and the Courts," review of *The Hollow Hope: Can Courts Bring About Social Change?*, 3rd ed., by Gerald R. Rosenberg, *New York Review of Books*, February 29, 2024.

48. Blackhawk, "Foreword," 89–115.

49. Rana, *Constitutional Bind*, 483–64; Gerstle, *Liberty and Coercion*, 284–310, quotation at 284.

50. The states that failed to ratify were from the Deep South, the ones that Du Bois in 1947 had pointed out as the most likely to block the will of large popular majorities through the concentrated power of small numbers of overrepresented voters, as well as several from the arid West, where sparse overall populations gave residents far more voting power than those in highly populous states.

51. Richardson, *How the South Won*, 166–91.

52. Gerstle, *Liberty and Coercion*, 311–18; Jonathan Rieder, "The Rise of the 'Silent Majority,'" in *The Rise and Fall of the New Deal Order*, ed. Steven Fraser and Gary Gerstle (Princeton University Press, 1989), 243–68; Daniel J. Sargent, *A Superpower Transformed: The Remaking of American Foreign Relations in the 1970s* (Oxford University Press, 2015).

53. The organization most responsible for promoting originalism in the legal profession calls itself the Federalist Society.

54. Jonathan Gienapp, *Against Constitutional Originalism: A Historical Critique* (Yale University Press, 2024); Sean Wilentz, *The Age of Reagan: A History, 1974–2008* (Harper Collins, 2008), 187–94.

55. Preston, *Total Defense*, 216.

56. Rana, *Constitutional Bind*, 639–53; Gerstle, *Liberty and Coercion*, 320–25; Wilentz, *Age of Reagan*, 637–38.

57. On the rise of originalism and its grounding in traditions of constitutional veneration, see Rana, *Constitutional Bind*, 639–53; Gerstle, *Liberty and Coercion*, 320–25; and Wilentz, *Age of Reagan*, 187–94.

58. Michael Sherry, *In the Shadow of War: The United States Since the 1930s* (Yale University Press, 1995), 392–416; Gerstle, *Liberty and Coercion*, 326–27.

59. Franklin D. Roosevelt, Excerpts from the Press Conference, December 28, 1943, *American Presidency Project*, https://www.presidency.ucsb.edu/node/209751.

60. James F. Childress, "The War Metaphor in Public Policy: Some Moral Reflections," in *The Leader's Imperative: Ethics, Integrity, and Responsibility*, ed. J. Carl Ficarrotta (Purdue University Press, 2001), 181–97.

61. "Global War on Terror," George W. Bush Presidential Library, https://www.georgewbushlibrary.gov/research/topic-guides/global-war-terror.

62. Elizabeth Hinton, *From the War on Poverty to the War on Crime: The Making of Mass Incarceration in America* (Harvard University Press, 2016); Michelle Alexander, *The New Jim Crow: Mass Incarceration in the Age of Colorblindness* (New Press, 2010).

63. For example, see "Protecting the American People Against Invasion," The White House, January 20, 2025, https://www.whitehouse.gov/presidential-actions/2025/01/protecting-the-american-people-against-invasion/.

64. Rana, *Constitutional Bind*, 652–56.

Epilogue: Toward 2090

1. *The Eisenhower Diaries*, ed. Robert H. Farrell (W. W. Norton, 1981), 210, quoted in Andrew Preston, *Total Defense: The New Deal and the Invention of National Security* (Harvard University Press, 2025), 219.

2. Bernard Bailyn, *The Ideological Origins of the American Revolution*, 50th anniv. ed. (Harvard University Press, 2017), xv–xx.

3. Rexford G. Tugwell, *The Emerging Constitution* (Harper's Magazine Press, 1974).

4. Tugwell, *Emerging Constitution*, 60–61.

5. Tugwell, *Emerging Constitution*, 592–621.

6. Tugwell, *Emerging Constitution*, 61.

ILLUSTRATION CREDITS

1.1. Original mapping created by Anna Powell-Smith is available at Open Domesday: https://opendomesday.org. Data courtesy of OpenStreetMap and is available under the Open Database License (for more information, see openstreetmap.org/copyright). Data compiled by Professor J.J.N Palmer and the team at University of Hull. The raw Domesday data is hosted by University of Hull here: https://www.hull.ac.uk/choose-hull/study-at-hull/library/resources/domesday-dataset.

1.2. Library of Congress, Geography and Map Division.

2.1. *Atlas of Early American History: The Revolutionary Era, 1760–1790*, ed. Lester J. Cappon (Princeton University Press, 1976), 23. The image is based on a manuscript map by Herman R. Friis, which comes from Friis's book, *A Series of Population Maps of the Colonies and the United States, 1625-1790*, rev., Amer. Geog. Soc., Mimeographed and Offset Publ., 3 (New York, 1968).

2.2. From the Norman B. Leventhal Map & Education Center at the Boston Public Library, https://collections.leventhalmap.org/search/commonwealth:z603vp51q.

2.3. William Faden, Cartographer, Publisher, Engraver, and Thomas Jefferys, *The North American Atlas, Selected from the Most Authentic Maps, Charts, Plans, &c. Hitherto Published* (London: Printed for William Faden, successor to the late Mr. Thomas Jeffreys, geographer to the King, the corner of St. Martin's-Lane, Charing-Cross, 1777). Library of Congress, Geography and Map Division., https://www.loc.gov/item/74180319/.

2.5. Abel Buell, *A New and Correct Map of the United States of North America: Layd down from the Latest Observations and Best Authorities Agreeable to the Peace of 1783…* (New Haven: Abel Buell, 1784). On deposit to the Library of Congress from David M. Rubenstein (005.00.00), https://www.loc.gov/exhibits/mapping-a-new-nation/online-exhibition.html#obj005.

4.1. In the digital collection of the William L. Clements Library Image Bank. William L. Clements Library, University of Michigan Library Digital Collections, available at https://quod.lib.umich.edu/w/wcl1ic/x-813/wcl000907.

4.2. Thomas Hutchins, William Barker, and Mathew Carey (Philadelphia: Mathew Carey, 1800), from the Norman B. Leventhal Map & Education Center, https://collections.leventhalmap.org/search/commonwealth:3f4630054.

5.1. Courtesy of the David Rumsey Map Collection, David Rumsey Map Center, Stanford Libraries.

9.1. Courtesy of the David Rumsey Map Collection, David Rumsey Map Center, Stanford Libraries.

9.2. United States Census Office, 11th Census, 1890, and Henry Gannett, *Statistical Atlas of the United States*, Based upon Results of the Eleventh Census (Washington, DC: Goverment Printing Offfice, 1898), https://www.loc.gov/item/07019233/.

9.3. Fletcher W. Hewes and Henry Gannett, *Scribner's Statistical Atlas of the United States, Showing by Graphic Methods Their Present Condition and Their Political, Social and Industrial Development.* (New York: C. Scribner's Sons, 1883), Map, https://www.loc.gov/item/a40001834/.

9.4. J. W. Powell, *Report on the Lands of the Arid Regions of the United States*, 2nd ed. (Washington. DC: Government Printing Office, 1879).

9.5. Washington, DC: Office of Indian Affairs, 1892. https://www.loc.gov/item/2009579467/. From Library of Congress, Geography and Map Division.

10.1. Library of Congress, Geography and Map Division. Originally published in E. Hergesheimer, *Map Showing the Distribution of the Slave Population of the Southern States of the United States Compiled from the Census of 1860* (Washington, DC: Henry S. Graham, 1861), https://www.loc.gov/item/99447026/.

10.2. Henry Gannett, *Statistical Atlas of the United States, Based upon Results of the Eleventh Census* (Washington, DC: Government Printing Office, 1898), plate 10, https://www.loc.gov/item/07019233/.

10.3. Gannett, *Statistical Atlas*, plate 11, https://www.loc.gov/item/07019233/.

10.4. Gannett, *Statistical Atlas*, fig. 36, plate 16, https://www.loc.gov/item/07019233/.

10.5. Gannett, *Statistical Atlas*, plate 12, https://www.loc.gov/item/07019233/.

10.6. Gannett, *Statistical Atlas*, plate 13, https://www.loc.gov/item/07019233/.

10.7. Gannett, *Statistical Atlas*, plate 42, https://www.loc.gov/item/07019233/.

10.8. Gannett, *Statistical Atlas*, plate 61, https://www.loc.gov/item/07019233/.

11.1. Trudy Suchan, Marc J. Perry, James D. Fitzsimmons, Anika Juhn, Alexander M. Tait, and Cynthia A. Brewer, *Census Atlas of the United States*, Series CENSR-29 (U.S. Census Bureau, 2007), 16.

11.2. Bradford Luckingham, *Phoenix: The History of a Southwestern Metropolis* (University of Arizona Press, 2016), 235.

11.3. Trudy Suchan, Marc J. Perry, James D. Fitzsimmons, Anika Juhn, Alexander M. Tait, and Cynthia A. Brewer, *Census Atlas of the United States*, Series CENSR-29 (U.S. Census Bureau, 2007), 9.

11.4. Suchan et al., *Census Atlas*, 29.

11.5. Suchan et al., *Census Atlas*, 93.

11.6. Suchan et al., *Census Atlas*, 161.

11.7. Suchan et al., *Census Atlas*, 227.

11.8. Suchan et al., *Census Atlas*, 213.

11.9. Suchan et al., *Census Atlas*, 188.

11.10. Suchan et al., *Census Atlas*, 188.

11.11. Suchan et al., *Census Atlas*, 189.

11.12. Suchan et al., *Census Atlas*, 184.

11.13. Suchan et al., *Census Atlas*, 187.

12.1. *An Appeal to the World!*, ed. W. E. Burghardt Du Bois (NAACP, 1947), back cover.

E.1. John L. Brooke, *Climate Change and the Course of Global History: A Rough Journey* (Cambridge University Press, 2014).

INDEX

Page references in italics indicate figures.

A NOTE ON THE TYPE

This book has been composed in Arno, an Old-style serif typeface in the classic Venetian tradition, designed by Robert Slimbach at Adobe.